To Tommy
Merry Xmas 2015

D0065571

THE COMPLETE
RUGBY UNION
COMPENDIUM

THE COMPLETE
RUGBY UNION
COMPENDIUM

KEITH YOUNG

First published in Great Britain in 2015 by
ARENA SPORT
An imprint of Birlinn Limited
West Newington House
10 Newington Road
Edinburgh
EH9 1QS

www.arenasportbooks.co.uk

ISBN: 978-1-909715-34-9
eBook ISBN: 978-0-85790-326-6

British Library Cataloguing-in-Publication Data
A catalogue record for this book is available on request from the
British Library.

Plate section images: Fotosport and Arena Sport Archive

Designed and typeset by Polaris Publishing, Edinburgh

Printed and bound by Grafica Veneta, Italy

**The author and publisher are grateful to Lockton Companies LLP
for a subvention in aid of publication.**

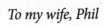

To my wife, Phil

ACKNOWLEDGEMENTS

I would like to thank my three sons, Gareth, Brendan and Damian for their support over the last couple of years, and a special thanks to my daughter Gwenda who gave me advice on the writing of the narrative section of the *Compendium*.

I am indebted to Nigel Owens who kindly agreed to write the foreword, and I also thank Jerry White and Cecil McCabe for their help.

Finally, a special note of thanks to my literary agent, Jonathan Williams who offered such meticulous attention to detail during the editing phase of the book, and to Peter Burns at Arena Sports for bringing together this project so expertly.

Keith Young, 2015

CONTENTS

FOREWORD
BY NIGEL OWENS

I first met Keith Young in Dublin at the signing of my autobiography, *Half Time*. He showed me the manuscript of his *Rugby Compendium* and I was amazed at the level of detail and research. When he asked me to write the foreword, I was more than happy to do so.

Keith has been a rugby enthusiast for over fifty years, and a mathematician by training; he has combined these passions to produce a book that contains a wealth of information that will delight not only rugby enthusiasts, but also anyone who is interested in sports generally and sporting statistics. This book contains data on every rugby union International (Test) match played by each of the major rugby-playing nations, laid out in a simple to read format.

There is also an analysis of the head-to-head records of the top twenty-one teams, and a summary of the results of each of the World Cup tournaments since 1987. Augmenting all this is a wonderful trivia section.

This publication is a must for the rugby enthusiast. It is more than a statistical reference book: it is a valuable compendium that would be a welcome addition to any sports fan's collection.

EXPLANATORY NOTES

THE TEN MAJOR RUGBY NATIONS

The ten major rugby nations are those defined as TIER 1 teams by the International Rugby Board, now known as World Rugby. They are:

Argentina, Australia, England, France, Ireland, Italy,
New Zealand, Scotland, South Africa and Wales.

The first section of this book contains a brief history of each of the ten teams and a match by match record of all the internationals played by each country.

In addition, it also includes a summary of each nation's head to head matches.

FORMAT OF EACH MATCH RECORD

Each match is recorded on a single line, divided into eight columns as follows:

Column 1 The match sequence in chronological order (1,2,3...)
Column 2 The exact date of the match (day/month/year)
Column 3 The opposing team (opponents)
Column 4 The tournament / trophy code
Column 5 The match status (home 'H', away 'A' or neutral 'N' ground)
Column 6 The match venue (name and/or location of the stadium)
Column 7 The match result (win 'W', loss 'L' or draw 'D')
Column 8 The final score (points for, points against)

THE OTHER ELEVEN RUGBY NATIONS

Seven Tier 2 and four Tier 3 teams, as presently defined by World Rugby, have been selected on the basis of having competed in the 2011 World Cup and/or qualified for the 2015 World Cup. They are:

TIER 2
Canada, Fiji, Japan, Romania, Samoa, Tonga and United States

TIER 3
Georgia, Namibia, Russia and Uruguay.

Section two of this book contains a brief history of each of the eleven teams and a summary of each nation's head to head matches.

THE POINTS SYSTEM

	Try	Convert	Pen Goal	Drop G	Goal from Mark
up to 1890-1891	1	2	2	3	3
1891-1893	2	3	3	4	4
1893-1905	3	2	3	4	4
1905-1948	3	2	3	4	3
1948-1971	3	2	3	3	3
1971-1977	4	2	3	3	3
1977-1992	4	2	3	3	discontinued
1992 onwards	5	2	3	3	discontinued

THE LIONS

In many publications, various teams representing the four Home Nations on tour to the Southern Hemisphere during the early twentieth century were called Great Britain and later the British Isles. It wasn't until the 1950s that they became known as Lions.

For consistency, and to avoid confusion, the name Lions has been used in this book for all the matches played by the four Home Nations touring teams.

However, there is one exception. In 1904 a touring Anglo-Welsh team played three Tests against New Zealand; the Lions name has not been used in these matches.

ABBREVIATIONS AND ACRONYMS

a.e.t – after extra time

SANZAR – South Africa, New Zealand, Australia Rugby

TOURNAMENT & TROPHY ABBREVIATIONS

MAIN TOURNAMENTS	CODE	ON TOUR
		(Away Team)
4 NATIONS	4N	
4 NATIONS & CALCUTTA CUP	4N-CC	
5 NATIONS	5N	
5 NATIONS & CALCUTTA CUP	5N-CC	
5 NATIONS & QUAICH TROPHY	5N-CQ	
5 NATIONS & MILLENNIUM TROPHY	5N-MT	
6 NATIONS	6N	
6 NATIONS & CALCUTTA CUP	6N-CC	
6 NATIONS & QUAICH TROPHY	6N-CQ	
6 NATIONS & GARIBALDI TROPHY	6N-GG	
6 NATIONS & MILLENNIUM TROPHY	6N-MT	
ADMIRAL WILLIAM BROWN CUP	ABC	ABC-T
ANTIM CUP	AC	AC-T
TROPHEE DES BICENTENAIRES	BIC	BIC-T
BLEDISLOE CUP	Bled	Bled-T
CALCUTTA CUP	CC	
COOK CUP	CKC	CKC-T
CENTENARY QUAICH TROPHY	CQT	
CONSUR CUP	CSC	
DAVE GALLAHER TROPHY	DGT	DGT-T
DOUGLAS HORN TROPHY	DHT	DHT-T
SIR EDMUND HILLARY SHIELD	EHS	EHS-T
FREEDOM CUP	FC	FC-T
FIRA EUROPEAN CUP (1952-54)	FEC	
FIRA EUROPEAN TROPHY (1936-38)	FET	
FIRA CHAMPIONSHIP (from 1965)	FIRA	
GIUSEPPE GARIBALDI TROPH	GGT	
HOPETOUN CUP	HC	HC-T
INVESTEC CHALLENGE CUP	ICC	ICC-T
FRIENDLY INTERNATIONALS	Int	Int-T
CENTENARY INTERNATIONAL	Int-C	
JAMES BEVAN TROPHY	JBT	JBT-T
LANSDOWNE CUP	LC	LC-T

MAIN TOURNAMENTS	CODE	ON TOUR
		(Away Team)
LIONS / SOUTH AFRICA SERIES (from 2009)	LSA	
LATIN CUP (1995-97)	LTC	
MANDELA CHALLENGE PLATE	MCP	MCP-T
MEDITERRANEAN CUP (1955-93)	MED	
MILLENNIUM TROPHY	MT	MT-T
OLYMPIC GAMES / pre-OLYMPIC GAMES	OG	pOG
PAN AMERICAN CHAMPIONSHIP (from 1995)	PAC	
PUMA TROPHY	PT	PT-T
PRINCE WILLIAM CUP	PWC	PWC-T
RUGBY CHAMPIONSHIP	RC	
RUGBY CHAMPIONSHIP & BLEDISLOE CUP	RC-B	
RUGBY CHAMPIONSHIP & FREEDOM CUP	RC-F	
RUG. CHAMP. & MANDELA CHALLENGE PLATE	RC-M	
RUGBY CHAMPIONSHIP & PUMA TROPHY	RC-P	
SOUTH AMERICAN CHAMPIONSHIP	SAC	
TRI NATIONS	TN	
TRI NATIONS & BLEDISLOE CUP	TN-B	
TRI NATIONS & FREEDOM CUP	TN-F	
TRI NATIONS & MANDELA CHALLENGE PLATE	TN-M	
TOM RICHARDS TROPHY	TRT	
WEBB ELLIS WORLD CUP FINAL	WCf	
WORLD CUP QUALIFYING ROUNDS	WCQ	
WORLD CUP POOL STAGES	WCp	
WORLD CUP PLAY-OFFS	WCpo	
WORLD CUP QUARTER-FINALS	WCqf	
WORLD CUP SEMI-FINALS	WCsf	
WORLD CUP THIRD / FOURTH PLACE	WC34	

THE MAJOR NATIONS

ARGENTINA

In 1899, four rugby-playing clubs in Buenos Aires got together and formed the River Plate Rugby Football Union. This led to the birth of the Argentina national team that played its first International match against a touring Great Britain XV in 1910, and lost by 28 points to 3. Seventeen years elapsed before they played their next four games, this time against a touring Great Britain XV in 1927. All four games were lost.

Five years later, in July 1932, the Junior Springboks visited Buenos Aires and they too defeated the home side in both games played. Argentina finally tasted success in their ninth match, away to Chile in Valparaiso, when they beat the home side in both matches by margins of nearly thirty points. In 1949, Argentina hosted France, and although losing both matches, they acquitted themselves well in their first encounter against a major nation. The South American Championship began in 1951 with Argentina, the hosts, winning the tournament by defeating Uruguay, Brazil and Chile. When France returned in 1954, the Argentinians were soundly beaten in both matches. The second South American Championship, held in Chile in 1958, was again won by Argentina: Peru and Uruguay were well beaten, but Chile did offer some resistance. In 1960, on their third visit, France exposed the huge gap between Five Nations rugby and South American rugby when they won all three matches. The Argentinians were again South American champions in 1961 and 1964, demolishing all opposition.

In 1965, Argentina embarked on their first tour outside South America, when they travelled to South Africa to play two Internationals. The team lost against Rhodesia (now Zimbabwe) in their first game, but in their second match in Johannesburg they avenged their four previous defeats to the Junior Springboks. The team's impressive power and stamina won them the nickname 'Los Pumas'. During the period 1968 to 1979, Argentina played a total of twenty-two matches against seven of the eight IRB founding members. Despite winning only five of these games and drawing three more, the Pumas gained tremendously from the experience, and proved that they could now compete with the best.

They continued to challenge the top teams throughout the 1980s, defeating Australia in Brisbane in 1983, and again, at home in Buenos Aires, in 1987. They also defeated France on three occasions at home: in 1985, 1986 and 1988. However, the highlight of the decade occurred on 2 November 1985, when the Pumas held the mighty All Blacks to a 21-all draw in Buenos Aires. They could now face the 1987 World Cup with some confidence of reaching the quarter-final, but an unexpected loss to Fiji at the pool stage thwarted those ambitions. Worse was to follow at the next two World Cup competitions, in 1991 and 1995, when they finished bottom of their pool.

However the Pumas did have some success in the early 1990s: ten successive wins between September 1992 and October 1993 included a first win over France on French soil, but the run was eventually ended by a 2-0 series loss to South Africa. Proving their resilience, the Pumas staged a comeback in June 1994 with a 2-0 series win over Scotland in Buenos Aires. A drawn series with England in May/June 1997, followed by another drawn series with Australia in November, enhanced Argentina's reputation as a Tier 1 nation. This formed the basis of their success in the 1999 World Cup. In that tournament, the Argentinians reached the quarter-final stage by eliminating Ireland in a play-off, their first win against a full Irish side, and two years later, in 2001, they defeated the Welsh in Cardiff. The Argentinians were not so successful at the 2003 World Cup, when they were eliminated at the pool stage of the tournament.

Argentina registered wins against all the Six Nations teams between 2004 and 2007; these included a 2-0 home series win against Wales in June 2006, followed by another series win, also at home, against Ireland in May and June 2007. The kind of form that the team was exhibiting enabled them to reach the semi-final stage of the 2007 World Cup by eliminating Ireland at the pool stage, and going on to overcome Scotland in the quarter-final. Their winning streak was cut short, however, by a defeat to South Africa (the World Cup winners of 2007) in the semi-final. Yet not all was lost: the Pumas ended on a high note as they beat France, the host nation, in the 3rd/4th place play-off match.

Such success aided Argentina's aspiration of gaining entry to the Tri Nations tournament, but poor results against Tier 1 teams in 2008 and 2009 did little to help their cause. However, on 14 September 2009, SANZAR (which stands for South Africa, New Zealand and Australia Rugby) issued a provisional invitation to Argentina to join an expanded Southern Hemisphere competition. The invitation contained certain conditions and also took into account that the existing TV rights did not expire until 2010.

Three wins in nine matches against Tier 1 sides, in 2010 and 2011, was no improvement on Argentina's performance in the previous two years, but in spite of this, at a meeting in Buenos Aires on 23 November 2011, it was decided that a new competition called The Rugby Championship should be formed. The competition would comprise the three Tri Nations teams (Australia, New Zealand and South Africa) and Argentina, with the first tournament starting in August 2012.

During 2012 the Pumas won three matches from six against the Northern Hemisphere Tier 1 teams, but in the inaugural Southern Hemisphere Rugby Championship they lost five out of the six matches, with one drawn game against South Africa, in Mendoza. Argentina's only victory against a Tier 1 country in 2013 was against Italy in November. This sole win followed a disastrous run of six defeats in that year's Rugby Championship.

In the less demanding South American Championship, a tournament that was established in 1951, the Pumas have been champions thirty-four times and, in fact, between 1951 and 2013 they did not lose a single game. A new tournament was instituted in 2014, the Consur Cup, which involved Argentina, who were seeded, and Uruguay and Chile, the top two teams of the previous year's South American Championship. The Pumas were easy winners of the inaugural competition.

Later in June, they lost twice to Ireland and once to Scotland but worse was to come in the Rugby Championship, when they lost the first five matches of the competition. There was some compensation, however: they won their final match against Australia, and finished the year in style by defeating both Italy and France on their autumn tour of the Northern Hemisphere.

ARGENTINA

HEAD TO HEAD RESULTS TO 31 MARCH 2015

	P	W	D	L	%	F	A
v TIER 1 Teams							
v Australia	23	5	1	17	23.9	363	610
v England	19	4	1	14	23.7	282	488
v France	48	13	1	34	28.1	754	1169
v Ireland	15	5	0	10	33.3	283	331
v Italy	20	14	1	5	72.5	496	344
v New Zealand	20	0	1	19	2.5	260	816
v Scotland	15	9	0	6	60.0	268	309
v South Africa	19	0	1	18	2.6	361	728
v Wales	15	5	0	10	33.3	350	428
Sub-Total	**194**	**55**	**6**	**133**	**29.9**	**3417**	**5223**
v TIER 2/3 Group							
v Canada	8	6	0	2	75.0	262	137
v Fiji	4	3	0	1	75.0	130	96
v Japan	5	4	0	1	80.0	205	139
v Romania	8	8	0	0	100.0	317	97
v Samoa	4	1	0	3	25.0	82	111
v Tonga	0	0	0	0	0.0	0	0
v United States	8	8	0	0	100.0	247	119
v Georgia	3	3	0	0	100.0	87	28
v Namibia	2	2	0	0	100.0	130	17
v Russia	0	0	0	0	0.0	0	0
v Uruguay	39	39	0	0	100.0	1666	391
Sub-Total	**81**	**74**	**0**	**7**	**91.4**	**3126**	**1135**
v TIER 3 Selection							
v Brazil	13	13	0	0	100.0	1054	47
v Chile	37	37	0	0	100.0	1716	243
v Paraguay	16	16	0	0	100.0	1311	58
v Spain	4	4	0	0	100.0	149	75
Sub-Total	**70**	**70**	**0**	**0**	**100.0**	**4230**	**423**
v Other Teams	**46**	**13**	**4**	**29**	**32.6**	**546**	**774**
All Internationals	**391**	**212**	**10 1**	**69**	**55.5**	**11319**	**7555**

5

No	Date	Opponents	Tmt	Match Venue	Result	
1	12-Jun-10	Gt Britain XV	Int	H	Polo Ground Flores, Buenos Aires	L	3-28
2	31-Jul-27	Gt Britain XV	Int	H	Estadio G.E.B.A., Buenos Aires	L	0-37
3	7-Aug-27	Gt Britain XV	Int	H	Estadio G.E.B.A., Buenos Aires	L	0-46
4	14-Aug-27	Gt Britain XV	Int	H	Estadio G.E.B.A., Buenos Aires	L	3-34
5	21-Aug-27	Gt Britain XV	Int	H	Estadio G.E.B.A., Buenos Aires	L	0-43
6	16-Jul-32	Jnr Springboks	Int	H	Ferro Carril Oeste Stadium, B Aires	L	0-42
7	23-Jul-32	Jnr Springboks	Int	H	Ferro Carril Oeste Stadium, B Aires	L	3-34
8	16-Aug-36	Gt Britain XV	Int	H	Estadio G.E.B.A., Buenos Aires	L	0-23
9	20-Sep-36	Chile	Int-T	A	Estadio Playa Ancha, Valparaiso	W	29-0
10	27-Sep-36	Chile	Int-T	A	Estadio Playa Ancha, Valparaiso	W	31-3
11	21-Aug-38	Chile	Int	H	Estadio G.E.B.A., Buenos Aires	W	33-3
12	29-Aug-48	Oxford & Cam.	Int	H	Estadio G.E.B.A., Buenos Aires	L	0-17
13	5-Sep-48	Oxford & Cam.	Int	H	Estadio G.E.B.A., Buenos Aires	L	0-39
14	28-Aug-49	France	Int	H	Estadio G.E.B.A., Buenos Aires	L	0-5
15	4-Sep-49	France	Int	H	Estadio G.E.B.A., Buenos Aires	L	3-12
16	9-Sep-51	Uruguay	SAC	H	Estadio G.E.B.A., Buenos Aires	W	62-0
17	13-Sep-51	Brazil	SAC	H	Estadio G.E.B.A., Buenos Aires	W	72-0
18	16-Sep-51	Chile	SAC	H	Estadio G.E.B.A., Buenos Aires	W	13-3
19	24-Aug-52	Ireland XV	Int	H	Estadio G.E.B.A., Buenos Aires	D	3-3
20	31-Aug-52	Ireland XV	Int	H	Estadio G.E.B.A., Buenos Aires	L	0-6
21	29-Aug-54	France	Int	H	Ferro Carril Oeste Stadium, B Aires	L	8-22
22	12-Sep-54	France	Int	H	Ferro Carril Oeste Stadium, B Aires	L	3-30
23	26-Aug-56	Oxford & Cam.	Int	H	Estadio G.E.B.A., Buenos Aires	L	6-25
24	16-Sep-56	Oxford & Cam.	Int	H	Estadio G.E.B.A., Buenos Aires	L	3-11
25	11-Sep-58	Peru	SAC	N	Stade Français, Santiago	W	44-0
26	15-Sep-58	Uruguay	SAC	N	Estadio Sausalito, Viña del Mar	W	50-3
27	18-Sep-58	Chile	SAC	A	Prince of Wales Country Club, Santiago	W	14-0
28	12-Sep-59	Jnr Springboks	Int	H	Estadio G.E.B.A., Buenos Aires	L	6-14
29	3-Oct-59	Jnr Springboks	Int	H	Estadio G.E.B.A., Buenos Aires	L	6-20
30	23-Jul-60	France	Int	H	Estadio G.E.B.A., Buenos Aires	L	3-37
31	6-Aug-60	France	Int	H	Estadio G.E.B.A., Buenos Aires	L	3-12
32	17-Aug-60	France	Int	H	Estadio G.E.B.A., Buenos Aires	L	6-29
33	7-Oct-61	Chile	SAC	N	Camino Carrasco Polo Club, Montevideo	W	11-3
34	12-Oct-61	Brazil	SAC	N	Camino Carrasco Polo Club, Montevideo	W	60-0
35	14-Oct-61	Uruguay	SAC	A	Camino Carrasco Polo Club, Montevideo	W	36-3
36	15-Aug-64	Uruguay	SAC	N	San Pablo Athletic Ground, São Paulo	W	25-6
37	19-Aug-64	Brazil	SAC	A	San Pablo Athletic Ground, São Paulo	W	30-8
38	22-Aug-64	Chile	SAC	N	San Pablo Athletic Ground, São Paulo	W	30-8
39	8-May-65	Rhodesia	Int-T	A	Police Grounds, Salisbury	L	12-17
40	19-Jun-65	Jnr Springboks	Int-T	A	Ellis Park, Johannesburg	W	11-6

No	Date	Opponents	Tmt		Match Venue	Result	
41	11-Sep-65	Oxford & Cam.	Int	H	Estadio G.E.B.A., Buenos Aires	D	19-19
42	18-Sep-65	Oxford & Cam.	Int	H	Estadio G.E.B.A., Buenos Aires	L	3-9
43	26-Sep-65	Chile	Int-T	A	Prince of Wales Country Club, Santiago	W	23-11
44	24-Sep-66	SA Gazelles	Int	H	Estadio G.E.B.A., Buenos Aires	L	3-9
45	1-Oct-66	SA Gazelles	Int	H	Estadio G.E.B.A., Buenos Aires	L	15-20
46	27-Sep-67	Uruguay	SAC	H	Club Atlético San Isidro, Buenos Aires	W	38-6
47	30-Sep-67	Chile	SAC	H	Club Atlético San Isidro, Buenos Aires	W	18-0
48	14-Sep-68	Wales XV	Int	H	Estadio G.E.B.A., Buenos Aires	W	9-5
49	28-Sep-68	Wales XV	Int	H	Estadio G.E.B.A., Buenos Aires	D	9-9
50	13-Sep-69	Scotland XV	Int	H	Estadio G.E.B.A., Buenos Aires	W	20-3
51	27-Sep-69	Scotland XV	Int	H	Estadio G.E.B.A., Buenos Aires	L	3-6
52	4-Oct-69	Uruguay	SAC	N	Prince of Wales Country Club, Santiago	W	41-6
53	11-Oct-69	Chile	SAC	A	Prince of Wales Country Club, Santiago	W	54-0
54	13-Sep-70	Ireland XV	Int	H	Ferro Carril Oeste Stadium, B Aires	W	8-3
55	20-Sep-70	Ireland XV	Int	H	Ferro Carril Oeste Stadium, B Aires	W	6-3
56	17-Jul-71	SA Gazelles	Int-T	A	Boet Erasmus Stadium, Port Elizabeth	L	6-12
57	7-Aug-71	SA Gazelles	Int-T	A	Loftus Versfeld Stadium, Pretoria	W	12-0
58	28-Aug-71	Oxford & Cam.	Int	H	Ferro Carril Oeste Stadium, B Aires	W	11-3
59	4-Sep-71	Oxford & Cam.	Int	H	Ferro Carril Oeste Stadium, B Aires	W	6-3
60	10-Oct-71	Chile	SAC	N	Camino Carrasco Polo Club, Montevideo	W	20-3
61	12-Oct-71	Brazil	SAC	N	Camino Carrasco Polo Club, Montevideo	W	50-6
62	16-Oct-71	Paraguay	SAC	N	Camino Carrasco Polo Club, Montevideo	W	61-0
63	17-Oct-71	Uruguay	SAC	A	Camino Carrasco Polo Club, Montevideo	W	55-6
64	21-Oct-72	SA Gazelles	Int	H	Ferro Carril Oeste Stadium, B Aires	L	6-14
65	4-Nov-72	SA Gazelles	Int	H	Ferro Carril Oeste Stadium, B Aires	W	18-16
66	8-Sep-73	Romania	Int	H	Ferro Carril Oeste Stadium, B Aires	W	15-9
67	15-Sep-73	Romania	Int	H	Ferro Carril Oeste Stadium, B Aires	W	24-3
68	14-Oct-73	Paraguay	SAC	N	Clube Atlético Ground, São Paulo	W	98-3
69	16-Oct-73	Uruguay	SAC	N	Clube Atlético Ground, São Paulo	W	55-0
70	20-Oct-73	Brazil	SAC	A	Clube Atlético Ground, São Paulo	W	96-0
71	21-Oct-73	Chile	SAC	N	Clube Atlético Ground-São Paulo	W	60-3
72	10-Nov-73	Ireland XV	Int-T	A	Lansdowne Road, Dublin	L	8-21
73	24-Nov-73	Scotland XV	Int-T	A	Murrayfield, Edinburgh	L	11-12
74	20-Jun-74	France	Int	H	Ferro Carril Oeste Stadium, B Aires	L	15-20
75	29-Jun-74	France	Int	H	Ferro Carril Oeste Stadium, B Aires	L	27-31
76	21-Sep-75	Uruguay	SAC	N	Estadio del Colegio San José, Asunción	W	30-15
77	25-Sep-75	Paraguay	SAC	A	Estadio del Colegio San José, Asunción	W	93-0
78	27-Sep-75	Brazil	SAC	N	Estadio del Colegio San José, Asunción	W	64-6
79	28-Sep-75	Chile	SAC	N	Estadio del Colegio San José, Asunción	W	45-3
80	19-Oct-75	France	Int-T	A	Stade de Gerland, Lyon	L	6-29

No	Date	Opponents	Tmt		Match Venue		Result
81	25-Oct-75	France	Int-T	A	Parc des Princess, Paris	L	21-36
82	16-Oct-76	Wales XV	Int-T	A	National Stadium, Cardiff	L	19-20
83	30-Oct-76	NZ XV	Int	H	Ferro Carril Oeste Stadium, B Aires	L	9-21
84	6-Nov-76	NZ XV	Int	H	Ferro Carril Oeste Stadium, B Aires	L	6-26
85	25-Jun-77	France	Int	H	Ferro Carril Oeste Stadium, B Aires	L	3-26
86	2-Jul-77	France	Int	H	Ferro Carril Oeste Stadium, B Aires	D	18-18
87	24-Oct-77	Brazil	SAC	H	Estadio Monumental José Fierro, Tucumán	W	78-6
88	28-Oct-77	Uruguay	SAC	H	Estadio Monumental José Fierro, Tucumán	W	70-0
89	29-Oct-77	Paraguay	SAC	H	Estadio Monumental José Fierro, Tucumán	W	77-3
90	30-Oct-77	Chile	SAC	H	Estadio Monumental José Fierro, Tucumán	W	25-10
91	14-Oct-78	England XV	Int-T	A	Twickenham, London	D	13-13
92	24-Oct-78	Italy	Int-T	A	Stadio Mario Battaglini, Rovigo	L	6-19
93	8-Sep-79	NZ XV	Int-T	A	Carisbrook, Dunedin	L	9-18
94	15-Sep-79	NZ XV	Int-T	A	Athletic Park, Wellington	L	6-15
95	4-Oct-79	Uruguay	SAC	N	Stade Français, Santiago	W	19-16
96	6-Oct-79	Chile	SAC	A	Stade Français, Santiago	W	34-15
97	7-Oct-79	Paraguay	SAC	N	Estadio Sausalito, Viña del Mar	W	76-13
98	9-Oct-79	Brazil	SAC	N	Stade Français, Santiago	W	109-3
99	27-Oct-79	Australia	Int	H	Ferro Carril Oeste Stadium, B Aires	W	24-13
100	3-Nov-79	Australia	Int	H	Ferro Carril Oeste Stadium, B Aires	L	12-17
101	9-Aug-80	World XV	Int	H	Ferro Carril Oeste Stadium, B Aires	W	36-22
102	1-Nov-80	Fiji	Int	H	Ferro Carril Oeste Stadium, B Aires	W	34-22
103	8-Nov-80	Fiji	Int	H	Ferro Carril Oeste Stadium, B Aires	W	38-16
104	30-May-81	England	Int	H	Ferro Carril Oeste Stadium, B Aires	D	19-19
105	6-Jun-81	England	Int	H	Ferro Carril Oeste Stadium, B Aires	L	6-12
106	3-Oct-81	Canada	Int	H	Estadio G.E.B.A., Buenos Aires	W	35-0
107	14-Nov-82	France	Int-T	A	Stade Municipal de Toulouse, Toulouse	L	12-25
108	20-Nov-82	France	Int-T	A	Parc des Princess, Paris	L	6-13
109	23-Nov-82	Spain	Int-T	A	Campo Ciudad Universitaria, Madrid	W	28-19
110	25-Jun-83	World XV	Int	H	Club Atlético Atlanta, Buenos Aires	W	28-20
111	16-Jul-83	Chile	SAC	H	Club Atlético San Isidro, Buenos Aires	W	46-6
112	20-Jul-83	Paraguay	SAC	H	Club Atlético San Isidro, Buenos Aires	W	43-3
113	23-Jul-83	Uruguay	SAC	H	Club Atlético San Isidro, Buenos Aires	W	29-6
114	31-Jul-83	Australia	Int-T	A	Ballymore Oval, Brisbane	W	18-3
115	7-Aug-83	Australia	Int-T	A	Cricket Ground, Sydney	L	13-29
116	22-Jun-85	France	Int	H	Ferro Carril Oeste Stadium, B Aires	W	24-16
117	29-Jun-85	France	Int	H	Ferro Carril Oeste Stadium, B Aires	L	15-23
118	17-Sep-85	Uruguay	SAC	N	Estadio General Pablo Rojas, Asunción	W	63-16
119	19-Sep-85	Chile	SAC	N	Estadio General Pablo Rojas, Asunción	W	59-6
120	21-Sep-85	Paraguay	SAC	A	Estadio General Pablo Rojas, Asunción	W	102-3

No	Date	Opponents	Tmt		Match Venue	Result	
121	26-Oct-85	New Zealand	Int	H	Ferro Carril Oeste Stadium, B Aires	L	20-33
122	2-Nov-85	New Zealand	Int	H	Ferro Carril Oeste Stadium, B Aires	D	21-21
123	31-May-86	France	Int	H	Vélez Sarsfield Stadium, Buenos Aires	W	15-13
124	7-Jun-86	France	Int	H	Vélez Sarsfield Stadium, Buenos Aires	L	9-22
125	6-Jul-86	Australia	Int-T	A	Ballymore Oval, Brisbane	L	19-39
126	12-Jul-86	Australia	Int-T	A	Cricket Ground, Sydney	L	0-26
127	3-May-87	Uruguay	Int-T	A	Estadio Gran Parque Central, Montevideo	W	38-3
128	24-May-87	Fiji	WCp	N	Rugby Park, Hamilton	L	9-28
129	28-May-87	Italy	WCp	N	Lancaster Park Oval, Christchurch	W	25-16
130	1-Jun-87	New Zealand	WCp	A	Athletic Park, Wellington	L	15-46
131	17-Aug-87	Spain	Int	H	Estadio José Maria Minella, Mar del Plata	W	40-12
132	27-Sep-87	Uruguay	SAC	N	Stade Français, Santiago	W	41-21
133	30-Sep-87	Paraguay	SAC	N	Stade Français, Santiago	W	62-4
134	3-Oct-87	Chile	SAC	A	Stade Français, Santiago	W	47-9
135	31-Oct-87	Australia	Int	H	Vélez Sarsfield Stadium, Buenos Aires	D	19-19
136	7-Nov-87	Australia	Int	H	Vélez Sarsfield Stadium, Buenos Aires	W	27-19
137	18-Jun-88	France	Int	H	Vélez Sarsfield Stadium, Buenos Aires	L	15-18
138	25-Jun-88	France	Int	H	Vélez Sarsfield Stadium, Buenos Aires	W	18-6
139	5-Nov-88	France	Int-T	A	Stade de la Beaujoire, Nantes	L	9-29
140	11-Nov-88	France	Int-T	A	Stade Lille-Métropole, Villeneuve	L	18-28
141	24-Jun-89	Italy	Int	H	Vélez Sarsfield Stadium, Buenos Aires	W	21-16
142	15-Jul-89	New Zealand	Int-T	A	Carisbrook, Dunedin	L	9-60
143	29-Jul-89	New Zealand	Int-T	A	Athletic Park, Wellington	L	12-49
144	8-Oct-89	Brazil	SAC	N	Estadio Charrúa, Montevideo	W	103-9
145	10-Oct-89	Chile	SAC	N	Estadio Charrúa, Montevideo	W	36-9
146	12-Oct-89	Paraguay	SAC	N	Estadio Charrúa, Montevideo	W	75-7
147	14-Oct-89	Uruguay	SAC	A	Estadio Charrúa, Montevideo	W	34-14
148	8-Nov-89	United States	WCQ	H	Vélez Sarsfield Stadium, Buenos Aires	W	23-6
149	30-Mar-90	Canada	WCQ	A	Swanguard Stadium, Burnaby Lake, BC	L	6-15
150	7-Apr-90	United States	WCQ	A	Harder Stadium, Santa Barbara, CA	W	13-6
151	16-Jun-90	Canada	WCQ	H	Vélez Sarsfield Stadium, Buenos Aires	L	15-19
152	28-Jul-90	England	Int	H	Vélez Sarsfield Stadium, Buenos Aires	L	12-25
153	4-Aug-90	England	Int	H	Vélez Sarsfield Stadium, Buenos Aires	W	15-13
154	27-Oct-90	Ireland	Int-T	A	Lansdowne Road, Dublin	L	18-20
155	3-Nov-90	England	Int-T	A	Twickenham, London	L	0-51
156	10-Nov-90	Scotland	Int-T	A	Murrayfield, Edinburgh	L	3-49
157	6-Jul-91	New Zealand	Int	H	Vélez Sarsfield Stadium, Buenos Aires	L	14-28
158	13-Jul-91	New Zealand	Int	H	Vélez Sarsfield Stadium, Buenos Aires	L	6-36
159	15-Aug-91	Chile	SAC	A	Prince of Wales Country Club, Santiago	W	41-6
160	21-Sep-91	Uruguay	SAC	H	Club Atlético San Isidro, Buenos Aires	W	32-9

No	Date	Opponents	Tmt		Match Venue	Result	
161	28-Sep-91	Paraguay	SAC	A	Estadio del Colegio San José, Asunción	W	37-10
162	1-Oct-91	Brazil	SAC	H	Belgrano Stadium, Buenos Aires	W	84-6
163	4-Oct-91	Australia	WCp	N	Stradey Park, Llanelli	L	19-32
164	9-Oct-91	Wales	WCp	A	National Stadium, Cardiff	L	7-16
165	13-Oct-91	Western Samoa	WCp	N	Sardis Road, Pontypridd	L	12-35
166	4-Jul-92	France	Int	H	Vélez Sarsfield Stadium, Buenos Aires	L	12-27
167	11-Jul-92	France	Int	H	Vélez Sarsfield Stadium, Buenos Aires	L	9-33
168	26-Sep-92	Spain	Int	H	Vélez Sarsfield Stadium, Buenos Aires	W	38-10
169	24-Oct-92	Spain	Int-T	A	Campo Ciudad Universitaria, Madrid	W	43-34
170	31-Oct-92	Romania	Int-T	A	Stadionul 23 August, Bucharest	W	21-18
171	14-Nov-92	France	Int-T	A	Stade de la Beaujoire, Nantes	W	24-20
172	15-May-93	Japan	Int	H	Estadio G.E.B.A., Buenos Aires	W	30-27
173	22-May-93	Japan	Int	H	Ferro Carril Oeste Stadium, B Aires	W	45-20
174	2-Oct-93	Brazil	SAC	A	Clube Atlético Ground, São Paulo	W	114-3
175	11-Oct-93	Chile (SAC)	WCQ	H	Estadio G.E.B.A., Buenos Aires	W	70-7
176	16-Oct-93	Paraguay (SAC)	WCQ	H	Estadio G.E.B.A., Buenos Aires	W	51-3
177	23-Oct-93	Uruguay (SAC)	WCQ	A	Estadio Gran Parque Central, Montevideo	W	19-10
178	6-Nov-93	South Africa	Int	H	Ferro Carril Oeste Stadium, B Aires	L	26-29
179	13-Nov-93	South Africa	Int	H	Ferro Carril Oeste Stadium, B Aires	L	23-52
180	28-May-94	United States	WCQ	A	George Allen Memorial Field, Long Beach	W	28-22
181	4-Jun-94	Scotland	Int	H	Ferro Carril Oeste Stadium, B Aires	W	16-15
182	11-Jun-94	Scotland	Int	H	Ferro Carril Oeste Stadium, B Aires	W	19-17
183	20-Jun-94	United States	WCQ	H	Ferro Carril Oeste Stadium, B Aires	W	16-11
184	8-Oct-94	South Africa	Int-T	A	Boet Erasmus Stadium, Port Elizabeth	L	22-42
185	15-Oct-94	South Africa	Int-T	A	Ellis Park, Johannesburg	L	26-46
186	4-Mar-95	Uruguay	PAC	H	Ferro Carril Oeste Stadium, B Aires	W	44-3
187	10-Mar-95	Canada	PAC	H	Ferro Carril Oeste Stadium, B Aires	W	29-26
188	30-Apr-95	Australia	Int-T	A	Ballymore Oval, Brisbane	L	7-53
189	6-May-95	Australia	Int-T	A	Football Stadium, Sydney	L	13-30
190	27-May-95	England	WCp	N	Kings Park Stadium, Durban	L	18-24
191	30-May-95	Western Samoa	WCp	N	Basil Kenyon Stadium, East London	L	26-32
192	4-Jun-95	Italy	WCp	N	Basil Kenyon Stadium, East London	L	25-31
193	24-Sep-95	Paraguay	SAC	A	Estadio de las Fuerzas, Asunción	W	103-9
194	30-Sep-95	Chile	SAC	A	Prince of Wales Country Club, Santiago	W	78-3
195	8-Oct-95	Uruguay	SAC	H	Tacuru Social Club Posadas, Misiones	W	52-37
196	14-Oct-95	Romania	LTC	H	Ferro Carril Oeste Stadium, B Aires	W	51-16
197	17-Oct-95	Italy	LTC	H	Estadio Monumental José Fierro, Tucumán	W	26-6
198	21-Oct-95	France	LTC	H	Ferro Carril Oeste Stadium, B Aires	L	12-47
199	8-Jun-96	Uruguay	Int-T	A	Camino Carrasco Polo Club, Montevideo	W	37-18
200	22-Jun-96	France	Int	H	Ferro Carril Oeste Stadium, B Aires	L	27-34

No	Date	Opponents	Tmt	Match Venue	Result	
201	29-Jun-96	France	Int	H Ferro Carril Oeste Stadium, B Aires	L	15-34
202	14-Sep-96	United States	PAC	N Twin Elms Rugby Park, Nepean, Ontario	W	29-26
203	18-Sep-96	Uruguay	PAC	N Mohawk Sports Park, Hamilton, Ontario	W	54-20
204	21-Sep-96	Canada	PAC	A Fletcher's Field, Markham, Toronto	W	41-21
205	9-Nov-96	South Africa	Int	H Ferro Carril Oeste Stadium, B Aires	L	15-46
206	16-Nov-96	South Africa	Int	H Ferro Carril Oeste Stadium, B Aires	L	21-44
207	14-Dec-96	England	Int-T	A Twickenham, London	L	18-20
208	31-May-97	England	Int	H Ferro Carril Oeste Stadium, B Aires	L	20-46
209	7-Jun-97	England	Int	H Ferro Carril Oeste Stadium, B Aires	W	33-13
210	21-Jun-97	New Zealand	Int-T	A Athletic Park, Wellington	L	8-93
211	28-Jun-97	New Zealand	Int-T	A Rugby Park, Hamilton	L	10-62
212	13-Sep-97	Paraguay	SAC	H Aranduroga Rugby Club, Corrientes	W	78-0
213	27-Sep-97	Uruguay	SAC	A Camino Carrasco Polo Club, Montevideo	W	56-17
214	4-Oct-97	Chile	SAC	H Estadio La Carrodilla, Mendoza	W	50-10
215	18-Oct-97	Romania	LTC	N Stade Jacques Fouroux, Auch	W	45-18
216	22-Oct-97	Italy	LTC	N Stade Antoine Béguère, Lourdes	D	18-18
217	26-Oct-97	France	LTC	A Stade Maurice Trélut, Tarbes	L	27-32
218	1-Nov-97	Australia	Int	H Ferro Carril Oeste Stadium, B Aires	L	15-23
219	8-Nov-97	Australia	Int	H Ferro Carril Oeste Stadium, B Aires	W	18-16
220	13-Jun-98	France	Int	H Vélez Sarsfield Stadium, Buenos Aires	L	18-35
221	20-Jun-98	France	Int	H Vélez Sarsfield Stadium, Buenos Aires	L	12-37
222	8-Aug-98	Romania	Int	H Estadio Gabino Sosa, Rosario	W	68-22
223	15-Aug-98	U. States(PAC)	WCQ	H Cricket and Rugby Club, Buenos Aires	W	52-24
224	18-Aug-98	Uruguay (PAC)	WCQ	H Club Atlético San Isidro, Buenos Aires	W	55-0
225	22-Aug-98	Canada (PAC)	WCQ	H Cricket and Rugby Club, Buenos Aires	W	54-28
226	15-Sep-98	Japan	Int-T	A Prince Chichibu Memorial Ground, Tokyo	L	29-44
227	3-Oct-98	Paraguay	SAC	A Estadio del Colegio San José, Asunción	W	59-0
228	10-Oct-98	Chile	SAC	A Prince of Wales Country Club, Santiago	W	25-17
229	17-Oct-98	Uruguay	SAC	H Club Atlético San Isidro, Buenos Aires	W	30-14
230	7-Nov-98	Italy	Int-T	A Stadio Comunale Beltrametti, Piacenza	L	19-23
231	14-Nov-98	France	Int-T	A Stade de la Beaujoire, Nantes	L	14-34
232	21-Nov-98	Wales	Int-T	A Stradey Park, Llanelli	L	30-43
233	5-Jun-99	Wales	Int	H Ferro Carril Oeste Stadium, B Aires	L	26-36
234	12-Jun-99	Wales	Int	H Ferro Carril Oeste Stadium, B Aires	L	16-23
235	21-Aug-99	Scotland	Int-T	A Murrayfield, Edinburgh	W	31-22
236	28-Aug-99	Ireland	Int-T	A Lansdowne Road, Dublin	L	24-32
237	1-Oct-99	Wales	WCp	A Millennium Stadium, Cardiff	L	18-23
238	10-Oct-99	Samoa	WCp	N Stradey Park, Llanelli	W	32-16
239	16-Oct-99	Japan	WCp	N Millennium Stadium, Cardiff	W	33-12
240	20-Oct-99	Ireland	WCpo	N Stade Félix Bollaert, Lens	W	28-24

No	Date	Opponents	Tmt		Match Venue	Result	
241	24-Oct-99	France	WCqf	N	Lansdowne Road, Dublin	L	26-47
242	3-Jun-00	Ireland	Int	H	Ferro Carril Oeste Stadium, B Aires	W	34-23
243	17-Jun-00	Australia	PT-T	A	Ballymore Oval, Brisbane	L	6-53
244	24-Jun-00	Australia	PT-T	A	Canberra Stadium, Canberra	L	25-32
245	12-Nov-00	South Africa	Int	H	Estadio Monumental A V Liberti, B Aires	L	33-37
246	25-Nov-00	England	Int-T	A	Twickenham, London	L	0-19
247	19-May-01	Uruguay	PAC	N	Richardson Stadium, Kingston, Ontario	W	32-27
248	23-May-01	United States	PAC	N	Mohawk Sports Park, Hamilton, Ontario	W	44-16
249	26-May-01	Canada	PAC	A	Fletcher's Field, Markham, Toronto	W	20-6
250	23-Jun-01	New Zealand	Int-T	A	Jade Stadium, Christchurch	L	19-67
251	14-Jul-01	Italy	Int	H	Ferro Carril Oeste Stadium, B Aires	W	38-17
252	10-Nov-01	Wales	Int-T	A	Millennium Stadium, Cardiff	W	30-16
253	18-Nov-01	Scotland	Int-T	A	Murrayfield, Edinburgh	W	25-16
254	1-Dec-01	New Zealand	Int	H	Estadio Monumental A V Liberti, B Aires	L	20-24
255	28-Apr-02	Uruguay	SAC	H	Estadio Bautista Gargantini, Mendoza	W	35-21
256	1-May-02	Paraguay	SAC	H	Estadio Bautista Gargantini, Mendoza	W	152-0
257	4-May-02	Chile	SAC	H	Estadio Bautista Gargantini, Mendoza	W	57-13
258	15-Jun-02	France	Int	H	Vélez Sarsfield Stadium, Buenos Aires	W	28-27
259	22-Jun-02	England	Int	H	Vélez Sarsfield Stadium, Buenos Aires	L	18-26
260	29-Jun-02	South Africa	Int-T	A	P A M Brink Stadium, Springs	L	29-49
261	2-Nov-02	Australia	PT	H	Estadio Monumental, River Plate, B Aires	L	6-17
262	16-Nov-02	Italy	Int-T	A	Stadio Flaminio, Rome	W	36-6
263	23-Nov-02	Ireland	Int-T	A	Lansdowne Road, Dublin	L	7-16
264	27-Apr-03	Paraguay	SAC	N	Estadio Luis Franzini, Montevideo	W	144-0
265	30-Apr-03	Chile	SAC	N	Estadio Luis Franzini, Montevideo	W	49-3
266	3-May-03	Uruguay	SAC	A	Estadio Luis Franzini, Montevideo	W	32-0
267	14-Jun-03	France	Int	H	Vélez Sarsfield Stadium, Buenos Aires	W	10-6
268	20-Jun-03	France	Int	H	Vélez Sarsfield Stadium, Buenos Aires	W	33-32
269	28-Jun-03	South Africa	Int-T	A	EPRFU Stadium, Port Elizabeth	L	25-26
270	18-Aug-03	Fiji	Int	H	Estadio Olimpico Château Carreras, Córdoba	W	49-30
271	23-Aug-03	United States	PAC	H	Cricket and Rugby Club, Buenos Aires	W	42-8
272	27-Aug-03	Uruguay	PAC	H	Club Atlético San Isidro, Buenos Aires	W	57-0
273	30-Aug-03	Canada	PAC	H	Cricket and Rugby Club, Buenos Aires	W	62-22
274	10-Oct-03	Australia	WCp	A	Telstra Stadium, Sydney	L	8-24
275	14-Oct-03	Namibia	WCp	N	Central Coast Stadium, Gosford, NSW	W	67-14
276	22-Oct-03	Romania	WCp	N	Aussie Stadium, Sydney	W	50-3
277	26-Oct-03	Ireland	WCp	N	Adelaide Oval, Adelaide	L	15-16
278	25-Apr-04	Chile	SAC	A	Prince of Wales Country Club, Santiago	W	45-3
279	28-Apr-04	Uruguay	SAC	N	Prince of Wales Country Club, Santiago	W	69-10
280	1-May-04	Venezuela	SAC	N	Prince of Wales Country Club, Santiago	W	147-7

No	Date	Opponents	Tmt		Match Venue	Result	
281	12-Jun-04	Wales	Int	H	Estadio Monumental José Fierro, Tucumán	W	50-44
282	19-Jun-04	Wales	Int	H	Vélez Sarsfield Stadium, Buenos Aires	L	20-35
283	26-Jun-04	New Zealand	Int-T	A	Waikato Stadium, Hamilton	L	7-41
284	20-Nov-04	France	Int-T	A	Stade Vélodrome, Marseille	W	24-14
285	27-Nov-04	Ireland	Int-T	A	Lansdowne Road, Dublin	L	19-21
286	4-Dec-04	South Africa	Int	H	Vélez Sarsfield Stadium, Buenos Aires	L	7-39
287	23-Apr-05	Japan	Int	H	Cricket and Rugby Club, Buenos Aires	W	68-36
288	8-May-05	Chile	SAC	H	Club Monte Grande, Buenos Aires	W	48-13
289	15-May-05	Uruguay	SAC	H	Club Los Matreros, Buenos Aires	W	27-21
290	11-Jun-05	Italy	Int	H	Estadio Padre Ernesto Martearena, Salta	W	35-21
291	17-Jun-05	Italy	Int	H	Estadio Olimpico Château Carreras, Córdoba	L	29-30
292	5-Nov-05	South Africa	Int	H	Vélez Sarsfield Stadium, Buenos Aires	L	23-34
293	12-Nov-05	Scotland	Int-T	A	Murrayfield, Edinburgh	W	23-19
294	19-Nov-05	Italy	Int-T	A	Stadio Luigi Ferraris, Genova	W	39-22
295	3-Dec-05	Samoa	Int	H	Cricket and Rugby Club, Buenos Aires	L	12-28
296	11-Jun-06	Wales	Int	H	Estadio Raúl Conti, Puerto Madryn	W	27-25
297	17-Jun-06	Wales	Int	H	Vélez Sarsfield Stadium, Buenos Aires	W	45-27
298	24-Jun-06	New Zealand	Int	H	Vélez Sarsfield Stadium, Buenos Aires	L	19-25
299	1-Jul-06	Chile (SAC)	WCQ	A	Prince of Wales Country Club, Santiago	W	60-13
300	8-Jul-06	Uruguay (SAC)	WCQ	H	Club Atlético San Isidro, Buenos Aires	W	26-0
301	11-Nov-06	England	Int-T	A	Twickenham, London	W	25-18
302	18-Nov-06	Italy	Int-T	A	Stadio Flaminio, Rome	W	23-16
303	25-Nov-06	France	Int-T	A	Stade de France, Paris	L	26-27
304	26-May-07	Ireland	Int	H	Estadio Brig General E. López, Santa Fe	W	22-20
305	2-Jun-07	Ireland	Int	H	Vélez Sarsfield Stadium, Buenos Aires	W	16-0
306	9-Jun-07	Italy	Int	H	Estadio Malvinas Argentinas, Mendoza	W	24-6
307	18-Aug-07	Wales	Int-T	A	Millennium Stadium, Cardiff	L	20-27
308	7-Sep-07	France	WCp	A	Stade de France, Paris	W	17-12
309	11-Sep-07	Georgia	WCp	N	Stade de Gerland, Lyon	W	33-3
310	22-Sep-07	Namibia	WCp	N	Stade Vélodrome, Marseille	W	63-3
311	30-Sep-07	Ireland	WCp	N	Parc des Princess, Paris	W	30-15
312	7-Oct-07	Scotland	WCqf	N	Stade de France, Paris	W	19-13
313	14-Oct-07	South Africa	WCsf	N	Stade de France, Paris	L	13-37
314	19-Oct-07	France	WC34	A	Parc des Princess, Paris	W	34-10
315	15-Dec-07	Chile	SAC	H	Estadio San Martin de San Juan, San Juan	W	79-8
316	31-May-08	Uruguay	SAC	A	Estadio Charrúa, Montevideo	W	43-8
317	7-Jun-08	Scotland	Int	H	Estadio Gigante de Arroyito, Rosario	W	21-15
318	14-Jun-08	Scotland	Int	H	Vélez Sarsfield Stadium, Buenos Aires	L	14-26
319	28-Jun-08	Italy	Int	H	Estadio Olimpico Château Carreras, Córdoba	L	12-13
320	9-Aug-08	South Africa	Int-T	A	Coca Cola Park, Johannesburg	L	9-63

No	Date	Opponents	Tmt		Match Venue	Result	
321	8-Nov-08	Chile	SAC	A	Prince of Wales Country Club, Santiago	W	71-3
322	8-Nov-08	France	Int-T	A	Stade Vélodrome, Marseille	L	6-12
323	15-Nov-08	Italy	Int-T	A	Stadio Olimpico, di Torino	W	22-14
324	22-Nov-08	Ireland	Int-T	A	Croke Park, Dublin	L	3-17
325	20-May-09	Chile	SAC	N	Estadio Charrúa, Montevideo	W	89-6
326	23-May-09	Uruguay	SAC	A	Estadio Charrúa, Montevideo	W	33-9
327	6-Jun-09	England	Int-T	A	Old Trafford, Manchester	L	15-37
328	13-Jun-09	England	Int	H	Estadio Padre Ernesto Martearena, Salta	W	24-22
329	14-Nov-09	England	Int-T	A	Twickenham, London	L	9-16
330	21-Nov-09	Wales	Int-T	A	Millennium Stadium, Cardiff	L	16-33
331	28-Nov-09	Scotland	Int-T	A	Murrayfield, Edinburgh	W	9-6
332	21-May-10	Uruguay	SAC	N	Parque Mahuida CARR La Reina, Santiago	W	38-0
333	23-May-10	Chile	SAC	A	Parque Mahuida CARR La Reina, Santiago	W	48-9
334	12-Jun-10	Scotland	Int	H	Estadio Monumental José Fierro, Tucumán	L	16-24
335	19-Jun-10	Scotland	Int	H	Estad. Mundialista J M Minella, Mar d. Plata	L	9-13
336	26-Jun-10	France	Int	H	Vélez Sarsfield Stadium, Buenos Aires	W	41-13
337	13-Nov-10	Italy	Int-T	A	Stadio Marc'Antonio Bentegodi, Verona	W	22-16
338	20-Nov-10	France	Int-T	A	Stade de la Mosson, Montpellier	L	9-15
339	28-Nov-10	Ireland	Int-T	A	Aviva Stadium, Dublin	L	9-29
340	22-May-11	Chile	SAC	H	Cataratus Rugby Club, Puerto Iguazu	W	61-6
341	25-May-11	Uruguay	SAC	H	Tacuru Social Club Posadas, Misiones	W	75-14
342	20-Aug-11	Wales	Int-T	A	Millennium Stadium, Cardiff	L	13-28
343	10-Sep-11	England	WCp	N	Otago Stadium, Dunedin	L	9-13
344	17-Sep-11	Romania	WCp	N	Rugby Park Stadium, Invercargill	W	43-8
345	25-Sep-11	Scotland	WCp	N	Wellington Regional Stadium, Wellington	W	13-12
346	2-Oct-11	Georgia	WCp	N	Arena Manawatu, Palmerston North	W	25-7
347	9-Oct-11	New Zealand	WCqf	A	Eden Park, Auckland	L	10-33
348	20-May-12	Uruguay	SAC	N	Parque Mahuida CARR La Reina, Santiago	W	40-5
349	23-May-12	Brazil	SAC	N	Parque Mahuida CARR La Reina, Santiago	W	111-0
350	26-May-12	Chile	SAC	A	Parque Mahuida CARR La Reina, Santiago	W	59-6
351	9-Jun-12	Italy	Int	H	Estadio S. Juan del Bicentenario, San Juan	W	37-22
352	16-Jun-12	France	Int	H	Estadio Olimpico Château Carreras, Córdoba	W	23-20
353	23-Jun-12	France	Int	H	Estadio Monumental José Fierro, Tucumán	L	10-49
354	18-Aug-12	South Africa	RC	A	Newlands Stadium, Cape Town	L	6-27
355	25-Aug-12	South Africa	RC	H	Estadío Malvinas Argentinas, Mendoza	D	16-16
356	8-Sep-12	New Zealand	RC	A	Westpac Stadium, Wellington	L	5-21
357	15-Sep-12	Australia	RC-P	A	Skilled Park, Robina, Gold Coast, Q'land	L	19-23
358	29-Sep-12	New Zealand	RC	H	Estadio Ciudad de la Plata, La Plata	L	15-54
359	6-Oct-12	Australia	RC-P	H	Estadio Gigante de Arroyito, Rosario	L	19-25
360	10-Nov-12	Wales	Int-T	A	Millennium Stadium, Cardiff	W	26-12

No	Date	Opponents	Tmt		Match Venue	Result	
361	17-Nov-12	France	Int-T	A	Grand Stade, Lille Métropole	L	22-39
362	24-Nov-12	Ireland	ABC-T	A	Aviva Stadium, Dublin	L	24-46
363	27-Apr-13	Uruguay	SAC	A	Estadio Charrúa, Montevideo	W	29-18
364	1-May-13	Chile	SAC	N	Estadio Charrúa, Montevideo	W	85-10.
365	4-May-13	Brazil	SAC	N	Estadio Charrúa, Montevideo	W	83-0
366	8-Jun-13	England	Int	H	Estadio Padre Ernesto Martearena, Salta	L	3-32
367	15-Jun-13	England	Int	H	Vélez Sarsfield Stadium, Buenos Aires	L	26-51
368	22-Jun-13	Georgia	Int	H	Estadio S. Juan del Bicentenario, San Juan	W	29-18
369	17-Aug-13	South Africa	RC	A	FNB Stadium, Soweto, Johannesburg	L	13-73
370	24-Aug-13	South Africa	RC	H	Estadio Malvinas Argentinas, Mendoza	L	17-22
371	7-Sep-13	New Zealand	RC	A	Waikato Stadium, Hamilton	L	13-28
372	14-Sep-13	Australia	RC-P	A	Patersons Stadium, Perth	L	13-14
373	28-Sep-13	New Zealand	RC	H	Estadio Ciudad de la Plata, La Plata	L	15-33
374	5-Oct-13	Australia	RC-P	H	Estadio Gigante de Arroyito, Rosario	L	17-54
375	9-Nov-13	England	ICC-T	A	Twickenham, London	L	12-31
376	16-Nov-13	Wales	Int-T	A	Millennium Stadium, Cardiff	L	6-40
377	23-Nov-13	Italy	Int-T	A	Stadio Olimpico, Rome	W	19-14
378	17-May-14	Uruguay	CSC	A	Estadio Parque Artigas, Paysandú	W	65-9
379	24-May-14	Chile	CSC	A	Estadio S. Carlos de Apoquindo, Santiago	W	73-12
380	7-Jun-14	Ireland	ABC	H	Estadio Centenario, Resistencia	L	17-29
381	14-Jun-14	Ireland	ABC	H	Estadio Monumental José Fierro, Tucumán	L	17-23
382	21-Jun-14	Scotland	Int	H	Estadio Olimpico Château Carreras, Córdoba	L	19-21
383	16-Aug-14	South Africa	RC	A	Loftus Versfeld Stadium, Pretoria	L	6-13
384	23-Aug-14	South Africa	RC	H	Estadio Padre Ernesto Martearena, Salta	L	31-33
385	6-Sep-14	New Zealand	RC	A	McLean Park, Napier	L	9-28
386	13-Sep-14	Australia	RC-P	A	Skilled Park, Robina, Gold Coast, Q'land	L	25-32
387	27-Sep-14	New Zealand	RC	H	Estadio Ciudad de la Plata, La Plata	L	13-34
388	4-Oct-14	Australia	RC-P	H	Estadio Malvinas Argentinas, Mendoza	W	21-17
389	8-Nov-14	Scotland	Int-T	A	Murrayfield, Edinburgh	L	31-41
390	14-Nov-14	Italy	Int-T	A	Stadio Luigi Ferraris, Genova	W	20-18
391	22-Nov-14	France	Int-T	A	Stade de France, Paris	W	18-13

AUSTRALIA

In 1884, the first New Zealand representative side visited Australia, winning all nine matches against provincial sides. Four years later, in 1888, a team drawn from the four unions, known at that time as Great Britain, set off on a first-ever rugby tour to Australia and New Zealand. They played sixteen matches in Australia, winning fourteen and drawing two. No Internationals were played on that tour, but in 1899, on a second visit to Australia, four Internationals were played. The Aussies won the first Test by 13 points to 3, but lost the series 3-1. A loss in their first International against New Zealand in 1903 was followed the next year by a 3-0 series loss to the touring Great Britain side. Nicknamed the 'Wallabies' on their first tour of Britain in 1908-09, the Australian team lost by 9 points to 6 to Wales in the first International, but was successful against England in the second. Between 1905 and 1914, Australia played New Zealand thirteen times but won only two of those games.

From the end of the First World War to 1928, Australia played twenty-four Internationals against a New Zealand XV and three Internationals against a South African XV. Neither opponent accepted these games as full Internationals, but on their 1927-28 Northern Hemisphere tour all five International matches played were recognized as full Internationals. The Wallabies defeated Ireland, Wales and France for the first time on that tour, but lost to both England and Scotland. Then, in 1929, the Aussies won a first-ever home series against All Blacks, by defeating them in all three Internationals.

In 1931, the Bledisloe Cup, a competition between Australia and New Zealand, was founded and in 1932 the All Blacks won the inaugural series, held in Australia, 2-1. On their first tour of South Africa in 1933 the Wallabies lost a series of five Internationals 3-2, and between 1936 and 1938 they lost three further series to their Southern Hemisphere rivals.

With the outbreak of the Second World War, Australia's 1939 Northern Hemisphere tour was cancelled. It was eventually re-scheduled for the 1947-48 season and it proved to be quite successful for the Wallabies as they lost only to Wales and to France in the five Internationals played. In 1948 Australia was invited to join the International Rugby Board (IRB), which led to the inaugural meeting of the Australian RFU in November 1949. In June of that year the Wallabies shared a three-match series with the New Zealand Maoris, and in September they regained the Bledisloe Cup, last won in 1934, by winning the series 2-0, this time on New Zealand soil.

The 1950s was a poor decade for Australia, with only seven wins in thirty-five matches, which included: two 2-0 series losses to the Lions in 1950 and 1959; a 3-1 series loss to the Springboks in 1953; and a 2-0 series loss again to South Africa in 1956. Their lowest point occurred on their 1958 Northern Hemisphere tour when they lost all five matches against the Northern Hemisphere Five Nations teams.

The 1960s and early 1970s weren't much better for the team in their encounters with the Lions, South Africa and New Zealand: they suffered another 2-0 series loss to the Lions in 1966, three series losses to the Springboks, in 1961, 1969 and 1971, losing all eight Internationals, and three Bledisloe series losses to the All Blacks in 1962, 1964 and 1968. However, on the credit side the Wallabies did draw the 1963 series with South Africa 2-2, and followed it with a 2-0 win over the Springboks in the 1965 series. Despite these positive results, between 1966 and 1974 the Aussies won only seven games out of thirty-eight played.

An improvement in the 1980s included their own 'grand slam' of four wins against the Home Nations in 1984. The Wallabies also reached the semi-final of the inaugural World Cup in 1987. That achievement was bettered in 1991 when they won the trophy by defeating England, the host nation, in the final at Twickenham.

Between August 1990 and July 1993, the Wallabies played twenty matches and won eighteen. That run was bettered in the three-year period 1998 to 2000, when a superb Australian side won thirty Internationals out of thirty-six. Their run of victories included a second World Cup triumph in Cardiff in 1999. The dawn of the new millennium saw the Wallabies continuing their success and in 2001 they achieved a 2-1 series win against the Lions, followed by a second successive Tri Nations title, and the retention of the Bledisloe Cup for the fourth time in a row. However, this phenomenal run eventually ended in disappointment: a third World Cup trophy eluded them in 2003, when they lost to England in the final in Sydney.

During the period November 2004 to November 2005, results were mixed for the team: a sequence of six wins was followed by a run of seven losses, which included a loss of all four matches in the 2005 Tri Nations campaign. Five defeats in thirteen Internationals during 2006 was something of an improvement on the previous two years, but losing to England in the quarter-final of the 2007 World Cup was another big disappointment for the team.

In the three Tri Nations championships held between 2008 and 2010, the Aussies won only six times in eighteen matches, but bounced back in 2011 by winning their third title. The Wallabies then lost to Ireland in the 2011 World Cup pool match, but defeated South Africa in the quarter-final, before losing to New Zealand in the semi-final. They soon recovered by taking bronze in defeating Wales in the play-off match for third place. The Tri Nations tournament was expanded in 2012 when Argentina was invited to join and the tournament which was subsequently renamed The Rugby Championship: Australia finished in second place on points difference in that first year. A 2-1 series defeat to the Lions in 2013 was followed by a mediocre Rugby Championship campaign, which yielded only two wins in six games.

Australia's performance has been poor in the sixteen Tri Nations tournaments held annually between 1996 and 2011: only three titles have been won, in 2000, 2001 and 2011.

However, the team's performance against the All Blacks in the Bledisloe Cup series has even been worse: the Wallabies have won only twelve titles, to New Zealand's forty-three, in the tournament's history (between 1931 and 2014).

The team's fortunes was mixed in 2014: an impressive 3-0 home series win against France was followed by only two wins from six in the Rugby Championship, and just one win from four on their autumn tour of the Northern Hemisphere.

AUSTRALIA

HEAD TO HEAD RESULTS TO 31 MARCH 2015

	P	W	D	L	%	F	A
v TIER 1 Teams							
v Argentina	23	17	1	5	76.1	610	363
v England	43	24	1	18	57.0	907	661
v France	46	26	2	18	58.7	991	802
v Ireland	32	21	1	10	67.2	657	453
v Italy	16	16	0	0	100.0	565	217
v New Zealand	152	41	7	104	29.3	2103	3066
v Scotland	28	19	0	9	67.9	671	330
v South Africa	80	34	1	45	43.1	1391	1552
v Wales	38	27	1	10	72.4	897	590
v Lions	23	6	0	17	26.1	248	414
Sub-Total	**481**	**231**	**14**	**236**	**49.5**	**9040**	**8448**
v TIER 2/3 Group							
v Canada	6	6	0	0	100.0	283	60
v Fiji	19	16	1	2	86.8	546	221
v Japan	4	4	0	0	100.0	220	58
Romania	3	3	0	0	100.0	189	20
v moa	5	4	0	1	80.0	204	58
v Tonga	4	3	0	1	75.0	167	42
v United States	7	7	0	0	100.0	321	68
v Georgia	0	0	0	0	0.0	0	0
v Namibia	1	1	0	0	100.0	142	0
v Russia	1	1	0	0	100.0	68	22
v Uruguay	0	0	0	0	0.0	0	0
Sub-Total	**50**	**45**	**1**	**4**	**91.0**	**2140**	**549**
v Other Teams							
v Korea	1	1	0	0	100.0	65	18
v Spain	1	1	0	0	100.0	92	10
v New Zealand Maori	16	8	2	6	56.3	240	203
v New Zealand XV	24	6	0	18	25.0	257	459
v South African XV	3	0	0	3	0.0	30	69
v Pacific Islanders	1	1	0	0	100.0	29	14
Sub-Total	**46**	**17**	**2**	**27**	**39.1**	**713**	**773**
All Internationals	**577**	**293**	**17**	**267**	**52.3**	**11893**	**9770**

No	Date	Opponents	Tmt		Match Venue		Result
1	24-Jun-99	Lions	Int	H	Cricket Ground, Sydney	W	13-3
2	22-Jul-99	Lions	Int	H	Exhibition Ground, Brisbane	L	0-11
3	5-Aug-99	Lions	Int	H	Cricket Ground, Sydney	L	10-11
4	12-Aug-99	Lions	Int	H	Cricket Ground, Sydney	L	0-13
5	15-Aug-03	New Zealand	Int	H	Cricket Ground, Sydney	L	3-22
6	2-Jul-04	Lions	Int	H	Cricket Ground, Sydney	L	0-17
7	23-Jul-04	Lions	Int	H	Exhibition Ground, Brisbane	L	3-17
8	30-Jul-04	Lions	Int	H	Cricket Ground, Sydney	L	0-16
9	2-Sep-05	New Zealand	Int-T	A	Tahuna Park, Dunedin	L	3-14
10	20-Jul-07	New Zealand	Int	H	Cricket Ground, Sydney	L	6-26
11	3-Aug-07	New Zealand	Int	H	The Gabba Cricket Ground, Brisbane	L	5-14
12	10-Aug-07	New Zealand	Int	H	Cricket Ground, Sydney	D	5-5
13	12-Dec-08	Wales	Int-T	A	Arms Park, Cardiff	L	6-9
14	9-Jan-09	England	Int-T	A	Rectory Field, Blackheath	W	9-3
15	25-Jun-10	New Zealand	Int	H	Cricket Ground, Sydney	L	0-6
16	27-Jun-10	New Zealand	Int	H	Cricket Ground, Sydney	W	11-0
17	2-Jul-10	New Zealand	Int	H	Cricket Ground, Sydney	L	13-28
18	16-Nov-12	United States	Int-T	A	St Ignatius, California Field, Berkeley	W	12-8
19	6-Sep-13	New Zealand	Int-T	A	Athletic Park, Wellington	L	5-30
20	13-Sep-13	New Zealand	Int-T	A	Carisbrook, Dunedin	L	13-25
21	20-Sep-13	New Zealand	Int-T	A	Lancaster Park Oval, Christchurch	W	16-5
22	18-Jul-14	New Zealand	Int	H	Sports Ground, Sydney	L	0-5
23	1-Aug-14	New Zealand	Int	H	The Gabba Cricket Ground, Brisbane	L	0-17
24	15-Aug-14	New Zealand	Int	H	Sports Ground, Sydney	L	7-22
25	24-Jul-20	N.Z. XV	Int	H	Sports Ground, Sydney	L	15-26
26	31-Jul-20	N.Z. XV	Int	H	Sports Ground, Sydney	L	6-14
27	7-Aug-20	N.Z. XV	Int	H	Sports Ground, Sydney	L	13-24
28	25-Jun-21	S.A. XV	Int	H	Royal Agricultural Showground, Sydney	L	10-25
29	27-Jun-21	S.A. XV	Int	H	Royal Agricultural Showground, Sydney	L	11-16
30	2-Jul-21	S.A. XV	Int	H	University Ground, Sydney	L	9-28
31	3-Sep-21	N.Z. XV	Int-T	A	Lancaster Park Oval, Christchurch	W	17-0
32	24-Jun-22	N.Z Maori	Int	H	Royal Agricultural Showground, Sydney	L	22-25
33	26-Jun-22	N.Z Maori	Int	H	Royal Agricultural Showground, Sydney	W	28-13
34	8-Jul-22	N.Z Maori	Int	H	University Ground, Sydney	L	22-23
35	29-Jul-22	N.Z. XV	Int	H	Royal Agricultural Showground, Sydney	L	19-26
36	5-Aug-22	N.Z. XV	Int	H	Royal Agricultural Showground, Sydney	W	14-8
37	7-Aug-22	N.Z. XV	Int	H	Royal Agricultural Showground, Sydney	W	8-6
38	16-Jun-23	NZ Maori	Int	H	Royal Agricultural Showground, Sydney	W	27-23
39	23-Jun-23	NZ Maori	Int	H	Royal Agricultural Showground, Sydney	W	21-16
40	25-Jun-23	NZ Maori	Int	H	Royal Agricultural Showground, Sydney	W	14-12

No	Date	Opponents	Tmt		Match Venue	Result	
41	25-Aug-23	N.Z. XV	Int-T	A	Carisbrook, Dunedin	L	9-19
42	1-Sep-23	N.Z. XV	Int-T	A	Lancaster Park Oval, Christchurch	L	6-34
43	15-Sep-23	N.Z. XV	Int-T	A	Athletic Park, Wellington	L	11-38
44	5-Jul-24	N.Z. XV	Int	H	Royal Agricultural Showground, Sydney	W	20-16
45	12-Jul-24	N.Z. XV	Int	H	Royal Agricultural Showground, Sydney	L	5-21
46	16-Jul-24	N.Z. XV	Int	H	Royal Agricultural Showground, Sydney	L	8-38
47	13-Jun-25	N.Z. XV	Int	H	Royal Agricultural Showground, Sydney	L	3-26
48	20-Jun-25	N.Z. XV	Int	H	Royal Agricultural Showground, Sydney	L	0-4
49	23-Jun-25	N.Z. XV	Int	H	Royal Agricultural Showground, Sydney	L	3-11
50	19-Sep-25	N.Z. XV	Int-T	A	Eden Park, Auckland	L	10-36
51	10-Jul-26	N.Z. XV	Int	H	Royal Agricultural Showground, Sydney	W	26-20
52	17-Jul-26	N.Z. XV	Int	H	Royal Agricultural Showground, Sydney	L	6-11
53	20-Jul-26	N.Z. XV	Int	H	Royal Agricultural Showground, Sydney	L	0-14
54	29-Jul-26	N.Z. XV	Int	H	Royal Agricultural Showground, Sydney	L	21-28
55	12-Nov-27	Ireland	Int-T	A	Lansdowne Road, Dublin	W	5-3
56	26-Nov-27	Wales	Int-T	A	Arms Park, Cardiff	W	18-8
57	17-Dec-27	Scotland	Int-T	A	Murrayfield, Edinburgh	L	8-10
58	7-Jan-28	England	Int-T	A	Twickenham, London	L	11-18
59	22-Jan-28	France	Int-T	A	Stade Colombes, Paris	W	11-8
60	5-Sep-28	N.Z. XV	Int-T	A	Athletic Park, Wellington	L	12-15
61	8-Sep-28	N.Z. XV	Int-T	A	Carisbrook, Dunedin	L	14-16
62	15-Sep-28	N.Z. XV	Int-T	A	Lancaster Park Oval, Christchurch	W	11-8
63	22-Sep-28	N.Z Maori	Int-T	A	Athletic Park, Wellington	L	8-9
64	6-Jul-29	New Zealand	Int	H	Cricket Ground, Sydney	W	9-8
65	20-Jul-29	New Zealand	Int	H	Exhibition Ground, Brisbane	W	17-9
66	27-Jul-29	New Zealand	Int	H	Cricket Ground, Sydney	W	15-13
67	30-Aug-30	Lions	Int	H	Cricket Ground, Sydney	W	6-5
68	9-Sep-31	N.Z Maori	Int-T	A	Showgrounds Oval, Palmerston North	W	14-3
69	12-Sep-31	New Zealand	Bled-T	A	Eden Park, Auckland	L	13-20
70	2-Jul-32	New Zealand	Bled	H	Cricket Ground, Sydney	W	22-17
71	16-Jul-32	New Zealand	Bled	H	Exhibition Ground, Brisbane	L	3-21
72	23-Jul-32	New Zealand	Bled	H	Cricket Ground, Sydney	L	13-21
73	8-Jul-33	South Africa	Int-T	A	Newlands Stadium, Cape Town	L	3-17
74	22-Jul-33	South Africa	Int-T	A	Kingsmead Ground, Durban	W	21-6
75	12-Aug-33	South Africa	Int-T	A	Ellis Park, Johannesburg	L	3-12
76	26-Aug-33	South Africa	Int-T	A	Crusaders Ground, Port Elizabeth	L	0-11
77	2-Sep-33	South Africa	Int-T	A	Springbok Park, Bloemfontein	W	15-4
78	11-Aug-34	New Zealand	Bled	H	Cricket Ground, Sydney	W	25-11
79	25-Aug-34	New Zealand	Bled	H	Cricket Ground, Sydney	D	3-3
80	5-Sep-36	New Zealand	Bled-T	A	Athletic Park, Wellington	L	6-11

No	Date	Opponents	Tmt		Match Venue	Result	
81	12-Sep-36	New Zealand	Bled-T	A	Carisbrook, Dunedin	L	13-38
82	23-Sep-36	N.Z Maori	Int-T	A	Showgrounds Oval, Palmerston North	W	31-6
83	26-Jun-37	South Africa	Int	H	Cricket Ground, Sydney	L	5-9
84	17-Jul-37	South Africa	Int	H	Cricket Ground, Sydney	L	17-26
85	23-Jul-38	New Zealand	Bled	H	Cricket Ground, Sydney	L	9-24
86	6-Aug-38	New Zealand	Bled	H	Exhibition Ground, Brisbane	L	14-20
87	13-Aug-38	New Zealand	Bled	H	Cricket Ground, Sydney	L	6-14
88	14-Sep-46	New Zealand	Bled-T	A	Carisbrook, Dunedin	L	8-31
89	25-Sep-46	N.Z Maori	Int-T	A	Rugby Park, Hamilton	L	0-20
90	28-Sep-46	New Zealand	Bled-T	A	Eden Park, Auckland	L	10-14
91	14-Jun-47	New Zealand	Bled	H	Exhibition Ground, Brisbane	L	5-13
92	28-Jun-47	New Zealand	Bled	H	Cricket Ground, Sydney	L	14-27
93	22-Nov-47	Scotland	Int-T	A	Murrayfield, Edinburgh	W	16-7
94	6-Dec-47	Ireland	Int-T	A	Lansdowne Road, Dublin	W	16-3
95	20-Dec-47	Wales	Int-T	A	Arms Park, Cardiff	L	0-6
96	3-Jan-48	England	Int-T	A	Twickenham, London	W	11-0
97	11-Jan-48	France	Int-T	A	Stade Colombes, Paris	L	6-13
98	4-Jun-49	N.Z Maori	Int	H	Cricket Ground, Sydney	L	3-12
99	11-Jun-49	N.Z Maori	Int	H	Exhibition Ground, Brisbane	D	8-8
100	25-Jun-49	N.Z Maori	Int	H	Cricket Ground, Sydney	W	18-3
101	3-Sep-49	New Zealand	Bled-T	A	Athletic Park, Wellington	W	11-6
102	24-Sep-49	New Zealand	Bled-T	A	Eden Park, Auckland	W	16-9
103	19-Aug-50	Lions	Int	H	The Gabba Cricket Ground, Brisbane	L	6-19
104	26-Aug-50	Lions	Int	H	Cricket Ground, Sydney	L	3-24
105	23-Jun-51	New Zealand	Bled	H	Cricket Ground, Sydney	L	0-8
106	7-Jul-51	New Zealand	Bled	H	Cricket Ground, Sydney	L	11-17
107	21-Jul-51	New Zealand	Bled	H	The Gabba Cricket Ground, Brisbane	L	6-16
108	26-Jul-52	Fiji	Int	H	Cricket Ground, Sydney	W	15-9
109	9-Aug-52	Fiji	Int	H	Cricket Ground, Sydney	L	15-17
110	6-Sep-52	New Zealand	Bled-T	A	Lancaster Park Oval, Christchurch	W	14-9
111	13-Sep-52	New Zealand	Bled-T	A	Athletic Park, Wellington	L	8-15
112	22-Aug-53	South Africa	Int-T	A	Ellis Park, Johannesburg	L	3-25
113	5-Sep-53	South Africa	Int-T	A	Newlands Stadium, Cape Town	W	18-14
114	19-Sep-53	South Africa	Int-T	A	Kingsmead Ground, Durban	L	8-18
115	26-Sep-53	South Africa	Int-T	A	Crusaders Ground, Port Elizabeth	L	9-22
116	6-Jun-54	Fiji	Int	H	Exhibition Ground, Brisbane	W	22-19
117	26-Jun-54	Fiji	Int	H	Cricket Ground, Sydney	L	16-18
118	20-Aug-55	New Zealand	Bled-T	A	Athletic Park, Wellington	L	8-16
119	3-Sep-55	New Zealand	Bled-T	A	Carisbrook, Dunedin	L	0-8
120	17-Sep-55	New Zealand	Bled-T	A	Eden Park, Auckland	W	8-3

No	Date	Opponents	Tmt		Match Venue	Result	
121	26-May-56	South Africa	Int	H	Cricket Ground, Sydney	L	0-9
122	2-Jun-56	South Africa	Int	H	Exhibition Ground, Brisbane	L	0-9
123	25-May-57	New Zealand	Bled	H	Cricket Ground, Sydney	L	11-25
124	1-Jun-57	New Zealand	Bled	H	Exhibition Ground, Brisbane	L	9-22
125	4-Jan-58	Wales	Int-T	A	Arms Park, Cardiff	L	3-9
126	18-Jan-58	Ireland	Int-T	A	Lansdowne Road, Dublin	L	6-9
127	1-Feb-58	England	Int-T	A	Twickenham, London	L	6-9
128	15-Feb-58	Scotland	Int-T	A	Murrayfield, Edinburgh	L	8-12
129	9-Mar-58	France	Int-T	A	Stade Colombes, Paris	L	0-19
130	14-Jun-58	N.Z Maori	Int	H	Exhibition Ground, Brisbane	W	15-14
131	28-Jun-58	N.Z Maori	Int	H	Cricket Ground, Sydney	D	3-3
132	5-Jul-58	N.Z Maori	Int	H	Olympic Park Stadium, Melbourne	L	6-13
133	23-Aug-58	New Zealand	Bled-T	A	Athletic Park, Wellington	L	3-25
134	6-Sep-58	New Zealand	Bled-T	A	Lancaster Park Oval, Christchurch	W	6-3
135	20-Sep-58	New Zealand	Bled-T	A	Epsom Showgrounds, Auckland	L	8-17
136	6-Jun-59	Lions	Int	H	Exhibition Ground, Brisbane	L	6-17
137	13-Jun-59	Lions	Int	H	Sports Ground, Sydney	L	3-24
138	10-Jun-61	Fiji	Int	H	Exhibition Ground, Brisbane	W	24-6
139	17-Jun-61	Fiji	Int	H	Cricket Ground, Sydney	W	20-14
140	1-Jul-61	Fiji	Int	H	Olympic Park Stadium, Melbourne	D	3-3
141	5-Aug-61	South Africa	Int-T	A	Ellis Park, Johannesburg	L	3-28
142	12-Aug-61	South Africa	Int-T	A	Boet Erasmus Stadium, Port Elizabeth	L	11-23
143	26-Aug-61	France	Int	H	Cricket Ground, Sydney	L	8-15
144	26-May-62	New Zealand	Bled	H	Exhibition Ground, Brisbane	L	6-20
145	4-Jun-62	New Zealand	Bled	H	Cricket Ground, Sydney	L	5-14
146	25-Aug-62	New Zealand	Bled-T	A	Athletic Park, Wellington	D	9-9
147	8-Sep-62	New Zealand	Bled-T	A	Carisbrook, Dunedin	L	0-3
148	22-Sep-62	New Zealand	Bled-T	A	Eden Park, Auckland	L	8-16
149	4-Jun-63	England	Int	H	Sports Ground, Sydney	W	18-9
150	13-Jul-63	South Africa	Int-T	A	Loftus Versfeld Stadium, Pretoria	L	3-14
151	10-Aug-63	South Africa	Int-T	A	Newlands Stadium, Cape Town	W	9-5
152	24-Aug-63	South Africa	Int-T	A	Ellis Park, Johannesburg	W	11-9
153	7-Sep-63	South Africa	Int-T	A	Boet Erasmus Stadium, Port Elizabeth	L	6-22
154	15-Aug-64	New Zealand	Bled-T	A	Carisbrook, Dunedin	L	9-14
155	22-Aug-64	New Zealand	Bled-T	A	Lancaster Park Oval, Christchurch	L	3-18
156	29-Aug-64	New Zealand	Bled-T	A	Athletic Park, Wellington	W	20-5
157	19-Jun-65	South Africa	Int	H	Cricket Ground, Sydney	W	18-11
158	26-Jun-65	South Africa	Int	H	Lang Park, Brisbane	W	12-8
159	28-May-66	Lions	Int	H	Cricket Ground, Sydney	L	8-11
160	4-Jun-66	Lions	Int	H	Lang Park, Brisbane	L	0-31

No	Date	Opponents	Tmt		Match Venue	Result	
161	3-Dec-66	Wales	Int-T	A	Arms Park, Cardiff	W	14-11
162	17-Dec-66	Scotland	Int-T	A	Murrayfield, Edinburgh	L	5-11
163	7-Jan-67	England	Int-T	A	Twickenham, London	W	23-11
164	21-Jan-67	Ireland	Int-T	A	Lansdowne Road, Dublin	L	8-15
165	11-Feb-67	France	Int-T	A	Stade Colombes, Paris	L	14-20
166	13-May-67	Ireland	Int	H	Cricket Ground, Sydney	L	5-11
167	19-Aug-67	New Zealand	Bled-T	A	Athletic Park, Wellington	L	9-29
168	15-Jun-68	New Zealand	Bled	H	Cricket Ground, Sydney	L	11-27
169	22-Jun-68	New Zealand	Bled	H	Ballymore Oval, Brisbane	L	18-19
170	17-Aug-68	France	Int	H	Cricket Ground, Sydney	W	11-10
171	26-Oct-68	Ireland	Int-T	A	Lansdowne Road, Dublin	L	3-10
172	2-Nov-68	Scotland	Int-T	A	Murrayfield, Edinburgh	L	3-9
173	21-Jun-69	Wales	Int	H	Cricket Ground, Sydney	L	16-19
174	2-Aug-69	South Africa	Int-T	A	Ellis Park, Johannesburg	L	11-30
175	16-Aug-69	South Africa	Int-T	A	Kings Park Stadium, Durban	L	9-16
176	6-Sep-69	South Africa	Int-T	A	Newlands Stadium, Cape Town	L	3-11
177	20-Sep-69	South Africa	Int-T	A	Free State Stadium, Bloemfontein	L	8-19
178	6-Jun-70	Scotland	Int	H	Cricket Ground, Sydney	W	23-3
179	17-Jul-71	South Africa	Int	H	Cricket Ground, Sydney	L	11-19
180	31-Jul-71	South Africa	Int	H	Exhibition Ground, Brisbane	L	6-14
181	7-Aug-71	South Africa	Int	H	Cricket Ground, Sydney	L	6-18
182	20-Nov-71	France	Int-T	A	Stade Municipal de Toulouse, Toulouse	W	13-11
183	27-Nov-71	France	Int-T	A	Stade Colombes, Paris	L	9-18
184	17-Jun-72	France	Int	H	Cricket Ground, Sydney	D	14-14
185	25-Jun-72	France	Int	H	Ballymore Oval, Brisbane	L	15-16
186	19-Aug-72	New Zealand	Bled-T	A	Athletic Park, Wellington	L	6-29
187	2-Sep-72	New Zealand	Bled-T	A	Lancaster Park Oval, Christchurch	L	17-30
188	16-Sep-72	New Zealand	Bled-T	A	Eden Park, Auckland	L	3-38
189	19-Sep-72	Fiji	Int-T	A	Buckhurst Park, Suva	W	21-19
190	23-Jun-73	Tonga	Int	H	Cricket Ground, Sydney	W	30-12
191	30-Jun-73	Tonga	Int	H	Ballymore Oval, Brisbane	L	11-16
192	10-Nov-73	Wales	Int-T	A	National Stadium, Cardiff	L	0-24
193	17-Nov-73	England	Int-T	A	Twickenham, London	L	3-20
194	25-May-74	New Zealand	Bled	H	Cricket Ground, Sydney	L	6-11
195	1-Jun-74	New Zealand	Bled	H	Ballymore Oval, Brisbane	D	16-16
196	8-Jun-74	New Zealand	Bled	H	Cricket Ground, Sydney	L	6-16
197	24-May-75	England	Int	H	Cricket Ground, Sydney	W	16-9
198	31-May-75	England	Int	H	Ballymore Oval, Brisbane	W	30-21
199	2-Aug-75	Japan	Int	H	Cricket Ground, Sydney	W	37-7
200	17-Aug-75	Japan	Int	H	Ballymore Oval, Brisbane	W	50-25

No	Date	Opponents	Tmt		Match Venue	Result	
201	6-Dec-75	Scotland	Int-T	A	Murrayfield, Edinburgh	L	3-10
202	20-Dec-75	Wales	Int-T	A	National Stadium, Cardiff	L	3-28
203	3-Jan-76	England	Int-T	A	Twickenham, London	L	6-23
204	17-Jan-76	Ireland	Int-T	A	Lansdowne Road, Dublin	W	20-10
205	31-Jan-76	United States	Int-T	A	Glover Field Anaheim, Los Angeles	W	24-12
206	12-Jun-76	Fiji	Int	H	Cricket Ground, Sydney	W	22-6
207	19-Jun-76	Fiji	Int	H	Ballymore Oval, Brisbane	W	21-9
208	26-Jun-76	Fiji	Int	H	Cricket Ground, Sydney	W	27-17
209	24-Oct-76	France	Int-T	A	Stade du Parc Lescure, Bordeaux	L	15-18
210	30-Oct-76	France	Int-T	A	Parc des Princes, Paris	L	6-34
211	11-Jun-78	Wales	Int	H	Ballymore Oval, Brisbane	W	18-8
212	17-Jun-78	Wales	Int	H	Cricket Ground, Sydney	W	19-17
213	19-Aug-78	New Zealand	Bled-T	A	Athletic Park, Wellington	L	12-13
214	26-Aug-78	New Zealand	Bled-T	A	Lancaster Park Oval, Christchurch	L	6-22
215	9-Sep-78	New Zealand	Bled-T	A	Eden Park, Auckland	W	30-16
216	3-Jun-79	Ireland	Int	H	Ballymore Oval, Brisbane	L	12-27
217	16-Jun-79	Ireland	Int	H	Cricket Ground, Sydney	L	3-9
218	28-Jul-79	New Zealand	Bled	H	Cricket Ground, Sydney	W	12-6
219	27-Oct-79	Argentina	Int-T	A	Ferro Carril Oeste Stadium, B Aires	L	13-24
220	3-Nov-79	Argentina	Int-T	A	Ferro Carril Oeste Stadium, B Aires	W	17-12
221	24-May-80	Fiji	Int-T	A	National Stadium, Suva	W	22-9
222	21-Jun-80	New Zealand	Bled	H	Cricket Ground, Sydney	W	13-9
223	28-Jun-80	New Zealand	Bled	H	Ballymore Oval, Brisbane	L	9-12
224	12-Jul-80	New Zealand	Bled	H	Cricket Ground, Sydney	W	26-10
225	5-Jul-81	France	Int	H	Ballymore Oval, Brisbane	W	17-15
226	11-Jul-81	France	Int	H	Cricket Ground, Sydney	W	24-14
227	21-Nov-81	Ireland	Int-T	A	Lansdowne Road, Dublin	W	16-12
228	5-Dec-81	Wales	Int-T	A	National Stadium, Cardiff	L	13-18
229	19-Dec-81	Scotland	Int-T	A	Murrayfield, Edinburgh	L	15-24
230	2-Jan-82	England	Int-T	A	Twickenham, London	L	11-15
231	4-Jul-82	Scotland	Int	H	Ballymore Oval, Brisbane	L	7-12
232	10-Jul-82	Scotland	Int	H	Cricket Ground, Sydney	W	33-9
233	14-Aug-82	New Zealand	Bled-T	A	Lancaster Park Oval, Christchurch	L	16-23
234	28-Aug-82	New Zealand	Bled-T	A	Athletic Park, Wellington	W	19-16
235	11-Sep-82	New Zealand	Bled-T	A	Eden Park, Auckland	L	18-33
236	9-Jul-83	United States	Int	H	Cricket Ground, Sydney	W	49-3
237	31-Jul-83	Argentina	Int	H	Ballymore Oval, Brisbane	L	3-18
238	7-Aug-83	Argentina	Int	H	Cricket Ground, Sydney	W	29-13
239	20-Aug-83	New Zealand	Bled	H	Cricket Ground, Sydney	L	8-18
240	22-Oct-83	Italy	Int-T	A	Stadio Mario Battaglini, Rovigo	W	29-7

No	Date	Opponents	Tmt		Match Venue	Result	
241	13-Nov-83	France	Int-T	A	Stade Marcel Michelin, Clermont Ferrand	D	15-15
242	19-Nov-83	France	Int-T	A	Parc des Princes, Paris	L	6-15
243	9-Jun-84	Fiji	Int-T	A	National Stadium, Suva	W	16-3
244	21-Jul-84	New Zealand	Bled	H	Cricket Ground, Sydney	W	16-9
245	4-Aug-84	New Zealand	Bled	H	Ballymore Oval, Brisbane	L	15-19
246	18-Aug-84	New Zealand	Bled	H	Cricket Ground, Sydney	L	24-25
247	3-Nov-84	England	Int-T	A	Twickenham, London	W	19-3
248	10-Nov-84	Ireland	Int-T	A	Lansdowne Road, Dublin	W	16-9
249	24-Nov-84	Wales	Int-T	A	National Stadium, Cardiff	W	28-9
250	8-Dec-84	Scotland	Int-T	A	Murrayfield, Edinburgh	W	37-12
251	15-Jun-85	Canada	Int	H	Cricket Ground, Sydney	W	59-3
252	23-Jun-85	Canada	Int	H	Ballymore Oval, Brisbane	W	43-15
253	29-Jun-85	New Zealand	Bled-T	A	Eden Park, Auckland	L	9-10
254	10-Aug-85	Fiji	Int	H	Ballymore Oval, Brisbane	W	52-28
255	17-Aug-85	Fiji	Int	H	Cricket Ground, Sydney	W	31-9
256	1-Jun-86	Italy	Int	H	Ballymore Oval, Brisbane	W	39-18
257	21-Jun-86	France	Int	H	Cricket Ground, Sydney	W	27-14
258	6-Jul-86	Argentina	Int	H	Ballymore Oval, Brisbane	W	39-19
259	12-Jul-86	Argentina	Int	H	Cricket Ground, Sydney	W	26-0
260	9-Aug-86	New Zealand	Bled-T	A	Athletic Park, Wellington	W	13-12
261	23-Aug-86	New Zealand	Bled-T	A	Carisbrook, Dunedin	L	12-13
262	6-Sep-86	New Zealand	Bled-T	A	Eden Park, Auckland	W	22-9
263	17-May-87	Korea	Int	H	Ballymore Oval, Brisbane	W	65-18
264	23-May-87	England	WCp	H	Concord Oval, Sydney	W	19-6
265	31-May-87	United States	WCp	H	Ballymore Oval, Brisbane	W	47-12
266	3-Jun-87	Japan	WCp	H	Concord Oval, Sydney	W	42-23
267	7-Jun-87	Ireland	WCqf	H	Concord Oval, Sydney	W	33-15
268	13-Jun-87	France	WCsf	H	Concord Oval, Sydney	L	24-30
269	18-Jun-87	Wales	WC34	N	Rotorua International Stadium, Rotorua	L	21-22
270	25-Jul-87	New Zealand	Bled	H	Concord Oval, Sydney	L	16-30
271	31-Oct-87	Argentina	Int-T	A	Vélez Sarsfield Stadium, Buenos Aires	D	19-19
272	7-Nov-87	Argentina	Int-T	A	Vélez Sarsfield Stadium, Buenos Aires	L	19-27
273	29-May-88	England	Int	H	Ballymore Oval, Brisbane	W	22-16
274	12-Jun-88	England	Int	H	Concord Oval, Sydney	W	28-8
275	3-Jul-88	New Zealand	Bled	H	Concord Oval, Sydney	L	7-32
276	16-Jul-88	New Zealand	Bled	H	Ballymore Oval, Brisbane	D	19-19
277	30-Jul-88	New Zealand	Bled	H	Concord Oval, Sydney	L	9-30
278	5-Nov-88	England	Int-T	A	Twickenham, London	L	19-28
279	19-Nov-88	Scotland	Int-T	A	Murrayfield, Edinburgh	W	32-13
280	3-Dec-88	Italy	Int-T	A	Stadio Flaminio, Rome	W	55-6

No	Date	Opponents	Tmt		Match Venue	Result	
281	1-Jul-89	Lions	Int	H	Football Stadium, Sydney	W	30-12
282	8-Jul-89	Lions	Int	H	Ballymore Oval, Brisbane	L	12-19
283	15-Jul-89	Lions	Int	H	Football Stadium, Sydney	L	18-19
284	5-Aug-89	New Zealand	Bled-T	A	Eden Park, Auckland	L	12-24
285	4-Nov-89	France	BIC-T	A	Stade de la Meinau, Strasbourg	W	32-15
286	11-Nov-89	France	BIC-T	A	Stade Nord-Lille, Métropole	L	19-25
287	9-Jun-90	France	BIC	H	Football Stadium, Sydney	W	21-9
288	24-Jun-90	France	BIC	H	Ballymore Oval, Brisbane	W	48-31
289	30-Jun-90	France	BIC	H	Football Stadium, Sydney	L	19-28
290	8-Jul-90	United States	Int	H	Ballymore Oval, Brisbane	W	67-9
291	21-Jul-90	New Zealand	Bled-T	A	Lancaster Park Oval, Christchurch	L	6-21
292	4-Aug-90	New Zealand	Bled-T	A	Eden Park, Auckland	L	17-27
293	18-Aug-90	New Zealand	Bled-T	A	Athletic Park, Wellington	W	21-9
294	22-Jul-91	Wales	Int	H	Ballymore Oval, Brisbane	W	63-6
295	27-Jul-91	England	Int	H	Football Stadium, Sydney	W	40-15
296	10-Aug-91	New Zealand	Bled	H	Football Stadium, Sydney	W	21-12
297	24-Aug-91	New Zealand	Bled-T	A	Eden Park, Auckland	L	3-6
298	4-Oct-91	Argentina	WCp	N	Stradey Park, Llanelli	W	32-19
299	9-Oct-91	Western Samoa	WCp	N	Pontypool Park, Pontypool	W	9-3
300	12-Oct-91	Wales	WCp	A	National Stadium, Cardiff	W	38-3
301	20-Oct-91	Ireland	WCqf	A	Lansdowne Road, Dublin	W	19-18
302	27-Oct-91	New Zealand	WCsf	N	Lansdowne Road, Dublin	W	16-6
303	2-Nov-91	England	WCf	A	Twickenham, London	W	12-6
304	13-Jun-92	Scotland	Int	H	Football Stadium, Sydney	W	27-12
305	21-Jun-92	Scotland	Int	H	Ballymore Oval, Brisbane	W	37-13
306	4-Jul-92	New Zealand	Bled	H	Football Stadium, Sydney	W	16-15
307	19-Jul-92	New Zealand	Bled	H	Ballymore Oval, Brisbane	W	19-17
308	25-Jul-92	New Zealand	Bled	H	Football Stadium, Sydney	L	23-26
309	22-Aug-92	South Africa	Int-T	A	Newlands Stadium, Cape Town	W	26-3
310	31-Oct-92	Ireland	Int-T	A	Lansdowne Road, Dublin	W	42-17
311	21-Nov-92	Wales	Int-T	A	National Stadium, Cardiff	W	23-6
312	4-Jul-93	Tonga	Int	H	Ballymore Oval, Brisbane	W	52-14
313	17-Jul-93	New Zealand	Bled-T	A	Carisbrook, Dunedin	L	10-25
314	31-Jul-93	South Africa	Int	H	Football Stadium, Sydney	L	12-19
315	14-Aug-93	South Africa	Int	H	Ballymore Oval, Brisbane	W	28-20
316	21-Aug-93	South Africa	Int	H	Football Stadium, Sydney	W	19-12
317	9-Oct-93	Canada	Int-T	A	Kingsland Rugby Park, Calgary	W	43-16
318	30-Oct-93	France	BIC-T	A	Stade du Parc Lescure, Bordeaux	L	13-16
319	6-Nov-93	France	BIC-T	A	Parc des Princes, Paris	W	24-3
320	5-Jun-94	Ireland	Int	H	Ballymore Oval, Brisbane	W	33-13

No	Date	Opponents	Tmt		Match Venue	Result	
321	11-Jun-94	Ireland	Int	H	Football Stadium, Sydney	W	32-18
322	18-Jun-94	Italy	Int	H	Ballymore Oval, Brisbane	W	23-20
323	25-Jun-94	Italy	Int	H	Olympic Park Stadium, Melbourne	W	20-7
324	6-Aug-94	Western Samoa	Int	H	Football Stadium, Sydney	W	73-3
325	17-Aug-94	New Zealand	Bled	H	Football Stadium, Sydney	W	20-16
326	30-Apr-95	Argentina	Int	H	Ballymore Oval, Brisbane	W	53-7
327	6-May-95	Argentina	Int	H	Football Stadium, Sydney	W	30-13
328	25-May-95	South Africa	WCp	A	Newlands Stadium, Cape Town	L	18-27
329	31-May-95	Canada	WCp	N	Boet Erasmus Stadium, Port Elizabeth	W	27-11
330	3-Jun-95	Romania	WCp	N	Danie Craven Stadium, Stellenbosch	W	42-3
331	11-Jun-95	England	WCqf	N	Newlands Stadium, Cape Town	L	22-25
332	22-Jul-95	New Zealand	Bled-T	A	Eden Park, Auckland	L	16-28
333	29-Jul-95	New Zealand	Bled	H	Football Stadium, Sydney	L	23-34
334	9-Jun-96	Wales	Int	H	Ballymore Oval, Brisbane	W	56-25
335	22-Jun-96	Wales	Int	H	Football Stadium, Sydney	W	42-3
336	29-Jun-96	Canada	Int	H	Ballymore Oval, Brisbane	W	74-9
337	6-Jul-96	New Zealand	TN-B	A	Athletic Park, Wellington	L	6-43
338	13-Jul-96	South Africa	TN	H	Football Stadium, Sydney	W	21-16
339	27-Jul-96	New Zealand	TN-B	H	Suncorp Stadium, Brisbane	L	25-32
340	3-Aug-96	South Africa	TN	A	Free State Stadium, Bloemfontein	L	19-25
341	23-Oct-96	Italy	Int-T	A	Stadio Plebiscito, Padova	W	40-18
342	9-Nov-96	Scotland	Int-T	A	Murrayfield, Edinburgh	W	29-19
343	23-Nov-96	Ireland	Int-T	A	Lansdowne Road, Dublin	W	22-12
344	1-Dec-96	Wales	Int-T	A	National Stadium, Cardiff	W	28-19
345	21-Jun-97	France	BIC	H	Football Stadium, Sydney	W	29-15
346	28-Jun-97	France	BIC	H	Ballymore Oval, Brisbane	W	26-19
347	5-Jul-97	New Zealand	Bled-T	A	Lancaster Park Oval, Christchurch	L	13-30
348	12-Jul-97	England	CKC	H	Football Stadium, Sydney	W	25-6
349	26-Jul-97	New Zealand	TN-B	H	Cricket Ground, Melbourne	L	18-33
350	2-Aug-97	South Africa	TN	H	Suncorp Stadium, Brisbane	W	32-20
351	16-Aug-97	New Zealand	TN-B	A	Carisbrook, Dunedin	L	24-36
352	23-Aug-97	South Africa	TN	A	Loftus Versfeld Stadium, Pretoria	L	22-61
353	1-Nov-97	Argentina	Int-T	A	Ferro Carril Oeste Stadium, B Aires	W	23-15
354	8-Nov-97	Argentina	Int-T	A	Ferro Carril Oeste Stadium, B Aires	L	16-18
355	15-Nov-97	England	CKC-T	A	Twickenham, London	D	15-15
356	22-Nov-97	Scotland	Int-T	A	Murrayfield, Edinburgh	W	37-8
357	6-Jun-98	England	CKC	H	Suncorp Stadium, Brisbane	W	76-0
358	13-Jun-98	Scotland	HT	H	Football Stadium, Sydney	W	45-3
359	20-Jun-98	Scotland	HT	H	Ballymore Oval, Brisbane	W	33-11
360	11-Jul-98	New Zealand	TN-B	H	Cricket Ground, Melbourne	W	24-16

No	Date	Opponents	Tmt		Match Venue	Result	
361	18-Jul-98	South Africa	TN	H	Subiaco Oval, Perth	L	13-14
362	1-Aug-98	New Zealand	TN-B	A	Jade Stadium, Christchurch	W	27-23
363	22-Aug-98	South Africa	TN	A	Ellis Park, Johannesburg	L	15-29
364	29-Aug-98	New Zealand	Bled	H	Football Stadium, Sydney	W	19-14
365	18-Sep-98	Fiji	WCQ	H	Parramatta Stadium, Sydney	W	66-20
366	22-Sep-98	Tonga	WCQ	H	Bruce Stadium, Canberra	W	74-0
367	26-Sep-98	Samoa	WCQ	H	Ballymore Oval, Brisbane	W	25-13
368	21-Nov-98	France	BIC-T	A	Stade de France, Paris	W	32-21
369	28-Nov-98	England	CKC-T	A	Twickenham, London	W	12-11
370	12-Jun-99	Ireland	LC	H	Ballymore Oval, Brisbane	W	46-10
371	19-Jun-99	Ireland	LC	H	Subiaco Oval, Perth	W	32-26
372	26-Jun-99	England	CKC	H	Stadium Australia, Sydney	W	22-15
373	17-Jul-99	South Africa	TN	H	Suncorp Stadium, Brisbane	W	32-6
374	24-Jul-99	New Zealand	TN-B	A	Eden Park, Auckland	L	15-34
375	14-Aug-99	South Africa	TN	A	Newlands Stadium, Cape Town	L	9-10
376	28-Aug-99	New Zealand	TN-B	H	Stadium Australia, Sydney	W	28-7
377	3-Oct-99	Romania	WCp	N	Ravenhill, Belfast	W	57-9
378	10-Oct-99	Ireland	WCp	A	Lansdowne Road, Dublin	W	23-3
379	14-Oct-99	United States	WCp	N	Thomond Park, Limerick	W	55-19
380	23-Oct-99	Wales	WCqf	A	Millennium Stadium, Cardiff	W	24-9
381	30-Oct-99	South Africa	WCsf	N	Twickenham, London	W	27-21
382	6-Nov-99	France	WCf	N	Millennium Stadium, Cardiff	W	35-12
383	17-Jun-00	Argentina	PT	H	Ballymore Oval, Brisbane	W	53-6
384	24-Jun-00	Argentina	PT	H	Canberra Stadium, Canberra	W	32-25
385	8-Jul-00	South Africa	MCP	H	Colonial Stadium, Melbourne	W	44-23
386	15-Jul-00	New Zealand	TN-B	H	Stadium Australia, Sydney	L	35-39
387	29-Jul-00	South Africa	TN	H	Stadium Australia, Sydney	W	26-6
388	5-Aug-00	New Zealand	TN-B	A	Westpac Trust Stadium, Wellington	W	24-23
389	26-Aug-00	South Africa	TN	A	ABSA Stadium, Durban	W	19-18
390	4-Nov-00	France	BIC-T	A	Stade de France, Paris	W	18-13
391	11-Nov-00	Scotland	HT-T	A	Murrayfield, Edinburgh	W	30-9
392	18-Nov-00	England	CKC-T	A	Twickenham, London	L	19-22
393	30-Jun-01	Lions	TRT	H	The Gabba Cricket Ground, Brisbane	L	13-29
394	7-Jul-01	Lions	TRT	H	Colonial Stadium, Melbourne	W	35-14
395	14-Jul-01	Lions	TRT	H	Stadium Australia, Sydney	W	29-23
396	28-Jul-01	South Africa	TN	A	Minolta Loftus Stadium, Pretoria	L	15-20
397	11-Aug-01	New Zealand	TN-B	A	Carisbrook, Dunedin	W	23-15
398	18-Aug-01	South Africa	TN	H	Subiaco Oval, Perth	D	14-14
399	1-Sep-01	New Zealand	TN-B	H	Stadium Australia, Sydney	W	29-26
400	1-Nov-01	Spain	Int-T	A	Campo Ciudad Universitaria, Madrid	W	92-10

No	Date	Opponents	Tmt		Match Venue	Result	
401	10-Nov-01	England	CKC-T	A	Twickenham, London	L	15-21
402	17-Nov-01	France	BIC-T	A	Stade Vélodrome, Marseille	L	13-14
403	25-Nov-01	Wales	Int-T	A	Millennium Stadium, Cardiff	W	21-13
404	22-Jun-02	France	BIC	H	Colonial Stadium, Melbourne	W	29-17
405	29-Jun-02	France	BIC	H	Stadium Australia, Sydney	W	31-25
406	13-Jul-02	New Zealand	TN-B	A	Jade Stadium, Christchurch	L	6-12
407	27-Jul-02	South Africa	TN	H	The Gabba Cricket Ground, Brisbane	W	38-27
408	3-Aug-02	New Zealand	TN-B	H	Telstra Stadium, Sydney	W	16-14
409	17-Aug-02	South Africa	TN-M	A	Ellis Park, Johannesburg	L	31-33
410	2-Nov-02	Argentina	PT-T	A	River Plate Stadium, Buenos Aires	W	17-6
411	9-Nov-02	Ireland	LC-T	A	Lansdowne Road, Dublin	L	9-18
412	16-Nov-02	England	CKC-T	A	Twickenham, London	L	31-32
413	23-Nov-02	Italy	Int-T	A	Stadio Luigi Ferraris, Genova	W	34-3
414	7-Jun-03	Ireland	LC	H	Subiaco Oval, Perth	W	45-16
415	14-Jun-03	Wales	Int	H	Telstra Stadium, Sydney	W	30-10
416	21-Jun-03	England	CKC	H	Telstra Dome, Melbourne	L	14-25
417	12-Jul-03	South Africa	TN	A	Newlands Stadium, Cape Town	L	22-26
418	26-Jul-03	New Zealand	TN-B	H	Telstra Stadium, Sydney	L	21-50
419	2-Aug-03	South Africa	TN	H	Suncorp Stadium, Brisbane	W	29-9
420	16-Aug-03	New Zealand	TN-B	A	Eden Park, Auckland	L	17-21
421	10-Oct-03	Argentina	WCp	H	Telstra Stadium, Sydney	W	24-8
422	18-Oct-03	Romania	WCp	H	Suncorp Stadium, Brisbane	W	90-8
423	25-Oct-03	Namibia	WCp	H	Adelaide Oval, Adelaide	W	142-0
424	1-Nov-03	Ireland	WCp	H	Telstra Dome, Melbourne	W	17-16
425	8-Nov-03	Scotland	WCqf	H	Suncorp Stadium, Brisbane	W	33-16
426	15-Nov-03	New Zealand	WCsf	H	Telstra Stadium, Sydney	W	22-10
427	22-Nov-03	England	WCf	H	Telstra Stadium, Sydney (a-e-t)	L	17-20
428	13-Jun-04	Scotland	HT	H	Telstra Dome, Melbourne	W	35-15
429	19-Jun-04	Scotland	HT	H	Telstra Stadium, Sydney	W	34-13
430	26-Jun-04	England	CKC	H	Suncorp Stadium, Brisbane	W	51-15
431	3-Jul-04	Pacific Islands	Int	H	Adelaide Oval, Adelaide	W	29-14
432	17-Jul-04	New Zealand	TN-B	A	Westpac Stadium, Wellington	L	7-16
433	31-Jul-04	South Africa	TN	H	Subiaco Oval, Perth	W	30-26
434	7-Aug-04	New Zealand	TN-B	H	Telstra Stadium, Sydney	W	23-18
435	21-Aug-04	South Africa	TN	A	ABSA Stadium, Durban	L	19-23
436	6-Nov-04	Scotland	HT-T	A	Murrayfield, Edinburgh	W	31-14
437	13-Nov-04	France	BIC-T	A	Stade de France, Paris	L	14-27
438	20-Nov-04	Scotland	HT-T	A	Hampden Park, Glasgow	W	31-17
439	27-Nov-04	England	CKC-T	A	Twickenham, London	W	21-19
440	11-Jun-05	Samoa	Int	H	Telstra Stadium, Sydney	W	74-7

No	Date	Opponents	Tmt		Match Venue	Result	
441	25-Jun-05	Italy	Int	H	Telstra Dome, Melbourne	W	69-21
442	2-Jul-05	France	BIC	H	Suncorp Stadium, Brisbane	W	37-31
443	9-Jul-05	South Africa	MCP	H	Telstra Stadium, Sydney	W	30-12
444	23-Jul-05	South Africa	MCP-T	A	Ellis Park, Johannesburg	L	20-33
445	30-Jul-05	South Africa	TN	A	Securicor Loftus Stadium, Pretoria	L	16-22
446	13-Aug-05	New Zealand	TN-B	H	Telstra Stadium, Sydney	L	13-30
447	20-Aug-05	South Africa	TN	H	Subiaco Oval, Perth	L	19-22
448	3-Sep-05	New Zealand	TN-B	A	Eden Park, Auckland	L	24-34
449	5-Nov-05	France	BIC-T	A	Stade Vélodrome, Marseille	L	16-26
450	12-Nov-05	England	CKC-T	A	Twickenham, London	L	16-26
451	19-Nov-05	Ireland	LC-T	A	Lansdowne Road, Dublin	W	30-14
452	26-Nov-05	Wales	Int-T	A	Millennium Stadium, Cardiff	L	22-24
453	11-Jun-06	England	CKC	H	Telstra Stadium, Sydney	W	34-3
454	17-Jun-06	England	CKC	H	Telstra Dome, Melbourne	W	43-18
455	24-Jun-06	Ireland	LC	H	Subiaco Oval, Perth	W	37-15
456	8-Jul-06	New Zealand	TN-B	A	Jade Stadium, Christchurch	L	12-32
457	15-Jul-06	South Africa	TN-M	H	Suncorp Stadium, Brisbane	W	49-0
458	29-Jul-06	New Zealand	TN-B	H	Suncorp Stadium, Brisbane	L	9-13
459	5-Aug-06	South Africa	TN-M	H	Telstra Stadium, Sydney	W	20-18
460	19-Aug-06	New Zealand	TN-B	A	Eden Park, Auckland	L	27-34
461	9-Sep-06	South Africa	TN-M	A	Ellis Park, Johannesburg	L	16-24
462	4-Nov-06	Wales	Int-T	A	Millennium Stadium, Cardiff	D	29-29
463	11-Nov-06	Italy	Int-T	A	Stadio Flaminio, Rome	W	25-18
464	19-Nov-06	Ireland	LC-T	A	Lansdowne Road, Dublin	L	6-21
465	25-Nov-06	Scotland	HT-T	A	Murrayfield, Edinburgh	W	44-15
466	26-May-07	Wales	JBT	H	Telstra Stadium, Sydney	W	29-23
467	2-Jun-07	Wales	JBT	H	Suncorp Stadium, Brisbane	W	31-0
468	9-Jun-07	Fiji	Int	H	Subiaco Oval, Perth	W	49-0
469	16-Jun-07	South Africa	TN-M	A	Newlands Stadium, Cape Town	L	19-22
470	30-Jun-07	New Zealand	TN-B	H	Cricket Ground, Melbourne	W	20-15
471	7-Jul-07	South Africa	TN-M	H	Telstra Stadium, Sydney	W	25-17
472	21-Jul-07	New Zealand	TN-B	A	Eden Park, Auckland	L	12-26
473	8-Sep-07	Japan	WCp	N	Stade de Gerland, Lyon	W	91-3
474	15-Sep-07	Wales	WCp	A	Millennium Stadium, Cardiff	W	32-20
475	23-Sep-07	Fiji	WCp	N	Stade de la Mosson, Montpellier	W	55-12
476	29-Sep-07	Canada	WCp	N	Stade Chaban-Delmas, Bordeaux	W	37-6
477	6-Oct-07	England	WCqf	N	Stade Vélodrome, Marseille	L	10-12
478	14-Jun-08	Ireland	LC	H	Telstra Dome, Melbourne	W	18-12
479	28-Jun-08	France	BIC	H	ANZ Stadium, Sydney	W	34-13
480	5-Jul-08	France	BIC	H	Suncorp Stadium, Brisbane	W	40-10

No	Date	Opponents	Tmt		Match Venue	Result	
481	19-Jul-08	South Africa	TN-M	H	Subiaco Oval, Perth	W	16-9
482	26-Jul-08	New Zealand	TN-B	H	ANZ Stadium, Sydney	W	34-19
483	2-Aug-08	New Zealand	TN-B	A	Eden Park, Auckland	L	10-39
484	23-Aug-08	South Africa	TN-M	A	The ABSA Stadium, Durban	W	27-15
485	30-Aug-08	South Africa	TN-M	A	Coca Cola Park, Johannesburg	L	8-53
486	13-Sep-08	New Zealand	TN-B	H	Suncorp Stadium, Brisbane	L	24-28
487	1-Nov-08	New Zealand	Bled	N	So Kon Po Stadium, Hong Kong	L	14-19
488	8-Nov-08	Italy	Int-T	A	Stadio Euganeo, Padova	W	30-20
489	15-Nov-08	England	CKC-T	A	Twickenham, London	W	28-14
490	22-Nov-08	France	BIC-T	A	Stade de France, Paris	W	18-13
491	29-Nov-08	Wales	JBT-T	A	Millennium Stadium, Cardiff	L	18-21
492	13-Jun-09	Italy	Int	H	Canberra Stadium, Canberra	W	31-8
493	20-Jun-09	Italy	Int	H	Etihad Stadium, Docklands, Melbourne	W	34-12
494	27-Jun-09	France	BIC	H	ANZ Stadium, Sydney	W	22-6
495	18-Jul-09	New Zealand	TN-B	A	Eden Park, Auckland	L	16-22
496	8-Aug-09	South Africa	TN-M	A	Newlands Stadium, Cape Town	L	17-29
497	22-Aug-09	New Zealand	TN-B	H	ANZ Stadium, Sydney	L	18-19
498	29-Aug-09	South Africa	TN-M	H	Subiaco Oval, Perth	L	25-32
499	5-Sep-09	South Africa	TN-M	H	Suncorp Stadium, Brisbane	W	21-6
500	19-Sep-09	New Zealand	TN-B	A	Westpac Stadium, Wellington	L	6-33
501	31-Oct-09	New Zealand	Bled	N	National Olympic Stadium, Tokyo	L	19-32
502	7-Nov-09	England	CKC-T	A	Twickenham, London	W	18-9
503	15-Nov-09	Ireland	LC-T	A	Croke Park, Dublin	D	20-20
504	21-Nov-09	Scotland	HT-T	A	Murrayfield, Edinburgh	L	8-9
505	28-Nov-09	Wales	JBT-T	A	Millennium Stadium, Cardiff	W	33-12
506	5-Jun-10	Fiji	Int	H	Canberra Stadium, Canberra	W	49-3
507	12-Jun-10	England	CKC	H	Subiaco Oval, Perth	W	27-17
508	19-Jun-10	England	CKC	H	ANZ Stadium, Sydney	L	20-21
509	26-Jun-10	Ireland	LC	H	Suncorp Stadium, Brisbane	W	22-15
510	24-Jul-10	South Africa	TN-M	H	Suncorp Stadium, Brisbane	W	30-13
511	31-Jul-10	New Zealand	TN-B	H	Etihad Stadium, Docklands, Melbourne	L	28-49
512	7-Aug-10	New Zealand	TN-B	A	AMI Stadium, Christchurch	L	10-20
513	28-Aug-10	South Africa	TN-M	A	Loftus Versfeld Stadium, Pretoria	L	31-44
514	4-Sep-10	South Africa	TN-M	A	Vodacom Park Stadium, Bloemfontein	W	41-39
515	11-Sep-10	New Zealand	TN-B	H	ANZ Stadium, Sydney	L	22-23
516	30-Oct-10	New Zealand	Bled	N	So Kon Po Stadium, Hong Kong	W	26-24
517	6-Nov-10	Wales	JBT-T	A	Millennium Stadium, Cardiff	W	25-16
518	13-Nov-10	England	CKC-T	A	Twickenham, London	L	18-35
519	20-Nov-10	Italy	Int-T	A	Stadio Artemio Franchi, Florence	W	32-14
520	27-Nov-10	France	BIC-T	A	Stade de France, Paris	W	59-16

No	Date	Opponents	Tmt		Match Venue	Result	
521	17-Jul-11	Samoa	Int	H	ANZ Stadium, Sydney	L	23-32
522	23-Jul-11	South Africa	TN-M	H	ANZ Stadium, Sydney	W	39-20
523	6-Aug-11	New Zealand	TN-B	A	Eden Park, Auckland	L	14-30
524	13-Aug-11	South Africa	TN-M	A	Kings Park Stadium, Durban	W	14-9
525	27-Aug-11	New Zealand	TN-B	H	Suncorp Stadium, Brisbane	W	25-20
526	11-Sep-11	Italy	WCp	N	North Harbour Stadium, Albany	W	32-6
527	17-Sep-11	Ireland	WCp	N	Eden Park, Auckland	L	6-15
528	23-Sep-11	United States	WCp	N	Wellington Regional Stadium, Wellington	W	67-5
529	1-Oct-11	Russia	WCp	N	Trafalgar Park, Nelson	W	68-22
530	9-Oct-11	South Africa	WCqf	N	Wellington Regional Stadium, Wellington	W	11-9
531	16-Oct-11	New Zealand	WCsf	A	Eden Park, Auckland	L	6-20
532	21-Oct-11	Wales	WC34	N	Eden Park, Auckland	W	21-18
533	3-Dec-11	Wales	JBT-T	A	Millennium Stadium, Cardiff	W	24-18
534	5-Jun-12	Scotland	HT	H	Ausgrid Stadium, Newcastle, NSW	L	6-9
535	9-Jun-12	Wales	JBT	H	Suncorp Stadium, Brisbane	W	27-19
536	16-Jun-12	Wales	JBT	H	Etihad Stadium, Docklands, Melbourne	W	25-23
537	23-Jun-12	Wales	JBT	H	Football Stadium, Sydney	W	20-19
538	18-Aug-12	New Zealand	RC-B	H	ANZ Stadium, Sydney	L	19-27
539	25-Aug-12	New Zealand	RC-B	A	Eden Park, Auckland	L	0-22
540	8-Sep-12	South Africa	RC-M	H	Patersons Stadium, Perth	W	26-19
541	15-Sep-12	Argentina	RC-P	H	Skilled Park, Robina, Gold Coast, Q'land	W	23-19
542	29-Sep-12	South Africa	RC-M	A	Loftus Versfeld Stadium, Pretoria	L	8-31
543	6-Oct-12	Argentina	RC-P	A	Estadio Gigante de Arroyito, Rosario	W	25-19
544	20-Oct-12	New Zealand	Bled	H	Suncorp Stadium, Brisbane	D	18-18
545	10-Nov-12	France	BIC-T	A	Stade de France, Paris	L	6-33
546	17-Nov-12	England	CKC-T	A	Twickenham, London	W	20-14
547	24-Nov-12	Italy	Int-T	A	Stadio Artemio Franchi, Florence	W	22-19
548	1-Dec-12	Wales	JBT-T	A	Millennium Stadium, Cardiff	W	14-12
549	22-Jun-13	Lions	TRT	H	Suncorp Stadium, Brisbane	L	21-23
550	29-Jun-13	Lions	TRT	H	Etihad Stadium, Docklands, Melbourne	W	16-15
551	6-Jul-13	Lions	TRT	H	ANZ Stadium, Sydney	L	16-41
552	17-Aug-13	New Zealand	RC-B	H	ANZ Stadium, Sydney	L	29-47
553	24-Aug-13	New Zealand	RC-B	A	Westpac Stadium, Wellington	L	16-27
554	7-Sep-13	South Africa	RC-M	H	Suncorp Stadium, Brisbane	L	12-38
555	14-Sep-13	Argentina	RC-P	H	Patersons Stadium, Perth	W	14-13
556	28-Sep-13	South Africa	RC-M	A	Newlands Stadium, Cape Town	L	8-28
557	5-Oct-13	Argentina	RC-P	A	Estadio Gigante de Arroyito, Rosario	W	54-17
558	19-Oct-13	New Zealand	Bled-T	A	Forsyth Barr Stadium, Dunedin	L	33-41
559	2-Nov-13	England	CKC-T	A	Twickenham, London	L	13-20
560	9-Nov-13	Italy	Int-T	A	Stadio Olimpico di Torino, Torino	W	50-20

No	Date	Opponents	Tmt		Match Venue	Result	
561	16-Nov-13	Ireland	LC-T	A	Aviva Stadium, Dublin	W	32-15
562	23-Nov-13	Scotland	HT-T	A	Murrayfield, Edinburgh	W	21-15
563	30-Nov-13	Wales	JBT-T	A	Millennium Stadium, Cardiff	W	30-26
564	7-Jun-14	France	BIC	H	Suncorp Stadium, Brisbane	W	50-23
565	14-Jun-14	France	BIC	H	Etihad Stadium, Docklands, Melbourne	W	6-0
566	21-Jun-14	France	BIC	H	Football Stadium, Sydney	W	39-13
567	16-Aug-14	New Zealand	RC-B	H	ANZ Stadium, Sydney	D	12-12
568	23-Aug-14	New Zealand	RC-B	A	Eden Park, Auckland	L	20-51
569	6-Sep-14	South Africa	RC-M	H	Patersons Stadium, Perth	W	24-23
570	13-Sep-14	Argentina	RC-P	H	Skilled Park, Robina, Gold Coast, Q'land	W	32-25
571	27-Sep-14	South Africa	RC-M	A	Newlands Stadium, Cape Town	L	10-28
572	4-Oct-14	Argentina	RC-P	A	Estadio Malvinas Argentinas, Mendoza	L	17-21
573	11-Oct-14	New Zealand	RC-B	H	Suncorp Stadium, Brisbane	L	28-29
574	8-Nov-14	Wales	JBT-T	A	Millennium Stadium, Cardiff	W	33-28
575	15-Nov-14	France	BIC-T	A	Stade de France, Paris	L	26-29
576	22-Nov-14	Ireland	LC-T	A	Aviva Stadium, Dublin	L	23-26
577	29-Nov-14	England	CKC-T	A	Twickenham, London	L	17-26

ENGLAND

The very first rugby International was played at Raeburn Place in Edinburgh on 27 March 1871, when Scotland defeated England in a challenge match. Scotland won by one goal and one try to one try; that is, four points to one if we adopt the scoring system of the time. Four years later, England played their first game against Ireland at the Oval in London, winning by seven points to nil. Another six years elapsed before they played Wales for the first time, in Blackheath in 1881. They also won that match by the huge margin of thirty points to nil. England were very successful in those early years, losing only six times in their first forty-five Internationals to the end of the 1892 season.

In 1883 a tournament contested by England, Ireland, Scotland and Wales was launched and called the Four (or Home) Nations Championship and with it the Triple Crown, a mythical trophy won by the team that defeated the other three competitors: England were Triple Crown winners in 1883 and in 1884.

In 1910 the French team was invited to participate in the Four Nations Championship, which was renamed the Five Nations Championship. If a team won all four matches in a season, it was then said to have achieved the Grand Slam. England's next period of success came on either side of the First World War, when the team won five Grand Slams in seven seasons between 1913 and 1924, losing only twice over twenty-eight matches.

In the next match, in January 1925, a sequence of nine wins was ended when England lost for the second time to New Zealand, but in 1928 the team achieved a sixth Grand Slam title.

In 1931 the French were expelled from the competition when they contravened the amateur status of the game, so in 1932, the tournament reverted to its original name: the Home Nations Championship. After a period of fifteen years, France was readmitted and the Home Nations Championship again became the Five Nations Championship in 1947. England had to wait ten years before winning their seventh Grand Slam in 1957, and a further twenty-three years before achieving an eighth success in 1980. However, wins against South Africa in 1969 and 1972, and against both New Zealand and Australia in 1973, made up for the lean times experienced on the domestic front during the 1960s, 1970s and 1980s.

Hosting the World Cup in 1991 provided the much-needed catalyst for the English team to improve, and they certainly rose to the challenge that year. In March 1991 the team was crowned Grand Slam champions, and World Cup runners-up to Australia in November.

This was followed by a second successive Grand Slam in 1992, and a home win against South Africa later that year. A rare win against New Zealand, also at Twickenham, followed in November 1993. Winning their eleventh Grand Slam in 1995 was a big incentive for England to perform well in the 1995 World Cup, held in South Africa. In that tournament they defeated Australia, the holders, in the quarter-finals, before losing to New Zealand the semi-final. The team also lost to France in the play-off for third place.

England commenced the new Millennium in 2000 by winning the inaugural Six Nations Championship title (an expanded Five Nations Championship with the entry of Italy). This was followed by an unprecedented sequence of wins, which started with an away victory against South Africa in Bloemfontein on 24 June 2000.

In forty-three matches up to 21 February 2004, England lost only three times: once to Ireland in 2001, and twice to France in 2002 and 2003. During that period they recorded one run of eleven consecutive wins and another of fourteen. The loss to Ireland in 2001 and to France in 2002 denied them the Grand Slam in both years. A sole defeat to Wales in 1999, and to Scotland in 2000, had also denied England two earlier Grand Slams.

In 2003 the English finally achieved the Grand Slam that had eluded them for four years, and topped that by winning the biggest prize of all, the World Cup, the following October. Winning the competition by defeating Australia, the host nation, on their home ground at the Telstra Stadium in Sydney, was the high point of English rugby history.

England's fortunes took a turn for the worse in 2004, when over a span of fifteen Six Nations matches between 2004 and 2006 they won on only seven occasions. The year 2006 was a particularly disappointing for the team as they suffered a sequence of seven consecutive defeats. The following year also started badly with just four wins from ten matches up to August. The English team's fortune changed in the 2007 World Cup, when they reached their third final, before losing to South Africa in an extremely close game. The period 2008 to 2010 was again a lean time for England, with only fourteen wins in thirty-two games. Things got better in 2011, when the English team won the first four matches in the Six Nations Championship, but failed to win the Grand Slam when they lost to Ireland in Dublin.

Elimination by France in the 2011 World Cup quarter-final was followed by an encouraging 2012 Six Nations campaign in which England's only loss in the Championship was to Wales, the team that went on to win the Grand Slam. After losing three times to South Africa and once to Australia later that year, the English produced a magnificent display in December 2012, when they defeated the All Blacks at Twickenham by 38 points to 21. The team was again denied a Grand Slam in 2013, when they were beaten by Wales in the final match of the tournament.

In the 2014 Six Nations Championship England lost the first match, but won the next four, only to be denied the title by finishing as runners-up, to Ireland, on points difference. Three months later, on the tour to New Zealand, the English team's run of four wins in the Six Nations campaign came to an end, when they suffered three consecutive defeats to the home side. The losing sequence was extended to five in November when they lost for the fourth successive time to the All Blacks and then to the Springboks a week later. However, a win against the Wallabies in the final match of 2014 did ease the situation.

In the 2015 Six Nations Championship, England, as in the previous year, with four wins, had to settle for the runners-up spot again, when the team lost on points difference to Ireland.

ENGLAND

HEAD TO HEAD RESULTS TO 31 MARCH 2015

	P	W	D	L	%	F	A
v TIER 1 Teams							
v Argentina	19	14	1	4	76.3	488	282
v Australia	43	18	1	24	43.0	661	907
v France	99	54	7	38	58.1	1553	1230
v Ireland *	129	74	8	47	60.5	1484	1056
v Italy	21	21	0	0	100.0	842	266
v New Zealand	40	7	1	32	18.7	560	969
v Scotland *	133	73	18	42	61.7	1547	1132
v South Africa	37	12	2	23	35.1	592	780
v Wales *	126	58	12	56	50.8	1596	1456
Sub-Total	**647**	**331**	**50**	**266**	**55.0**	**9323**	**8078**
v TIER 2/3 Group							
v Canada	6	6	0	0	100.0	273	73
v Fiji	5	5	0	0	100.0	210	83
v Japan	1	1	0	0	100.0	60	7
v Romania	5	5	0	0	100.0	335	24
v Samoa	7	7	0	0	100.0	244	100
v Tonga	2	2	0	0	100.0	137	30
v United States	5	5	0	0	100.0	253	52
v Georgia	2	2	0	0	100.0	125	16
v Namibia	0	0	0	0	0.0	0	0
v Russia	0	0	0	0	0.0	0	0
v Uruguay	1	1	0	0	100.0	111	13
Sub-Total	**34**	**34**	**0**	**0**	**100.0**	**1748**	**398**
v Other Teams							
v Netherlands	1	1	0	0	100.0	110	0
v Pacific Islanders	1	1	0	0	100.0	39	13
v President's XV	1	0	0	1	0.0	11	28
v New Zealand Natives	1	1	0	0	100.0	7	0
Sub-Total	**4**	**3**	**0**	**1**	**75.0**	**167**	**41**
All Internationals	**685**	**368**	**50**	**267**	**57.4**	**11238**	**8517**

* excludes points scored before the introduction of the modern points system

No	Date	Opponents	Tmt		Match Venue		Result
1	27-Mar-71	Scotland	Int	A	Raeburn Place, Edinburgh	L	1-4
2	5-Feb-72	Scotland	Int	H	Kennington Oval, London	W	8-3
3	3-Mar-73	Scotland	Int	A	Hamilton Crescent, Glasgow	D	0-0
4	23-Feb-74	Scotland	Int	H	Kennington Oval, London	W	3-1
5	15-Feb-75	Ireland	Int	H	Kennington Oval, London	W	7-0
6	8-Mar-75	Scotland	Int	A	Raeburn Place, Edinburgh	D	0-0
7	13-Dec-75	Ireland	Int	A	Leinster CC, Rathmines, Dublin	W	4-0
8	6-Mar-76	Scotland	Int	H	Kennington Oval, London	W	4-0
9	5-Feb-77	Ireland	Int	H	Kennington Oval, London	W	8-0
10	5-Mar-77	Scotland	Int	A	Raeburn Place, Edinburgh	L	0-3
11	4-Mar-78	Scotland	Int	H	Kennington Oval, London	D	0-0
12	11-Mar-78	Ireland	Int	A	Lansdowne Road, Dublin	W	7-0
13	10-Mar-79	Scotland	CC	A	Raeburn Place, Edinburgh	D	3-3
14	24-Mar-79	Ireland	Int	H	Kennington Oval, London	W	11-0
15	30-Jan-80	Ireland	Int	A	Lansdowne Road, Dublin	W	4-1
16	28-Feb-80	Scotland	CC	H	Whalley Range, Manchester	W	9-3
17	5-Feb-81	Ireland	Int	H	Whalley Range, Manchester	W	8-0
18	19-Feb-81	Wales	Int	H	Richardson's Field, Blackheath	W	30-0
19	19-Mar-81	Scotland	CC	A	Raeburn Place, Edinburgh	D	4-4
20	6-Feb-82	Ireland	Int	A	Lansdowne Road, Dublin	D	2-2
21	4-Mar-82	Scotland	CC	H	Whalley Range, Manchester	L	0-2
22	16-Dec-82	Wales	4N	A	St Helen's, Swansea	W	10-0
23	5-Feb-83	Ireland	4N	H	Whalley Range, Manchester	W	6-1
24	3-Mar-83	Scotland	4N-CC	A	Raeburn Place, Edinburgh	W	2-1
25	5-Jan-84	Wales	4N	H	Cardigan Fields, Leeds	W	5-3
26	4-Feb-84	Ireland	4N	A	Lansdowne Road, Dublin	W	3-0
27	1-Mar-84	Scotland	4N-CC	H	Rectory Field, Blackheath	W	3-1
28	3-Jan-85	Wales	4N	A	St Helen's, Swansea	W	7-4
29	7-Feb-85	Ireland	4N	H	Whalley Range, Manchester	W	2-1
30	2-Jan-86	Wales	4N	H	Rectory Field, Blackheath	W	5-3
31	6-Feb-86	Ireland	4N	A	Lansdowne Road, Dublin	W	1-0
32	13-Mar-86	Scotland	4N-CC	A	Raeburn Place, Edinburgh	D	0-0
33	8-Jan-87	Wales	4N	A	Stradey Park, Llanelli	D	0-0
34	5-Feb-87	Ireland	4N	A	Lansdowne Road, Dublin	L	0-6
35	5-Mar-87	Scotland	4N-CC	H	Whalley Range, Manchester	D	1-1
36	16-Feb-89	N Z Natives	Int	H	Rectory Field, Blackheath	W	7-0
37	15-Feb-90	Wales	4N	H	Crown Flatt, Dewsbury	L	0-1
38	1-Mar-90	Scotland	4N-CC	A	Raeburn Place, Edinburgh	W	6-0
39	15-Mar-90	Ireland	4N	H	Rectory Field, Blackheath	W	3-0
40	3-Jan-91	Wales	4N	A	Rodney Parade, Newport	W	7-3

No	Date	Opponents	Tmt		Match Venue	Result	
41	7-Feb-91	Ireland	4N	A	Lansdowne Road, Dublin	W	9-0
42	7-Mar-91	Scotland	4N-CC	H	Athletic Ground, Richmond	L	3-9
43	2-Jan-92	Wales	4N	H	Rectory Field, Blackheath	W	17-0
44	6-Feb-92	Ireland	4N	H	Whalley Range, Manchester	W	7-0
45	5-Mar-92	Scotland	4N-CC	A	Raeburn Place, Edinburgh	W	5-0
46	7-Jan-93	Wales	4N	A	Arms Park, Cardiff	L	11-12
47	4-Feb-93	Ireland	4N	A	Lansdowne Road, Dublin	W	4-0
48	4-Mar-93	Scotland	4N-CC	H	Headingley Stadium, Leeds	L	0-8
49	6-Jan-94	Wales	4N	H	Upper Park, Birkenhead Park	W	24-3
50	3-Feb-94	Ireland	4N	H	Rectory Field, Blackheath	L	5-7
51	17-Mar-94	Scotland	4N-CC	A	Raeburn Place, Edinburgh	L	0-6
52	5-Jan-95	Wales	4N	A	St Helen's, Swansea	W	14-6
53	2-Feb-95	Ireland	4N	A	Lansdowne Road, Dublin	W	6-3
54	9-Mar-95	Scotland	4N-CC	H	Athletic Ground, Richmond	L	3-6
55	4-Jan-96	Wales	4N	H	Rectory Field, Blackheath	W	25-0
56	1-Feb-96	Ireland	4N	H	Meanwood Road, Leeds	L	4-10
57	14-Mar-96	Scotland	4N-CC	A	Old Hampden Park, Glasgow	L	0-11
58	9-Jan-97	Wales	4N	A	Rodney Parade, Newport	L	0-11
59	6-Feb-97	Ireland	4N	A	Lansdowne Road, Dublin	L	9-13
60	13-Mar-97	Scotland	4N-CC	H	Fallowfield, Manchester	W	12-3
61	5-Feb-98	Ireland	4N	H	Athletic Ground, Richmond	L	6-9
62	12-Mar-98	Scotland	4N-CC	A	Powderhall, Edinburgh	D	3-3
63	2-Apr-98	Wales	4N	H	Rectory Field, Blackheath	W	14-7
64	7-Jan-99	Wales	4N	A	St Helen's, Swansea	L	3-26
65	4-Feb-99	Ireland	4N	A	Lansdowne Road, Dublin	L	0-6
66	11-Mar-99	Scotland	4N-CC	H	Rectory Field, Blackheath	L	0-5
67	6-Jan-00	Wales	4N	H	Kingsholm, Gloucester	L	3-13
68	3-Feb-00	Ireland	4N	H	Athletic Ground, Richmond	W	15-4
69	10-Mar-00	Scotland	4N-CC	A	Inverleith, Edinburgh	D	0-0
70	5-Jan-01	Wales	4N	A	Arms Park, Cardiff	L	0-13
71	9-Feb-01	Ireland	4N	A	Lansdowne Road, Dublin	L	6-10
72	9-Mar-01	Scotland	4N-CC	H	Rectory Field, Blackheath	L	3-18
73	11-Jan-02	Wales	4N	H	Rectory Field, Blackheath	L	8-9
74	8-Feb-02	Ireland	4N	H	Welford Road, Leicester	W	6-3
75	15-Mar-02	Scotland	4N-CC	A	Inverleith, Edinburgh	W	6-3
76	10-Jan-03	Wales	4N	A	St Helen's, Swansea	L	5-21
77	14-Feb-03	Ireland	4N	A	Lansdowne Road, Dublin	L	0-6
78	21-Mar-03	Scotland	4N-CC	H	Athletic Ground, Richmond	L	6-10
79	9-Jan-04	Wales	4N	H	Welford Road, Leicester	D	14-14
80	13-Feb-04	Ireland	4N	H	Rectory Field, Blackheath	W	19-0

No	Date	Opponents	Tmt		Match Venue	Result	
161	25-Feb-28	France	5N	H	Twickenham, London	W	18-8
162	17-Mar-28	Scotland	5N-CC	H	Twickenham, London	W	6-0
163	19-Jan-29	Wales	5N	H	Twickenham, London	W	8-3
164	9-Feb-29	Ireland	5N	H	Twickenham, London	L	5-6
165	16-Mar-29	Scotland	5N-CC	A	Murrayfield, Edinburgh	L	6-12
166	1-Apr-29	France	5N	A	Stade Colombes, Paris	W	16-6
167	18-Jan-30	Wales	5N	A	Arms Park, Cardiff	W	11-3
168	8-Feb-30	Ireland	5N	A	Lansdowne Road, Dublin	L	3-4
169	22-Feb-30	France	5N	H	Twickenham, London	W	11-5
170	15-Mar-30	Scotland	5N-CC	H	Twickenham, London	D	0-0
171	17-Jan-31	Wales	5N	H	Twickenham, London	D	11-11
172	14-Feb-31	Ireland	5N	H	Twickenham, London	L	5-6
173	21-Mar-31	Scotland	5N-CC	A	Murrayfield, Edinburgh	L	19-28
174	6-Apr-31	France	5N	A	Stade Colombes, Paris	L	13-14
175	2-Jan-32	South Africa	Int	H	Twickenham, London	L	0-7
176	16-Jan-32	Wales	4N	A	St Helen's, Swansea	L	5-12
177	13-Feb-32	Ireland	4N	A	Lansdowne Road, Dublin	W	11-8
178	19-Mar-32	Scotland	4N-CC	H	Twickenham, London	W	16-3
179	21-Jan-33	Wales	4N	H	Twickenham, London	L	3-7
180	11-Feb-33	Ireland	4N	H	Twickenham, London	W	17-6
181	18-Mar-33	Scotland	4N-CC	A	Murrayfield, Edinburgh	L	0-3
182	20-Jan-34	Wales	4N	A	Arms Park, Cardiff	W	9-0
183	10-Feb-34	Ireland	4N	A	Lansdowne Road, Dublin	W	13-3
184	17-Mar-34	Scotland	4N-CC	H	Twickenham, London	W	6-3
185	19-Jan-35	Wales	4N	H	Twickenham, London	D	3-3
186	9-Feb-35	Ireland	4N	H	Twickenham, London	W	14-3
187	16-Mar-35	Scotland	4N-CC	A	Murrayfield, Edinburgh	L	7-10
188	4-Jan-36	New Zealand	Int	H	Twickenham, London	W	13-0
189	18-Jan-36	Wales	4N	A	St Helen's, Swansea	D	0-0
190	8-Feb-36	Ireland	4N	A	Lansdowne Road, Dublin	L	3-6
191	21-Mar-36	Scotland	4N-CC	H	Twickenham, London	W	9-8
192	16-Jan-37	Wales	4N	H	Twickenham, London	W	4-3
193	13-Feb-37	Ireland	4N	H	Twickenham, London	W	9-8
194	20-Mar-37	Scotland	4N-CC	A	Murrayfield, Edinburgh	W	6-3
195	15-Jan-38	Wales	4N	A	Arms Park, Cardiff	L	8-14
196	12-Feb-38	Ireland	4N	A	Lansdowne Road, Dublin	W	36-14
197	19-Mar-38	Scotland	4N-CC	H	Twickenham, London	L	16-21
198	21-Jan-39	Wales	4N	H	Twickenham, London	W	3-0
199	11-Feb-39	Ireland	4N	H	Twickenham, London	L	0-5
200	18-Mar-39	Scotland	4N-CC	A	Murrayfield, Edinburgh	W	9-6

No	Date	Opponents	Tmt		Match Venue	Result	
201	18-Jan-47	Wales	5N	A	Arms Park, Cardiff	W	9-6
202	8-Feb-47	Ireland	5N	A	Lansdowne Road, Dublin	L	0-22
203	15-Mar-47	Scotland	5N-CC	H	Twickenham, London	W	24-5
204	19-Apr-47	France	5N	H	Twickenham, London	W	6-3
205	3-Jan-48	Australia	Int	H	Twickenham, London	L	0-11
206	17-Jan-48	Wales	5N	H	Twickenham, London	D	3-3
207	14-Feb-48	Ireland	5N	H	Twickenham, London	L	10-11
208	20-Mar-48	Scotland	5N-CC	A	Murrayfield, Edinburgh	L	3-6
209	29-Mar-48	France	5N	A	Stade Colombes, Paris	L	0-15
210	15-Jan-49	Wales	5N	A	Arms Park, Cardiff	L	3-9
211	12-Feb-49	Ireland	5N	A	Lansdowne Road, Dublin	L	5-14
212	26-Feb-49	France	5N	H	Twickenham, London	W	8-3
213	19-Mar-49	Scotland	5N-CC	H	Twickenham, London	W	19-3
214	21-Jan-50	Wales	5N	H	Twickenham, London	L	5-11
215	11-Feb-50	Ireland	5N	H	Twickenham, London	W	3-0
216	25-Feb-50	France	5N	A	Stade Colombes, Paris	L	3-6
217	18-Mar-50	Scotland	5N-CC	A	Murrayfield, Edinburgh	L	11-13
218	20-Jan-51	Wales	5N	A	St Helen's, Swansea	L	5-23
219	10-Feb-51	Ireland	5N	A	Lansdowne Road, Dublin	L	0-3
220	24-Feb-51	France	5N	H	Twickenham, London	L	3-11
221	17-Mar-51	Scotland	5N-CC	H	Twickenham, London	W	5-3
222	5-Jan-52	South Africa	Int	H	Twickenham, London	L	3-8
223	19-Jan-52	Wales	5N	H	Twickenham, London	L	6-8
224	15-Mar-52	Scotland	5N-CC	A	Murrayfield, Edinburgh	W	19-3
225	29-Mar-52	Ireland	5N	H	Twickenham, London	W	3-0
226	5-Apr-52	France	5N	A	Stade Colombes, Paris	W	6-3
227	17-Jan-53	Wales	5N	A	Arms Park, Cardiff	W	8-3
228	14-Feb-53	Ireland	5N	A	Lansdowne Road, Dublin	D	9-9
229	28-Feb-53	France	5N	H	Twickenham, London	W	11-0
230	21-Mar-53	Scotland	5N-CC	H	Twickenham, London	W	26-8
231	16-Jan-54	Wales	5N	H	Twickenham, London	W	9-6
232	30-Jan-54	New Zealand	Int	H	Twickenham, London	L	0-5
233	13-Feb-54	Ireland	5N	H	Twickenham, London	W	14-3
234	20-Mar-54	Scotland	5N-CC	A	Murrayfield, Edinburgh	W	13-3
235	10-Apr-54	France	5N	A	Stade Colombes, Paris	L	3-11
236	22-Jan-55	Wales	5N	A	Arms Park, Cardiff	L	0-3
237	12-Feb-55	Ireland	5N	A	Lansdowne Road, Dublin	D	6-6
238	26-Feb-55	France	5N	H	Twickenham, London	L	9-16
239	19-Mar-55	Scotland	5N-CC	H	Twickenham, London	W	9-6
240	21-Jan-56	Wales	5N	H	Twickenham, London	L	3-8

No	Date	Opponents	Tmt		Match Venue	Result	
241	11-Feb-56	Ireland	5N	H	Twickenham, London	W	20-0
242	17-Mar-56	Scotland	5N-CC	A	Murrayfield, Edinburgh	W	11-6
243	14-Apr-56	France	5N	A	Stade Colombes, Paris	L	9-14
244	19-Jan-57	Wales	5N	A	Arms Park, Cardiff	W	3-0
245	9-Feb-57	Ireland	5N	A	Lansdowne Road, Dublin	W	6-0
246	23-Feb-57	France	5N	H	Twickenham, London	W	9-5
247	16-Mar-57	Scotland	5N-CC	H	Twickenham, London	W	16-3
248	18-Jan-58	Wales	5N	H	Twickenham, London	D	3-3
249	1-Feb-58	Australia	Int	H	Twickenham, London	W	9-6
250	8-Feb-58	Ireland	5N	H	Twickenham, London	W	6-0
251	1-Mar-58	France	5N	A	Stade Colombes, Paris	W	14-0
252	15-Mar-58	Scotland	5N-CC	A	Murrayfield, Edinburgh	D	3-3
253	17-Jan-59	Wales	5N	A	Arms Park, Cardiff	L	0-5
254	14-Feb-59	Ireland	5N	A	Lansdowne Road, Dublin	W	3-0
255	28-Feb-59	France	5N	H	Twickenham, London	D	3-3
256	21-Mar-59	Scotland	5N-CC	H	Twickenham, London	D	3-3
257	16-Jan-60	Wales	5N	H	Twickenham, London	W	14-6
258	13-Feb-60	Ireland	5N	H	Twickenham, London	W	8-5
259	27-Feb-60	France	5N	A	Stade Colombes, Paris	D	3-3
260	19-Mar-60	Scotland	5N-CC	A	Murrayfield, Edinburgh	W	21-12
261	7-Jan-61	South Africa	Int	H	Twickenham, London	L	0-5
262	21-Jan-61	Wales	5N	A	Arms Park, Cardiff	L	3-6
263	11-Feb-61	Ireland	5N	A	Lansdowne Road, Dublin	L	8-11
264	25-Feb-61	France	5N	H	Twickenham, London	D	5-5
265	18-Mar-61	Scotland	5N-CC	H	Twickenham, London	W	6-0
266	20-Jan-62	Wales	5N	H	Twickenham, London	D	0-0
267	10-Feb-62	Ireland	5N	H	Twickenham, London	W	16-0
268	24-Feb-62	France	5N	A	Stade Colombes, Paris	L	0-13
269	17-Mar-62	Scotland	5N-CC	A	Murrayfield, Edinburgh	D	3-3
270	19-Jan-63	Wales	5N	A	Arms Park, Cardiff	W	13-6
271	9-Feb-63	Ireland	5N	A	Lansdowne Road, Dublin	D	0-0
272	23-Feb-63	France	5N	H	Twickenham, London	W	6-5
273	16-Mar-63	Scotland	5N-CC	H	Twickenham, London	W	10-8
274	25-May-63	New Zealand	Int-T	A	Eden Park, Auckland	L	11-21
275	1-Jun-63	New Zealand	Int-T	A	Lancaster Park Oval, Christchurch	L	6-9
276	4-Jun-63	Australia	Int-T	A	Sports Ground, Sydney	L	9-18
277	4-Jan-64	New Zealand	Int	H	Twickenham, London	L	0-14
278	18-Jan-64	Wales	5N	H	Twickenham, London	D	6-6
279	8-Feb-64	Ireland	5N	H	Twickenham, London	L	5-18
280	22-Feb-64	France	5N	A	Stade Colombes, Paris	W	6-3

No	Date	Opponents	Tmt		Match Venue	Result	
281	21-Mar-64	Scotland	5N-CC	A	Murrayfield, Edinburgh	L	6-15
282	16-Jan-65	Wales	5N	A	Arms Park, Cardiff	L	3-14
283	13-Feb-65	Ireland	5N	A	Lansdowne Road, Dublin	L	0-5
284	27-Feb-65	France	5N	H	Twickenham, London	W	9-6
285	20-Mar-65	Scotland	5N-CC	H	Twickenham, London	D	3-3
286	15-Jan-66	Wales	5N	H	Twickenham, London	L	6-11
287	12-Feb-66	Ireland	5N	H	Twickenham, London	D	6-6
288	26-Feb-66	France	5N	A	Stade Colombes, Paris	L	0-13
289	19-Mar-66	Scotland	5N-CC	A	Murrayfield, Edinburgh	L	3-6
290	7-Jan-67	Australia	Int	H	Twickenham, London	L	11-23
291	11-Feb-67	Ireland	5N	A	Lansdowne Road, Dublin	W	8-3
292	25-Feb-67	France	5N	H	Twickenham, London	L	12-16
293	18-Mar-67	Scotland	5N-CC	H	Twickenham, London	W	27-14
294	15-Apr-67	Wales	5N	A	Arms Park, Cardiff	L	21-34
295	4-Nov-67	New Zealand	Int	H	Twickenham, London	L	11-23
296	20-Jan-68	Wales	5N	H	Twickenham, London	D	11-11
297	10-Feb-68	Ireland	5N	H	Twickenham, London	D	9-9
298	24-Feb-68	France	5N	A	Stade Colombes, Paris	L	9-14
299	16-Mar-68	Scotland	5N-CC	A	Murrayfield, Edinburgh	W	8-6
300	8-Feb-69	Ireland	5N	A	Lansdowne Road, Dublin	L	15-17
301	22-Feb-69	France	5N	H	Twickenham, London	W	22-8
302	15-Mar-69	Scotland	5N-CC	H	Twickenham, London	W	8-3
303	12-Apr-69	Wales	5N	A	National Stadium, Cardiff	L	9-30
304	20-Dec-69	South Africa	Int	H	Twickenham, London	W	11-8
305	14-Feb-70	Ireland	5N	H	Twickenham, London	W	9-3
306	28-Feb-70	Wales	5N	H	Twickenham, London	L	13-17
307	21-Mar-70	Scotland	5N-CC	A	Murrayfield, Edinburgh	L	5-14
308	18-Apr-70	France	5N	A	Stade Colombes, Paris	L	13-35
309	16-Jan-71	Wales	5N	A	National Stadium, Cardiff	L	6-22
310	13-Feb-71	Ireland	5N	A	Lansdowne Road, Dublin	W	9-6
311	27-Feb-71	France	5N	H	Twickenham, London	D	14-14
312	20-Mar-71	Scotland	5N-CC	H	Twickenham, London	L	15-16
313	27-Mar-71	Scotland	Int-C	A	Murrayfield, Edinburgh	L	6-26
314	17-Apr-71	President's XV	Int-C	H	Twickenham, London	L	11-28
315	15-Jan-72	Wales	5N	H	Twickenham, London	L	3-12
316	12-Feb-72	Ireland	5N	H	Twickenham, London	L	12-16
317	26-Feb-72	France	5N	A	Stade Colombes, Paris	L	12-37
318	18-Mar-72	Scotland	5N-CC	A	Murrayfield, Edinburgh	L	9-23
319	3-Jun-72	South Africa	Int-T	A	Ellis Park, Johannesburg	W	18-9
320	6-Jan-73	New Zealand	Int	H	Twickenham, London	L	0-9

No	Date	Opponents	Tmt		Match Venue	Result	
321	20-Jan-73	Wales	5N	A	National Stadium, Cardiff	L	9-25
322	10-Feb-73	Ireland	5N	A	Lansdowne Road, Dublin	L	9-18
323	24-Feb-73	France	5N	H	Twickenham, London	W	14-6
324	17-Mar-73	Scotland	5N-CC	H	Twickenham, London	W	20-13
325	15-Sep-73	New Zealand	Int-T	A	Eden Park, Auckland	W	16-10
326	17-Nov-73	Australia	Int	H	Twickenham, London	W	20-3
327	2-Feb-74	Scotland	5N-CC	A	Murrayfield, Edinburgh	L	14-16
328	16-Feb-74	Ireland	5N	H	Twickenham, London	L	21-26
329	2-Mar-74	France	5N	A	Parc des Princess, Paris	D	12-12
330	16-Mar-74	Wales	5N	H	Twickenham, London	W	16-12
331	18-Jan-75	Ireland	5N	A	Lansdowne Road, Dublin	L	9-12
332	1-Feb-75	France	5N	H	Twickenham, London	L	20-27
333	15-Feb-75	Wales	5N	A	National Stadium, Cardiff	L	4-20
334	15-Mar-75	Scotland	5N-CC	H	Twickenham, London	W	7-6
335	24-May-75	Australia	Int-T	A	Cricket Ground, Sydney	L	9-16
336	31-May-75	Australia	Int-T	A	Ballymore Oval, Brisbane	L	21-30
337	3-Jan-76	Australia	Int	H	Twickenham, London	W	23-6
338	17-Jan-76	Wales	5N	H	Twickenham, London	L	9-21
339	21-Feb-76	Scotland	5N-CC	A	Murrayfield, Edinburgh	L	12-22
340	6-Mar-76	Ireland	5N	H	Twickenham, London	L	12-13
341	20-Mar-76	France	5N	A	Parc des Princess, Paris	L	9-30
342	15-Jan-77	Scotland	5N-CC	H	Twickenham, London	W	26-6
343	5-Feb-77	Ireland	5N	A	Lansdowne Road, Dublin	W	4-0
344	19-Feb-77	France	5N	H	Twickenham, London	L	3-4
345	5-Mar-77	Wales	5N	A	National Stadium, Cardiff	L	9-14
346	21-Jan-78	France	5N	A	Parc des Princess, Paris	L	6-15
347	4-Feb-78	Wales	5N	H	Twickenham, London	L	6-9
348	4-Mar-78	Scotland	5N-CC	A	Murrayfield, Edinburgh	W	15-0
349	18-Mar-78	Ireland	5N	H	Twickenham, London	W	15-9
350	25-Nov-78	New Zealand	Int	H	Twickenham, London	L	6-16
351	3-Feb-79	Scotland	5N-CC	H	Twickenham, London	D	7-7
352	17-Feb-79	Ireland	5N	A	Lansdowne Road, Dublin	L	7-12
353	3-Mar-79	France	5N	H	Twickenham, London	W	7-6
354	17-Mar-79	Wales	5N	A	National Stadium, Cardiff	L	3-27
355	24-Nov-79	New Zealand	Int	H	Twickenham, London	L	9-10
356	19-Jan-80	Ireland	5N	H	Twickenham, London	W	24-9
357	2-Feb-80	France	5N	A	Parc des Princess, Paris	W	17-13
358	16-Feb-80	Wales	5N	H	Twickenham, London	W	9-8
359	15-Mar-80	Scotland	5N-CC	A	Murrayfield, Edinburgh	W	30-18
360	17-Jan-81	Wales	5N	A	National Stadium, Cardiff	L	19-21

No	Date	Opponents	Tmt		Match Venue	Result	
361	21-Feb-81	Scotland	5N-CC	H	Twickenham, London	W	23-17
362	7-Mar-81	Ireland	5N	A	Lansdowne Road, Dublin	W	10-6
363	21-Mar-81	France	5N	H	Twickenham, London	L	12-16
364	30-May-81	Argentina	Int-T	A	Ferro Carril Oeste Stadium, B Aires	D	19-19
365	6-Jun-81	Argentina	Int-T	A	Ferro Carril Oeste Stadium, B Aires	W	12-6
366	2-Jan-82	Australia	Int	H	Twickenham, London	W	15-11
367	16-Jan-82	Scotland	5N-CC	A	Murrayfield, Edinburgh	D	9-9
368	6-Feb-82	Ireland	5N	H	Twickenham, London	L	15-16
369	20-Feb-82	France	5N	A	Parc des Princess, Paris	W	27-15
370	6-Mar-82	Wales	5N	H	Twickenham, London	W	17-7
371	15-Jan-83	France	5N	H	Twickenham, London	L	15-19
372	5-Feb-83	Wales	5N	A	National Stadium, Cardiff	D	13-13
373	5-Mar-83	Scotland	5N-CC	H	Twickenham, London	L	12-22
374	19-Mar-83	Ireland	5N	A	Lansdowne Road, Dublin	L	15-25
375	19-Nov-83	New Zealand	Int	H	Twickenham, London	W	15-9
376	4-Feb-84	Scotland	5N-CC	A	Murrayfield, Edinburgh	L	6-18
377	18-Feb-84	Ireland	5N	H	Twickenham, London	W	12-9
378	3-Mar-84	France	5N	A	Parc des Princess, Paris	L	18-32
379	17-Mar-84	Wales	5N	H	Twickenham, London	L	15-24
380	2-Jun-84	South Africa	Int-T	A	Boet Erasmus Stadium, Port Elizabeth	L	15-33
381	9-Jun-84	South Africa	Int-T	A	Ellis Park, Johannesburg	L	9-35
382	3-Nov-84	Australia	Int	H	Twickenham, London	L	3-19
383	5-Jan-85	Romania	Int	H	Twickenham, London	W	22-15
384	2-Feb-85	France	5N	H	Twickenham, London	D	9-9
385	16-Mar-85	Scotland	5N-CC	H	Twickenham, London	W	10-7
386	30-Mar-85	Ireland	5N	A	Lansdowne Road, Dublin	L	10-13
387	20-Apr-85	Wales	5N	A	National Stadium, Cardiff	L	15-24
388	1-Jun-85	New Zealand	Int-T	A	Lancaster Park Oval, Christchurch	L	13-18
389	8-Jun-85	New Zealand	Int-T	A	Athletic Park, Wellington	L	15-42
390	18-Jan-86	Wales	5N	H	Twickenham, London	W	21-18
391	15-Feb-86	Scotland	5N-CC	A	Murrayfield, Edinburgh	L	6-33
392	1-Mar-86	Ireland	5N	H	Twickenham, London	W	25-20
393	15-Mar-86	France	5N	A	Parc des Princess, Paris	L	10-29
394	7-Feb-87	Ireland	5N	A	Lansdowne Road, Dublin	L	0-17
395	21-Feb-87	France	5N	H	Twickenham, London	L	15-19
396	7-Mar-87	Wales	5N	A	National Stadium, Cardiff	L	12-19
397	4-Apr-87	Scotland	5N-CC	H	Twickenham, London	W	21-12
398	23-May-87	Australia	WCp	A	Concord Oval, Sydney	L	6-19
399	30-May-87	Japan	WCp	N	Concord Oval, Sydney	W	60-7
400	3-Jun-87	United States	WCp	N	Concord Oval, Sydney	W	34-6

No	Date	Opponents	Tmt		Match Venue	Result	
401	8-Jun-87	Wales	WCqf	N	Ballymore Oval, Brisbane	L	3-16
402	16-Jan-88	France	5N	A	Parc des Princess, Paris	L	9-10
403	6-Feb-88	Wales	5N	H	Twickenham, London	L	3-11
404	5-Mar-88	Scotland	5N-CC	A	Murrayfield, Edinburgh	W	9-6
405	19-Mar-88	Ireland	5N	H	Twickenham, London	W	35-3
406	23-Apr-88	Ireland	MT	A	Lansdowne Road, Dublin	W	21-10
407	29-May-88	Australia	Int-T	A	Ballymore Oval, Brisbane	L	16-22
408	12-Jun-88	Australia	Int-T	A	Concord Oval, Sydney	L	8-28
409	16-Jun-88	Fiji	Int-T	A	National Stadium, Suva	W	25-12
410	5-Nov-88	Australia	Int	H	Twickenham, London	W	28-19
411	4-Feb-89	Scotland	5N-CC	H	Twickenham, London	D	12-12
412	18-Feb-89	Ireland	5N-MT	A	Lansdowne Road, Dublin	W	16-3
413	4-Mar-89	France	5N	H	Twickenham, London	W	11-0
414	18-Mar-89	Wales	5N	A	National Stadium, Cardiff	L	9-12
415	13-May-89	Romania	Int	A	Stadionul 23 August, Bucharest	W	58-3
416	4-Nov-89	Fiji	Int	H	Twickenham, London	W	58-23
417	20-Jan-90	Ireland	5N-MT	H	Twickenham, London	W	23-0
418	3-Feb-90	France	5N	A	Parc des Princess, Paris	W	26-7
419	17-Feb-90	Wales	5N	H	Twickenham, London	W	34-6
420	17-Mar-90	Scotland	5N-CC	A	Murrayfield, Edinburgh	L	7-13
421	28-Jul-90	Argentina	Int-T	A	Vélez Sarsfield Stadium, Buenos Aires	W	25-12
422	4-Aug-90	Argentina	Int-T	A	Vélez Sarsfield Stadium, Buenos Aires	L	13-15
423	3-Nov-90	Argentina	Int	H	Twickenham, London	W	51-0
424	19-Jan-91	Wales	5N	A	National Stadium, Cardiff	W	25-6
425	16-Feb-91	Scotland	5N-CC	H	Twickenham, London	W	21-12
426	2-Mar-91	Ireland	5N-MT	A	Lansdowne Road, Dublin	W	16-7
427	16-Mar-91	France	5N	H	Twickenham, London	W	21-19
428	20-Jul-91	Fiji	Int-T	A	National Stadium, Suva	W	28-12
429	27-Jul-91	Australia	Int-T	A	Football Stadium, Sydney	L	15-40
430	3-Oct-91	New Zealand	WCp	H	Twickenham, London	L	12-18
431	8-Oct-91	Italy	WCp	H	Twickenham, London	W	36-6
432	11-Oct-91	United States	WCp	H	Twickenham, London	W	37-9
433	19-Oct-91	France	WCqf	A	Parc des Princess, Paris	W	19-10
434	26-Oct-91	Scotland	WCsf	A	Murrayfield, Edinburgh	W	9-6
435	2-Nov-91	Australia	WCf	H	Twickenham, London	L	6-12
436	18-Jan-92	Scotland	5N-CC	A	Murrayfield, Edinburgh	W	25-7
437	1-Feb-92	Ireland	5N-MT	H	Twickenham, London	W	38-9
438	15-Feb-92	France	5N	A	Parc des Princess, Paris	W	31-13
439	7-Mar-92	Wales	5N	H	Twickenham, London	W	24-0
440	17-Oct-92	Canada	Int	H	Wembley Stadium, London	W	26-13

No	Date	Opponents	Tmt		Match Venue	Result	
441	14-Nov-92	South Africa	Int	H	Twickenham, London	W	33-16
442	16-Jan-93	France	5N	H	Twickenham, London	W	16-15
443	6-Feb-93	Wales	5N	A	National Stadium, Cardiff	L	9-10
444	6-Mar-93	Scotland	5N-CC	H	Twickenham, London	W	26-12
445	20-Mar-93	Ireland	5N-MT	A	Lansdowne Road, Dublin	L	3-17
446	27-Nov-93	New Zealand	Int	H	Twickenham, London	W	15-9
447	5-Feb-94	Scotland	5N-CC	A	Murrayfield, Edinburgh	W	15-14
448	19-Feb-94	Ireland	5N-MT	H	Twickenham, London	L	12-13
449	5-Mar-94	France	5N	A	Parc des Princess, Paris	W	18-14
450	19-Mar-94	Wales	5N	H	Twickenham, London	W	15-8
451	4-Jun-94	South Africa	Int-T	A	Loftus Versfeld Stadium, Pretoria	W	32-15
452	11-Jun-94	South Africa	Int-T	A	Newlands Stadium, Cape Town	L	9-27
453	12-Nov-94	Romania	Int	H	Twickenham, London	W	54-3
454	10-Dec-94	Canada	Int	H	Twickenham, London	W	60-19
455	21-Jan-95	Ireland	5N-MT	A	Lansdowne Road, Dublin	W	20-8
456	4-Feb-95	France	5N	H	Twickenham, London	W	31-10
457	18-Feb-95	Wales	5N	A	National Stadium, Cardiff	W	23-9
458	18-Mar-95	Scotland	5N-CC	H	Twickenham, London	W	24-12
459	27-May-95	Argentina	WCp	N	Kings Park Stadium, Durban	W	24-18
460	31-May-95	Italy	WCp	N	Kings Park Stadium, Durban	W	27-20
461	4-Jun-95	Western Samoa	WCp	N	Kings Park Stadium, Durban	W	44-22
462	11-Jun-95	Australia	WCqf	N	Newlands Stadium, Cape Town	W	25-22
463	ı.·-Jun-95	New Zealand	WCsf	N	Newlands Stadium, Cape Town	L	29-45
464	22-Jun-95	France	WC34	N	Loftus Versfeld Stadium, Pretoria	L	9-19
465	18-Nov-95	South Africa	Int	H	Twickenham, London	L	14-24
466	16-Dec-95	Western Samoa	Int	H	Twickenham, London	W	27-9
467	20-Jan-96	France	5N	A	Parc des Princess, Paris	L	12-15
468	3-Feb-96	Wales	5N	H	Twickenham, London	W	21-15
469	2-Mar-96	Scotland	5N-CC	A	Murrayfield, Edinburgh	W	18-9
470	16-Mar-96	Ireland	5N-MT	H	Twickenham, London	W	28-15
471	23-Nov-96	Italy	Int	H	Twickenham, London	W	54-21
472	14-Dec-96	Argentina	Int	H	Twickenham, London	W	20-18
473	1-Feb-97	Scotland	5N-CC	H	Twickenham, London	W	41-13
474	15-Feb-97	Ireland	5N-MT	A	Lansdowne Road, Dublin	W	46-6
475	1-Mar-97	France	5N	H	Twickenham, London	L	20-23
476	15-Mar-97	Wales	5N	A	National Stadium, Cardiff	W	34-13
477	31-May-97	Argentina	Int-T	A	Ferro Carril Oeste Stadium, B Aires	W	46-20
478	7-Jun-97	Argentina	Int-T	A	Ferro Carril Oeste Stadium, B Aires	L	13-33
479	12-Jul-97	Australia	CKC-T	A	Football Stadium, Sydney	L	6-25
480	15-Nov-97	Australia	CKC	H	Twickenham, London	D	15-15

No	Date	Opponents	Tmt		Match Venue	Result	
481	22-Nov-97	New Zealand	Int	H	Old Trafford, Manchester	L	8-25
482	29-Nov-97	South Africa	Int	H	Twickenham, London	L	11-29
483	6-Dec-97	New Zealand	Int	H	Twickenham, London	D	26-26
484	7-Feb-98	France	5N	A	Stade de France, Paris	L	17-24
485	21-Feb-98	Wales	5N	H	Twickenham, London	W	60-26
486	22-Mar-98	Scotland	5N-CC	A	Murrayfield, Edinburgh	W	34-20
487	4-Apr-98	Ireland	5N-MT	H	Twickenham, London	W	35-17
488	6-Jun-98	Australia	CKC-T	A	Suncorp Stadium, Brisbane	L	0-76
489	20-Jun-98	New Zealand	Int-T	A	Carisbrook, Dunedin	L	22-64
490	27-Jun-98	New Zealand	Int-T	A	Eden Park, Auckland	L	10-40
491	4-Jul-98	South Africa	Int-T	A	Norwich Park, Newlands, Cape Town	L	0-18
492	14-Nov-98	Netherlands	WCQ	H	McAlpine Stadium, Huddersfield	W	110-0
493	22-Nov-98	Italy	WCQ	H	McAlpine Stadium, Huddersfield	W	23-15
494	28-Nov-98	Australia	CKC	H	Twickenham, London	L	11-12
495	5-Dec-98	South Africa	Int	H	Twickenham, London	W	13-7
496	20-Feb-99	Scotland	5N-CC	H	Twickenham, London	W	24-21
497	6-Mar-99	Ireland	5N-MT	A	Lansdowne Road, Dublin	W	27-15
498	20-Mar-99	France	5N	H	Twickenham, London	W	21-10
499	11-Apr-99	Wales	5N	N	Wembley Stadium, London	L	31-32
500	26-Jun-99	Australia	CKC-T	A	Stadium Australia, Sydney	L	15-22
501	21-Aug-99	United States	Int	H	Twickenham, London	W	106-8
502	28-Aug-99	Canada	Int	H	Twickenham, London	W	36-11
503	2-Oct-99	Italy	WCp	H	Twickenham, London	W	67-7
504	9-Oct-99	New Zealand	WCp	H	Twickenham, London	L	16-30
505	15-Oct-99	Tonga	WCp	H	Twickenham, London	W	101-10
506	20-Oct-99	Fiji	QFpo	H	Twickenham, London	W	45-24
507	24-Oct-99	South Africa	WCqf	N	Stade de France, Paris	L	21-44
508	5-Feb-00	Ireland	6N-MT	H	Twickenham, London	W	50-18
509	19-Feb-00	France	6N	A	Stade de France, Paris	W	15-9
510	4-Mar-00	Wales	6N	H	Twickenham, London	W	46-12
511	18-Mar-00	Italy	6N	A	Stadio Flaminio, Rome	W	59-12
512	2-Apr-00	Scotland	6N-CC	A	Murrayfield, Edinburgh	L	13-19
513	17-Jun-00	South Africa	Int-T	A	Minolta Loftus Stadium, Pretoria	L	13-18
514	24-Jun-00	South Africa	Int-T	A	Free State Stadium, Bloemfontein	W	27-22
515	18-Nov-00	Australia	CKC	H	Twickenham, London	W	22-19
516	25-Nov-00	Argentina	Int	H	Twickenham, London	W	19-0
517	2-Dec-00	South Africa	Int	H	Twickenham, London	W	25-17
518	3-Feb-01	Wales	6N	A	Millennium Stadium, Cardiff	W	44-15
519	17-Feb-01	Italy	6N	H	Twickenham, London	W	80-23
520	3-Mar-01	Scotland	6N-CC	H	Twickenham, London	W	43-3

No	Date	Opponents	Tmt		Match Venue	Result	
521	7-Apr-01	France	6N	H	Twickenham, London	W	48-19
522	2-Jun-01	Canada	Int-T	A	Fletcher's Field, Markham, Toronto	W	22-10
523	9-Jun-01	Canada	Int-T	A	Swanguard Stadium, Burnaby, B.C.	W	59-20
524	16-Jun-01	United States	Int-T	A	Boxer Stadium, San Francisco	W	48-19
525	20-Oct-01	Ireland	6N-MT	A	Lansdowne Road, Dublin	L	14-20
526	10-Nov-01	Australia	CKC	H	Twickenham, London	W	21-15
527	17-Nov-01	Romania	Int	H	Twickenham, London	W	134-0
528	24-Nov-01	South Africa	Int	H	Twickenham, London	W	29-9
529	2-Feb-02	Scotland	6N-CC	A	Murrayfield, Edinburgh	W	29-3
530	16-Feb-02	Ireland	6N-MT	H	Twickenham, London	W	45-11
531	2-Mar-02	France	6N	A	Stade de France, Paris	L	15-20
532	23-Mar-02	Wales	6N	H	Twickenham, London	W	50-10
533	7-Apr-02	Italy	6N	A	Stadio Flaminio, Rome	W	45-9
534	22-Jun-02	Argentina	Int-T	A	Vélez Sarsfield Stadium, Buenos Aires	W	26-18
535	9-Nov-02	New Zealand	Int	H	Twickenham, London	W	31-28
536	16-Nov-02	Australia	CKC	H	Twickenham, London	W	32-31
537	23-Nov-02	South Africa	Int	H	Twickenham, London	W	53-3
538	15-Feb-03	France	6N	H	Twickenham, London	W	25-17
539	22-Feb-03	Wales	6N	A	Millennium Stadium, Cardiff	W	26-9
540	9-Mar-03	Italy	6N	H	Twickenham, London	W	40-5
541	22-Mar-03	Scotland	6N-CC	H	Twickenham, London	W	40-9
542	30-Mar-03	Ireland	6N-MT	A	Lansdowne Road, Dublin	W	42-6
543	14-Jun-03	New Zealand	Int-T	A	Westpac Trust Stadium, Wellington	W	15-13
544	21-Jun-03	Australia	CKC-T	A	Telstra Dome, Melbourne	W	25-14
545	23-Aug-03	Wales	Int	A	Millennium Stadium, Cardiff	W	43-9
546	30-Aug-03	France	Int	A	Stade Vélodrome, Marseille	L	16-17
547	6-Sep-03	France	Int	H	Twickenham, London	W	45-14
548	12-Oct-03	Georgia	WCp	N	Subiaco Oval, Perth	W	84-6
549	18-Oct-03	South Africa	WCp	N	Subiaco Oval, Perth	W	25-6
550	26-Oct-03	Samoa	WCp	N	Telstra Dome, Melbourne	W	35-22
551	2-Nov-03	Uruguay	WCp	N	Suncorp Stadium, Brisbane	W	111-13
552	9-Nov-03	Wales	WCqf	N	Suncorp Stadium, Brisbane	W	28-17
553	16-Nov-03	France	WCsf	N	Telstra Stadium, Sydney	W	24-7
554	22-Nov-03	Australia	WCf	A	Telstra Stadium, Sydney (a-e-t)	W	20-17
555	15-Feb-04	Italy	6N	A	Stadio Flaminio, Rome	W	50-9
556	21-Feb-04	Scotland	6N-CC	A	Murrayfield, Edinburgh	W	35-13
557	6-Mar-04	Ireland	6N-MT	H	Twickenham, London	L	13-19
558	20-Mar-04	Wales	6N	H	Twickenham, London	W	31-21
559	27-Mar-04	France	6N	A	Stade de France, Paris	L	21-24
560	12-Jun-04	New Zealand	Int-T	A	Carisbrook, Dunedin	L	3-36

No	Date	Opponents	Tmt		Match Venue	Result	
561	19-Jun-04	New Zealand	Int-T	A	Eden Park, Auckland	L	12-36
562	26-Jun-04	Australia	CKC-T	A	Suncorp Stadium, Brisbane	L	15-51
563	13-Nov-04	Canada	Int	H	Twickenham, London	W	70-0
564	20-Nov-04	South Africa	Int	H	Twickenham, London	W	32-16
565	27-Nov-04	Australia	CKC	H	Twickenham, London	L	19-21
566	5-Feb-05	Wales	6N	A	Millennium Stadium, Cardiff	L	9-11
567	13-Feb-05	France	6N	H	Twickenham, London	L	17-18
568	27-Feb-05	Ireland	6N-MT	A	Lansdowne Road, Dublin	L	13-19
569	12-Mar-05	Italy	6N	H	Twickenham, London	W	39-7
570	19-Mar-05	Scotland	6N-CC	H	Twickenham, London	W	43-22
571	12-Nov-05	Australia	CKC	H	Twickenham, London	W	26-16
572	19-Nov-05	New Zealand	Int	H	Twickenham, London	L	19-23
573	26-Nov-05	Samoa	Int	H	Twickenham, London	W	40-3
574	4-Feb-06	Wales	6N	H	Twickenham, London	W	47-13
575	11-Feb-06	Italy	6N	A	Stadio Flaminio, Rome	W	31-6
576	25-Feb-06	Scotland	6N-CC	A	Murrayfield, Edinburgh	L	12-18
577	12-Mar-06	France	6N	A	Stade de France, Paris	L	6-31
578	18-Mar-06	Ireland	6N-MT	H	Twickenham, London	L	24-28
579	11-Jun-06	Australia	CKC-T	A	Telstra Stadium, Sydney	L	3-34
580	17-Jun-06	Australia	CKC-T	A	Telstra Dome, Melbourne	L	18-43
581	5-Nov-06	New Zealand	Int	H	Twickenham, London	L	20-41
582	11-Nov-06	Argentina	Int	H	Twickenham, London	L	18-25
583	18-Nov-06	South Africa	Int	H	Twickenham, London	W	23-21
584	25-Nov-06	South Africa	Int	H	Twickenham, London	L	14-25
585	3-Feb-07	Scotland	6N-CC	H	Twickenham, London	W	42-20
586	10-Feb-07	Italy	6N	H	Twickenham, London	W	20-7
587	24-Feb-07	Ireland	6N-MT	A	Croke Park, Dublin	L	13-43
588	11-Mar-07	France	6N	H	Twickenham, London	W	26-18
589	17-Mar-07	Wales	6N	A	Millennium Stadium, Cardiff	L	18-27
590	26-May-07	South Africa	Int-T	A	Vodacom Park Stadium, Bloemfontein	L	10-58
591	2-Jun-07	South Africa	Int-T	A	Loftus Versfeld Stadium, Pretoria	L	22-55
592	4-Aug-07	Wales	Int	H	Twickenham, London	W	62-5
593	11-Aug-07	France	Int	H	Twickenham, London	L	15-21
594	18-Aug-07	France	Int	A	Stade Vélodrome, Marseille	L	9-22
595	8-Sep-07	United States	WCp	N	Stade Félix Bollaert, Lens	W	28-10
596	14-Sep-07	South Africa	WCp	N	Stade de France, Paris	L	0-36
597	22-Sep-07	Samoa	WCp	N	Stade de la Beaujoire, Nantes	W	44-22
598	28-Sep-07	Tonga	WCp	N	Parc des Princess, Paris	W	36-20
599	6-Oct-07	Australia	WCqf	N	Stade Vélodrome, Marseille	W	12-10
600	13-Oct-07	France	WCsf	A	Stade de France, Paris	W	14-9

No	Date	Opponents	Tmt		Match Venue	Result	
601	20-Oct-07	South Africa	WCf	N	Stade de France, Paris	L	6-15
602	2-Feb-08	Wales	6N	H	Twickenham, London	L	19-26
603	10-Feb-08	Italy	6N	A	Stadio Flaminio, Rome	W	23-19
604	23-Feb-08	France	6N	A	Stade de France, Paris	W	24-13
605	8-Mar-08	Scotland	6N-CC	A	Murrayfield, Edinburgh	L	9-15
606	15-Mar-08	Ireland	6N-MT	H	Twickenham, London	W	33-10
607	14-Jun-08	New Zealand	Int-T	A	Eden Park, Auckland	L	20-37
608	21-Jun-08	New Zealand	Int-T	A	AMI Stadium, Christchurch	L	12-44
609	8-Nov-08	Pacific Islands	Int	H	Twickenham, London	W	39-13
610	15-Nov-08	Australia	CKC	H	Twickenham, London	L	14-28
611	22-Nov-08	South Africa	Int	H	Twickenham, London	L	6-42
612	29-Nov-08	New Zealand	EHS	H	Twickenham, London	L	6-32
613	7-Feb-09	Italy	6N	H	Twickenham, London	W	36-11
614	14-Feb-09	Wales	6N	A	Millennium Stadium, Cardiff	L	15-23
615	28-Feb-09	Ireland	6N-MT	A	Croke Park, Dublin	L	13-14
616	15-Mar-09	France	6N	H	Twickenham, London	W	34-10
617	21-Mar-09	Scotland	6N-CC	H	Twickenham, London	W	26-12
618	6-Jun-09	Argentina	Int	H	Old Trafford, Manchester	W	37-15
619	13-Jun-09	Argentina	Int-T	A	Estadio Padre Ernesto Martearena, Salta	L	22-24
620	7-Nov-09	Australia	CKC	H	Twickenham, London	L	9-18
621	14-Nov-09	Argentina	Int	H	Twickenham, London	W	16-9
622	21-Nov-09	New Zealand	EHS	H	Twickenham, London	L	6-19
623	6-Feb-10	Wales	6N	H	Twickenham, London	W	30-17
624	14-Feb-10	Italy	6N	A	Stadio Flaminio, Rome	W	17-12
625	27-Feb-10	Ireland	6N-MT	H	Twickenham, London	L	16-20
626	13-Mar-10	Scotland	6N-CC	A	Murrayfield, Edinburgh	D	15-15
627	20-Mar-10	France	6N	A	Stade de France, Paris	L	10-12
628	12-Jun-10	Australia	CKC-T	A	Subiaco Oval, Perth	L	17-27
629	19-Jun-10	Australia	CKC-T	A	ANZ Stadium, Sydney	W	21-20
630	6-Nov-10	New Zealand	EHS	H	Twickenham, London	L	16-26
631	13-Nov-10	Australia	CKC	H	Twickenham, London	W	35-18
632	20-Nov-10	Samoa	Int	H	Twickenham, London	W	26-13
633	27-Nov-10	South Africa	Int	H	Twickenham, London	L	11-21
634	4-Feb-11	Wales	6N	A	Millennium Stadium, Cardiff	W	26-19
635	12-Feb-11	Italy	6N	H	Twickenham, London	W	59-13
636	26-Feb-11	France	6N	H	Twickenham, London	W	17-9
637	13-Mar-11	Scotland	6N-CC	H	Twickenham, London	W	22-16
638	19-Mar-11	Ireland	6N-MT	A	Aviva Stadium, Dublin	L	8-24
639	6-Aug-11	Wales	Int	H	Twickenham, London	W	23-19
640	13-Aug-11	Wales	Int	A	Millennium Stadium, Cardiff	L	9-19

No	Date	Opponents	Tmt		Match Venue	Result	
641	27-Aug-11	Ireland	Int	A	Aviva Stadium, Dublin	W	20-9
642	10-Sep-11	Argentina	WCp	N	Otago Stadium, Dunedin	W	13-9
643	18-Sep-11	Georgia	WCp	N	Otago Stadium, Dunedin	W	41-10
644	24-Sep-11	Romania	WCp	N	Otago Stadium, Dunedin	W	67-3
645	1-Oct-11	Scotland	WCp	N	Eden Park, Auckland	W	16-12
646	8-Oct-11	France	WCqf	N	Eden Park, Auckland	L	12-19
647	4-Feb-12	Scotland	6N-CC	A	Murrayfield, Edinburgh	W	13-6
648	11-Feb-12	Italy	6N	A	Stadio Olimpico, Rome	W	19-15
649	25-Feb-12	Wales	6N	H	Twickenham, London	L	12-19
650	11-Mar-12	France	6N	A	Stade de France, Paris	W	24-22
651	17-Mar-12	Ireland	6N-MT	H	Twickenham, London	W	30-9
652	9-Jun-12	South Africa	Int-T	A	Kings Park Stadium, Durban	L	17-22
653	16-Jun-12	South Africa	Int-T	A	Ellis Park, Johannesburg	L	27-36
654	23-Jun-12	South Africa	Int-T	A	Nelson Mandela Bay Stadium, Pt Elizabeth	D	14-14
655	10-Nov-12	Fiji	Int	H	Twickenham, London	W	54-12
656	17-Nov-12	Australia	CKC	H	Twickenham, London	L	14-20
657	24-Nov-12	South Africa	Int	H	Twickenham, London	L	15-16
658	1-Dec-12	New Zealand	EHS	H	Twickenham, London	W	38-21
659	2-Feb-13	Scotland	6N-CC	H	Twickenham, London	W	38-18
660	10-Feb-13	Ireland	6N-MT	A	Aviva Stadium, Dublin	W	12-6
661	23-Feb-13	France	6N	H	Twickenham, London	W	23-13
662	10-Mar-13	Italy	6N	H	Twickenham, London	W	18-11
663	16-Mar-13	Wales	6N	A	Millennium Stadium, Cardiff	L	3-30
664	8-Jun-13	Argentina	Int-T	A	Estadio Padre Ernesto Martearena, Salta	W	32-3
665	15-Jun-13	Argentina	Int-T	A	Vélez Sarsfield Stadium, Buenos Aires	W	51-26
666	2-Nov-13	Australia	CKC	H	Twickenham, London	W	20-13
667	9-Nov-13	Argentina	ICC	H	Twickenham, London	W	31-12
668	16-Nov-13	New Zealand	EHS	H	Twickenham, London	L	22-30
669	1-Feb-14	France	6N	A	Stade de France, Paris	L	24-26
670	8-Feb-14	Scotland	6N-CC	A	Murrayfield, Edinburgh	W	20-0
671	22-Feb-14	Ireland	6N-MT	H	Twickenham, London	W	13-10
672	9-Mar-14	Wales	6N	H	Twickenham, London	W	29-18
673	15-Mar-14	Italy	6N	A	Stadio Olimpico, Rome	W	52-11
674	7-Jun-14	New Zealand	EHS-T	A	Eden Park, Auckland	L	15-20
675	14-Jun-14	New Zealand	EHS-T	A	Forsyth Barr Stadium, Dunedin	L	27-28
676	21-Jun-14	New Zealand	EHS-T	A	Waikato Stadium, Hamilton	L	13-36
677	8-Nov-14	New Zealand	EHS	H	Twickenham, London	L	21-24
678	15-Nov-14	South Africa	Int	H	Twickenham, London	L	28-31
679	22-Nov-14	Samoa	Int	H	Twickenham, London	W	28-9
680	29-Nov-14	Australia	CKC	H	Twickenham, London	W	26-17

No	Date	Opponents	Tmt		Match Venue		Result	
681	6-Feb-15	Wales	6N	A	Millennium Stadium, Cardiff	W	21-16
682	14-Feb-15	Italy	6N	H	Twickenham, London	W	47-17
683	1-Mar-15	Ireland	6N-MT	A	Aviva Stadium, Dublin	L	9-19
684	14-Mar-15	Scotland	6N-CC	H	Twickenham, London	W	25-13
685	21-Mar-15	France	6N	H	Twickenham, London	W	55-35

FRANCE

Although a French representative team competed, and won a gold medal, at the 1900 Summer Olympics in Paris, France's first official International did not take place until 1 January 1906, when they played New Zealand in Paris. They lost that match by 38 points to 3, and exactly four years later, on 1 January 1910, they faced Wales in the inaugural Five Nations Championship, which they lost by 49 points to 14.

The following year brought France their first victory, when they beat Scotland at Stade Colombes in Paris. France's triumph was short lived: they lost their next eighteen games and it wasn't until after the First World War that they finally registered a win, against Ireland in Dublin on 3 April 1920. A few months later, in October, France beat the United States and followed that victory with another win over Scotland in January 1921.

In 1924, France competed in the Olympic Games for the second time and, following a semi-final triumph over Romania, the French lost to the United States in the final.

Then, in 1927, France beat England by 3 points to nil in Paris, and a year later they finally defeated Wales, also in Paris, by 8 points to 3. In 1931, the French were expelled from the Five Nations Championship, accused of professionalism at a time when Rugby Union was strictly amateur. They were subsequently readmitted in 1947.

France played nineteen matches between 1954 and 1956 and lost only four: on three occasions to Wales and once to Scotland. During those three years they also achieved a famous victory against New Zealand, in February 1954. In 1958 the French toured South Africa and won the series by winning the second match after drawing the first. A year later, the French team won their first Five Nations Championship, a feat they repeated with back-to-back titles in 1961 and 1962. They secured another Five Nations title in 1967, and a first Grand Slam in 1968, closing out a very successful decade.

France's second Grand Slam came in 1977. In fact, from October 1975 to the end of 1978 France played twenty-five International matches and lost only four. Yet another Grand Slam was achieved in 1981, and a fourth in 1987, which augured well for France in the 1987 World Cup competition. They certainly rose to the occasion, performing strongly until the final, when they lost to New Zealand, the host nation, by 29 points to 9.

While England seemed to dominate the early part of the 1990s, the French came roaring back near the end of the decade, winning two consecutive Grand Slams in 1997 and 1998.

From 1965 to 1997 France also competed in a European tournament known as the Fédération Internationale de Rugby (FIRA). They played in all twenty-six competitions, securing the title on twenty occasions.

France's performance in the 1991 World Cup competition was, by their standard, disappointing: they were knocked out in the quarter-final by England. Their performance in the 1995 World Cup, however, was much better and, in the play-off for third place, they gained a revenge win over England after narrowly losing to the host nation, and eventual winners, South Africa, in the semi-final.

In 1999, France, commonly referred to as 'Les Bleus', reached the World Cup final for the second time, after defeating New Zealand in the semi-final, only to lose to Australia, in the final, by 35 points to 12. France reached the semi-final of the 2003 World Cup held in Australia, but were well beaten by England, the eventual winners, by 24 points to 7. They also lost to New Zealand in the third place play-off. In the 2007 World Cup, which they hosted, despite losing to Argentina in the pool game, they qualified for the quarter final and reached the semi-final by defeating New Zealand at the Millennium Stadium in Cardiff. They lost to England in that semi-final and subsequently lost to Argentina in the third place play-off at Parc des Princess in Paris.

The French did perform better in the 2011 World Cup by reaching the final for the third time, after defeating Wales in the semi-final. In the final they narrowly lost by just one point to the host nation, and tournament favourites, New Zealand.

The French team was the most consistent in the first twelve seasons of the Six Nations Championship held between 2000 and 2011, winning forty-four Internationals out of sixty: an impressive success rate of 73%. During that period they also won three Grand Slams: in 2002, 2004 and 2010. However, the team's success rate fell to below 47% during the next three Six Nations Championships held between 2012 and 2014, when they managed only six wins and two draws from fifteen matches.

Furthermore, during the period 2000 to 2013, France registered only thirteen wins and two draws out of a total of forty-five International matches against the Southern Hemisphere giants, Australia, New Zealand and South Africa, making for an even lower success rate of under 31%.

Another disappointing year for the French came in 2014 when, after finishing in fourth place in the Six Nations Championship, they suffered three losses to the Wallabies on their summer tour of Australia. They did, however, gain some revenge in November when they defeated the Aussies by 29 points to 26 in the Stade de France, but this was short-lived: they lost just a week later to Argentina at the same venue. Les Bleus finished in fourth place for the second year in succession in the 2015 Six Nations Championship.

FRANCE

HEAD TO HEAD RESULTS TO 31 MARCH 2015

v TIER 1 Teams	P	W	D	L	%	F	A
v Argentina	48	34	1	13	71.9	1169	754
v Australia	46	18	2	26	41.3	802	991
v England	99	38	7	54	41.9	1230	1553
v Ireland	93	55	7	31	62.9	1508	1084
v Italy	36	33	0	3	91.7	1069	382
v New Zealand	55	12	1	42	22.7	713	1345
v Scotland	88	51	3	34	59.7	1243	1057
v South Africa	39	11	6	22	35.9	578	783
v Wales	93	43	3	47	47.8	1338	1384
Sub-Total	**597**	**295**	**30**	**272**	**51.9**	**9650**	**9333**
v TIER 2/3 Group							
v Canada	8	7	0	1	87.5	274	101
v Fiji	9	9	0	0	100.0	359	111
v Japan	3	3	0	0	100.0	128	68
v Romania	49	39	2	8	81.6	1277	451
v Samoa	3	3	0	0	100.0	104	41
v Tonga	5	3	0	2	60.0	149	75
v United States	7	6	0	1	85.7	181	93
v Georgia	1	1	0	0	100.0	64	7
v Namibia	2	2	0	0	100.0	134	23
v Russia	0	0	0	0	0.0	0	0
v Uruguay	0	0	0	0	0.0	0	0
Sub-Total	**87**	**73**	**2**	**12**	**85.1**	**2670**	**970**
v Tier 3 Selection							
v Czechoslovakia *	2	2	0	0	100.0	47	9
v Germany **	15	13	0	2	86.7	298	89
v Côte d'Ivoire	1	1	0	0	100.0	54	18
v Zimbabwe	1	1	0	0	100.0	70	12
Sub-Total	**19**	**17**	**0**	**2**	**89.5**	**469**	**128**
v Other Teams	**11**	**5**	**0**	**6**	**45.5**	**137**	**155**
All Internationals	**714**	**390**	**32**	**292**	**56.9**	**12926**	**10586**

* 1956-68   ** 1927-38

No	Date	Opponents	Tmt		Match Venue	Result	
1	1-Jan-06	New Zealand	Int	H	Parc des Princess, Paris	L	8-38
2	22-Mar-06	England	Int	H	Parc des Princess, Paris	L	8-35
3	5-Jan-07	England	Int	A	Athletic Ground, Richmond	L	13-41
4	1-Jan-08	England	Int	H	Stade Colombes, Paris	L	0-19
5	2-Mar-08	Wales	Int	A	Arms Park, Cardiff	L	4-36
6	30-Jan-09	England	Int	A	Welford Road, Leicester	L	0-22
7	23-Feb-09	Wales	Int	H	Stade Colombes, Paris	L	5-47
8	20-Mar-09	Ireland	Int	A	Lansdowne Road, Dublin	L	8-19
9	1-Jan-10	Wales	5N	A	St Helen's, Swansea	L	14-49
10	22-Jan-10	Scotland	5N	A	Inverleith, Edinburgh	L	0-27
11	3-Mar-10	England	5N	H	Parc des Princess, Paris	L	3-11
12	28-Mar-10	Ireland	5N	H	Parc des Princess, Paris	L	3-8
13	2-Jan-11	Scotland	5N	H	Stade Colombes, Paris	W	16-15
14	28-Jan-11	England	5N	A	Twickenham, London	L	0-37
15	28-Feb-11	Wales	5N	H	Parc des Princess, Paris	L	0-15
16	25-Mar-11	Ireland	5N	A	Mardyke, Cork	L	5-25
17	1-Jan-12	Ireland	5N	H	Parc des Princess, Paris	L	6-11
18	20-Jan-12	Scotland	5N	A	Inverleith, Edinburgh	L	3-31
19	25-Mar-12	Wales	5N	A	Rodney Parade, Newport	L	8-14
20	8-Apr-12	England	5N	H	Parc des Princess, Paris	L	8-18
21	1-Jan-13	Scotland	5N	H	Parc des Princess, Paris	L	3-21
22	11-Jan-13	South Africa	Int	H	Route du Médoc, Le Bouscat, Bordeaux	L	5-38
23	25-Jan-13	England	5N	A	Twickenham, London	L	0-20
24	27-Feb-13	Wales	5N	H	Parc des Princess, Paris	L	8-11
25	24-Mar-13	Ireland	5N	A	Mardyke, Cork	L	0-24
26	1-Jan-14	Ireland	5N	H	Parc des Princess, Paris	L	6-8
27	2-Mar-14	Wales	5N	A	St Helen's, Swansea	L	0-31
28	13-Apr-14	England	5N	H	Stade Colombes, Paris	L	13-39
29	1-Jan-20	Scotland	5N	H	Parc des Princess, Paris	L	0-5
30	31-Jan-20	England	5N	A	Twickenham, London	L	3-8
31	17-Feb-20	Wales	5N	H	Stade Colombes, Paris	L	5-6
32	3-Apr-20	Ireland	5N	A	Lansdowne Road, Dublin	W	15-7
33	10-Oct-20	United States	Int	H	Stade Colombes, Paris	W	14-5
34	22-Jan-21	Scotland	5N	A	Inverleith, Edinburgh	W	3-0
35	26-Feb-21	Wales	5N	A	Arms Park, Cardiff	L	4-12
36	28-Mar-21	England	5N	H	Stade Colombes, Paris	L	6-10
37	9-Apr-21	Ireland	5N	H	Stade Colombes, Paris	W	20-10
38	2-Jan-22	Scotland	5N	H	Stade Colombes, Paris	D	3-3
39	25-Feb-22	England	5N	A	Twickenham, London	D	11-11
40	23-Mar-22	Wales	5N	H	Stade Colombes, Paris	L	3-11

No	Date	Opponents	Tmt		Match Venue	Result	
41	8-Apr-22	Ireland	5N	A	Lansdowne Road, Dublin	L	3-8
42	20-Jan-23	Scotland	5N	A	Inverleith, Edinburgh	L	3-16
43	24-Feb-23	Wales	5N	A	St Helen's, Swansea	L	8-16
44	2-Apr-23	England	5N	H	Stade Colombes, Paris	L	3-12
45	14-Apr-23	Ireland	5N	H	Stade Colombes, Paris	W	14-8
46	1-Jan-24	Scotland	5N	H	Stade Pershing, Vincennes, Paris	W	12-10
47	26-Jan-24	Ireland	5N	A	Lansdowne Road, Dublin	L	0-6
48	23-Feb-24	England	5N	A	Twickenham, London	L	7-19
49	27-Mar-24	Wales	5N	H	Stade Colombes, Paris	L	6-10
50	4-May-24	Romania	OGsf	H	Stade Colombes, Paris	W	61-3
51	18-May-24	United States	OGf	H	Stade Colombes, Paris	L	3-17
52	1-Jan-25	Ireland	5N	H	Stade Colombes, Paris	L	3-9
53	18-Jan-25	New Zealand	Int	H	Stade des Ponts, Jumeaux, Toulouse	L	6-30
54	24-Jan-25	Scotland	5N	A	Inverleith, Edinburgh	L	4-25
55	28-Feb-25	Wales	5N	A	Arms Park, Cardiff	L	5-11
56	13-Apr-25	England	5N	H	Stade Colombes, Paris	L	11-13
57	2-Jan-26	Scotland	5N	H	Stade Colombes, Paris	L	6-20
58	23-Jan-26	Ireland	5N	A	Ravenhill, Belfast	L	0-11
59	27-Feb-26	England	5N	A	Twickenham, London	L	0-11
60	5-Apr-26	Wales	5N	H	Stade Colombes, Paris	L	5-7
61	26-Dec-26	N Z Natives	Int	H	Stade Colombes, Paris	L	3-12
62	1-Jan-27	Ireland	5N	H	Stade Colombes, Paris	L	3-8
63	22-Jan-27	Scotland	5N	A	Murrayfield, Edinburgh	L	6-23
64	26-Feb-27	Wales	5N	A	St Helen's, Swansea	L	7-25
65	2-Apr-27	England	5N	H	Stade Colombes, Paris	W	3-0
66	17-Apr-27	Germany	Int	H	Stade Colombes, Paris	W	30-5
67	15-May-27	Germany	Int	A	Frankfurt	L	16-17
68	2-Jan-28	Scotland	5N	H	Stade Colombes, Paris	L	6-15
69	22-Jan-28	Australia	Int	H	Stade Colombes, Paris	L	8-11
70	28-Jan-28	Ireland	5N	A	Ravenhill, Belfast	L	8-12
71	25-Feb-28	England	5N	A	Twickenham, London	L	8-18
72	18-Mar-28	Germany	Int	A	Hanover	W	14-3
73	9-Apr-28	Wales	5N	H	Stade Colombes, Paris	W	8-3
74	31-Dec-28	Ireland	5N	H	Stade Colombes, Paris	L	0-6
75	19-Jan-29	Scotland	5N	A	Murrayfield, Edinburgh	L	3-6
76	23-Feb-29	Wales	5N	A	Arms Park, Cardiff	L	3-8
77	1-Apr-29	England	5N	H	Stade Colombes, Paris	L	6-16
78	28-Apr-29	Germany	Int	H	Stade Colombes, Paris	W	24-0
79	1-Jan-30	Scotland	5N	H	Stade Colombes, Paris	W	7-3
80	25-Jan-30	Ireland	5N	A	Ravenhill, Belfast	W	5-0

No	Date	Opponents	Tmt		Match Venue	Result	
81	22-Feb-30	England	5N	A	Twickenham, London	L	5-11
82	6-Apr-30	Germany	Int	A	Berlin	W	31-0
83	21-Apr-30	Wales	5N	H	Stade Colombes, Paris	L	0-11
84	1-Jan-31	Ireland	5N	H	Stade Colombes, Paris	W	3-0
85	24-Jan-31	Scotland	5N	A	Murrayfield, Edinburgh	L	4-6
86	28-Feb-31	Wales	5N	A	St Helen's, Swansea	L	3-35
87	6-Apr-31	England	5N	H	Stade Colombes, Paris	W	14-13
88	19-Apr-31	Germany	Int	H	Stade Colombes, Paris	W	34-0
89	17-Apr-32	Germany	Int	A	Frankfurt	W	20-4
90	26-Mar-33	Germany	Int	H	Parc des Princess, Paris	W	38-17
91	25-Mar-34	Germany	Int	A	Hanover	W	13-9
92	24-Mar-35	Germany	Int	H	Parc des Princess, Paris	W	18-3
93	17-May-36	Germany	FET	A	Berlin	W	19-14
94	1-Nov-36	Germany	Int	A	Hanover	W	6-3
95	18-Apr-37	Germany	Int	H	Parc des Princess, Paris	W	27-6
96	17-Oct-37	Italy	FET	H	Parc des Princess, Paris	W	43-5
97	27-Mar-38	Germany	Int	A	Frankfurt	L	0-3
98	15-May-38	Romania	FET	A	Stadionul ANEF, Bucharest	W	11-8
99	22-May-38	Germany	FET	N	Stadionul Dinamo, Bucharest	W	8-5
100	25-Feb-40	British Army	Int	H	Parc des Princess, Paris	L	3-36
101	1-Jan-45	British Army	Int	H	Parc des Princess, Paris	W	21-9
102	28-Apr-45	Empire XV	Int	A	Athletic Ground, Richmond	L	6-27
103	22-Dec-45	Wales XV	Int	A	St Helen's, Swansea	L	0-8
104	1-Jan-46	Empire XV	Int	H	Parc des Princess, Paris	W	10-0
105	26-Jan-46	Ireland XV	Int	A	Lansdowne Road, Dublin	W	4-3
106	10-Mar-46	Kiwis	Int	H	Stade Colombes, Paris	L	9-14
107	22-Apr-46	Wales XV	Int	H	Stade Colombes, Paris	W	12-0
108	1-Jan-47	Scotland	5N	H	Stade Colombes, Paris	W	8-3
109	25-Jan-47	Ireland	5N	A	Lansdowne Road, Dublin	W	12-8
110	22-Mar-47	Wales	5N	H	Stade Colombes, Paris	L	0-3
111	19-Apr-47	England	5N	A	Twickenham, London	L	3-6
112	1-Jan-48	Ireland	5N	H	Stade Colombes, Paris	L	6-13
113	11-Jan-48	Australia	Int	H	Stade Colombes, Paris	W	13-6
114	24-Jan-48	Scotland	5N	A	Murrayfield, Edinburgh	L	8-9
115	21-Feb-48	Wales	5N	A	St Helen's, Swansea	W	11-3
116	29-Mar-48	England	5N	H	Stade Colombes, Paris	W	15-0
117	15-Jan-49	Scotland	5N	H	Stade Colombes, Paris	L	0-8
118	29-Jan-49	Ireland	5N	A	Lansdowne Road, Dublin	W	16-9
119	26-Feb-49	England	5N	A	Twickenham, London	L	3-8
120	26-Mar-49	Wales	5N	H	Stade Colombes, Paris	W	5-3

No	Date	Opponents	Tmt		Match Venue	Result	
121	28-Aug-49	Argentina	Int-T	A	Estadio G.E.B.A, Buenos Aires	W	5-0
122	4-Sep-49	Argentina	Int-T	A	Estadio G.E.B.A, Buenos Aires	W	12-3
123	14-Jan-50	Scotland	5N	A	Murrayfield, Edinburgh	L	5-8
124	28-Jan-50	Ireland	5N	H	Stade Colombes, Paris	D	3-3
125	25-Feb-50	England	5N	H	Stade Colombes, Paris	W	6-3
126	25-Mar-50	Wales	5N	A	Arms Park, Cardiff	L	0-21
127	13-Jan-51	Scotland	5N	H	Stade Colombes, Paris	W	14-12
128	27-Jan-51	Ireland	5N	A	Lansdowne Road, Dublin	L	8-9
129	24-Feb-51	England	5N	A	Twickenham, London	W	11-3
130	7-Apr-51	Wales	5N	H	Stade Colombes, Paris	W	8-3
131	12-Jan-52	Scotland	5N	A	Murrayfield, Edinburgh	W	13-11
132	26-Jan-52	Ireland	5N	H	Stade Colombes, Paris	L	8-11
133	16-Feb-52	South Africa	Int	H	Stade Colombes, Paris	L	3-25
134	22-Mar-52	Wales	5N	A	St Helen's, Swansea	L	5-9
135	5-Apr-52	England	5N	H	Stade Colombes, Paris	L	3-6
136	17-May-52	Italy	FEC	A	Arena Civica, Milan	W	17-8
137	10-Jan-53	Scotland	5N	H	Stade Colombes, Paris	W	11-5
138	24-Jan-53	Ireland	5N	A	Ravenhill, Belfast	L	3-16
139	28-Feb-53	England	5N	A	Twickenham, London	L	0-11
140	28-Mar-53	Wales	5N	H	Stade Colombes, Paris	L	3-6
141	26-Apr-53	Italy	Int	H	Stade de Gerland, Lyon	W	22-8
142	9-Jan-54	Scotland	5N	A	Murrayfield, Edinburgh	W	3-0
143	23-Jan-54	Ireland	5N	H	Stade Colombes, Paris	W	8-0
144	27-Feb-54	New Zealand	Int	H	Stade Colombes, Paris	W	3-0
145	27-Mar-54	Wales	5N	A	Arms Park, Cardiff	L	13-19
146	10-Apr-54	England	5N	H	Stade Colombes, Paris	W	11-3
147	24-Apr-54	Italy	FEC	A	Stadio Olimpico, Rome	W	39-12
148	29-Aug-54	Argentina	Int-T	A	Ferro Carril Oeste Stadium, B Aires	W	22-8
149	12-Sep-54	Argentina	Int-T	A	Ferro Carril Oeste Stadium, B Aires	W	30-3
150	8-Jan-55	Scotland	5N	H	Stade Colombes, Paris	W	15-0
151	22-Jan-55	Ireland	5N	A	Lansdowne Road, Dublin	W	5-3
152	26-Feb-55	England	5N	A	Twickenham, London	W	16-9
153	26-Mar-55	Wales	5N	H	Stade Colombes, Paris	L	11-16
154	10-Apr-55	Italy	Int	H	Stade Lesdiguières, Grenoble	W	24-0
155	14-Jan-56	Scotland	5N	A	Murrayfield, Edinburgh	L	0-12
156	28-Jan-56	Ireland	5N	H	Stade Colombes, Paris	W	14-8
157	24-Mar-56	Wales	5N	A	Arms Park, Cardiff	L	3-5
158	2-Apr-56	Italy	Int	A	Stadio Silvio Appiani, Padova	W	16-3
159	14-Apr-56	England	5N	H	Stade Colombes, Paris	W	14-9
160	16-Dec-56	Czechoslovakia	Int	H	Stade Municipal de Toulouse, Toulouse	W	28-3

No	Date	Opponents	Tmt		Match Venue	Result	
161	12-Jan-57	Scotland	5N	H	Stade Colombes, Paris	L	0-6
162	26-Jan-57	Ireland	5N	A	Lansdowne Road, Dublin	L	6-11
163	23-Feb-57	England	5N	A	Twickenham, London	L	5-9
164	23-Mar-57	Wales	5N	H	Stade Colombes, Paris	L	13-19
165	21-Apr-57	Italy	Int	H	Stade Armandie, Agen	W	38-6
166	19-May-57	Romania	Int	A	Stadionul 23 August, Bucharest	W	18-15
167	15-Dec-57	Romania	Int	H	Stade du Parc Lescure, Bordeaux	W	39-0
168	11-Jan-58	Scotland	5N	A	Murrayfield, Edinburgh	L	9-11
169	1-Mar-58	England	5N	H	Stade Colombes, Paris	L	0-14
170	9-Mar-58	Australia	Int	H	Stade Colombes, Paris	W	19-0
171	29-Mar-58	Wales	5N	A	Arms Park, Cardiff	W	16-6
172	7-Apr-58	Italy	Int	A	Stadio Arturo Collana, Naples	W	11-3
173	19-Apr-58	Ireland	5N	H	Stade Colombes, Paris	W	11-6
174	26-Jul-58	South Africa	Int-T	A	Newlands Stadium, Cape Town	D	3-3
175	16-Aug-58	South Africa	Int-T	A	Ellis Park, Johannesburg	W	9-5
176	10-Jan-59	Scotland	5N	H	Stade Colombes, Paris	W	9-0
177	28-Feb-59	England	5N	A	Twickenham, London	D	3-3
178	29-Mar-59	Italy	Int	H	Stade Marcel Saupin, Nantes	W	22-0
179	4-Apr-59	Wales	5N	H	Stade Colombes, Paris	W	11-3
180	18-Apr-59	Ireland	5N	A	Lansdowne Road, Dublin	L	5-9
181	9-Jan-60	Scotland	5N	A	Murrayfield, Edinburgh	W	13-11
182	27-Feb-60	England	5N	H	Stade Colombes, Paris	D	3-3
183	26-Mar-60	Wales	5N	A	Arms Park, Cardiff	W	16-8
184	9-Apr-60	Ireland	5N	H	Stade Colombes, Paris	W	23-6
185	17-Apr-60	Italy	Int	A	Stadio Omobono Tenni, Treviso	W	26-0
186	5-Jun-60	Romania	Int	A	Stadionul Dinamo, Bucharest	L	5-11
187	23-Jul-60	Argentina	Int-T	A	Estadio G.E.B.A., Buenos Aires	W	37-3
188	6-Aug-60	Argentina	Int-T	A	Estadio G.E.B.A., Buenos Aires	W	12-3
189	17-Aug-60	Argentina	Int-T	A	Estadio G.E.B.A., Buenos Aires	W	29-6
190	7-Jan-61	Scotland	5N	H	Stade Colombes, Paris	W	11-0
191	18-Feb-61	South Africa	Int	H	Stade Colombes, Paris	D	0-0
192	25-Feb-61	England	5N	A	Twickenham, London	D	5-5
193	25-Mar-61	Wales	5N	H	Stade Colombes, Paris	W	8-6
194	2-Apr-61	Italy	Int	H	Stade Municipal, Chambéry	W	17-0
195	15-Apr-61	Ireland	5N	A	Lansdowne Road, Dublin	W	15-3
196	22-Jul-61	New Zealand	Int-T	A	Eden Park, Auckland	L	6-13
197	5-Aug-61	New Zealand	Int-T	A	Athletic Park, Wellington	L	3-5
198	19-Aug-61	New Zealand	Int-T	A	Lancaster Park Oval, Christchurch	L	3-32
199	26-Aug-61	Australia	Int-T	A	Cricket Ground, Sydney	W	15-8
200	12-Nov-61	Romania	Int	H	Parc Municipal des Sports, Bayonne	D	5-5

No	Date	Opponents	Tmt		Match Venue	Result	
201	13-Jan-62	Scotland	5N	A	Murrayfield, Edinburgh	W	11-3
202	24-Feb-62	England	5N	H	Stade Colombes, Paris	W	13-0
203	24-Mar-62	Wales	5N	A	Arms Park, Cardiff	L	0-3
204	14-Apr-62	Ireland	5N	H	Stade Colombes, Paris	W	11-0
205	22-Apr-62	Italy	Int	A	Stadio Mompiano, Brescia	W	6-3
206	11-Nov-62	Romania	Int	A	Stadionul 23 August, Bucharest	L	0-3
207	12-Jan-63	Scotland	5N	H	Stade Colombes, Paris	L	6-11
208	26-Jan-63	Ireland	5N	A	Lansdowne Road, Dublin	W	24-5
209	23-Feb-63	England	5N	A	Twickenham, London	L	5-6
210	23-Mar-63	Wales	5N	H	Stade Colombes, Paris	W	5-3
211	14-Apr-63	Italy	Int	H	Stade Lesdiguières, Grenoble	W	14-12
212	15-Dec-63	Romania	Int	H	Stade Municipal de Toulouse, Toulouse	D	6-6
213	4-Jan-64	Scotland	5N	A	Murrayfield, Edinburgh	L	0-10
214	8-Feb-64	New Zealand	Int	H	Stade Colombes, Paris	L	3-12
215	22-Feb-64	England	5N	H	Stade Colombes, Paris	L	3-6
216	21-Mar-64	Wales	5N	A	Arms Park, Cardiff	D	11-11
217	29-Mar-64	Italy	Int	A	Stadio Comunale Ennio Tardini, Parma	W	12-3
218	11-Apr-64	Ireland	5N	H	Stade Colombes, Paris	W	27-6
219	25-Jul-64	South Africa	Int-T	A	P A M Brink Stadium, Springs	W	8-6
220	17-Oct-64	Fiji	Int	H	Stade Colombes, Paris	W	21-3
221	29-Nov-64	Romania	Int	A	Stadionul Dinamo, Bucharest	W	9-6
222	9-Jan-65	Scotland	5N	H	Stade Colombes, Paris	W	16-8
223	23-Jan-65	Ireland	5N	A	Lansdowne Road, Dublin	D	3-3
224	27-Feb-65	England	5N	A	Twickenham, London	L	6-9
225	27-Mar-65	Wales	5N	H	Stade Colombes, Paris	W	22-13
226	18-Apr-65	Italy	Int	H	Stade de la Croix du Prince, Pau	W	21-0
227	28-Nov-65	Romania	FIRA	H	Stade de Gerland, Lyon	W	8-3
228	15-Jan-66	Scotland	5N	A	Murrayfield, Edinburgh	D	3-3
229	29-Jan-66	Ireland	5N	H	Stade Colombes, Paris	W	11-6
230	26-Feb-66	England	5N	H	Stade Colombes, Paris	W	13-0
231	26-Mar-66	Wales	5N	A	Arms Park, Cardiff	L	8-9
232	9-Apr-66	Italy	FIRA	A	Naples	W	21-0
233	27-Nov-66	Romania	FIRA	A	Stadionul Republicii, Bucharest	W	9-3
234	14-Jan-67	Scotland	5N	H	Stade Colombes, Paris	L	8-9
235	11-Feb-67	Australia	Int	H	Stade Colombes, Paris	W	20-14
236	25-Feb-67	England	5N	A	Twickenham, London	W	16-12
237	26-Mar-67	Italy	FIRA	H	Stade Félix Mayol, Toulon	W	60-13
238	1-Apr-67	Wales	5N	H	Stade Colombes, Paris	W	20-14
239	15-Apr-67	Ireland	5N	A	Lansdowne Road, Dublin	W	11-6
240	15-Jul-67	South Africa	Int-T	A	Kings Park Stadium, Durban	L	3-26

No	Date	Opponents	Tmt		Match Venue	Result	
241	22-Jul-67	South Africa	Int-T	A	Free State Stadium, Bloemfontein	L	3-16
242	29-Jul-67	South Africa	Int-T	A	Ellis Park, Johannesburg	W	19-14
243	12-Aug-67	South Africa	Int-T	A	Newlands Stadium, Cape Town	D	6-6
244	25-Nov-67	New Zealand	Int	H	Stade Colombes, Paris	L	15-21
245	10-Dec-67	Romania	FIRA	H	Stade Marcel Saupin, Nantes	W	11-3
246	13-Jan-68	Scotland	5N	A	Murrayfield, Edinburgh	W	8-6
247	27-Jan-68	Ireland	5N	H	Stade Colombes, Paris	W	16-6
248	24-Feb-68	England	5N	H	Stade Colombes, Paris	W	14-9
249	23-Mar-68	Wales	5N	A	Arms Park, Cardiff	W	14-9
250	5-May-68	Czechoslovakia	FIRA	A	Stadion Krč, Prague	W	19-6
251	13-Jul-68	New Zealand	Int-T	A	Lancaster Park Oval, Christchurch	L	9-12
252	27-Jul-68	New Zealand	Int-T	A	Athletic Park, Wellington	L	3-9
253	10-Aug-68	New Zealand	Int-T	A	Eden Park, Auckland	L	12-19
254	17-Aug-68	Australia	Int-T	A	Cricket Ground, Sydney	L	10-11
255	9-Nov-68	South Africa	Int	H	Stade du Parc Lescure, Bordeaux	L	9-12
256	16-Nov-68	South Africa	Int	H	Stade Colombes, Paris	L	11-16
257	1-Dec-68	Romania	FIRA	A	Stadionul 23 August, Bucharest	L	14-15
258	11-Jan-69	Scotland	5N	H	Stade Colombes, Paris	L	3-6
259	25-Jan-69	Ireland	5N	A	Lansdowne Road, Dublin	L	9-17
260	22-Feb-69	England	5N	A	Twickenham, London	L	8-22
261	22-Mar-69	Wales	5N	H	Stade Colombes, Paris	D	8-8
262	14-Dec-69	Romania	FIRA	H	Stade Maurice Trélut, Tarbes	W	14-9
263	10-Jan-70	Scotland	5N	A	Murrayfield, Edinburgh	W	11-9
264	24-Jan-70	Ireland	5N	H	Stade Colombes, Paris	W	8-0
265	4-Apr-70	Wales	5N	A	National Stadium, Cardiff	L	6-11
266	18-Apr-70	England	5N	H	Stade Colombes, Paris	W	35-13
267	29-Nov-70	Romania	FIRA	A	Stadionul Giuleşti-V Stănescu, Bucharest	W	14-3
268	16-Jan-71	Scotland	5N	H	Stade Colombes, Paris	W	13-8
269	30-Jan-71	Ireland	5N	A	Lansdowne Road, Dublin	D	9-9
270	27-Feb-71	England	5N	A	Twickenham, London	D	14-14
271	27-Mar-71	Wales	5N	H	Stade Colombes, Paris	L	5-9
272	12-Jun-71	South Africa	Int-T	A	Free State Stadium, Bloemfontein	L	9-22
273	19-Jun-71	South Africa	Int-T	A	Kings Park Stadium, Durban	D	8-8
274	20-Nov-71	Australia	Int	H	Stade Municipal de Toulouse, Toulouse	L	11-13
275	27-Nov-71	Australia	Int	H	Stade Colombes, Paris	W	18-9
276	11-Dec-71	Romania	FIRA	H	Parc des Sports de Sauclières, Béziers	W	31-12
277	15-Jan-72	Scotland	5N	A	Murrayfield, Edinburgh	L	9-20
278	29-Jan-72	Ireland	5N	H	Stade Colombes, Paris	L	9-14
279	26-Feb-72	England	5N	H	Stade Colombes, Paris	W	37-12
280	25-Mar-72	Wales	5N	A	National Stadium, Cardiff	L	6-20

No	Date	Opponents	Tmt		Match Venue	Result	
281	29-Apr-72	Ireland	Int	A	Lansdowne Road, Dublin	L	14-24
282	17-Jun-72	Australia	Int-T	A	Cricket Ground, Sydney	D	14-14
283	25-Jun-72	Australia	Int-T	A	Ballymore Oval, Brisbane	W	16-15
284	26-Nov-72	Romania	FIRA	A	Stadionul 1 Mai, Constanta	W	15-6
285	13-Jan-73	Scotland	5N	H	Parc des Princess, Paris	W	16-13
286	10-Feb-73	New Zealand	Int	H	Parc des Princess, Paris	W	13-6
287	24-Feb-73	England	5N	A	Twickenham, London	L	6-14
288	24-Mar-73	Wales	5N	H	Parc des Princess, Paris	W	12-3
289	14-Apr-73	Ireland	5N	A	Lansdowne Road, Dublin	L	4-6
290	27-Oct-73	Japan	Int	H	Stade du Parc Lescure, Bordeaux	W	30-18
291	11-Nov-73	Romania	FIRA	H	Stade de la Chamberliére, Valence	W	7-6
292	19-Jan-74	Ireland	5N	H	Parc des Princess, Paris	W	9-6
293	16-Feb-74	Wales	5N	A	National Stadium, Cardiff	D	16-16
294	2-Mar-74	England	5N	H	Parc des Princess, Paris	D	12-12
295	16-Mar-74	Scotland	5N	A	Murrayfield, Edinburgh	L	6-19
296	20-Jun-74	Argentina	Int-T	A	Ferro Carril Oeste Stadium, B Aires	W	20-15
297	29-Jun-74	Argentina	Int-T	A	Ferro Carril Oeste Stadium, B Aires	W	31-27
298	13-Oct-74	Romania	FIRA	A	Stadionul 23 August, Bucharest	L	10-15
299	23-Nov-74	South Africa	Int	H	Stade Municipal de Toulouse, Toulouse	L	4-13
300	30-Nov-74	South Africa	Int	H	Parc des Princess, Paris	L	8-10
301	18-Jan-75	Wales	5N	H	Parc des Princess, Paris	L	10-25
302	1-Feb-75	England	5N	A	Twickenham, London	W	27-20
303	15-Feb-75	Scotland	5N	H	Parc des Princess, Paris	W	10-9
304	1-Mar-75	Ireland	5N	A	Lansdowne Road, Dublin	L	6-25
305	21-Jun-75	South Africa	Int-T	A	Free State Stadium, Bloemfontein	L	25-38
306	28-Jun-75	South Africa	Int-T	A	Loftus Versfeld Stadium, Pretoria	L	18-33
307	19-Oct-75	Argentina	Int	H	Stade de Gerland, Lyon	W	29-6
308	25-Oct-75	Argentina	Int	H	Parc des Princess, Paris	W	36-21
309	23-Nov-75	Romania	FIRA	H	Stade du Parc Lescure, Bordeaux	W	36-12
310	10-Jan-76	Scotland	5N	A	Murrayfield, Edinburgh	W	13-6
311	7-Feb-76	Ireland	5N	H	Parc des Princess, Paris	W	26-3
312	6-Mar-76	Wales	5N	A	National Stadium, Cardiff	L	13-19
313	20-Mar-76	England	5N	H	Parc des Princess, Paris	W	30-9
314	12-Jun-76	United States	Int-T	A	Rockne Stadium, Northfield, Chicago	W	33-14
315	24-Oct-76	Australia	Int	H	Stade du Parc Lescure, Bordeaux	W	18-15
316	30-Oct-76	Australia	Int	H	Parc des Princess, Paris	W	34-6
317	14-Nov-76	Romania	FIRA	A	Stadionul Giuleşti-V Stănescu, Bucharest	L	12-15
318	5-Feb-77	Wales	5N	H	Parc des Princess, Paris	W	16-9
319	19-Feb-77	England	5N	A	Twickenham, London	W	4-3
320	5-Mar-77	Scotland	5N	H	Parc des Princess, Paris	W	23-3

No	Date	Opponents	Tmt		Match Venue		Result
401	13-Jun-87	Australia	WCsf	A	Concord Oval, Sydney	W	30-24
402	20-Jun-87	New Zealand	WCf	A	Eden Park, Auckland	L	9-29
403	11-Nov-87	Romania	FIRA	H	Stade Armandie, Agen	W	49-3
404	16-Jan-88	England	5N	H	Parc des Princess, Paris	W	10-9
405	6-Feb-88	Scotland	5N	A	Murrayfield, Edinburgh	L	12-23
406	20-Feb-88	Ireland	5N	H	Parc des Princess, Paris	W	25-6
407	19-Mar-88	Wales	5N	A	National Stadium, Cardiff	W	10-9
408	18-Jun-88	Argentina	Int-T	A	Vélez Sarsfield Stadium, Buenos Aires	W	18-15
409	25-Jun-88	Argentina	Int-T	A	Vélez Sarsfield Stadium, Buenos Aires	L	6-18
410	5-Nov-88	Argentina	Int	H	Stade de la Beaujoire, Nantes	W	29-9
411	11-Nov-88	Argentina	Int	H	Stade Nord Lille Métropole	W	28-18
412	26-Nov-88	Romania	FIRA	A	Stadionul Giuleşti-V Stănescu, Bucharest	W	16-12
413	21-Jan-89	Ireland	5N	A	Lansdowne Road, Dublin	W	26-21
414	18-Feb-89	Wales	5N	H	Parc des Princess, Paris	W	31-12
415	4-Mar-89	England	5N	A	Twickenham, London	L	0-11
416	18-Mar-89	Scotland	5N	H	Parc des Princess, Paris	W	19-3
417	17-Jun-89	New Zealand	Int-T	A	Lancaster Park Oval, Christchurch	L	17-25
418	1-Jul-89	New Zealand	Int-T	A	Eden Park, Auckland	L	20-34
419	4-Oct-89	Lions XV	Int	H	Parc des Princess, Paris	L	27-29
420	4-Nov-89	Australia	BIC	H	Stade de la Meinau, Strasbourg	L	15-32
421	11-Nov-89	Australia	BIC	H	Stade Nord Lille Métropole	W	25-19
422	20-Jan-90	Wales	5N	A	National Stadium, Cardiff	W	29-19
423	3-Feb-90	England	5N	H	Parc des Princess, Paris	L	7-26
424	17-Feb-90	Scotland	5N	A	Murrayfield, Edinburgh	L	0-21
425	3-Mar-90	Ireland	5N	H	Parc des Princess, Paris	W	31-12
426	24-May-90	Romania	FIRA	H	Stade Jacques Fouroux, Auch	L	6-12
427	9-Jun-90	Australia	BIC-T	A	Football Stadium, Sydney	L	9-21
428	24-Jun-90	Australia	BIC-T	A	Ballymore Oval, Brisbane	L	31-48
429	30-Jun-90	Australia	BIC-T	A	Football Stadium, Sydney	W	28-19
430	3-Nov-90	New Zealand	Int	H	Stade de la Beaujoire, Nantes	L	3-24
431	10-Nov-90	New Zealand	Int	H	Parc des Princess, Paris	L	12-30
432	19-Jan-91	Scotland	5N	H	Parc des Princess, Paris	W	15-9
433	2-Feb-91	Ireland	5N	A	Lansdowne Road, Dublin	W	21-13
434	2-Mar-91	Wales	5N	H	Parc des Princess, Paris	W	36-3
435	16-Mar-91	England	5N	A	Twickenham, London	L	19-21
436	22-Jun-91	Romania	FIRA	A	Stadionul 23 August, Bucharest	W	33-21
437	13-Jul-91	United States	Int-T	A	Observatory Park, Denver, Colorado	W	41-9
438	20-Jul-91	United States	Int-T	A	Colorado Springs	W	10-3
439	4-Sep-91	Wales	Int	A	National Stadium, Cardiff	W	22-9
440	4-Oct-91	Romania	WCp	H	Stade de la Méditerranée, Béziers	W	30-3

No	Date	Opponents	Tmt		Match Venue	Result	
441	8-Oct-91	Fiji	WCp	H	Stade Lesdiguières, Grenoble	W	33-9
442	13-Oct-91	Canada	WCp	H	Stade Armandie, Agen	W	19-13
443	19-Oct-91	England	WCqf	H	Parc des Princess, Paris	L	10-19
444	1-Feb-92	Wales	5N	A	National Stadium, Cardiff	W	12-9
445	15-Feb-92	England	5N	H	Parc des Princess, Paris	L	13-31
446	7-Mar-92	Scotland	5N	A	Murrayfield, Edinburgh	L	6-10
447	21-Mar-92	Ireland	5N	H	Parc des Princess, Paris	W	44-12
448	28-May-92	Romania	FIRA	H	Stade Jules Deschaseaux, Le Havre	W	25-6
449	4-Jul-92	Argentina	Int-T	A	Vélez Sarsfield Stadium, Buenos Aires	W	27-12
450	11-Jul-92	Argentina	Int-T	A	Vélez Sarsfield Stadium, Buenos Aires	W	33-9
451	17-Oct-92	South Africa	Int	H	Stade de Gerland, Lyon	L	15-20
452	24-Oct-92	South Africa	Int	H	Parc des Princess, Paris	W	29-16
453	14-Nov-92	Argentina	Int	H	Stade de la Beaujoire, Nantes	L	20-24
454	16-Jan-93	England	5N	A	Twickenham, London	L	15-16
455	6-Feb-93	Scotland	5N	H	Parc des Princess, Paris	W	11-3
456	20-Feb-93	Ireland	5N	A	Lansdowne Road, Dublin	W	21-6
457	20-Mar-93	Wales	5N	H	Parc des Princess, Paris	W	26-10
458	20-May-93	Romania	Int	A	Stadionul Dinamo, Bucharest	W	37-20
459	26-Jun-93	South Africa	Int-T	A	Kings Park Stadium, Durban	D	20-20
460	3-Jul-93	South Africa	Int-T	A	Ellis Park, Johannesburg	W	18-17
461	17-Oct-93	Romania	FIRA	H	Stade Parc Municipal des Sports, Brive	W	51-0
462	30-Oct-93	Australia	BIC	H	Stade du Parc Lescure, Bordeaux	W	16-13
463	6-Nov-93	Australia	BIC	H	Parc des Princess, Paris	L	3-24
464	15-Jan-94	Ireland	5N	H	Parc des Princess, Paris	W	35-15
465	19-Feb-94	Wales	5N	A	National Stadium, Cardiff	L	15-24
466	5-Mar-94	England	5N	H	Parc des Princess, Paris	L	14-18
467	19-Mar-94	Scotland	5N	A	Murrayfield, Edinburgh	W	20-12
468	4-Jun-94	Canada	Int-T	A	Twin Elms Rugby Park, Nepean, Ontario	L	16-18
469	26-Jun-94	New Zealand	Int-T	A	Lancaster Park Oval, Christchurch	W	22-8
470	3-Jul-94	New Zealand	Int-T	A	Eden Park, Auckland	W	23-20
471	17-Dec-94	Canada	Int	H	Stade Leo Lagrange, Besançon	W	28-9
472	21-Jan-95	Wales	5N	H	Parc des Princess, Paris	W	21-9
473	4-Feb-95	England	5N	A	Twickenham, London	L	10-31
474	18-Feb-95	Scotland	5N	H	Parc des Princess, Paris	L	21-23
475	4-Mar-95	Ireland	5N	A	Lansdowne Road, Dublin	W	25-7
476	8-Apr-95	Romania	Int	A	Stadionul 23 August, Bucharest	W	24-15
477	26-May-95	Tonga	WCp	N	Loftus Versfeld Stadium, Pretoria	W	38-10
478	30-May-95	Côte d'Ivoire	WCp	N	Olympia Park, Rustenburg	W	54-18
479	3-Jun-95	Scotland	WCp	N	Loftus Versfeld Stadium, Pretoria	W	22-19
480	10-Jun-95	Ireland	WCqf	N	Kings Park Stadium, Durban	W	36-12

No	Date	Opponents	Tmt		Match Venue	Result	
481	17-Jun-95	South Africa	WCsf	A	Kings Park Stadium, Durban	L	15-19
482	22-Jun-95	England	WC34	N	Loftus Versfeld Stadium, Pretoria	W	19-9
483	14-Oct-95	Italy	LTC	N	Ferro Carril Oeste Stadium, B Aires	W	34-22
484	17-Oct-95	Romania	LTC	N	Estadio Monumental José Fierro, Tucumán	W	52-8
485	21-Oct-95	Argentina	LTC	A	Ferro Carril Oeste Stadium, B Aires	W	47-12
486	11-Nov-95	New Zealand	Int	H	Stade Municipal de Toulouse, Toulouse	W	22-15
487	18-Nov-95	New Zealand	Int	H	Parc des Princess, Paris	L	12-37
488	20-Jan-96	England	5N	H	Parc des Princess, Paris	W	15-12
489	3-Feb-96	Scotland	5N	A	Murrayfield, Edinburgh	L	14-19
490	17-Feb-96	Ireland	5N	H	Parc des Princess, Paris	W	45-10
491	16-Mar-96	Wales	5N	A	National Stadium, Cardiff	L	15-16
492	20-Apr-96	Romania	Int	H	Stade Jean Alric, Aurillac	W	64-12
493	22-Jun-96	Argentina	Int-T	A	Ferro Carril Oeste Stadium, B Aires	W	34-27
494	29-Jun-96	Argentina	Int-T	A	Ferro Carril Oeste Stadium, B Aires	W	34-15
495	25-Sep-96	Wales	Int	A	National Stadium, Cardiff	W	40-33
496	30-Nov-96	South Africa	Int	H	Stade du Parc Lescure, Bordeaux	L	12-22
497	7-Dec-96	South Africa	Int	H	Parc des Princess, Paris	L	12-13
498	18-Jan-97	Ireland	5N	A	Lansdowne Road, Dublin	W	32-15
499	15-Feb-97	Wales	5N	H	Parc des Princess, Paris	W	27-22
500	1-Mar-97	England	5N	A	Twickenham, London	W	23-20
501	15-Mar-97	Scotland	5N	H	Parc des Princess, Paris	W	47-20
502	22-Mar-97	Italy	FIRA	H	Stade Lesdiguières, Grenoble	L	32-40
503	1-Jun-97	Romania	Int	A	Stadionul Dinamo, Bucharest	W	51-20
504	21-Jun-97	Australia	BIC-T	A	Football Stadium, Sydney	L	15-29
505	28-Jun-97	Australia	BIC-T	A	Ballymore Oval, Brisbane	L	19-26
506	18-Oct-97	Italy	LTC	H	Stade Jacques Fouroux, Auch	W	30-19
507	22-Oct-97	Romania	LTC	H	Stade Antoine Béguère, Lourdes	W	39-3
508	26-Oct-97	Argentina	LTC	H	Stade Maurice Trélut, Tarbes	W	32-27
509	15-Nov-97	South Africa	Int	H	Stade de Gerland, Lyon	L	32-36
510	22-Nov-97	South Africa	Int	H	Parc des Princess, Paris	L	10-52
511	7-Feb-98	England	5N	H	Stade de France, Paris	W	24-17
512	21-Feb-98	Scotland	5N	A	Murrayfield, Edinburgh	W	51-16
513	7-Mar-98	Ireland	5N	H	Stade de France, Paris	W	18-16
514	5-Apr-98	Wales	5N	N	Wembley Stadium, London	W	51-0
515	13-Jun-98	Argentina	Int-T	A	Vélez Sarsfield Stadium, Buenos Aires	W	35-18
516	20-Jun-98	Argentina	Int-T	A	Vélez Sarsfield Stadium, Buenos Aires	W	37-12
517	27-Jun-98	Fiji	Int-T	A	National Stadium, Suva	W	34-9
518	14-Nov-98	Argentina	Int	H	Stade de la Beaujoire, Nantes	W	34-14
519	21-Nov-98	Australia	BIC	H	Stade de France, Paris	L	21-32
520	6-Feb-99	Ireland	5N	A	Lansdowne Road, Dublin	W	10-9

No	Date	Opponents	Tmt		Match Venue	Result	
521	6-Mar-99	Wales	5N	H	Stade de France, Paris	L	33-34
522	20-Mar-99	England	5N	A	Twickenham, London	L	10-21
523	10-Apr-99	Scotland	5N	H	Stade de France, Paris	L	22-36
524	3-Jun-99	Romania	Int	H	Stade Pierre-Antoine, Castres	W	62-8
525	12-Jun-99	Samoa	Int-T	A	Apia Park, Apia	W	39-22
526	16-Jun-99	Tonga	Int-T	A	Teufaiva Sport Stadium, Nuku'alofa	L	16-20
527	26-Jun-99	New Zealand	Int-T	A	Athletic Park, Wellington	L	7-54
528	28-Aug-99	Wales	Int	A	Millennium Stadium, Cardiff	L	23-34
529	2-Oct-99	Canada	WCp	H	Stade de la Méditerranée, Béziers	W	33-20
530	8-Oct-99	Namibia	WCp	H	Stade du Parc Lescure, Bordeaux	W	47-13
531	16-Oct-99	Fiji	WCp	H	Stade Municipal de Toulouse, Toulouse	W	28-19
532	24-Oct-99	Argentina	Wcqf	N	Lansdowne Road, Dublin	W	47-26
533	31-Oct-99	New Zealand	WCsf	N	Twickenham, London	W	43-31
534	6-Nov-99	Australia	WCf	N	Millennium Stadium, Cardiff	L	12-35
535	5-Feb-00	Wales	6N	A	Millennium Stadium, Cardiff	W	36-3
536	19-Feb-00	England	6N	H	Stade de France, Paris	L	9-15
537	4-Mar-00	Scotland	6N	A	Murrayfield, Edinburgh	W	28-16
538	19-Mar-00	Ireland	6N	H	Stade de France, Paris	L	25-27
539	1-Apr-00	Italy	6N	H	Stade de France, Paris	W	42-31
540	28-May-00	Romania	Int	A	Stadionul Dinamo, Bucharest	W	67-20
541	4-Nov-00	Australia	BIC	H	Stade de France, Paris	L	13-18
542	11-Nov-00	New Zealand	DGT	H	Stade de France, Paris	L	26-39
543	18-Nov-00	New Zealand	Int	H	Stade Vélodrome, Marseille	W	42-33
544	4-Feb-01	Scotland	6N	H	Stade de France, Paris	W	16-6
545	17-Feb-01	Ireland	6N	A	Lansdowne Road, Dublin	L	15-22
546	3-Mar-01	Italy	6N	A	Stadio Flaminio, Rome	W	30-19
547	17-Mar-01	Wales	6N	H	Stade de France, Paris	L	35-43
548	7-Apr-01	England	6N	A	Twickenham, London	L	19-48
549	16-Jun-01	South Africa	Int-T	A	Ellis Park, Johannesburg	W	32-23
550	23-Jun-01	South Africa	Int-T	A	ABSA Stadium, Durban	L	15-20
551	30-Jun-01	New Zealand	DGT-T	A	Westpac Trust Stadium, Wellington	L	12-37
552	10-Nov-01	South Africa	Int	H	Stade de France, Paris	W	20-10
553	17-Nov-01	Australia	BIC	H	Stade Vélodrome, Marseille	W	14-13
554	24-Nov-01	Fiji	Int	H	Stade Geoffroy-Guichard, St Étienne	W	77-10
555	2-Feb-02	Italy	6N	H	Stade de France, Paris	W	33-12
556	16-Feb-02	Wales	6N	A	Millennium Stadium, Cardiff	W	37-33
557	2-Mar-02	England	6N	H	Stade de France, Paris	W	20-15
558	23-Mar-02	Scotland	6N	A	Murrayfield, Edinburgh	W	22-10
559	6-Apr-02	Ireland	6N	H	Stade de France, Paris	W	44-5
560	15-Jun-02	Argentina	Int-T	A	Vélez Sarsfield Stadium, Buenos Aires	L	27-28

No	Date	Opponents	Tmt	Match Venue	Result	
561	22-Jun-02	Australia	BIC-T	A Colonial Stadium, Melbourne	L	17-29
562	29-Jun-02	Australia	BIC-T	A Stadium Australia, Sydney	L	25-31
563	9-Nov-02	South Africa	Int	H Stade Vélodrome, Marseille	W	30-10
564	16-Nov-02	New Zealand	DGT	H Stade de France, Paris	D	20-20
565	23-Nov-02	Canada	Int	H Stade de France, Paris	W	35-3
566	15-Feb-03	England	6N	A Twickenham, London	L	17-25
567	23-Feb-03	Scotland	6N	H Stade de France, Paris	W	38-3
568	8-Mar-03	Ireland	6N	A Lansdowne Road, Dublin	L	12-15
569	23-Mar-03	Italy	6N	A Stadio Flaminio, Rome	W	53-27
570	29-Mar-03	Wales	6N	H Stade de France, Paris	W	33-5
571	14-Jun-03	Argentina	Int-T	A Vélez Sarsfield Stadium, Buenos Aires	L	6-10
572	20-Jun-03	Argentina	Int-T	A Vélez Sarsfield Stadium, Buenos Aires	L	32-33
573	28-Jun-03	New Zealand	DGT-T	A Jade Stadium, Christchurch	L	23-31
574	22-Aug-03	Romania	Int	H Stade Félix Bollaert, Lens	W	56-8
575	30-Aug-03	England	Int	H Stade Vélodrome, Marseille	W	17-16
576	6-Sep-03	England	Int	A Twickenham, London	L	14-45
577	11-Oct-03	Fiji	WCp	N Suncorp Stadium, Brisbane	W	61-18
578	18-Oct-03	Japan	WCp	N Dairy Farmers Stadium, Townsville	W	51-29
579	25-Oct-03	Scotland	WCp	N Telstra Stadium, Sydney	W	51-9
580	31-Oct-03	United States	WCp	N WIN Stadium, Wollongong	W	41-14
581	9-Nov-03	Ireland	WCqf	N Telstra Dome, Melbourne	W	43-21
582	16-Nov-03	England	WCsf	N Telstra Stadium, Sydney	L	7-24
583	20-Nov-03	New Zealand	WC34	N Telstra Stadium, Sydney	L	13-40
584	14-Feb-04	Ireland	6N	H Stade de France, Paris	W	35-17
585	21-Feb-04	Italy	6N	H Stade de France, Paris	W	25-0
586	7-Mar-04	Wales	6N	A Millennium Stadium, Cardiff	W	29-22
587	21-Mar-04	Scotland	6N	A Murrayfield, Edinburgh	W	31-0
588	27-Mar-04	England	6N	H Stade de France, Paris	W	24-21
589	3-Jul-04	United States	Int-T	A Rentschler Field, Hartford, Connecticut	W	39-31
590	10-Jul-04	Canada	Int-T	A York Stadium, Toronto	W	47-13
591	13-Nov-04	Australia	BIC	H Stade de France, Paris	W	27-14
592	20-Nov-04	Argentina	Int	H Stade Vélodrome, Marseille	L	14-24
593	27-Nov-04	New Zealand	DGT	H Stade de France, Paris	L	6-45
594	5-Feb-05	Scotland	6N	H Stade de France, Paris	W	16-9
595	13-Feb-05	England	6N	A Twickenham, London	W	18-17
596	26-Feb-05	Wales	6N	H Stade de France, Paris	L	18-24
597	12-Mar-05	Ireland	6N	A Lansdowne Road, Dublin	W	26-19
598	19-Mar-05	Italy	6N	A Stadio Flaminio, Rome	W	56-13
599	18-Jun-05	South Africa	Int-T	A The ABSA Stadium, Durban	D	30-30
600	25-Jun-05	South Africa	Int-T	A EPRFU Stadium, Port Elizabeth	L	13-27

No	Date	Opponents	Tmt	Match Venue	Result	
601	2-Jul-05	Australia	BIC-T	A Suncorp Stadium, Brisbane	L	31-37
602	5-Nov-05	Australia	BIC	H Stade Vélodrome, Marseille	W	26-16
603	12-Nov-05	Canada	Int	H Stade de la Beaujoire, Nantes	W	50-6
604	19-Nov-05	Tonga	Int	H Stade Municipal de Toulouse, Toulouse	W	43-8
605	26-Nov-05	South Africa	Int	H Stade de France, Paris	W	26-20
606	5-Feb-06	Scotland	6N	A Murrayfield, Edinburgh	L	16-20
607	11-Feb-06	Ireland	6N	H Stade de France, Paris	W	43-31
608	25-Feb-06	Italy	6N	H Stade de France, Paris	W	37-12
609	12-Mar-06	England	6N	H Stade de France, Paris	W	31-6
610	18-Mar-06	Wales	6N	A Millennium Stadium, Cardiff	W	21-16
611	17-Jun-06	Romania	Int	A Stadionul Cotroceni, Bucharest	W	62-14
612	24-Jun-06	South Africa	Int-T	A Newlands Stadium, Cape Town	W	36-26
613	11-Nov-06	New Zealand	DGT	H Stade de Gerland, Lyon	L	3-47
614	18-Nov-06	New Zealand	Int	H Stade de France, Paris	L	11-23
615	25-Nov-06	Argentina	Int	H Stade de France, Paris	W	27-26
616	3-Feb-07	Italy	6N-GG	A Stadio Flaminio, Rome	W	39-3
617	11-Feb-07	Ireland	6N	A Croke Park, Dublin	W	20-17
618	24-Feb-07	Wales	6N	H Stade de France, Paris	W	32-21
619	11-Mar-07	England	6N	A Twickenham, London	L	18-26
620	17-Mar-07	Scotland	6N	H Stade de France, Paris	W	46-19
621	2-Jun-07	New Zealand	DGT-T	A Eden Park, Auckland	L	11-42
622	9-Jun-07	New Zealand	Int-T	A Westpac Stadium, Wellington	L	10-61
623	11-Aug-07	England	Int	A Twickenham, London	W	21-15
624	18-Aug-07	England	Int	H Stade Vélodrome, Marseille	W	22-9
625	26-Aug-07	Wales	Int	A Millennium Stadium, Cardiff	W	34-7
626	7-Sep-07	Argentina	WCp	H Stade de France, Paris	L	12-17
627	16-Sep-07	Namibia	WCp	H Stade Municipal de Toulouse, Toulouse	W	87-10
628	21-Sep-07	Ireland	WCp	H Stade de France, Paris	W	25-3
629	30-Sep-07	Georgia	WCp	H Stade Vélodrome, Marseille	W	64-7
630	6-Oct-07	New Zealand	WCqf	N Millennium Stadium, Cardiff	W	20-18
631	13-Oct-07	England	WCsf	H Stade de France, Paris	L	9-14
632	19-Oct-07	Argentina	WC34	H Parc des Princess, Paris	L	10-34
633	3-Feb-08	Scotland	6N	A Murrayfield, Edinburgh	W	27-6
634	9-Feb-08	Ireland	6N	H Stade de France, Paris	W	26-21
635	23-Feb-08	England	6N	H Stade de France, Paris	L	13-24
636	9-Mar-08	Italy	6N-GG	H Stade de France, Paris	W	25-13
637	15-Mar-08	Wales	6N	A Millennium Stadium, Cardiff	L	12-29
638	28-Jun-08	Australia	BIC-T	A ANZ Stadium, Sydney	L	13-34
639	5-Jul-08	Australia	BIC-T	A Suncorp Stadium, Brisbane	L	10-40
640	8-Nov-08	Argentina	Int	H Stade Vélodrome, Marseille	W	12-6

No	Date	Opponents	Tmt		Match Venue	Result	
641	15-Nov-08	Pacific Islands	Int	H	Stade Auguste Bonal, Montbéliard	W	42-17
642	22-Nov-08	Australia	BIC	H	Stade de France, Paris	L	13-18
643	7-Feb-09	Ireland	6N	A	Croke Park, Dublin	L	21-30
644	14-Feb-09	Scotland	6N	H	Stade de France, Paris	W	22-13
645	27-Feb-09	Wales	6N	H	Stade de France, Paris	W	21-16
646	15-Mar-09	England	6N	A	Twickenham, London	L	10-34
647	21-Mar-09	Italy	6N-GG	A	Stadio Flaminio, Rome	W	50-8
648	13-Jun-09	New Zealand	DGT-T	A	Carisbrook, Dunedin	W	27-22
649	20-Jun-09	New Zealand	DGT-T	A	Westpac Stadium, Wellington	L	10-14
650	27-Jun-09	Australia	BIC-T	A	ANZ Stadium, Sydney	L	6-22
651	13-Nov-09	South Africa	Int	H	Stade Municipal de Toulouse, Toulouse	W	20-13
652	21-Nov-09	Samoa	Int	H	Stade de France, Paris	W	43-5
653	28-Nov-09	New Zealand	DGT	H	Stade Vélodrome, Marseille	L	12-39
654	7-Feb-10	Scotland	6N	A	Murrayfield, Edinburgh	W	18-9
655	13-Feb-10	Ireland	6N	H	Stade de France, Paris	W	33-10
656	26-Feb-10	Wales	6N	A	Millennium Stadium, Cardiff	W	26-20
657	14-Mar-10	Italy	6N-GG	H	Stade de France, Paris	W	46-20
658	20-Mar-10	England	6N	H	Stade de France, Paris	W	12-10
659	12-Jun-10	South Africa	Int-T	A	Newlands Stadium, Cape Town	L	17-42
660	26-Jun-10	Argentina	Int	A	Vélez Sarsfield Stadium, Buenos Aires	L	13-41
661	13-Nov-10	Fiji	Int-T	H	Stade de la Beaujoire, Nantes	W	34-12
662	20-Nov-10	Argentina	Int	H	Stade de la Mosson, Montpellier	W	15-9
663	27-Nov-10	Australia	BIC	H	Stade de France, Paris	L	16-59
664	5-Feb-11	Scotland	6N	H	Stade de France, Paris	W	34-21
665	13-Feb-11	Ireland	6N	A	Aviva Stadium, Dublin	W	25-22
666	26-Feb-11	England	6N	A	Twickenham, London	L	9-17
667	12-Mar-11	Italy	6N-GG	A	Stadio Flaminio, Rome	L	21-22
668	19-Mar-11	Wales	6N	H	Stade de France, Paris	W	28-9
669	13-Aug-11	Ireland	Int	H	Stade Chaban-Delmas, Bordeaux	W	19-12
670	20-Aug-11	Ireland	Int	A	Aviva Stadium, Dublin	W	26-22
671	10-Sep-11	Japan	WCp	N	North Harbour Stadium, Albany	W	47-21
672	18-Sep-11	Canada	WCp	N	McLean Park, Napier	W	46-19
673	24-Sep-11	New Zealand	WCp	A	Eden Park, Auckland	L	17-37
674	1-Oct-11	Tonga	WCp	N	Wellington Regional Stadium, Wellington	L	14-19
675	8-Oct-11	England	WCqf	N	Eden Park, Auckland	W	19-12
676	15-Oct-11	Wales	WCsf	N	Eden Park, Auckland	W	9-8
677	21-Oct-11	New Zealand	WCf	A	Eden Park, Auckland	L	7-8
678	4-Feb-12	Italy	6N-GG	H	Stade de France, Paris	W	30-12
679	26-Feb-12	Scotland	6N	A	Murrayfield, Edinburgh	W	23-17
680	4-Mar-12	Ireland	6N	H	Stade de France, Paris	D	17-17

No	Date	Opponents	Tmt	Match Venue		Result
681	11-Mar-12	England	6N	H	Stade de France, Paris	L 22-24
682	17-Mar-12	Wales	6N	A	Millennium Stadium, Cardiff	L 9-16
683	16-Jun-12	Argentina	Int-T	A	Estadio Olimpico Château Carreras,Córdoba	L 20-23
684	23-Jun-12	Argentina	Int-T	A	Estadio Monumental José Fierro, Tucumán	W 49-10
685	10-Nov-12	Australia	BIC	H	Stade de France, Paris	W 33-6
686	17-Nov-12	Argentina	Int	H	Grand Stade, Lille Métropole	W 39-22
687	24-Nov-12	Samoa	Int	H	Stade de France, Paris	W 22-14
688	3-Feb-13	Italy	6N-GG	A	Stadio Olimpico, Rome	L 18-23
689	9-Feb-13	Wales	6N	H	Stade de France, Paris	L 6-16
690	23-Feb-13	England	6N	A	Twickenham, London	L 13-23
691	9-Mar-13	Ireland	6N	A	Aviva Stadium, Dublin	D 13-13
692	16-Mar-13	Scotland	6N	H	Stade de France, Paris	W 23-16
693	8-Jun-13	New Zealand	DGT-T	A	Eden Park, Auckland	L 13-23
694	15-Jun-13	New Zealand	DGT-T	A	AMI Stadium, Addington	L 0-30
695	22-Jun-13	New Zealand	DGT-T	A	Yarrow Stadium, New Plymouth	L 9-24
696	9-Nov-13	New Zealand	DGT	H	Stade de France, Paris	L 19-26
697	16-Nov-13	Tonga	Int	H	Stade Océane, Le Havre	W 38-18
698	23-Nov-13	South Africa	Int	H	Stade de France, Paris	L 10-19
699	1-Feb-14	England	6N	H	Stade de France, Paris	W 26-24
700	9-Feb-14	Italy	6N-GG	H	Stade de France, Paris	W 30-10
701	21-Feb-14	Wales	6N	A	Millennium Stadium, Cardiff	L 6-27
702	8-Mar-14	Scotland	6N	A	Murrayfield, Edinburgh	W 19-17
703	15-Mar-14	Ireland	6N	H	Stade de France, Paris	L 20-22
704	7-Jun-14	Australia	BIC-T	A	Suncorp Stadium, Brisbane	L 23-50
705	14-Jun-14	Australia	BIC-T	A	Etihad Stadium, Docklands, Melbourne	L 0-6
706	21-Jun-14	Australia	BIC-T	A	Football Stadium, Sydney	L 13-39
707	8-Nov-14	Fiji	Int	H	Stade Vélodrome, Marseille	W 40-15
708	15-Nov-14	Australia	BIC	H	Stade de France, Paris	W 29-26
709	22-Nov-14	Argentina	Int	H	Stade de France, Paris	L 13-18
710	7-Feb-15	Scotland	6N	H	Stade de France, Paris	W 15-8
711	14-Feb-15	Ireland	6N	A	Aviva Stadium, Dublin	L 11-18
712	28-Feb-15	Wales	6N	H	Stade de France, Paris	L 13-20
713	15-Mar-15	Italy	6N-GG	A	Stadio Olimpico, Rome	W 29-0
714	21-Mar-15	England	6N	A	Twickenham, London	L 35-55

IRELAND

The Irish Rugby Football Union, formed in 1874, resulted from the unification of the Irish Football Union and the North of Ireland Union. A year later, the Irish played their first International match against England at the Kennington Oval in London, which they lost by seven points to nil. The next nine matches also ended in defeat for the Irish, and even after forty-four games, to the end of the 1893 season, the men in green had won only five times. There was, however, a dramatic turnaround in 1894 when Ireland won its first Triple Crown by defeating the other three Home Nations. The achievement was repeated five years later, in 1899.

Apart from winning the Four Nations Championship in 1935, and only sharing the title six times, the Irish team's performance was very mediocre during the first forty-seven years of the twentieth century. In that lean period the Irish also lost all seven matches against the three touring Southern Hemisphere teams, losing once to Australia and three times to both New Zealand and South Africa. The tide then changed, and the four seasons from 1948 to 1951 turned out to be very successful for the Irish team. In 1948 they won their first Grand Slam and followed it with a third Triple Crown in 1949. Only a draw in Paris that year prevented Ireland from winning back-to-back Grand Slams. Another draw in Cardiff in 1951 also denied the Irish a second Grand Slam.

In 1958 Ireland secured their first win over Southern Hemisphere opposition when they defeated Australia by 9 points to 6, but losses to the other two touring sides continued when they were beaten twice by New Zealand and three times by South Africa between 1951 and 1963. The second of those defeats by the

Springboks took place in Cape Town on Ireland's first tour to the Southern Hemisphere.

During the same period, the Irish performed miserably in the Five Nations Championship, gaining only the occasional win each year and suffering some indignity in 1960 when they lost all four Championship matches. Things improved in 1965 when the Irish team narrowly lost a Triple Crown decider to Wales in Cardiff in March, having drawn with France in Dublin earlier in the campaign. They defeated South Africa for the first time at Lansdowne Road, a month later, in April.

In January 1967, Ireland defeated Australia, again at Lansdowne Road, and four months later became the first Home Nations team to win in the Southern Hemisphere, when they beat Australia at the Cricket Ground in Sydney. The following year was also a good one for Ireland with just one defeat in the Five Nations and a fourth successive win, on home ground, against the Wallabies in October. In 1969 Ireland won in Paris for the first time in ten years but were denied a Grand Slam in Cardiff in the final game of the Championship. Three years later, in 1972, they missed an opportunity of a Grand Slam yet again, when, having won both their away games, the Five Nations Championship was not completed owing to unrest in Northern Ireland (both Scotland and Wales refused to travel to Dublin for security reasons).

A Championship title in 1974 was followed by a series of poor Irish performances to the end of 1978 when they mustered only four wins in twenty-one matches. Things improved for the team on their tour to Australia in June 1979, when they defeated the home side in both Internationals, staged in Brisbane and Sydney.

In 1982 Ireland won the Triple Crown for the first time in thirty-three years, a feat they repeated in 1985 (on that occasion a draw against France denied them that elusive second Grand Slam). Following losses to Australia at the quarter-final stage in both the 1987 and the 1991 World Cup, Ireland's performances throughout the 1990s were disappointing, especially during the period from 1996 to 1998 when the Irish team managed just six wins in twenty-four matches, with four of these being against the weaker Tier 2/3 sides namely Canada, Georgia, Romania and the United States.

The new millennium, however, hailed a marked improvement for the Irish, especially during the period 2004 to 2007, when they won three Triple Crowns. This success gave the whole of Ireland high expectations for the 2007 World Cup, but unfortunately hopes were dashed when the team was eliminated at the pool stage by Argentina and France. Two years later, in 2009, the Irish rallied and that elusive second Grand Slam was finally won, bridging a sixty-one-year gap since their only other success in 1948.

The success continued into the autumn of that year with a drawn game against Australia and a win against South Africa, but 2010 proved to be less fruitful when Ireland managed only five wins in eleven matches.

Three wins from five in the 2011 Six Nations Championship and four defeats in the August warm-up games did not inspire much confidence as the team prepared for the World Cup in New Zealand later that year, but the team rose to the occasion and fully deserved their win against Australia to top their pool. Unfortunately, high expectations were dashed yet again when they were beaten three weeks later by an inspired Welsh team in the quarter-final.

A mediocre period followed with only three wins from ten matches in 2012 and four wins from ten games in 2013. Fortunes, however, changed in the 2014 Six Nations Championship when the Irish claimed their first title, apart from the 2009 Grand Slam, since 1985. The good form continued on their Argentinian tour in June with a 2-0 series win over the host nation, and it reached a peak during the autumn Internationals when Ireland defeated both South Africa and Australia. Ireland had thus achieved a remarkable record of nine wins from ten matches in 2014, which included seven in a row. By winning the first three matches in the 2015 Six Nations Championship, the Irish had now achieved ten consecutive wins. The run came to an end when they lost to Wales in the fourth game of the Championship, but in winning the fifth match against Scotland, Ireland claimed the title, on points difference, from both England and Wales for the second successive year.

IRELAND

HEAD TO HEAD RESULTS TO 31 MARCH 2015

	P	W	D	L	%	F	A
v TIER 1 Teams							
v Argentina	15	10	0	5	66.7	331	283
v Australia	32	10	1	21	32.8	453	657
v England *	129	47	8	74	39.5	1056	1484
v France	93	31	7	55	37.1	1084	1508
v Italy	24	20	0	4	83.3	772	382
v New Zealand	28	0	1	27	1.8	310	812
v Scotland * / **	130	59	5	65	47.7	1412	1333
v South Africa	22	5	1	16	25.0	277	432
v Wales *	121	49	6	66	43.0	1320	1424
Sub-Total	**594**	**231**	**29**	**333**	**41.3**	**7015**	**8315**
v TIER 2/3 Group							
v Canada	6	5	1	0	91.7	226	77
v Fiji	3	3	0	0	100.0	149	31
v Japan	5	5	0	0	100.0	251	83
v Romania	8	8	0	0	100.0	346	92
v Samoa	6	5	0	1	83.3	209	103
v Tonga	2	2	0	0	100.0	72	28
v United States	8	8	0	0	100.0	306	82
v Georgia	4	4	0	0	100.0	196	31
v Namibia	4	2	0	2	50.00	117	65
v Russia	2	2	0	0	100.0	97	15
v Uruguay	0	0	0	0	0.0	0	0
Sub-Total	**48**	**44**	**1**	**3**	**92.7**	**1969**	**607**
v Other Teams							
v Zimbabwe	1	1	0	0	100.0	55	11
v New Zealand Natives *	1	0	0	1	0.0	-	-
v Pacific Islanders	1	1	0	0	100.0	61	17
v President's XV	1	0	1	0	50.0	18	18
Sub-Total	**4**	**2**	**1**	**1**	**62.5**	**134**	**46**
All Internationals	**646**	**277**	**31**	**337**	**45.3**	**9118**	**8968**

* excludes points scored before the introduction of the modern points system
** excludes the abandoned match on 21 February 1885 (Ireland 0 Scotland 1)

No	Date	Opponents	Tmt		Match Venue	Result	
1	15-Feb-75	England	Int	A	Kennington Oval, London	L	0-7
2	13-Dec-75	England	Int	H	Leinster CC, Rathmines, Dublin	L	0-4
3	5-Feb-77	England	Int	A	Kennington Oval, London	L	0-8
4	19-Feb-77	Scotland	Int	H	Ormeau, Belfast	L	0-20
5	11-Mar-78	England	Int	H	Lansdowne Road, Dublin	L	0-7
6	17-Feb-79	Scotland	Int	H	Ormeau, Belfast	L	0-7
7	24-Mar-79	England	Int	A	Kennington Oval, London	L	0-11
8	30-Jan-80	England	Int	H	Lansdowne Road, Dublin	L	1-4
9	14-Feb-80	Scotland	Int	A	Hamilton Crescent, Glasgow	L	0-11
10	5-Feb-81	England	Int	A	Whalley Range, Manchester	L	0-8
11	19-Feb-81	Scotland	Int	H	Ormeau, Belfast	W	3-1
12	28-Jan-82	Wales	Int	H	Lansdowne Road, Dublin	L	0-8
13	6-Feb-82	England	Int	H	Lansdowne Road, Dublin	D	2-2
14	18-Feb-82	Scotland	Int	A	Hamilton Crescent, Glasgow	L	0-2
15	5-Feb-83	England	4N	A	Whalley Range, Manchester	L	1-6
16	17-Feb-83	Scotland	4N	H	Ormeau, Belfast	L	0-4
17	4-Feb-84	England	4N	H	Lansdowne Road, Dublin	L	0-3
18	16-Feb-84	Scotland	4N	A	Raeburn Place, Edinburgh	L	1-8
19	12-Apr-84	Wales	4N	A	Arms Park, Cardiff	L	0-5
20	7-Feb-85	England	4N	A	Whalley Range, Manchester	L	1-2
21	21-Feb-85	Scotland	4N	H	Ormeau, Belfast (abandoned)	A	0-1
22	7-Mar-85	Scotland	4N	A	Raeburn Place, Edinburgh	L	0-5
23	6-Feb-86	England	4N	H	Lansdowne Road, Dublin	L	0-1
24	20-Feb-86	Scotland	4N	A	Raeburn Place, Edinburgh	L	0-14
25	5-Feb-87	England	4N	H	Lansdowne Road, Dublin	W	6-0
26	19-Feb-87	Scotland	4N	H	Ormeau, Belfast	L	0-8
27	12-Mar-87	Wales	4N	N	Upper Park, Birkenhead Park	L	3-4
28	3-Mar-88	Wales	4N	H	Lansdowne Road, Dublin	W	7-0
29	10-Mar-88	Scotland	4N	A	Raeburn Place, Edinburgh	L	0-3
30	1-Dec-88	N Z Natives	Int	H	Lansdowne Road, Dublin	L	4-13
31	16-Feb-89	Scotland	4N	H	Ormeau, Belfast	L	0-3
32	2-Mar-89	Wales	4N	A	St Helen's, Swansea	W	2-0
33	22-Feb-90	Scotland	4N	A	Raeburn Place, Edinburgh	L	0-5
34	1-Mar-90	Wales	4N	H	Lansdowne Road, Dublin	D	3-3
35	15-Mar-90	England	4N	A	Rectory Field, Blackheath	L	0-3
36	7-Feb-91	England	4N	H	Lansdowne Road, Dublin	L	0-9
37	21-Feb-91	Scotland	4N	H	Ballynafeigh, Belfast	L	0-14
38	7-Mar-91	Wales	4N	A	Stradey Park, Llanelli	L	4-6
39	6-Feb-92	England	4N	A	Whalley Range, Manchester	L	0-7
40	20-Feb-92	Scotland	4N	A	Raeburn Place, Edinburgh	L	0-2

No	Date	Opponents	Tmt	Match Venue	Result	
41	5-Mar-92	Wales	4N	H Lansdowne Road, Dublin	W	9-0
42	4-Feb-93	England	4N	H Lansdowne Road, Dublin	L	0-4
43	18-Feb-93	Scotland	4N	H Ballynafeigh, Belfast	D	0-0
44	11-Mar-93	Wales	4N	A Stradey Park, Llanelli	L	0-2
45	3-Feb-94	England	4N	A Rectory Field, Blackheath	W	7-5
46	24-Feb-94	Scotland	4N	H Lansdowne Road, Dublin	W	5-0
47	10-Mar-94	Wales	4N	H Ballynafeigh, Belfast	W	3-0
48	2-Feb-95	England	4N	H Lansdowne Road, Dublin	L	3-6
49	2-Mar-95	Scotland	4N	A Raeburn Place, Edinburgh	L	0-6
50	16-Mar-95	Wales	4N	A Arms Park, Cardiff	L	3-5
51	1-Feb-96	England	4N	A Meanwood Road, Leeds	W	10-4
52	15-Feb-96	Scotland	4N	H Lansdowne Road, Dublin	D	0-0
53	14-Mar-96	Wales	4N	H Lansdowne Road, Dublin	W	8-4
54	6-Feb-97	England	4N	H Lansdowne Road, Dublin	W	13-9
55	20-Feb-97	Scotland	4N	A Powderhall, Edinburgh	L	3-8
56	5-Feb-98	England	4N	A Athletic Ground, Richmond	W	9-6
57	19-Feb-98	Scotland	4N	H Balmoral Showgrounds, Belfast	L	0-8
58	19-Mar-98	Wales	4N	H Thomond Park, Limerick	L	3-11
59	4-Feb-99	England	4N	H Lansdowne Road, Dublin	W	6-0
60	18-Feb-99	Scotland	4N	A Inverleith, Edinburgh	W	9-3
61	18-Mar-99	Wales	4N	A Arms Park, Cardiff	W	3-0
62	3-Feb-00	England	4N	A Athletic Ground, Richmond	L	4-15
63	24-Feb-00	Scotland	4N	H Lansdowne Road, Dublin	D	0-0
64	17-Mar-00	Wales	4N	H Balmoral Showgrounds, Belfast	L	0-3
65	9-Feb-01	England	4N	H Lansdowne Road, Dublin	W	10-6
66	23-Feb-01	Scotland	4N	A Inverleith, Edinburgh	L	5-9
67	16-Mar-01	Wales	4N	A St Helen's, Swansea	L	9-10
68	8-Feb-02	England	4N	A Welford Road, Leicester	L	3-6
69	22-Feb-02	Scotland	4N	H Balmoral Showgrounds, Belfast	W	5-0
70	8-Mar-02	Wales	4N	H Lansdowne Road, Dublin	L	0-15
71	14-Feb-03	England	4N	H Lansdowne Road, Dublin	W	6-0
72	28-Feb-03	Scotland	4N	A Inverleith, Edinburgh	L	0-3
73	14-Mar-03	Wales	4N	A Arms Park, Cardiff	L	0-18
74	13-Feb-04	England	4N	A Rectory Field, Blackheath	L	0-19
75	27-Feb-04	Scotland	4N	H Lansdowne Road, Dublin	L	3-19
76	12-Mar-04	Wales	4N	H Balmoral Showgrounds, Belfast	W	14-12
77	11-Feb-05	England	4N	H Mardyke, Cork	W	17-3
78	25-Feb-05	Scotland	4N	A Inverleith, Edinburgh	W	11-5
79	11-Mar-05	Wales	4N	A St Helen's, Swansea	L	3-10
80	25-Nov-05	New Zealand	Int	H Lansdowne Road, Dublin	L	0-15

No	Date	Opponents	Tmt		Match Venue		Result	
81	10-Feb-06	England	4N	A	Welford Road, Leicester	W	16-6
82	24-Feb-06	Scotland	4N	H	Lansdowne Road, Dublin	L	6-13
83	10-Mar-06	Wales	4N	H	Balmoral Showgrounds, Belfast	W	11-6
84	24-Nov-06	South Africa	Int	H	Balmoral Showgrounds, Belfast	L	12-15
85	9-Feb-07	England	4N	H	Lansdowne Road, Dublin	W	17-9
86	23-Feb-07	Scotland	4N	A	Inverleith, Edinburgh	L	3-15
87	9-Mar-07	Wales	4N	A	Arms Park, Cardiff	L	0-29
88	8-Feb-08	England	4N	A	Athletic Ground, Richmond	L	3-13
89	29-Feb-08	Scotland	4N	H	Lansdowne Road, Dublin	W	16-11
90	14-Mar-08	Wales	4N	H	Balmoral Showgrounds, Belfast	L	5-11
91	13-Feb-09	England	4N	H	Lansdowne Road, Dublin	L	5-11
92	27-Feb-09	Scotland	4N	A	Inverleith, Edinburgh	L	3-9
93	13-Mar-09	Wales	4N	A	St Helen's, Swansea	L	5-18
94	20-Mar-09	France	Int	H	Lansdowne Road, Dublin	W	19-8
95	12-Feb-10	England	5N	A	Twickenham, London	D	0-0
96	26-Feb-10	Scotland	5N	H	Balmoral Showgrounds, Belfast	L	0-14
97	12-Mar-10	Wales	5N	H	Lansdowne Road, Dublin	L	3-19
98	28-Mar-10	France	5N	A	Parc des Princess, Paris	W	8-3
99	11-Feb-11	England	5N	H	Lansdowne Road, Dublin	W	3-0
100	25-Feb-11	Scotland	5N	A	Inverleith, Edinburgh	W	16-10
101	11-Mar-11	Wales	5N	A	Arms Park, Cardiff	L	0-16
102	25-Mar-11	France	5N	H	Mardyke, Cork	W	25-5
103	1-Jan-12	France	5N	A	Parc des Princess, Paris	W	11-6
104	10-Feb-12	England	5N	A	Twickenham, London	L	0-15
105	24-Feb-12	Scotland	5N	H	Lansdowne Road, Dublin	W	10-8
106	9-Mar-12	Wales	5N	H	Balmoral Showgrounds, Belfast	W	12-5
107	30-Nov-12	South Africa	Int	H	Lansdowne Road, Dublin	L	0-38
108	8-Feb-13	England	5N	H	Lansdowne Road, Dublin	L	4-15
109	22-Feb-13	Scotland	5N	A	Inverleith, Edinburgh	L	14-29
110	8-Mar-13	Wales	5N	A	St Helen's, Swansea	L	13-16
111	24-Mar-13	France	5N	H	Mardyke, Cork	W	24-0
112	1-Jan-14	France	5N	A	Parc des Princess, Paris	W	8-6
113	14-Feb-14	England	5N	A	Twickenham, London	L	12-17
114	28-Feb-14	Scotland	5N	H	Lansdowne Road, Dublin	W	6-0
115	14-Mar-14	Wales	5N	H	Balmoral Showgrounds, Belfast	L	3-11
116	14-Feb-20	England	5N	H	Lansdowne Road, Dublin	L	11-14
117	28-Feb-20	Scotland	5N	A	Inverleith, Edinburgh	L	0-19
118	13-Mar-20	Wales	5N	A	Arms Park, Cardiff	L	4-28
119	3-Apr-20	France	5N	H	Lansdowne Road, Dublin	L	7-15
120	12-Feb-21	England	5N	A	Twickenham, London	L	0-15

No	Date	Opponents	Tmt	Match Venue	Result
121	26-Feb-21	Scotland	5N	H Lansdowne Road, Dublin	W 9-8
122	12-Mar-21	Wales	5N	H Balmoral Showgrounds, Belfast	L 0-6
123	9-Apr-21	France	5N	A Stade Colombes, Paris	L 10-20
124	11-Feb-22	England	5N	H Lansdowne Road, Dublin	L 3-12
125	25-Feb-22	Scotland	5N	A Inverleith, Edinburgh	L 3-6
126	11-Mar-22	Wales	5N	A St Helen's, Swansea	L 5-11
127	8-Apr-22	France	5N	H Lansdowne Road, Dublin	W 8-3
128	10-Feb-23	England	5N	A Welford Road, Leicester	L 5-23
129	24-Feb-23	Scotland	5N	H Lansdowne Road, Dublin	L 3-13
130	10-Mar-23	Wales	5N	H Lansdowne Road, Dublin	W 5-4
131	14-Apr-23	France	5N	A Stade Colombes, Paris	L 8-14
132	26-Jan-24	France	5N	H Lansdowne Road, Dublin	W 6-0
133	9-Feb-24	England	5N	H Lansdowne Road, Dublin	L 3-14
134	23-Feb-24	Scotland	5N	A Inverleith, Edinburgh	L 8-13
135	8-Mar-24	Wales	5N	A Arms Park, Cardiff	W 13-10
136	1-Nov-24	New Zealand	Int	H Lansdowne Road, Dublin	L 0-6
137	1-Jan-25	France	5N	A Stade Colombes, Paris	W 9-3
138	14-Feb-25	England	5N	A Twickenham, London	D 6-6
139	28-Feb-25	Scotland	5N	H Lansdowne Road, Dublin	L 8-14
140	14-Mar-25	Wales	5N	H Ravenhill, Belfast	W 19-3
141	23-Jan-26	France	5N	H Ravenhill, Belfast	W 11-0
142	13-Feb-26	England	5N	H Lansdowne Road, Dublin	W 19-15
143	27-Feb-26	Scotland	5N	A Murrayfield, Edinburgh	W 3-0
144	13-Mar-26	Wales	5N	A St Helen's, Swansea	L 8-11
145	1-Jan-27	France	5N	A Stade Colombes, Paris	W 8-3
146	12-Feb-27	England	5N	A Twickenham, London	L 6-8
147	26-Feb-27	Scotland	5N	H Lansdowne Road, Dublin	W 6-0
148	12-Mar-27	Wales	5N	H Lansdowne Road, Dublin	W 19-9
149	12-Nov-27	Australia	Int	H Lansdowne Road, Dublin	L 3-5
150	28-Jan-28	France	5N	H Ravenhill, Belfast	W 12-8
151	11-Feb-28	England	5N	H Lansdowne Road, Dublin	L 6-7
152	25-Feb-28	Scotland	5N	A Murrayfield, Edinburgh	W 13-5
153	10-Mar-28	Wales	5N	A Arms Park, Cardiff	W 13-10
154	31-Dec-28	France	5N	A Stade Colombes, Paris	W 6-0
155	9-Feb-29	England	5N	A Twickenham, London	W 6-5
156	23-Feb-29	Scotland	5N	H Lansdowne Road, Dublin	L 7-16
157	9-Mar-29	Wales	5N	H Ravenhill, Belfast	D 5-5
158	25-Jan-30	France	5N	H Ravenhill, Belfast	L 0-5
159	8-Feb-30	England	5N	H Lansdowne Road, Dublin	W 4-3
160	22-Feb-30	Scotland	5N	A Murrayfield, Edinburgh	W 14-11

No	Date	Opponents	Tmt		Match Venue	Result	
161	8-Mar-30	Wales	5N	A	St Helen's, Swansea	L	7-12
162	1-Jan-31	France	5N	A	Stade Colombes, Paris	L	0-3
163	14-Feb-31	England	5N	A	Twickenham, London	W	6-5
164	28-Feb-31	Scotland	5N	H	Lansdowne Road, Dublin	W	8-5
165	14-Mar-31	Wales	5N	H	Ravenhill, Belfast	L	3-15
166	19-Dec-31	South Africa	Int	H	Lansdowne Road, Dublin	L	3-8
167	13-Feb-32	England	4N	H	Lansdowne Road, Dublin	L	8-11
168	27-Feb-32	Scotland	4N	A	Murrayfield, Edinburgh	W	20-8
169	12-Mar-32	Wales	4N	A	Arms Park, Cardiff	W	12-10
170	11-Feb-33	England	4N	A	Twickenham, London	L	6-17
171	11-Mar-33	Wales	4N	H	Ravenhill, Belfast	W	10-5
172	1-Apr-33	Scotland	4N	H	Lansdowne Road, Dublin	L	6-8
173	10-Feb-34	England	4N	H	Lansdowne Road, Dublin	L	3-13
174	24-Feb-34	Scotland	4N	A	Murrayfield, Edinburgh	L	9-16
175	10-Mar-34	Wales	4N	A	St Helen's, Swansea	L	0-13
176	9-Feb-35	England	4N	A	Twickenham, London	L	3-14
177	23-Feb-35	Scotland	4N	H	Lansdowne Road, Dublin	W	12-5
178	9-Mar-35	Wales	4N	H	Ravenhill, Belfast	W	9-3
179	7-Dec-35	New Zealand	Int	H	Lansdowne Road, Dublin	L	9-17
180	8-Feb-36	England	4N	H	Lansdowne Road, Dublin	W	6-3
181	22-Feb-36	Scotland	4N	A	Murrayfield, Edinburgh	W	10-4
182	14-Mar-36	Wales	4N	A	Arms Park, Cardiff	L	0-3
183	13-Feb-37	England	4N	A	Twickenham, London	L	8-9
184	27-Feb-37	Scotland	4N	H	Lansdowne Road, Dublin	W	11-4
185	3-Apr-37	Wales	4N	H	Ravenhill, Belfast	W	5-3
186	12-Feb-38	England	4N	H	Lansdowne Road, Dublin	L	14-36
187	26-Feb-38	Scotland	4N	A	Murrayfield, Edinburgh	L	14-23
188	12-Mar-38	Wales	4N	A	St Helen's, Swansea	L	5-11
189	11-Feb-39	England	4N	A	Twickenham, London	W	5-0
190	25-Feb-39	Scotland	4N	H	Lansdowne Road, Dublin	W	12-3
191	11-Mar-39	Wales	4N	H	Ravenhill, Belfast	L	0-7
192	25-Jan-47	France	5N	H	Lansdowne Road, Dublin	L	8-12
193	8-Feb-47	England	5N	H	Lansdowne Road, Dublin	W	22-0
194	22-Feb-47	Scotland	5N	A	Murrayfield, Edinburgh	W	3-0
195	29-Mar-47	Wales	5N	A	St Helen's, Swansea	L	0-6
196	6-Dec-47	Australia	Int	H	Lansdowne Road, Dublin	L	3-16
197	1-Jan-48	France	5N	A	Stade Colombes, Paris	W	13-6
198	14-Feb-48	England	5N	A	Twickenham, London	W	11-10
199	28-Feb-48	Scotland	5N	H	Lansdowne Road, Dublin	W	6-0
200	13-Mar-48	Wales	5N	H	Ravenhill, Belfast	W	6-3

No	Date	Opponents	Tmt		Match Venue		Result
201	29-Jan-49	France	5N	H	Lansdowne Road, Dublin	L	9-16
202	12-Feb-49	England	5N	H	Lansdowne Road, Dublin	W	14-5
203	26-Feb-49	Scotland	5N	A	Murrayfield, Edinburgh	W	13-3
204	12-Mar-49	Wales	5N	A	St Helen's, Swansea	W	5-0
205	28-Jan-50	France	5N	A	Stade Colombes, Paris	D	3-3
206	11-Feb-50	England	5N	A	Twickenham, London	L	0-3
207	25-Feb-50	Scotland	5N	H	Lansdowne Road, Dublin	W	21-0
208	11-Mar-50	Wales	5N	H	Ravenhill, Belfast	L	3-6
209	27-Jan-51	France	5N	H	Lansdowne Road, Dublin	W	9-8
210	10-Feb-51	England	5N	H	Lansdowne Road, Dublin	W	3-0
211	24-Feb-51	Scotland	5N	A	Murrayfield, Edinburgh	W	6-5
212	10-Mar-51	Wales	5N	A	Arms Park, Cardiff	D	3-3
213	8-Dec-51	South Africa	Int	H	Lansdowne Road, Dublin	L	5-17
214	26-Jan-52	France	5N	A	Stade Colombes, Paris	W	11-8
215	23-Feb-52	Scotland	5N	H	Lansdowne Road, Dublin	W	12-8
216	8-Mar-52	Wales	5N	H	Lansdowne Road, Dublin	L	3-14
217	29-Mar-52	England	5N	A	Twickenham, London	L	0-3
218	24-Jan-53	France	5N	H	Ravenhill, Belfast	W	16-3
219	14-Feb-53	England	5N	H	Lansdowne Road, Dublin	D	9-9
220	28-Feb-53	Scotland	5N	A	Murrayfield, Edinburgh	W	26-8
221	14-Mar-53	Wales	5N	A	St Helen's, Swansea	L	3-5
222	9-Jan-54	New Zealand	Int	H	Lansdowne Road, Dublin	L	3-14
223	23-Jan-54	France	5N	A	Stade Colombes, Paris	L	0-8
224	13-Feb-54	England	5N	A	Twickenham, London	L	3-14
225	27-Feb-54	Scotland	5N	H	Ravenhill, Belfast	W	6-0
226	13-Mar-54	Wales	5N	H	Lansdowne Road, Dublin	L	9-12
227	22-Jan-55	France	5N	H	Lansdowne Road, Dublin	L	3-5
228	12-Feb-55	England	5N	H	Lansdowne Road, Dublin	D	6-6
229	26-Feb-55	Scotland	5N	A	Murrayfield, Edinburgh	L	3-12
230	12-Mar-55	Wales	5N	A	Arms Park, Cardiff	L	3-21
231	28-Jan-56	France	5N	A	Stade Colombes, Paris	L	8-14
232	11-Feb-56	England	5N	A	Twickenham, London	L	0-20
233	25-Feb-56	Scotland	5N	H	Lansdowne Road, Dublin	W	14-10
234	10-Mar-56	Wales	5N	H	Lansdowne Road, Dublin	W	11-3
235	26-Jan-57	France	5N	H	Lansdowne Road, Dublin	W	11-6
236	9-Feb-57	England	5N	H	Lansdowne Road, Dublin	L	0-6
237	23-Feb-57	Scotland	5N	A	Murrayfield, Edinburgh	W	5-3
238	9-Mar-57	Wales	5N	A	Arms Park, Cardiff	L	5-6
239	18-Jan-58	Australia	Int	H	Lansdowne Road, Dublin	W	9-6
240	8-Feb-58	England	5N	A	Twickenham, London	L	0-6

No	Date	Opponents	Tmt		Match Venue	Result	
241	1-Mar-58	Scotland	5N	H	Lansdowne Road, Dublin	W	12-6
242	15-Mar-58	Wales	5N	H	Lansdowne Road, Dublin	L	6-9
243	19-Apr-58	France	5N	A	Stade Colombes, Paris	L	6-11
244	14-Feb-59	England	5N	H	Lansdowne Road, Dublin	L	0-3
245	28-Feb-59	Scotland	5N	A	Murrayfield, Edinburgh	W	8-3
246	14-Mar-59	Wales	5N	A	Arms Park, Cardiff	L	6-8
247	18-Apr-59	France	5N	H	Lansdowne Road, Dublin	W	9-5
248	13-Feb-60	England	5N	A	Twickenham, London	L	5-8
249	27-Feb-60	Scotland	5N	H	Lansdowne Road, Dublin	L	5-6
250	12-Mar-60	Wales	5N	H	Lansdowne Road, Dublin	L	9-10
251	9-Apr-60	France	5N	A	Stade Colombes, Paris	L	6-23
252	17-Dec-60	South Africa	Int	H	Lansdowne Road, Dublin	L	3-8
253	11-Feb-61	England	5N	H	Lansdowne Road, Dublin	W	11-8
254	25-Feb-61	Scotland	5N	A	Murrayfield, Edinburgh	L	8-16
255	11-Mar-61	Wales	5N	A	Arms Park, Cardiff	L	0-9
256	15-Apr-61	France	5N	H	Lansdowne Road, Dublin	L	3-15
257	13-May-61	South Africa	Int-T	A	Newlands Stadium, Cape Town	L	8-24
258	10-Feb-62	England	5N	A	Twickenham, London	L	0-16
259	24-Feb-62	Scotland	5N	H	Lansdowne Road, Dublin	L	6-20
260	14-Apr-62	France	5N	A	Stade Colombes, Paris	L	0-11
261	17-Nov-62	Wales	5N	H	Lansdowne Road, Dublin	D	3-3
262	26-Jan-63	France	5N	H	Lansdowne Road, Dublin	L	5-24
263	9-Feb-63	England	5N	H	Lansdowne Road, Dublin	D	0-0
264	23-Feb-63	Scotland	5N	A	Murrayfield, Edinburgh	L	0-3
265	9-Mar-63	Wales	5N	A	Arms Park, Cardiff	W	14-6
266	7-Dec-63	New Zealand	Int	H	Lansdowne Road, Dublin	L	5-6
267	8-Feb-64	England	5N	A	Twickenham, London	W	18-5
268	22-Feb-64	Scotland	5N	H	Lansdowne Road, Dublin	L	3-6
269	7-Mar-64	Wales	5N	H	Lansdowne Road, Dublin	L	6-15
270	11-Apr-64	France	5N	A	Stade Colombes, Paris	L	6-27
271	23-Jan-65	France	5N	H	Lansdowne Road, Dublin	D	3-3
272	13-Feb-65	England	5N	H	Lansdowne Road, Dublin	W	5-0
273	27-Feb-65	Scotland	5N	A	Murrayfield, Edinburgh	W	16-6
274	13-Mar-65	Wales	5N	A	Arms Park, Cardiff	L	8-14
275	10-Apr-65	South Africa	Int	H	Lansdowne Road, Dublin	W	9-6
276	29-Jan-66	France	5N	A	Stade Colombes, Paris	L	6-11
277	12-Feb-66	England	5N	A	Twickenham, London	D	6-6
278	26-Feb-66	Scotland	5N	H	Lansdowne Road, Dublin	L	3-11
279	12-Mar-66	Wales	5N	H	Lansdowne Road, Dublin	W	9-6
280	21-Jan-67	Australia	Int	H	Lansdowne Road, Dublin	W	15-8

No	Date	Opponents	Tmt		Match Venue		Result	
281	11-Feb-67	England	5N	H	Lansdowne Road, Dublin	L	3-8
282	25-Feb-67	Scotland	5N	A	Murrayfield, Edinburgh	W	5-3
283	11-Mar-67	Wales	5N	A	Arms Park, Cardiff	W	3-0
284	15-Apr-67	France	5N	H	Lansdowne Road, Dublin	L	6-11
285	13-May-67	Australia	Int-T	A	Cricket Ground, Sydney	W	11-5
286	27-Jan-68	France	5N	A	Stade Colombes, Paris	L	6-16
287	10-Feb-68	England	5N	A	Twickenham, London	D	9-9
288	24-Feb-68	Scotland	5N	H	Lansdowne Road, Dublin	W	14-6
289	9-Mar-68	Wales	5N	H	Lansdowne Road, Dublin	W	9-6
290	26-Oct-68	Australia	Int	H	Lansdowne Road, Dublin	W	10-3
291	25-Jan-69	France	5N	H	Lansdowne Road, Dublin	W	17-9
292	8-Feb-69	England	5N	H	Lansdowne Road, Dublin	W	17-15
293	22-Feb-69	Scotland	5N	A	Murrayfield, Edinburgh	W	16-0
294	8-Mar-69	Wales	5N	A	National Stadium, Cardiff	L	11-24
295	10-Jan-70	South Africa	Int	H	Lansdowne Road, Dublin	D	8-8
296	24-Jan-70	France	5N	A	Stade Colombes, Paris	L	0-8
297	14-Feb-70	England	5N	A	Twickenham, London	L	3-9
298	28-Feb-70	Scotland	5N	H	Lansdowne Road, Dublin	W	16-11
299	14-Mar-70	Wales	5N	H	Lansdowne Road, Dublin	W	14-0
300	30-Jan-71	France	5N	H	Lansdowne Road, Dublin	D	9-9
301	13-Feb-71	England	5N	H	Lansdowne Road, Dublin	L	6-9
302	27-Feb-71	Scotland	5N	A	Murrayfield, Edinburgh	W	17-5
303	13-Mar-71	Wales	5N	A	National Stadium, Cardiff	L	9-23
304	29-Jan-72	France	5N	A	Stade Colombes, Paris	W	14-9
305	12-Feb-72	England	5N	A	Twickenham, London	W	16-12
306	29-Apr-72	France	Int	H	Lansdowne Road, Dublin	W	24-14
307	20-Jan-73	New Zealand	Int	H	Lansdowne Road, Dublin	D	10-10
308	10-Feb-73	England	5N	H	Lansdowne Road, Dublin	W	18-9
309	24-Feb-73	Scotland	5N	A	Murrayfield, Edinburgh	L	14-19
310	10-Mar-73	Wales	5N	A	National Stadium, Cardiff	L	12-16
311	14-Apr-73	France	5N	H	Lansdowne Road, Dublin	W	6-4
312	19-Jan-74	France	5N	A	Parc des Princess, Paris	L	6-9
313	2-Feb-74	Wales	5N	H	Lansdowne Road, Dublin	D	9-9
314	16-Feb-74	England	5N	A	Twickenham, London	W	26-21
315	2-Mar-74	Scotland	5N	H	Lansdowne Road, Dublin	W	9-6
316	7-Sep-74	President's XV	Int	H	Lansdowne Road, Dublin	D	18-18
317	23-Nov-74	New Zealand	Int	H	Lansdowne Road, Dublin	L	6-15
318	18-Jan-75	England	5N	H	Lansdowne Road, Dublin	W	12-9
319	1-Feb-75	Scotland	5N	A	Murrayfield, Edinburgh	L	13-20
320	1-Mar-75	France	5N	H	Lansdowne Road, Dublin	W	25-6

No	Date	Opponents	Tmt		Match Venue	Result	
321	15-Mar-75	Wales	5N	A	National Stadium, Cardiff	L	4-32
322	17-Jan-76	Australia	Int	H	Lansdowne Road, Dublin	L	10-20
323	7-Feb-76	France	5N	A	Parc des Princess, Paris	L	3-26
324	21-Feb-76	Wales	5N	H	Lansdowne Road, Dublin	L	9-34
325	6-Mar-76	England	5N	A	Twickenham, London	W	13-12
326	20-Mar-76	Scotland	5N	H	Lansdowne Road, Dublin	L	6-15
327	5-Jun-76	New Zealand	Int-T	A	Athletic Park, Wellington	L	3-11
328	15-Jan-77	Wales	5N	A	National Stadium, Cardiff	L	9-25
329	5-Feb-77	England	5N	H	Lansdowne Road, Dublin	L	0-4
330	19-Feb-77	Scotland	5N	A	Murrayfield, Edinburgh	L	18-21
331	19-Mar-77	France	5N	H	Lansdowne Road, Dublin	L	6-15
332	21-Jan-78	Scotland	5N	H	Lansdowne Road, Dublin	W	12-9
333	18-Feb-78	France	5N	A	Parc des Princess, Paris	L	9-10
334	4-Mar-78	Wales	5N	H	Lansdowne Road, Dublin	L	16-20
335	18-Mar-78	England	5N	A	Twickenham, London	L	9-15
336	4-Nov-78	New Zealand	Int	H	Lansdowne Road, Dublin	L	6-10
337	20-Jan-79	France	5N	H	Lansdowne Road, Dublin	D	9-9
338	3-Feb-79	Wales	5N	A	National Stadium, Cardiff	L	21-24
339	17-Feb-79	England	5N	H	Lansdowne Road, Dublin	W	12-7
340	3-Mar-79	Scotland	5N	A	Murrayfield, Edinburgh	D	11-11
341	3-Jun-79	Australia	Int-T	A	Ballymore Oval, Brisbane	W	27-12
342	16-Jun-79	Australia	Int-T	A	Cricket Ground, Sydney	W	9-3
343	19-Jan-80	England	5N	A	Twickenham, London	L	9-24
344	2-Feb-80	Scotland	5N	H	Lansdowne Road, Dublin	W	22-15
345	1-Mar-80	France	5N	A	Parc des Princess, Paris	L	18-19
346	15-Mar-80	Wales	5N	H	Lansdowne Road, Dublin	W	21-7
347	7-Feb-81	France	5N	H	Lansdowne Road, Dublin	L	13-19
348	21-Feb-81	Wales	5N	A	National Stadium, Cardiff	L	8-9
349	7-Mar-81	England	5N	H	Lansdowne Road, Dublin	L	6-10
350	21-Mar-81	Scotland	5N	A	Murrayfield, Edinburgh	L	9-10
351	30-May-81	South Africa	Int-T	A	Newlands Stadium, Cape Town	L	15-23
352	6-Jun-81	South Africa	Int-T	A	Kings Park Stadium, Durban	L	10-12
353	21-Nov-81	Australia	Int	H	Lansdowne Road, Dublin	L	12-16
354	23-Jan-82	Wales	5N	H	Lansdowne Road, Dublin	W	20-12
355	6-Feb-82	England	5N	A	Twickenham, London	W	16-15
356	20-Feb-82	Scotland	5N	H	Lansdowne Road, Dublin	W	21-12
357	20-Mar-82	France	5N	A	Parc des Princess, Paris	L	9-22
358	15-Jan-83	Scotland	5N	A	Murrayfield, Edinburgh	W	15-13
359	19-Feb-83	France	5N	H	Lansdowne Road, Dublin	W	22-16
360	5-Mar-83	Wales	5N	A	National Stadium, Cardiff	L	9-23

No	Date	Opponents	Tmt		Match Venue	Result	
361	19-Mar-83	England	5N	H	Lansdowne Road, Dublin	W	25-15
362	21-Jan-84	France	5N	A	Parc des Princess, Paris	L	12-25
363	4-Feb-84	Wales	5N	H	Lansdowne Road, Dublin	L	9-18
364	18-Feb-84	England	5N	A	Twickenham, London	L	9-12
365	3-Mar-84	Scotland	5N	H	Lansdowne Road, Dublin	L	9-32
366	10-Nov-84	Australia	Int	H	Lansdowne Road, Dublin	L	9-16
367	2-Feb-85	Scotland	5N	A	Murrayfield, Edinburgh	W	18-15
368	2-Mar-85	France	5N	H	Lansdowne Road, Dublin	D	15-15
369	16-Mar-85	Wales	5N	A	National Stadium, Cardiff	W	21-9
370	30-Mar-85	England	5N	H	Lansdowne Road, Dublin	W	13-10
371	1-Feb-86	France	5N	A	Parc des Princess, Paris	L	9-29
372	15-Feb-86	Wales	5N	H	Lansdowne Road, Dublin	L	12-19
373	1-Mar-86	England	5N	A	Twickenham, London	L	20-25
374	15-Mar-86	Scotland	5N	H	Lansdowne Road, Dublin	L	9-10
375	1-Nov-86	Romania	Int	H	Lansdowne Road, Dublin	W	60-0
376	7-Feb-87	England	5N	H	Lansdowne Road, Dublin	W	17-0
377	21-Feb-87	Scotland	5N	A	Murrayfield, Edinburgh	L	12-16
378	21-Mar-87	France	5N	H	Lansdowne Road, Dublin	L	13-19
379	4-Apr-87	Wales	5N	A	National Stadium, Cardiff	W	15-11
380	25-May-87	Wales	WCp	N	Athletic Park, Wellington	L	6-13
381	30-May-87	Canada	WCp	N	Carisbrook, Dunedin	W	46-19
382	3-Jun-87	Tonga	WCp	N	Ballymore Oval, Brisbane	W	32-9
383	7-Jun-87	Australia	WCp	A	Concord Oval, Sydney	L	15-33
384	16-Jan-88	Scotland	5N	H	Lansdowne Road, Dublin	W	22-18
385	20-Feb-88	France	5N	A	Parc des Princess, Paris	L	6-25
386	5-Mar-88	Wales	5N	H	Lansdowne Road, Dublin	L	9-12
387	19-Mar-88	England	5N	A	Twickenham, London	L	3-35
388	23-Apr-88	England	MT	H	Lansdowne Road, Dublin	L	10-21
389	29-Oct-88	Western Samoa	Int	H	Lansdowne Road, Dublin	W	49-22
390	31-Dec-88	Italy	Int	H	Lansdowne Road, Dublin	W	31-15
391	21-Jan-89	France	5N	H	Lansdowne Road, Dublin	L	21-26
392	4-Feb-89	Wales	5N	A	National Stadium, Cardiff	W	19-13
393	18-Feb-89	England	5N-MT	H	Lansdowne Road, Dublin	L	3-16
394	4-Mar-89	Scotland	5N-CQ	A	Murrayfield, Edinburgh	L	21-37
395	18-Nov-89	New Zealand	Int	H	Lansdowne Road, Dublin	L	6-23
396	20-Jan-90	England	5N-MT	A	Twickenham, London	L	0-23
397	3-Feb-90	Scotland	5N-CQ	H	Lansdowne Road, Dublin	L	10-13
398	3-Mar-90	France	5N	A	Parc des Princess, Paris	L	12-31
399	24-Mar-90	Wales	5N	H	Lansdowne Road, Dublin	W	14-8
400	27-Oct-90	Argentina	Int	H	Lansdowne Road, Dublin	W	20-18

No	Date	Opponents	Tmt		Match Venue	Result	
401	2-Feb-91	France	5N	H	Lansdowne Road, Dublin	L	13-21
402	16-Feb-91	Wales	5N	A	National Stadium, Cardiff	D	21-21
403	2-Mar-91	England	5N-MT	H	Lansdowne Road, Dublin	L	7-16
404	16-Mar-91	Scotland	5N-CQ	A	Murrayfield, Edinburgh	L	25-28
405	20-Jul-91	Namibia	Int-T	A	South West Stadium, Windhoek	L	6-15
406	27-Jul-91	Namibia	Int-T	A	South West Stadium, Windhoek	L	15-26
407	6-Oct-91	Zimbabwe	WCp	H	Lansdowne Road, Dublin	W	55-11
408	9-Oct-91	Japan	WCp	H	Lansdowne Road, Dublin	W	32-16
409	12-Oct-91	Scotland	WCp	A	Murrayfield, Edinburgh	L	15-24
410	20-Oct-91	Australia	WCq	H	Lansdowne Road, Dublin	L	18-19
411	18-Jan-92	Wales	5N	H	Lansdowne Road, Dublin	L	15-16
412	1-Feb-92	England	5N-MT	A	Twickenham, London	L	9-38
413	15-Feb-92	Scotland	5N-CQ	H	Lansdowne Road, Dublin	L	10-18
414	21-Mar-92	France	5N	A	Parc des Princess, Paris	L	12-44
415	30-May-92	New Zealand	Int-T	A	Carisbrook, Dunedin	L	21-24
416	6-Jun-92	New Zealand	Int-T	A	Athletic Park, Wellington	L	6-59
417	31-Oct-92	Australia	Int	H	Lansdowne Road, Dublin	L	17-42
418	16-Jan-93	Scotland	5N-CQ	A	Murrayfield, Edinburgh	L	3-15
419	20-Feb-93	France	5N	H	Lansdowne Road, Dublin	L	6-21
420	6-Mar-93	Wales	5N	A	National Stadium, Cardiff	W	19-14
421	20-Mar-93	England	5N-MT	H	Lansdowne Road, Dublin	W	17-3
422	13-Nov-93	Romania	Int	H	Lansdowne Road, Dublin	W	25-3
423	15-Jan-94	France	5N	A	Parc des Princess, Paris	L	15-35
424	5-Feb-94	Wales	5N	H	Lansdowne Road, Dublin	L	15-17
425	19-Feb-94	England	5N-MT	A	Twickenham, London	W	13-12
426	5-Mar-94	Scotland	5N-CQ	H	Lansdowne Road, Dublin	D	6-6
427	5-Jun-94	Australia	Int-T	A	Ballymore Oval, Brisbane	L	13-33
428	11-Jun-94	Australia	Int-T	A	Football Stadium, Sydney	L	18-32
429	5-Nov-94	United States	Int	H	Lansdowne Road, Dublin	W	26-15
430	21-Jan-95	England	5N-MT	H	Lansdowne Road, Dublin	L	8-20
431	4-Feb-95	Scotland	5N-CQ	A	Murrayfield, Edinburgh	L	13-26
432	4-Mar-95	France	5N	H	Lansdowne Road, Dublin	L	7-25
433	18-Mar-95	Wales	5N	A	National Stadium, Cardiff	W	16-12
434	6-May-95	Italy	Int	A	Stadio Comunale di Monigo, Treviso	L	12-22
435	27-May-95	New Zealand	WCp	N	Ellis Park, Johannesburg	L	19-43
436	31-May-95	Japan	WCp	N	Free State Stadium, Bloemfontein	W	50-28
437	4-Jun-95	Wales	WCp	N	Ellis Park, Johannesburg	W	24-23
438	10-Jun-95	France	WCqf	N	Kings Park Stadium, Durban	L	12-36
439	18-Nov-95	Fiji	Int	H	Lansdowne Road, Dublin	W	44-8
440	6-Jan-96	United States	Int-T	A	Life College Stadium, Atlanta, Georgia	W	25-18

No	Date	Opponents	Tmt		Match Venue	Result	
441	20-Jan-96	Scotland	5N-CQ	H	Lansdowne Road, Dublin	L	10-16
442	17-Feb-96	France	5N	A	Parc des Princess, Paris	L	10-45
443	2-Mar-96	Wales	5N	H	Lansdowne Road, Dublin	W	30-17
444	16-Mar-96	England	5N-MT	A	Twickenham, London	L	15-28
445	12-Nov-96	Western Samoa	Int	H	Lansdowne Road, Dublin	L	25-40
446	23-Nov-96	Australia	Int	H	Lansdowne Road, Dublin	L	12-22
447	4-Jan-97	Italy	Int	H	Lansdowne Road, Dublin	L	29-37
448	18-Jan-97	France	5N	H	Lansdowne Road, Dublin	L	15-32
449	1-Feb-97	Wales	5N	A	National Stadium, Cardiff	W	26-25
450	15-Feb-97	England	5N-MT	H	Lansdowne Road, Dublin	L	6-46
451	1-Mar-97	Scotland	5N-CQ	A	Murrayfield, Edinburgh	L	10-38
452	15-Nov-97	New Zealand	Int	H	Lansdowne Road, Dublin	L	15-63
453	30-Nov-97	Canada	Int	H	Lansdowne Road, Dublin	W	33-11
454	20-Dec-97	Italy	Int	A	Stadio Renato Dall'Ara, Bologna	L	22-37
455	7-Feb-98	Scotland	5N-CQ	H	Lansdowne Road, Dublin	L	16-17
456	7-Mar-98	France	5N	A	Stade de France, Paris	L	16-18
457	21-Mar-98	Wales	5N	H	Lansdowne Road, Dublin	L	21-30
458	4-Apr-98	England	5N-MT	A	Twickenham, London	L	17-35
459	13-Jun-98	South Africa	Int-T	A	Free State Stadium, Bloemfontein	L	13-37
460	20-Jun-98	South Africa	Int-T	A	Minolta Loftus Stadium, Pretoria	L	0-33
461	14-Nov-98	Georgia	WCQ	H	Lansdowne Road, Dublin	W	70-0
462	21-Nov-98	Romania	WCQ	H	Lansdowne Road, Dublin	W	53-35
463	28-Nov-98	South Africa	Int	H	Lansdowne Road, Dublin	L	13-27
464	6-Feb-99	France	5N	H	Lansdowne Road, Dublin	L	9-10
465	20-Feb-99	Wales	5N	N	Wembley Stadium, London	W	29-23
466	6-Mar-99	England	5N-MT	H	Lansdowne Road, Dublin	L	15-27
467	20-Mar-99	Scotland	5N-CQ	A	Murrayfield, Edinburgh	L	13-30
468	10-Apr-99	Italy	Int	H	Lansdowne Road, Dublin	W	39-30
469	12-Jun-99	Australia	LC-T	A	Ballymore Oval, Brisbane	L	10-46
470	19-Jun-99	Australia	LC-T	A	Subiaco Oval, Perth	L	26-32
471	28-Aug-99	Argentina	Int	H	Lansdowne Road, Dublin	W	32-24
472	2-Oct-99	United States	WCp	H	Lansdowne Road, Dublin	W	53-8
473	10-Oct-99	Australia	WCp	H	Lansdowne Road, Dublin	L	3-23
474	15-Oct-99	Romania	WCp	H	Lansdowne Road, Dublin	W	44-14
475	20-Oct-99	Argentina	QFpo	N	Stade Félix Bollaert, Lens	L	24-28
476	5-Feb-00	England	6N-MT	A	Twickenham, London	L	18-50
477	19-Feb-00	Scotland	6N-CQ	H	Lansdowne Road, Dublin	W	44-22
478	4-Mar-00	Italy	6N	H	Lansdowne Road, Dublin	W	60-13
479	19-Mar-00	France	6N	A	Stade de France, Paris	W	27-25
480	1-Apr-00	Wales	6N	H	Lansdowne Road, Dublin	L	19-23

No	Date	Opponents	Tmt		Match Venue	Result	
481	3-Jun-00	Argentina	Int-T	A	Ferro Carril Oeste Stadium, B Aires	L	23-34
482	10-Jun-00	United States	Int-T	A	Singer Family Park, Manchester, NH	W	83-3
483	17-Jun-00	Canada	Int-T	A	Fletcher's Fields, Markham, Toronto	D	27-27
484	11-Nov-00	Japan	Int	H	Lansdowne Road, Dublin	W	78-9
485	19-Nov-00	South Africa	Int	H	Lansdowne Road, Dublin	L	18-28
486	3-Feb-01	Italy	6N	A	Stadio Flaminio, Rome	W	41-22
487	17-Feb-01	France	6N	H	Lansdowne Road, Dublin	W	22-15
488	2-Jun-01	Romania	Int	A	Stadionul Dinamo, Bucharest	W	37-3
489	22-Sep-01	Scotland	6N-CQ	A	Murrayfield, Edinburgh	L	10-32
490	13-Oct-01	Wales	6N	A	Millennium Stadium, Cardiff	W	36-6
491	20-Oct-01	England	6N-MT	H	Lansdowne Road, Dublin	W	20-14
492	11-Nov-01	Samoa	Int	H	Lansdowne Road, Dublin	W	35-8
493	17-Nov-01	New Zealand	Int	H	Lansdowne Road, Dublin	L	29-40
494	3-Feb-02	Wales	6N	H	Lansdowne Road, Dublin	W	54-10
495	16-Feb-02	England	6N-MT	A	Twickenham, London	L	11-45
496	2-Mar-02	Scotland	6N-CQ	H	Lansdowne Road, Dublin	W	43-22
497	23-Mar-02	Italy	6N	H	Lansdowne Road, Dublin	W	32-17
498	6-Apr-02	France	6N	A	Stade de France, Paris	L	5-44
499	15-Jun-02	New Zealand	Int-T	A	Carisbrook, Dunedin	L	6-15
500	22-Jun-02	New Zealand	Int-T	A	Eden Park, Auckland	L	8-40
501	7-Sep-02	Romania	Int	H	Thomond Park, Limerick	W	39-8
502	21-Sep-02	Russia	WCQ	A	Central Stadium, Krasnoyarsk	W	35-3
503	28-Sep-02	Georgia	WCQ	H	Lansdowne Road, Dublin	W	63-14
504	9-Nov-02	Australia	LC	H	Lansdowne Road, Dublin	W	18-9
505	17-Nov-02	Fiji	Int	H	Lansdowne Road, Dublin	W	64-17
506	23-Nov-02	Argentina	Int	H	Lansdowne Road, Dublin	W	16-7
507	16-Feb-03	Scotland	6N-CQ	A	Murrayfield, Edinburgh	W	36-6
508	22-Feb-03	Italy	6N	A	Stadio Flaminio, Rome	W	37-13
509	8-Mar-03	France	6N	H	Lansdowne Road, Dublin	W	15-12
510	22-Mar-03	Wales	6N	A	Millennium Stadium, Cardiff	W	25-24
511	30-Mar-03	England	6N-MT	H	Lansdowne Road, Dublin	L	6-42
512	7-Jun-03	Australia	LC-T	A	Subiaco Oval, Perth	L	16-45
513	14-Jun-03	Tonga	Int-T	A	Teufaiva Sport Stadium, Nuku'alofa	W	40-19
514	20-Jun-03	Samoa	Int-T	A	Apia Park, Apia	W	40-14
515	16-Aug-03	Wales	Int	H	Lansdowne Road, Dublin	W	35-12
516	30-Aug-03	Italy	Int	H	Thomond Park, Limerick	W	61-6
517	6-Sep-03	Scotland	Int	A	Murrayfield, Edinburgh	W	29-10
518	11-Oct-03	Romania	WCp	N	Central Coast Stadium, Gosford, NSW	W	45-17
519	19-Oct-03	Namibia	WCp	N	Aussie Stadium, Sydney	W	64-7
520	26-Oct-03	Argentina	WCp	N	Adelaide Oval, Adelaide	W	16-15

No	Date	Opponents	Tmt		Match Venue	Result	
521	1-Nov-03	Australia	WCp	A	Telstra Dome, Melbourne	L	16-17
522	9-Nov-03	France	WCq	N	Telstra Dome, Melbourne	L	21-43
523	14-Feb-04	France	6N	A	Stade de France, Paris	L	17-35
524	22-Feb-04	Wales	6N	H	Lansdowne Road, Dublin	W	36-15
525	6-Mar-04	England	6N-MT	A	Twickenham, London	W	19-13
526	20-Mar-04	Italy	6N	H	Lansdowne Road, Dublin	W	19-3
527	27-Mar-04	Scotland	6N-CQ	H	Lansdowne Road, Dublin	W	37-16
528	12-Jun-04	South Africa	Int-T	A	Vodacom Park Stadium, Bloemfontein	L	17-31
529	19-Jun-04	South Africa	Int-T	A	Newlands Stadium, Cape Town	L	17-26
530	13-Nov-04	South Africa	Int	H	Lansdowne Road, Dublin	W	17-12
531	20-Nov-04	United States	Int	H	Lansdowne Road, Dublin	W	55-6
532	27-Nov-04	Argentina	Int	H	Lansdowne Road, Dublin	W	21-19
533	6-Feb-05	Italy	6N	A	Stadio Flaminio, Rome	W	28-17
534	12-Feb-05	Scotland	6N-CQ	A	Murrayfield, Edinburgh	W	40-13
535	27-Feb-05	England	6N-MT	H	Lansdowne Road, Dublin	W	19-13
536	12-Mar-05	France	6N	H	Lansdowne Road, Dublin	L	19-26
537	19-Mar-05	Wales	6N	A	Millennium Stadium, Cardiff	L	20-32
538	12-Jun-05	Japan	Int-T	A	Nagai Stadium, Osaka	W	44-12
539	19-Jun-05	Japan	Int-T	A	Prince Chichibu Memorial Ground, Tokyo	W	47-18
540	12-Nov-05	New Zealand	Int	H	Lansdowne Road, Dublin	L	7-45
541	19-Nov-05	Australia	LC	H	Lansdowne Road, Dublin	L	14-30
542	26-Nov-05	Romania	Int	H	Lansdowne Road, Dublin	W	43-12
543	4-Feb-06	Italy	6N	H	Lansdowne Road, Dublin	W	26-16
544	11-Feb-06	France	6N	A	Stade de France, Paris	L	31-43
545	26-Feb-06	Wales	6N	H	Lansdowne Road, Dublin	W	31-5
546	11-Mar-06	Scotland	6N-CQ	H	Lansdowne Road, Dublin	W	15-9
547	18-Mar-06	England	6N-MT	A	Twickenham, London	W	28-24
548	10-Jun-06	New Zealand	Int-T	A	Waikato Stadium, Hamilton	L	23-34
549	17-Jun-06	New Zealand	Int-T	A	Eden Park, Auckland	L	17-27
550	24-Jun-06	Australia	LC-T	A	Subiaco Oval, Perth	L	15-37
551	11-Nov-06	South Africa	Int	H	Lansdowne Road, Dublin	W	32-15
552	19-Nov-06	Australia	LC	H	Lansdowne Road, Dublin	W	21-6
553	26-Nov-06	Pacific Islands	Int	H	Lansdowne Road, Dublin	W	61-17
554	4-Feb-07	Wales	6N	A	Millennium Stadium, Cardiff	W	19-9
555	11-Feb-07	France	6N	H	Croke Park, Dublin	L	17-20
556	24-Feb-07	England	6N-MT	H	Croke Park, Dublin	W	43-13
557	10-Mar-07	Scotland	6N-CQ	A	Murrayfield, Edinburgh	W	19-18
558	17-Mar-07	Italy	6N	A	Stadio Flaminio, Rome	W	51-24
559	26-May-07	Argentina	Int-T	A	Estadio Brig General E. López, Santa Fe	L	20-22
560	2-Jun-07	Argentina	Int-T	A	Vélez Sarsfield Stadium, Buenos Aires	L	0-16

No	Date	Opponents	Tmt		Match Venue		Result	
561	11-Aug-07	Scotland	Int	A	Murrayfield, Edinburgh		L	21-31
562	24-Aug-07	Italy	Int	H	Ravenhill, Belfast		W	23-20
563	9-Sep-07	Namibia	WCp	N	Stade Chaban-Delmas, Bordeaux		W	32-17
564	15-Sep-07	Georgia	WCp	N	Stade Chaban-Delmas, Bordeaux		W	14-10
565	21-Sep-07	France	WCp	A	Stade de France, Paris		L	3-25
566	30-Sep-07	Argentina	WCp	N	Parc des Princess, Paris		L	15-30
567	2-Feb-08	Italy	6N	H	Croke Park, Dublin		W	16-11
568	9-Feb-08	France	6N	A	Stade de France, Paris		L	21-26
569	23-Feb-08	Scotland	6N-CQ	H	Croke Park, Dublin		W	34-13
570	8-Mar-08	Wales	6N	H	Croke Park, Dublin		L	12-16
571	15-Mar-08	England	6N-MT	A	Twickenham, London		L	10-33
572	7-Jun-08	New Zealand	Int-T	A	Westpac Stadium, Wellington		L	11-21
573	14-Jun-08	Australia	LC-T	A	Telstra Dome, Melbourne		L	12-18
574	8-Nov-08	Canada	Int	H	Thomond Park, Limerick		W	55-0
575	15-Nov-08	New Zealand	Int	H	Croke Park, Dublin		L	3-22
576	22-Nov-08	Argentina	Int	H	Croke Park, Dublin		W	17-3
577	7-Feb-09	France	6N	H	Croke Park, Dublin		W	30-21
578	15-Feb-09	Italy	6N	A	Stadio Flaminio, Rome		W	38-9
579	28-Feb-09	England	6N-MT	H	Croke Park, Dublin		W	14-13
580	14-Mar-09	Scotland	6N-CQ	A	Murrayfield, Edinburgh		W	22-15
581	21-Mar-09	Wales	6N	A	Millennium Stadium, Cardiff		W	17-15
582	23-May-09	Canada	Int-T	A	Thunderbird Stadium, Vancouver		W	25-6
583	31-May-09	United States	Int-T	A	Buck Shaw Stadium, Santa Clara		W	27-10
584	15-Nov-09	Australia	LC	H	Croke Park, Dublin		D	20-20
585	21-Nov-09	Fiji	Int	H	RDS Showgrounds, Dublin		W	41-6
586	28-Nov-09	South Africa	Int	H	Croke Park, Dublin		W	15-10
587	6-Feb-10	Italy	6N	H	Croke Park, Dublin		W	29-11
588	13-Feb-10	France	6N	A	Stade de France, Paris		L	10-33
589	27-Feb-10	England	6N-MT	A	Twickenham, London		W	20-16
590	13-Mar-10	Wales	6N	H	Croke Park, Dublin		W	27-12
591	20-Mar-10	Scotland	6N-CQ	H	Croke Park, Dublin		L	20-23
592	12-Jun-10	New Zealand	Int-T	A	Yarrow Stadium, New Plymouth		L	28-66
593	26-Jun-10	Australia	LC-T	A	Suncorp Stadium, Brisbane		L	15-22
594	6-Nov-10	South Africa	Int	H	Aviva Stadium, Dublin		L	21-23
595	13-Nov-10	Samoa	Int	H	Aviva Stadium, Dublin		W	20-10
596	20-Nov-10	New Zealand	Int	H	Aviva Stadium, Dublin		L	18-38
597	28-Nov-10	Argentina	Int	H	Aviva Stadium, Dublin		W	29-9
598	5-Feb-11	Italy	6N	A	Stadio Flaminio, Rome		W	13-11
599	13-Feb-11	France	6N	H	Aviva Stadium, Dublin		L	22-25
600	27-Feb-11	Scotland	6N-CQ	A	Murrayfield, Edinburgh		W	21-18

No	Date	Opponents	Tmt	Match Venue	Result	
601	12-Mar-11	Wales	6N	A	Millennium Stadium, Cardiff	L	13-19
602	19-Mar-11	England	6N-MT	H	Aviva Stadium, Dublin	W	24-8
603	6-Aug-11	Scotland	Int	A	Murrayfield, Edinburgh	L	6-10
604	13-Aug-11	France	Int	A	Stade Chaban-Delmas, Bordeaux	L	12-19
605	20-Aug-11	France	Int	H	Aviva Stadium, Dublin	L	22-26
606	27-Aug-11	England	Int	H	Aviva Stadium, Dublin	L	9-20
607	11-Sep-11	United States	WCp	N	Stadium Taranaki, New Plymouth	W	22-10
608	17-Sep-11	Australia	WCp	N	Eden Park, Auckland	W	15-6
609	25-Sep-11	Russia	WCp	N	Rotorua International Stadium, Rotorua	W	62-12
610	2-Oct-11	Italy	WCp	N	Otago Stadium, Dunedin	W	36-6
611	9-Oct-11	Wales	WCq	N	Wellington Regional Stadium, Wellington	L	10-22
612	5-Feb-12	Wales	6N	H	Aviva Stadium, Dublin	L	21-23
613	25-Feb-12	Italy	6N	H	Aviva Stadium, Dublin	W	42-10
614	4-Mar-12	France	6N	A	Stade de France, Paris	D	17-17
615	10-Mar-12	Scotland	6N-CQ	H	Aviva Stadium, Dublin	W	32-14
616	17-Mar-12	England	6N-MT	A	Twickenham, London	L	9-30
617	9-Jun-12	New Zealand	Int-T	A	Eden Park, Auckland	L	10-42
618	16-Jun-12	New Zealand	Int-T	A	Rugby League Park, Christchurch	L	19-22
619	23-Jun-12	New Zealand	Int-T	A	Waikato Stadium, Hamilton	L	0-60
620	10-Nov-12	South Africa	Int	H	Aviva Stadium, Dublin	L	12-16
621	24-Nov-12	Argentina	ABC	H	Aviva Stadium, Dublin	W	46-24
622	2-Feb-13	Wales	6N	A	Millennium Stadium, Cardiff	W	30-22
623	10-Feb-13	England	6N-MT	H	Aviva Stadium, Dublin	L	6-12
624	24-Feb-13	Scotland	6N-CQ	A	Murrayfield, Edinburgh	L	8-12
625	9-Mar-13	France	6N	H	Aviva Stadium, Dublin	D	13-13
626	16-Mar-13	Italy	6N	A	Stadio Olimpico, Rome	L	15-22
627	8-Jun-13	United States	Int-T	A	BBVA Compass Stadium, Houston	W	15-12
628	15-Jun-13	Canada	Int-T	A	BMO Stadium, Toronto	W	40-14
629	9-Nov-13	Samoa	Int	H	Aviva Stadium, Dublin	W	40-9
630	16-Nov-13	Australia	LC	H	Aviva Stadium, Dublin	L	15-32
631	24-Nov-13	New Zealand	Int	H	Aviva Stadium, Dublin	L	22-24
632	2-Feb-14	Scotland	6N-CQ	H	Aviva Stadium, Dublin	W	28-6
633	8-Feb-14	Wales	6N	H	Aviva Stadium, Dublin	W	26-3
634	22-Feb-14	England	6N-MT	A	Twickenham, London	L	10-13
635	8-Mar-14	Italy	6N	H	Aviva Stadium, Dublin	W	46-7
636	15-Mar-14	France	6N	A	Stade de France, Paris	W	22-20
637	7-Jun-14	Argentina	ABC-T	A	Estadio Centenario, Resistencia	W	29-17
638	14-Jun-14	Argentina	ABC-T	A	Estadio Monumental José Fierro, Tucumán	W	23-17
639	8-Nov-14	South Africa	Int	H	Aviva Stadium, Dublin	W	29-15
640	16-Nov-14	Georgia	Int	H	Aviva Stadium, Dublin	W	49-7

No	Date	Opponents	Tmt		Match Venue		Result	
641	22-Nov-14	Australia	LC	H	Aviva Stadium, Dublin		W	26-23
642	7-Feb-15	Italy	6N	A	Stadio Olimpico, Rome		W	26-3
643	14-Feb-15	France	6N	H	Aviva Stadium, Dublin		W	18-11
644	1-Mar-15	England	6N-MT	H	Aviva Stadium, Dublin		W	19-9
645	14-Mar-15	Wales	6N	A	Millennium Stadium, Cardiff		L	16-23
646	21-Mar-15	Scotland	6N-CQ	A	Murrayfield, Edinburgh		W	40-10

ITALY

On 25 July 1911, a 'Propaganda Committee' was formed to promote the game of rugby in Italy and, over a decade later, in 1928, the Federazione Italiana Rugby was formed.

The following year, Italy played its first International match, against Spain in Barcelona, and lost by 9 points to nil. In 1932 the Fédération Internationale de Rugby Amateur, better known as FIRA, was founded, and an association consisting of Italy, France, Romania, Czechoslovakia, Spain and Germany was created two years later.

The FIRA European Trophy tournament (FET) was staged between 1936 and 1938, with France winning the trophy in all three years, and the Italian team finishing in second place in 1937. The French team also won the first two FIRA European Cup (FEC) competitions held between 1952 and 1954, with Italy finishing runners-up in both years.

A third FIRA tournament, known as the Nations Cup, was inaugurated in 1965. France once again dominated this competition by winning eight out of the nine titles before the tournament's demise in 1973. Italy's best achievement during that period came in the first season, 1965-66, when they finished in second place.

In 1974, a new FIRA Championship was launched to provide an alternative European international competition to the Five Nations Championship. The tournament ran until 1997, with the French playing all their matches, except for games against Romania and Italy in 1997, as France 'A'. The French team won thirteen titles during that period, with the Romanians winning four times. Italy surprised everyone by winning the title in the final competition, held between 1995 and 1997, beating a full French side in the process.

The FIRA Championship was finally replaced three years later, in 2000, by the European Nations Cup (ENC), a tournament that currently runs in tandem with the Six Nations Championship. The Italians did not enter the ENC that year because they were invited to join the newly formed Six Nations Championship. Italy also competed in the two Latin Cup tournaments, the first held in Argentina in October 1995 and the second hosted by France in October 1997. The four nations taking part were Italy, Romania, France and Argentina, and the Italian team's performance was disappointing, winning just two matches out of the six they played over the two years.

Italy's first International against a major nation was in 1978 when they faced Argentina in Rovigo. They won that match comfortably by 19 points to 6, but it was another five years before they faced another major nation: Australia, also in Rovigo. On that occasion they were well beaten by 29 points to 7. The Italians lost again to Australia in Brisbane three years later, in 1986. In 1987 Italy lost both their matches against New Zealand and Argentina at the pool stage of the inaugural World Cup, and three more defeats to the top teams followed, with losses to Australia and Ireland in December 1988 and to Argentina in Buenos Aires in June 1989.

Throughout the 1990s, Italy had ambitions to play in an expanded Five Nations Championship, but it wasn't until the second half of the decade that they were able to achieve wins against the teams competing in that tournament. Wins against Ireland in 1995, against France and Ireland (twice) in 1997, and against Scotland in 1998 strengthened the Italians' case for entry to the Five Nations Championship, and in 2000 they were finally invited to join the tournament which was renamed the Six Nations Championship.

However, the 1990s didn't prove to be a successful decade for the 'Azzuri' as they were known, in the World Cup tournaments: in 1991 they lost to both England and New Zealand in the pool games. They fared slightly better in 1995, losing narrowly to England by 27 points to 20, before beating Argentina in their final pool match. In the 1999 World Cup, Italy lost all three pool games: firstly to England, then to Tonga and finally, in a devastating match against New Zealand, the Italians were overrun, scoring just 3 points to New Zealand's 101. Their World Cup record improved a little in 2003 and 2007 when they won two pool games out of four in each competition.

In thirty-six Internationals contested between the beginning of 2008 to March 2011, Italy suffered thirty defeats, including a sequence of thirteen straight losses. Going into the 2011 Rugby World Cup with that kind of record, it was not surprising that the team failed to qualify for the quarter-finals, and only won two pool games from four (against Russia and the United States). The Italians also lost four of the five matches in the 2012 Six Nations Championship, winning only the final game of the tournament against Scotland in Rome. There was an improvement in the 2013 Six Nations Championship, when they achieved two victories in the Championship for only the second time since their entry in 2000. They defeated France at home in their opening game of the campaign, and then went on to secure a first-ever Championship win against Ireland in the final match, also in Rome.

Italy's poor form returned when they lost all five matches in the 2014 Six Nations Championship. This was followed by three further defeats to Tier 2 teams: Fiji, Samoa and Japan, in June. The team's dismal results meant that they had suffered nine losses in a row, all in the space of seven months. The sequence was finally broken in November 2014 when they defeated

Samoa by 24 points to 14. The Azzuri have not had a happy time in the Six Nations Championships, having won on only twelve occasions in eighty matches played (15.6%) over the sixteen seasons to 2015.

ITALY

HEAD TO HEAD RESULTS TO 31 MARCH 2015

v TIER 1 Teams	P	W	D	L	%	F	A
v Argentina	20	5	1	14	27.5	344	496
v Australia	16	0	0	16	0.0	217	565
v England	21	0	0	21	0.0	266	842
v France	36	3	0	33	8.3	382	1069
v Ireland	24	4	0	20	16.7	382	772
v New Zealand	12	0	0	12	0.0	118	686
v Scotland	23	8	0	15	34.8	416	524
v South Africa	12	0	0	12	0.0	145	599
v Wales	22	2	1	19	11.4	367	725
Sub-Total	**186**	**22**	**2**	**162**	**12.4**	**2637**	**6278**
v TIER 2/3 Group							
v Canada	7	5	0	2	71.4	203	92
v Fiji	10	5	0	5	50.0	244	243
v Japan	6	5	0	1	83.3	199	90
v Romania	41	22	3	16	57.3	577	612
v Samoa	7	2	0	5	28.6	109	175
v Tonga	4	3	0	1	75.0	137	63
v United States	4	4	0	0	100.0	130	54
v Georgia	1	1	0	0	100.0	31	22
v Namibia	3	1	0	2	33.3	75	74
v Russia	4	4	0	0	100.0	198	61
v Uruguay	3	3	0	0	100.0	92	25
Sub-Total	**90**	**55**	**3**	**32**	**62.8**	**1995**	**1511**
v Tier 3 Selection							
v Czechoslovakia *	11	9	1	1	86.4	162	54
v Portugal	12	10	1	1	87.5	333	71
v Spain	27	23	1	3	87.0	581	187
v USSR **	14	4	1	9	32.1	171	165
v W. Germany ***	14	13	1	0	96.4	226	69
Sub-Total	**78**	**59**	**5**	**14**	**78.8**	**1473**	**546**
v Other Teams							
v France 'A'	30	1	1	28	5.0	289	751
v Various Teams	71	39	3	29	57.0	1418	927
All Internationals	**455**	**176**	**14**	**265**	**40.2**	**7812**	**10013**

* 1933-77   ** 1978-91   *** 1952-82

No	Date	Opponents	Tmt		Match Venue	Result	
1	20-May-29	Spain	Int	A	Estadi Olimpic de Montjuïc, Barcelona	L	0-9
2	29-May-30	Spain	Int	H	Arena Civica, Milan	W	3-0
3	12-Feb-33	Czechoslovakia	Int	H	Arena Civica, Milan	W	7-3
4	16-Apr-33	Czechoslovakia	Int	A	Great Strahov Stadium, Prague	W	12-3
5	14-Apr-34	Catalonia	Int	A	Estadi Olimpic de Montjuïc, Barcelona	D	5-5
6	26-Dec-34	Romania	Int	H	Arena Civica, Milan	W	7-0
7	24-Mar-35	Catalonia	Int	H	Stadio Luigi Ferraris, Genova	W	5-3
8	22-Apr-35	France XV	Int	H	Stadio Nazionale del Roma, Rome	L	6-44
9	14-May-36	Germany (pOG)	FET	A	Berlin	L	8-19
10	17-May-36	Romania (pOG)	FET	N	Berlin	W	8-7
11	1-Jan-37	Germany	Int	H	Arena Civica, Milan	L	3-6
12	25-Apr-37	Romania	Int	A	Stadionul Dinamo, Bucharest	D	0-0
13	10-Oct-37	Belgium	FET	N	Stade Sébastien, Charléty, Paris	W	45-0
14	14-Oct-37	Germany	FET	N	Stade Sébastien, Charléty, Paris	W	9-7
15	17-Oct-37	France	FET	A	Parc des Princess, Paris	L	5-43
16	6-Mar-38	Germany	Int	A	Stuttgart	L	0-10
17	11-Feb-39	Germany	Int	H	Arena Civica, Milan	L	3-12
18	29-Apr-39	Romania	Int	H	Stadio Testaccio, Rome	W	3-0
19	14-Apr-40	Romania	Int	A	Stadionul Dinamo, Bucharest	L	0-3
20	5-May-40	Germany	Int	A	Stuttgart	W	4-0
21	2-May-42	Romania	Int	H	Arena Civica, Milan	W	22-3
22	28-Mar-48	France XV	Int	H	Stadio Mario Battaglini, Rovigo	L	6-39
23	23-May-48	Czechoslovakia	Int	H	Stadio Comunale Ennio Tardini, Parma	W	17-0
24	27-Mar-49	France XV	Int	A	Stade Vélodrome, Marseille	L	0-27
25	22-May-49	Czechoslovakia	Int	A	Great Strahov Stadium, Prague	L	6-14
26	6-May-51	Spain	Int	H	Stadio Flaminio, Rome	W	12-0
27	13-Apr-52	Spain	FEC	A	Estadi Olimpic de Montjuïc, Barcelona	W	6-0
28	27-Apr-52	West Germany	FEC	H	Stadio Plebiscito, Padova	W	14-6
29	17-May-52	France	FEC	H	Arena Civica, Milan	L	8-17
30	26-Apr-53	France	Int	A	Stade de Gerland, Lyon	L	8-22
31	17-May-53	West Germany	Int	A	Hanover	W	21-3
32	24-May-53	Romania	Int	A	Stadionul Republicii, Bucharest	W	16-14
33	19-Apr-54	Spain	FEC	H	Naples	W	16-6
34	24-Apr-54	France	FEC	H	Stadio Olimpico, Rome	L	12-39
35	13-Mar-55	West Germany	Int	H	Arena Civica, Milan	W	24-8
36	10-Apr-55	France	Int	A	Stade Lesdiguières, Grenoble	L	0-24
37	18-Jul-55	Spain	MED	A	Estadi Olimpic de Montjuïc, Barcelona	W	8-0
38	21-Jul-55	France XV	MED	N	Estadi Olimpic de Montjuïc, Barcelona	L	8-16
39	11-Dec-55	Czechoslovakia	Int	H	Stadio Flaminio, Rome	W	17-6
40	25-Mar-56	West Germany	Int	A	Fritz Grunebaum-Sportpark, Heidelburg	W	12-3

No	Date	Opponents	Tmt		Match Venue		Result
41	2-Apr-56	France	Int	H	Stadio Silvio Appiani, Padova	L	3-16
42	29-Apr-56	Czechoslovakia	Int	A	Great Strahov Stadium, Prague	W	19-9
43	21-Apr-57	France	Int	A	Stade Armandie, Agen	L	6-38
44	7-Dec-57	West Germany	Int	H	Arena Civica, Milan	W	8-0
45	7-Apr-58	France	Int	H	Stadio Arturo Collana, Naples	L	3-11
46	7-Dec-58	Romania	Int	H	Stadio Santa Maria Goretti, Catania	W	6-3
47	29-Mar-59	France	Int	A	Stade Marcel Saupin, Nantes	L	0-22
48	10-Apr-60	West Germany	Int	A	Hanover	W	11-5
49	17-Apr-60	France	Int	H	Stadio Omobono Tenni, Treviso	L	0-26
50	15-Jan-61	West Germany	Int	H	Stadio Comunale Beltrametti, Piacenza	W	19-0
51	2-Apr-61	France	Int	A	Stade Municipal, Chambéry	L	0-17
52	22-Apr-62	France	Int	H	Stadio Mompiano, Brescia	L	3-6
53	27-May-62	West Germany	Int	A	Berlin	W	13-11
54	10-Jun-62	Romania	Int	A	Stadionul 23 August, Bucharest	L	6-14
55	14-Apr-63	France	Int	A	Stade Lesdiguières, Grenoble	L	12-14
56	22-Mar-64	West Germany	Int	H	Stadio Renato Dall'Ara, Bologna	W	17-3
57	29-Mar-64	France	Int	H	Stadio Comunale, Ennio Tardini, Parma	L	3-12
58	18-Apr-65	France	Int	A	Stade de la Croix du Prince, Pau	L	0-21
59	8-Dec-65	Czechoslovakia	FIRA	H	Stadio Comunale Carlo Montano, Livorno	W	11-0
60	9-Apr-66	France	FIRA	H	Naples	L	0-21
61	30-Oct-66	West Germany	FIRA	A	Berlin	D	3-3
62	6-Nov-66	Romania	FIRA	H	Stadio Tommaso Fattori, L'Aquila	W	3-0
63	26-Mar-67	France	FIRA	A	Stade Félix Mayol, Toulon	L	13-60
64	7-May-67	Portugal	FIRA	H	Stadio Luigi Ferraris, Genova	W	6-3
65	14-May-67	Romania	FIRA	A	Stadionul Republicii, Bucharest	L	3-24
66	12-May-68	Portugal	Int	A	Estádio Universitário de Lisboa, Lisbon	W	17-3
67	3-Nov-68	West Germany	Int	H	Stadio Pierluigi Penzo, Venice	W	22-14
68	29-Dec-68	Yugoslavia	FIRA	H	Stadio San Dona di Piave, Venice	W	22-3
69	2-Mar-69	Bulgaria	FIRA	A	Sofia	W	17-0
70	4-May-69	Spain	FIRA	H	Stadio Tommaso Fattori, L'Aquila	W	12-5
71	10-May-69	Belgium	FIRA	A	Stade Roi Baudouin, Brussels	W	30-0
72	9-Nov-69	France XV	FIRA	H	Stadio Santa Maria Goretti, Catania	L	8-22
73	26-Apr-70	Czechoslovakia	FIRA	A	Stadion Krč, Prague	W	11-3
74	24-May-70	Madagascar	Int-T	A	Mahamasina Stadium, Antananarivo	W	17-9
75	31-May-70	Madagascar	Int-T	A	Mahamasina Stadium, Antananarivo	W	9-6
76	25-Oct-70	Romania	FIRA	H	Stadio Mario Battaglini, Rovigo	L	3-14
77	21-Feb-71	Morocco	FIRA	H	Stadio San Paulo, Naples	L	6-8
78	28-Feb-71	France XV	FIRA	A	Stade du Ray, Nice	L	13-37
79	11-Apr-71	Romania	FIRA	A	Stadionul Dinamo, Bucharest	L	6-32
80	20-Feb-72	Portugal	FIRA	H	Stadio Plebiscito, Padova	D	0-0

No	Date	Opponents	Tmt		Match Venue	Result	
81	2-Apr-72	Portugal	FIRA	A	Estádio Universitário de Lisboa, Lisbon	W	15-7
82	14-May-72	Spain	FIRA	A	Campo Ciudad Universitaria, Madrid	L	0-10
83	21-May-72	Spain	FIRA	H	Stadio Gino Pistoni-Ivrea,Turin	D	6-6
84	26-Nov-72	Yugoslavia	FIRA	H	Stadio P. Perucca, St Vincent, Aosta	W	13-12
85	25-Feb-73	Portugal	FIRA	A	Estadio Sérgio Conceição, Coimbra	L	6-9
86	16-Jun-73	Rhodesia	Int-T	A	Police Ground, Salisbury	L	4-42
87	20-Jun-73	W. Transvaal	Int-T	A	Olën Park, Potchefstroom	L	6-32
88	23-Jun-73	Border	Int-T	A	Basil Kenyon Stadium, East London	L	12-25
89	27-Jun-73	N.E Transvaal	Int-T	A	Cradock RC ,Cradock, Eastern Cape	L	12-31
90	30-Jun-73	Natal	Int-T	A	Kings Park Stadium, Durban	L	3-23
91	4-Jul-73	S.E Transvaal	Int-T	A	Johann van Riebeeck Stad, Witbank	L	12-39
92	7-Jul-73	SA Africans	Int-T	A	Boet Erasmus Stadium, Port Elizabeth	W	24-4
93	9-Jul-73	N. Free State	Int-T	A	North West Stadium, Welkom	L	11-12
94	11-Jul-73	Transvaal 'B'	Int-T	A	Ellis Park, Johannesburg	L	24-28
95	4-Nov-73	Czechoslovakia	FIRA	H	Stadio Mario Battaglini, Rovigo	D	3-3
96	11-Nov-73	Yugoslavia	FIRA	A	Stadion Maksimir, Zagreb	W	25-7
97	21-Nov-73	Australia XV	Int	H	Stadio Tommaso Fattori, L'Aquila	L	21-59
98	10-Feb-74	Portugal	FIRA	A	Estádio Universitário de Lisboa, Lisbon	W	11-3
99	15-Mar-74	Middlesex	Int-T	A	Stoop Memorial Ground, London	L	12-28
100	17-Mar-74	Sussex	Int-T	A	Withdean Stadium, Brighton	L	7-16
101	20-Mar-74	Oxfordshire	Int-T	A	Iffley Road, Oxford	L	6-30
102	5-May-74	West Germany	FIRA	H	Stadio Comunale Rho, Rho	W	16-10
103	15-May-74	SA Africans	Int	H	Stadio Mompiano, Brescia	W	25-10
104	15-Feb-75	France XV	FIRA	H	Stadio Flaminio, Rome	L	9-16
105	6-Apr-75	Spain	FIRA	A	Campo Ciudad Universitaria, Madrid	W	19-3
106	27-Apr-75	Romania	FIRA	A	Dinamo Stadion, Bucharest	D	3-3
107	10-May-75	Czechoslovakia	FIRA	H	Stadio Oreste Granillo, Reggio di Calabria	W	49-9
108	13-Sep-75	England U 23	Int	A	County Ground, Gosforth	L	13-29
109	25-Oct-75	Poland	FIRA	H	Stadio Comunale di Monigo, Treviso	W	28-13
110	23-Nov-75	Netherlands	FIRA	A	Sports Park Berg and Bos, Apeldoorn	W	24-0
111	20-Dec-75	Spain	FIRA	A	Campo Ciudad Universitaria, Madrid	W	19-6
112	7-Feb-76	France XV	FIRA	H	Arena Civica, Milan	L	11-23
113	24-Apr-76	Romania	FIRA	H	Stadio Comunale, Ennio Tardini, Parma	W	13-12
114	21-Oct-76	Japan	Int	H	Stadio Silvio Appiani, Padova	W	25-3
115	4-Nov-76	Australia XV	Int	H	Arena Civica, Milan	L	15-16
116	27-Nov-76	Spain	FIRA	H	Stadio Flaminio, Rome	W	17-4
117	6-Feb-77	France XV	FIRA	A	Stade Lesdiguières, Grenoble	L	3-10
118	6-Mar-77	Morocco	FIRA	A	COC Stadium, Casablanca	L	9-10
119	2-Apr-77	Poland	FIRA	H	Stadio Santa Maria Goretti, Catania	W	29-3
120	1-May-77	Romania	FIRA	A	Stadionul Dinamo, Bucharest	L	0-69

No	Date	Opponents	Tmt	Match Venue	Result	
121	23-Oct-77	Poland	FIRA	A	Skra Stadium, Warsaw	L 6-12
122	29-Oct-77	Czechoslovakia	FIRA	A	Stadion Krč, Prague	W 10-4
123	26-Nov-77	Romania	FIRA	H	Stadio Oreste Granillo, Reggio di Calabria	D 10-10
124	17-Dec-77	Spain	FIRA	A	Campo Ciudad Universitaria, Madrid	L 3-10
125	4-Feb-78	France XV	FIRA	H	Stadio Tommaso Fattori, L'Aquila	L 9-31
126	24-Oct-78	Argentina	Int	H	Stadio Mario Battaglini, Rovigo	W 19-6
127	18-Nov-78	USSR	FIRA	H	Stadio Flaminio, Rome	L 9-11
128	17-Dec-78	Spain	FIRA	H	Stadio Comunale di Monigo, Treviso	W 35-3
129	18-Feb-79	France XV	FIRA	H	Stadio Plebiscito, Padova	L 9-15
130	14-Apr-79	Poland	FIRA	H	Stadio Tommaso Fattori, L'Aquila	W 18-3
131	22-Apr-79	Romania	FIRA	A	Stadionul Parcul Copilului, Bucharest	L 0-44
132	16-May-79	England U 23	Int	H	Stadio Mompiano, Brescia	D 6-6
133	18-Sep-79	Spain	MED	N	Makarska Stadium, Makaraska, Yugoslavia	W 16-9
134	20-Sep-79	Morocco	MED	N	Makarska Stadium, Makaraska, Yugoslavia	W 10-7
135	22-Sep-79	France XV	MED	N	Makarska Stadium, Makaraska, Yugoslavia	L 12-38
136	30-Sep-79	Poland	FIRA	A	Sochaczew, Poland	W 13-3
137	28-Oct-79	USSR	FIRA	A	Fili Stadion, Moscow	L 0-9
138	28-Nov-79	NZ XV	Int	H	Stadio Mario Battaglini, Rovigo	L 12-18
139	22-Dec-79	Morocco	FIRA	H	Stadio Santa Colomba, Benevento	W 34-6
140	17-Feb-80	France XV	FIRA	A	Stade Marcel Michelin, Clermont Ferrand	L 9-46
141	13-Apr-80	Romania	FIRA	H	Stadio Tommaso Fattori, L'Aquila	W 24-17
142	14-Jun-80	Fiji	Int-T	A	National Stadium, Suva	L 3-16
143	5-Jul-80	Jnr All Blacks	Int-T	A	Eden Park, Auckland	L 13-30
144	6-Jul-80	Cook Islands	Int-T	A	National Stadium, Avarua, Rarotonga	L 6-15
145	5-Oct-80	Poland	FIRA	H	Stadio Mario Battaglini, Rovigo	W 37-12
146	2-Nov-80	U S S R	FIRA	H	Stadio Mario Battaglini, Rovigo	L 3-4
147	21-Dec-80	Spain	FIRA	A	Campo Ciudad Universitaria, Madrid	W 18-13
148	8-Mar-81	France XV	FIRA	H	Stadio Mario Battaglini, Rovigo	L 9-17
149	12-Apr-81	Romania	FIRA	A	Stadionul Municipal, Brăilla	L 9-35
150	25-Oct-81	U S S R	FIRA	A	Nauka Stadion, Moscow	D 12-12
151	29-Nov-81	West Germany	FIRA	H	Stadio Mario Battaglini, Rovigo	W 23-0
152	21-Feb-82	France XV	FIRA	A	Stade Albert Domec, Carcassonne	L 19-25
153	11-Apr-82	Romania	FIRA	H	Stadio Mario Battaglini, Rovigo	W 21-15
154	22-May-82	England U 23	Int	H	Stadio Plebiscito, Padova	W 12-7
155	7-Nov-82	West Germany	FIRA	A	Hanover	W 23-3
156	19-Dec-82	Morocco	FIRA	A	COC Stadium, Casablanca	W 13-3
157	6-Feb-83	France XV	FIRA	H	Stadio Mario Battaglini, Rovigo	D 6-6
158	10-Apr-83	Romania	FIRA	A	Stadionul Municipal Gloria, Buzău	L 6-13
159	22-May-83	U S S R	FIRA	H	Stadio Santa Maria Goretti, Catania	W 12-10
160	25-Jun-83	Canada	Int-T	A	Swanguard Stadium, Burnaby Lake, BC	L 13-19

No	Date	Opponents	Tmt		Match Venue	Result	
161	1-Jul-83	Canada	Int-T	A	Varsity Stadium, Stanley Park, Toronto	W	37-9
162	7-Sep-83	Spain	MED	N	COC Stadium, Casablanca	W	27-9
163	10-Sep-83	Morocco	MED	A	COC Stadium, Casablanca	W	15-9
164	13-Sep-83	France XV	MED	N	COC Stadium, Casablanca	L	12-26
165	22-Oct-83	Australia	Int	H	Stadio Mario Battaglini, Rovigo	L	7-29
166	30-Oct-83	USSR	FIRA	A	Spartak Stadium, Kiev	L	7-16
167	19-Feb-84	France XV	FIRA	A	Stade Municipal, Chalon-sur-Saone	L	16-38
168	18-Mar-84	Morocco	FIRA	H	Stadio Comunale Beltrametti, Piacenza	W	27-0
169	22-Apr-84	Romania	FIRA	H	Stadio Tommaso Fattori, L'Aquila	W	12-6
170	20-Oct-84	Tunisia	FIRA	A	Stade Mustapha Ben Jannet, Monastir	W	20-6
171	18-Nov-84	USSR	FIRA	H	Stadio Tommaso Fattori, L'Aquila	W	13-12
172	3-Mar-85	France XV	FIRA	H	Stadio Comunale di Monigo, Treviso	L	9-22
173	14-Apr-85	Romania	FIRA	A	Stadionul Municipal, Brasov	L	6-7
174	17-Apr-85	England B	Int	A	Twickenham, London	L	9-21
175	18-May-85	Spain	FIRA	H	Stadio Danilo Martelli, Mantova	W	22-13
176	22-Jun-85	Zimbabwe	Int-T	A	Hartsfield Rugby Ground, Bulawayo	W	25-6
177	30-Jun-85	Zimbabwe	Int-T	A	Police Ground, Harare	W	12-10
178	10-Nov-85	USSR	FIRA	A	Fili Stadion, Moscow	L	13-15
179	7-Dec-85	Romania	FIRA	H	Stadio Tommaso Fattori, L'Aquila	W	19-3
180	8-Feb-86	Tunisia	FIRA	H	Stadio Mario Battaglini, Rovigo	W	18-4
181	15-Feb-86	France XV	FIRA	A	Union Sportif Annecy Rugby, Annecy	L	0-18
182	13-Apr-86	Portugal	FIRA	H	Stadio Jesi Arriva, Jesi	W	26-24
183	10-May-86	England XV	Int	H	Stadio Olimpico, Rome	D	15-15
184	1-Jun-86	Australia	Int-T	A	Ballymore Oval, Brisbane	L	18-39
185	18-Oct-86	Tunisia	FIRA	A	Stade Africain de Menzel, Bourghiba	W	22-9
186	16-Nov-86	USSR	FIRA	H	Stadio Luigi Ferraris, Genova	L	14-16
187	18-Jan-87	Portugal	FIRA	A	Estádio Universitário de Lisboa, Lisbon	W	41-3
188	22-Feb-87	France XV	FIRA	H	Stadio Plebiscito, Padova	L	6-22
189	12-Apr-87	Romania	FIRA	A	Stadionul 1 Mai, Constanta	L	3-9
190	22-May-87	New Zealand	WCp	A	Eden Park, Auckland	L	6-70
191	28-May-87	Argentina	WCp	N	Lancaster Park Oval, Christchurch	L	16-25
192	31-May-87	Fiji	WCp	A	Carisbrook, Dunedin	W	18-15
193	7-Nov-87	USSR	FIRA	A	Stadionul Republican Chişinău, Moldova	L	9-12
194	5-Dec-87	Spain	FIRA	A	Estadi Olímpic Lluís Companys, Barcelona	W	13-0
195	7-Feb-88	France XV	FIRA	A	Stade Louis II, Monte Carlo	L	9-19
196	2-Apr-88	Romania	FIRA	H	Stadio San Siro, Milan	L	3-12
197	5-Nov-88	USSR	FIRA	H	Stadio Comunale di Monigo, Treviso	L	12-18
198	3-Dec-88	Australia	Int	H	Stadio Flaminio, Rome	L	6-55
199	31-Dec-88	Ireland	Int	A	Lansdowne Road, Dublin	L	15-31
200	19-Feb-89	France XV	FIRA	H	Stadio Mompiano, Brescia	L	12-40

No	Date	Opponents	Tmt	Match Venue	Result
201	15-Apr-89	Romania	FIRA	A Stadionul Dinamo, Bucharest	L 4-28
202	2-Jun-89	Spain	FIRA	H Stadio Tommaso Fattori, L'Aquila	W 33-19
203	24-Jun-89	Argentina	Int-T	A Vélez Sarsfield Stadium, Buenos Aires	L 16-21
204	30-Sep-89	Zimbabwe	Int	H Stadio Comunale di Monigo, Treviso	W 33-9
205	5-Nov-89	USSR	FIRA	A Fili Stadion, Moscow	L 12-15
206	18-Feb-90	France XV	FIRA	A Stade Municipal, Albi	L 12-22
207	7-Apr-90	Poland	FIRA	H Naples	W 34-3
208	14-Apr-90	Romania	FIRA	H Frascati Rugby Stadium, Rome	L 9-16
209	30-Sep-90	Spain (WCQ)	FIRA	H Stadio Mario Battaglini, Rovigo	W 30-6
210	3-Oct-90	Netherlands	WCQ	H Stadio Comunale di Monigo, Treviso	W 24-11
211	7-Oct-90	Romania	WCQ	H Stadio Plebiscito, Padova	W 29-21
212	24-Nov-90	USSR	FIRA	H Stadio Mario Battaglini, Rovigo	W 34-12
213	2-Mar-91	France XV	FIRA	H Stadio Flaminio, Rome	L 9-15
214	21-Apr-91	Romania	FIRA	A Stadionul Dinamo, Bucharest	W 21-18
215	15-Jun-91	Namibia	Int-T	A South West Stadium, Windhoek	L 7-17
216	22-Jun-91	Namibia	Int-T	A South West Stadium, Windhoek	L 19-33
217	5-Oct-91	United States	WCp	N Cross Green, Otley, Yorkshire	W 30-9
218	8-Oct-91	England	WCP	A Twickenham, London	L 6-36
219	13-Oct-91	New Zealand	WCp	N Welford Road, Leicester	L 21-31
220	3-Nov-91	CIS	FIRA	A Fili Stadion, Moscow	W 21-3
221	9-Feb-92	Spain	FIRA	A Campo Ciudad Universitaria, Madrid	W 22-21
222	16-Feb-92	France Espoirs	FIRA	A Stade Maurice Trélut, Tarbes	L 18-21
223	18-Apr-92	Romania	FIRA	H Stadio Mario Battaglini, Rovigo	W 39-13
224	1-Oct-92	Romania	FIRA	H Stadio Flaminio, Rome	W 22-3
225	19-Dec-92	Scotland A	Int	A The Greenyards, Melrose	L 17-22
226	14-Feb-93	Spain	FIRA	A Campo Ciudad Universitaria, Madrid	W 52-0
227	20-Feb-93	France XV	Int	H Stadio Comunale di Monigo, Treviso	L 12-14
228	17-Apr-93	Portugal	FIRA	A Estádio Universitário de Coimbra, Còimbra	W 33-11
229	17-Jun-93	Croatia	MED	N Stade Aimé Giral, Perpignan	W 76-11
230	19-Jun-93	Morocco	MED	N Stade Albert Domec, Carcassonne	W 70-9
231	21-Jun-93	Spain	MED	N Stade Aimé Giral, Perpignan	W 38-6
232	25-Jun-93	France XV	MED	A Stade Méditerranée, Béziers	L 6-31
233	6-Nov-93	Russia	FIRA	A Fili Stadion, Moscow	W 30-19
234	11-Nov-93	France XV	FIRA	H Stadio Comunale di Monigo, Treviso	W 16-9
235	18-Dec-93	Scotland A	Int	H Stadio Mario Battaglini, Rovigo	W 18-15
236	7-May-94	Spain	FIRA	H Stadio Comunale Sergio Lanfrachi, Parma	W 62-15
237	14-May-94	Romania	FIRA	A Stadionul Dinamo, Bucharest	L 12-26
238	18-May-94	Czech Republic	WCQ	H Stadio Luigi Zaffanella, Viadana	W 104-8
239	21-May-94	Netherlands	WCQ	H Centro Sportivo San Michele, Calvisano	W 63-9
240	18-Jun-94	Australia	Int-T	A Ballymore Oval, Brisbane	L 20-23

No	Date	Opponents	Tmt		Match Venue	Result	
241	25-Jun-94	Australia	Int-T	A	Olympic Park Stadium, Melbourne	L	7-20
242	1-Oct-94	Romania	WCQ	H	Stadio Santa Maria Goretti, Catania	W	24-6
243	12-Oct-94	Wales	WCQ	A	National Stadium, Cardiff	L	19-29
244	4-Dec-94	France XV	Int	A	Stade Bourillot, Dijon	L	9-14
245	7-Jan-95	Scotland A	Int	A	McDiarmid Park, Perth	L	16-18
246	6-May-95	Ireland	Int	H	Stadio Comunale di Monigo, Treviso	W	22-12
247	27-May-95	Western Samoa	WCp	N	Basil Kenyon Stadium, East London	L	18-42
248	31-May-95	England	WCp	N	Kings Park Stadium, Durban	L	20-27
249	4-Jun-95	Argentina	WCp	N	Basil Kenyon Stadium, East London	W	31-25
250	14-Oct-95	France	LTC	N	Ferro Carril Oeste Stadium, B Aires	L	22-34
251	17-Oct-95	Argentina	LTC	A	Estadio Monumental José Fierro, Tucumán	L	6-26
252	21-Oct-95	Romania LTC	FIRA	N	Ferro Carril Oeste Stadium, B Aires	W	40-3
253	28-Oct-95	New Zealand	Int	H	Stadio Renato Dall'Ara, Bologna	L	6-70
254	12-Nov-95	South Africa	Int	H	Stadio Olimpico, Rome	L	21-40
255	16-Jan-96	Wales	Int	A	National Stadium, Cardiff	L	26-31
256	2-Mar-96	Portugal	FIRA	A	Estádio Universitário de Lisboa, Lisbon	W	64-3
257	5-Oct-96	Wales	Int	H	Stadio Olimpico, Rome	L	22-31
258	23-Oct-96	Australia	Int	H	Stadio Plebiscito, Padova	L	18-40
259	23-Nov-96	England	Int	A	Twickenham, London	L	21-54
260	14-Dec-96	Scotland	Int	A	Murrayfield, Edinburgh	L	22-29
261	4-Jan-97	Ireland	Int	A	Lansdowne Road, Dublin	W	37-29
262	22-Mar-97	France	FIRA	A	Stade Lesdiguières, Grenoble	W	40-32
263	18-Oct-97	France	LTC	A	Stade Jacques Fouroux, Auch	L	19-30
264	22-Oct-97	Argentina	LTC	N	Stade Antoine Béguère, Lourdes	D	18-18
265	26-Oct-97	Romania	LTC	N	Stade Maurice Trélut, Tarbes	W	55-32
266	8-Nov-97	South Africa	Int	H	Stadio Renato Dall'Ara, Bologna	L	31-62
267	20-Dec-97	Ireland	Int	H	Stadio Renato Dall'Ara, Bologna	W	37-22
268	24-Jan-98	Scotland	Int	H	Stadio Comunale di Monigo, Treviso	W	25-21
269	7-Feb-98	Wales	Int	A	Stradey Park, Llanelli	L	20-23
270	18-Apr-98	Russia	WCQ	A	Central Stadium, Krasnoyarsk	W	48-18
271	7-Nov-98	Argentina	Int	H	Stadio Comunale Beltrametti, Piacenza	W	23-19
272	18-Nov-98	Netherlands	WCQ	N	McAlpine Stadium, Huddersfield	W	67-7
273	22-Nov-98	England	WCQ	A	McAlpine Stadium, Huddersfield	L	15-23
274	30-Jan-99	France XV	Int	H	Stadio Luigi Ferraris, Genova	L	24-49
275	6-Mar-99	Scotland	Int	A	Murrayfield, Edinburgh	L	12-30
276	20-Mar-99	Wales	Int	H	Stadio Comunale di Monigo, Treviso	L	21-60
277	10-Apr-99	Ireland	Int	A	Lansdowne Road, Dublin	L	30-39
278	12-Jun-99	South Africa	Int-T	A	Telkom Park Stadium, Port Elizabeth	L	3-74
279	19-Jun-99	South Africa	Int-T	A	Kings Park Stadium, Durban	L	0-101
280	22-Aug-99	Uruguay	Int	H	Stadio Tommaso Fattori, L'Aquila	W	49-17

No	Date	Opponents	Tmt		Match Venue		Result
281	26-Aug-99	Spain	Int	H	Stadio Tommaso Fattori, L'Aquila	W	42-11
282	28-Aug-99	Fiji	Int	H	Stadio Tommaso Fattori, L'Aquila	L	32-50
283	2-Oct-99	England	WCp	A	Twickenham, London	L	7-67
284	10-Oct-99	Tonga	WCp	N	Welford Road, Leicester	L	25-28
285	14-Oct-99	New Zealand	WCp	N	McAlpine Stadium, Huddersfield	L	3-101
286	5-Feb-00	Scotland	6N	H	Stadio Flaminio, Rome	W	34-20
287	19-Feb-00	Wales	6N	A	Millennium Stadium, Cardiff	L	16-47
288	4-Mar-00	Ireland	6N	A	Lansdowne Road, Dublin	L	13-60
289	18-Mar-00	England	6N	H	Stadio Flaminio, Rome	L	12-59
290	1-Apr-00	France	6N	A	Stade de France, Paris	L	31-42
291	8-Jul-00	Samoa	Int-T	A	Apia Park, Apia	L	24-43
292	15-Jul-00	Fiji	Int-T	A	Churchill Park, Lautoka	L	9-43
293	11-Nov-00	Canada	Int	H	Stadio Mario Battaglini, Rovigo	L	17-22
294	18-Nov-00	Romania	Int	H	Stadio Santa Columba, Benevento	W	37-17
295	25-Nov-00	New Zealand	Int	H	Stadio Luigi Ferraris, Genova	L	19-56
296	3-Feb-01	Ireland	6N	H	Stadio Flaminio, Rome	L	22-41
297	17-Feb-01	England	6N	A	Twickenham, London	L	23-80
298	3-Mar-01	France	6N	H	Stadio Flaminio, Rome	L	19-30
299	17-Mar-01	Scotland	6N	A	Murrayfield, Edinburgh	L	19-23
300	8-Apr-01	Wales	6N	H	Stadio Flaminio, Rome	L	23-33
301	23-Jun-01	Namibia	Int-T	A	South West Stadium, Windhoek	W	49-24
302	30-Jun-01	South Africa	Int-T	A	Telkom Park Stadium, Port Elizabeth	L	14-60
303	7-Jul-01	Uruguay	Int-T	A	Estadio Gran Parque Central, Montevideo	W	14-3
304	14-Jul-01	Argentina	Int-T	A	Ferro Carril Oeste Stadium, B Aires	L	17-38
305	10-Nov-01	Fiji	Int	H	Stadio Comunale di Monigo, Treviso	W	66-10
306	17-Nov-01	South Africa	Int	H	Stadio Luigi Ferraris, Genova	L	26-54
307	24-Nov-01	Samoa	Int	H	Stadio Tommaso Fattori, L'Aquila	L	9-17
308	2-Feb-02	France	6N	A	Stade de France, Paris	L	12-33
309	16-Feb-02	Scotland	6N	H	Stadio Flaminio, Rome	L	12-29
310	2-Mar-02	Wales	6N	A	Millennium Stadium, Cardiff	L	20-44
311	23-Mar-02	Ireland	6N	A	Lansdowne Road, Dublin	L	17-32
312	7-Apr-02	England	6N	H	Stadio Flaminio, Rome	L	9-45
313	8-Jun-02	New Zealand	Int-T	A	Waikato Stadium, Hamilton	L	10-64
314	22-Sep-02	Spain	WCQ	A	Campo de Pepe Rojo, Valladolid		50-3
315	28-Sep-02	Romania	WCQ	H	Stadio Comunale Sergio Lanfrachi, Parma	W	25-17
316	16-Nov-02	Argentina	Int	H	Stadio Flaminio, Rome	L	6-36
317	23-Nov-02	Australia	Int	H	Stadio Luigi Ferraris, Genova	L	3-34
318	15-Feb-03	Wales	6N	H	Stadio Flaminio, Rome	W	30-22
319	22-Feb-03	Ireland	6N	H	Stadio Flaminio, Rome	L	13-37
320	9-Mar-03	England	6N	A	Twickenham, London	L	5-40

No	Date	Opponents	Tmt		Match Venue		Result	
321	23-Mar-03	France	6N	H	Stadio Flaminio, Rome	L	27-53
322	29-Mar-03	Scotland	6N	A	Murrayfield, Edinburgh	L	25-33
323	23-Aug-03	Scotland	Int	A	Murrayfield, Edinburgh	L	15-47
324	30-Aug-03	Ireland	Int	A	Thomond Park, Limerick	L	6-61
325	6-Sep-03	Georgia	Int	H	Stadio Comunale Censin Bosia, Asti	W	31-22
326	11-Oct-03	New Zealand	WCp	N	Telstra Dome, Melbourne	L	7-70
327	15-Oct-03	Tonga	WCp	N	Canberra Stadium, Canberra	W	36-12
328	21-Oct-03	Canada	WCp	N	Canberra Stadium, Canberra	W	19-14
329	25-Oct-03	Wales	WCp	N	Canberra Stadium, Canberra	L	15-27
330	15-Feb-04	England	6N	H	Stadio Flaminio, Rome	L	9-50
331	21-Feb-04	France	6N	A	Stade de France, Paris	L	0-25
332	6-Mar-04	Scotland	6N	H	Stadio Flaminio, Rome	W	20-14
333	20-Mar-04	Ireland	6N	A	Lansdowne Road, Dublin	L	3-19
334	27-Mar-04	Wales	6N	A	Millennium Stadium, Cardiff	L	10-44
335	26-Jun-04	Romania	Int	A	Lia Manoliu Stadium, Bucharest	L	24-25
336	4-Jul-04	Japan	Int-T	A	Prince Chichibu Memorial Ground, Tokyo	W	32-19
337	6-Nov-04	Canada	Int	H	Stadio Tommaso Fattori, L'Aquila	W	51-6
338	13-Nov-04	New Zealand	Int	H	Stadio Flaminio, Rome	L	10-59
339	27-Nov-04	United States	Int	H	Stadio Lamarmora, Biella-in-Piedmont	W	43-25
340	6-Feb-05	Ireland	6N	H	Stadio Flaminio, Rome	L	17-28
341	12-Feb-05	Wales	6N	H	Stadio Flaminio, Rome	L	8-38
342	26-Feb-05	Scotland	6N	A	Murrayfield, Edinburgh	L	10-18
343	12-Mar-05	England	6N	A	Twickenham, London	L	7-39
344	19-Mar-05	France	6N	H	Stadio Flaminio, Rome	L	13-56
345	11-Jun-05	Argentina	Int-T	A	Estadio Padre Ernesto Martearena, Salta	L	21-35
346	17-Jun-05	Argentina	Int-T	A	Estadio Olimpico Château Carreras, Córdoba	W	30-29
347	25-Jun-05	Australia	Int-T	A	Telstra Dome, Melbourne	L	21-69
348	12-Nov-05	Tonga	Int	H	Stadio Lungobisenzio, Prato	W	48-0
349	19-Nov-05	Argentina	Int	H	Stadio Luigi Ferraris, Genova	L	22-39
350	26-Nov-05	Fiji	Int	H	Stadio Brianteo, Monza, Milan	W	23-8
351	4-Feb-06	Ireland	6N	A	Lansdowne Road, Dublin	L	16-26
352	11-Feb-06	England	6N	H	Stadio Flaminio, Rome	L	16-31
353	25-Feb-06	France	6N	A	Stade de France, Paris	L	12-37
354	11-Mar-06	Wales	6N	A	Millennium Stadium, Cardiff	D	18-18
355	18-Mar-06	Scotland	6N	H	Stadio Flaminio, Rome	L	10-13
356	11-Jun-06	Japan	Int-T	A	Prince Chichibu Memorial Ground, Tokyo	W	52-6
357	17-Jun-06	Fiji	Int-T	A	Churchill Park, Lautoka	L	18-29
358	7-Oct-06	Portugal	WCQ	H	Stadio Tommaso Fattori, L'Aquila	W	83-0
359	14-Oct-06	Russia	WCQ	A	Slava Stadion, Moscow	W	67-7
360	11-Nov-06	Australia	Int	H	Stadio Flaminio, Rome	L	18-25

No	Date	Opponents	Tmt		Match Venue		Result
361	18-Nov-06	Argentina	Int	H	Stadio Flaminio, Rome	L	16-23
362	25-Nov-06	Canada	Int	H	Stadio Comprensoriale, Fontanafredda	W	41-6
363	3-Feb-07	France	6N-GG	H	Stadio Flaminio, Rome	L	3-39
364	10-Feb-07	England	6N	A	Twickenham, London	L	7-20
365	24-Feb-07	Scotland	6N	A	Murrayfield, Edinburgh	W	37-17
366	10-Mar-07	Wales	6N	H	Stadio Flaminio, Rome	W	23-20
367	17-Mar-07	Ireland	6N	H	Stadio Flaminio, Rome	L	24-51
368	2-Jun-07	Uruguay	Int-T	A	Estadio Gran Parque Central, Montevideo	W	29-5
369	9-Jun-07	Argentina	Int-T	A	Estadio Malvinas Argentinas, Mendoza	L	6-24
370	18-Aug-07	Japan	Int	H	Stadio P. Perucca, St Vincent, Aosta	W	36-12
371	24-Aug-07	Ireland	Int	A	Ravenhill, Belfast	L	20-23
372	8-Sep-07	New Zealand	WCp	N	Stade Vélodrome, Marseille	L	14-76
373	12-Sep-07	Romania	WCp	N	Stade Vélodrome, Marseille	W	24-18
374	19-Sep-07	Portugal	WCp	N	Parc des Princess, Paris	W	31-5
375	29-Sep-07	Scotland	WCp	N	Stade Geoffroy-Guichard, Saint Étienne	L	16-18
376	2-Feb-08	Ireland	6N	A	Croke Park, Dublin	L	11-16
377	10-Feb-08	England	6N	H	Stadio Flaminio, Rome	L	19-23
378	23-Feb-08	Wales	6N	A	Millennium Stadium, Cardiff	L	8-47
379	9-Mar-08	France	6N-GG	A	Stade de France, Paris	L	13-25
380	15-Mar-08	Scotland	6N	H	Stadio Flaminio, Rome	W	23-20
381	21-Jun-08	South Africa	Int-T	A	Newlands Stadium, Cape Town	L	0-26
382	28-Jun-08	Argentina	Int-T	A	Estadio Olimpico Château Carreras, Córdoba	W	13-12
383	8-Nov-08	Australia	Int	H	Stadio Euganeo, Padova	L	20-30
384	15-Nov-08	Argentina	Int	H	Stadio Olimpico di Torino, Turin	L	14-22
385	22-Nov-08	Pacific Islands	Int	H	Stadio Giglio, Reggio Emilia	L	17-25
386	7-Feb-09	England	6N	A	Twickenham, London	L	11-36
387	15-Feb-09	Ireland	6N	H	Stadio Flaminio, Rome	L	9-38
388	28-Feb-09	Scotland	6N	A	Murrayfield, Edinburgh	L	6-26
389	14-Mar-09	Wales	6N	H	Stadio Flaminio, Rome	L	15-20
390	21-Mar-09	France	6N-GG	H	Stadio Flaminio, Rome	L	8-50
391	13-Jun-09	Australia	Int-T	A	Canberra Stadium, Canberrra	L	8-31
392	20-Jun-09	Australia	Int-T	A	Etihad Stadium, Docklands, Melbourne	L	12-34
393	27-Jun-09	New Zealand	Int-T	A	AMI Stadium, Christchurch	L	6-27
394	14-Nov-09	New Zealand	Int	H	Stadio San Siro, Milan	L	6-20
395	21-Nov-09	South Africa	Int	H	Stadio Friuli, Udine	L	10-32
396	28-Nov-09	Samoa	Int	H	Stadio Cino e Lillo del Duca, Ascoli Piceno	W	24-6
397	6-Feb-10	Ireland	6N	A	Croke Park, Dublin	L	11-29
398	14-Feb-10	England	6N	H	Stadio Flaminio, Rome	L	12-17
399	27-Feb-10	Scotland	6N	H	Stadio Flaminio, Rome	W	16-12
400	14-Mar-10	France	6N-GG	A	Stade de France, Paris	L	20-46

No	Date	Opponents	Tmt		Match Venue	Result	
401	20-Mar-10	Wales	6N	A	Millennium Stadium, Cardiff	L	10-33
402	19-Jun-10	South Africa	Int-T	A	Johann van Riebeeck Stadium, Witbank	L	13-29
403	26-Jun-10	South Africa	Int-T	A	Buffalo City Stadium, East London	L	11-55
404	13-Nov-10	Argentina	Int	H	Stadio Marc'Antonio Bentegodi, Verona	L	16-22
405	20-Nov-10	Australia	Int	H	Stadio Artemio Franchi, Florence	L	14-32
406	27-Nov-10	Fiji	Int	H	Stadio Alberto Braglia, Modena	W	24-16
407	5-Feb-11	Ireland	6N	H	Stadio Flaminio, Rome	L	11-13
408	12-Feb-11	England	6N	A	Twickenham, London	L	13-59
409	26-Feb-11	Wales	6N	H	Stadio Flaminio, Rome	L	16-24
410	12-Mar-11	France	6N-GG	H	Stadio Flaminio, Rome	W	22-21
411	19-Mar-11	Scotland	6N	A	Murrayfield, Edinburgh	L	8-21
412	13-Aug-11	Japan	Int	H	Stadio Dino Manuzzi, Cesana, Trieste	W	31-24
413	20-Aug-11	Scotland	Int	A	Murrayfield, Edinburgh	L	12-23
414	11-Sep-11	Australia	WCp	N	North Harbour Stadium, Albany	L	6-32
415	20-Sep-11	Russia	WCp	N	Trafalgar Park, Nelson	W	53-17
416	27-Sep-11	United States	WCp	N	Trafalgar Park, Nelson	W	27-10
417	2-Oct-11	Ireland	WCp	N	Otago Stadium, Dunedin	L	6-36
418	4-Feb-12	France	6N-GG	A	Stade de France, Paris	L	12-30
419	11-Feb-12	England	6N	H	Stadio Olimpico, Rome	L	15-19
420	25-Feb-12	Ireland	6N	A	Aviva Stadium, Dublin	L	10-42
421	10-Mar-12	Wales	6N	A	Millennium Stadium, Cardiff	L	3-24
422	17-Mar-12	Scotland	6N	H	Stadio Olimpico, Rome	W	13-6
423	9-Jun-12	Argentina	Int-T	A	Estadio S. Juan del Bicentenario, San Juan	L	22-37
424	15-Jun-12	Canada	Int-T	A	BMO Stadium, Toronto	W	25-16
425	23-Jun-12	United States	Int-T	A	BBVA Compass Stadium, Houston	W	30-10
426	10-Nov-12	Tonga	Int-T	H	Stadio Mario Rigamonti, Brescia	W	28-23
427	17-Nov-12	New Zealand	Int-T	H	Stadio Olimpico, Rome	L	10-42
428	24-Nov-12	Australia	Int	H	Stadio Artemio Franchi, Florence	L	19-22
429	3-Feb-13	France	6N-GG	H	Stadio Olimpico, Rome	W	23-18
430	9-Feb-13	Scotland	6N	A	Murrayfield, Edinburgh	L	10-34
431	23-Feb-13	Wales	6N	H	Stadio Olimpico, Rome	L	9-26
432	10-Mar-13	England	6N	A	Twickenham, London	L	11-18
433	16-Mar-13	Ireland	6N	H	Stadio Olimpico, Rome	W	22-15
434	8-Jun-13	South Africa	quad	A	Kings Park Stadium, Durban	L	10-44
435	15-Jun-13	Samoa	quad	N	Mbombela Stadium, Nelspruit	L	10-39
436	22-Jun-13	Scotland	quad	N	Loftus Versfeld Stadium, Pretoria	L	29-30
437	9-Nov-13	Australia	Int	H	Stadio Olimpico di Torino, Turin	L	20-50
438	16-Nov-13	Fiji	Int	H	Stadio Giovanni Zini, Cremona	W	37-31
439	23-Nov-13	Argentina	Int	A	Stadio Olimpico, Rome	L	14-19
440	1-Feb-14	Wales	6N	A	Millennium Stadium, Cardiff	L	15-23

No	Date	Opponents	Tmt		Match Venue	Result	
441	9-Feb-14	France	6N-GG	A	Stade de France, Paris	L	10-30
442	22-Feb-14	Scotland	6N	H	Stadio Olimpico, Rome	L	20-21
443	8-Mar-14	Ireland	6N	A	Aviva Stadium, Dublin	L	7-46
444	15-Mar-14	England	6N	H	Stadio Olimpico, Rome	L	11-52
445	7-Jun-14	Fiji	Int-T	A	National Stadium, Suva	L	14-25
446	14-Jun-14	Samoa	Int-T	A	Apia Park, Apia	L	0-15
447	21-Jun-14	Japan	Int-T	A	Prince Chichibu Memorial Ground, Tokyo	L	23-26
448	8-Nov-14	Samoa	Int	H	Stadio Cino el Lillo del Duca, Ascoli Piceno	W	24-13
449	14-Nov-14	Argentina	Int	H	Stadio Luigi Ferraris, Genova	L	18-20
450	22-Nov-14	South Africa	Int	H	Stadio Euganeo, Padova	L	6-22
451	7-Feb-15	Ireland	6N	H	Stadio Olimpico, Rome	L	3-26
452	14-Feb-15	England	6N	A	Twickenham, London	L	17-47
453	28-Feb-15	Scotland	6N	A	Murrayfield, Edinburgh	W	22-19
454	15-Mar-15	France	6N-GG	H	Stadio Olimpico, Rome	L	0-29
455	28-Mar-15	Wales	6N	H	Stadio Olimpico, Rome	L	20-61

NEW ZEALAND

The New Zealand Rugby Football Union was founded in Wellington on 16 April 1892, at a meeting of the ten Provincial Unions, which had been formed over the previous twelve years. Despite the fact that New Zealand representative sides had toured Australia in 1884, 1893 and 1897, it was only on the 1903 tour that New Zealand actually played their first International against Australia in Sydney, which they won by 22 points to 3. In 1904, New Zealand defeated the visiting Great Britain team by 9 points to 3 and four years later they won a three-match series against the touring Anglo-Welsh team. It was during their first overseas tour of Britain, Ireland, France and the USA, in 1905-06, that the team became known as the All Blacks, and they certainly made an impression: they won thirty-four out of thirty-five games during that first tour, losing only to Wales by a try to nil. There were more triumphs to come in the following years, and on the 1924-25 Northern Hemisphere tour they won all thirty-two games, including the four International matches. Facing up to their Antipodean neighbours on twelve occasions between 1907 and 1914, New Zealand lost to the Australian team just twice.

After the First World War, in 1921, the All Blacks faced South Africa for the first time. The three-match series, played in New Zealand, was halved when the third International ended in a draw. Then, in 1928, it was South Africa's turn to host New Zealand and that four-match series was also shared, with two wins apiece. A 3-1 series win in 1930, against the touring Lions, was followed by a 2-1 series win in Australia in 1932. The team began to slip a little on the 1935-36 tour of the Northern Hemisphere when they won just two of the four Tests played against the Home Nations (losing to both Wales and England). The All Blacks also lost a home Test series 2-1 to the Springboks in 1937, but recovered to win the 1938 series in Australia, 3-0. They went on to beat the Wallabies four times in a row after the Second World War, only to suffer six successive defeats in 1949, when they lost two home Internationals to Australia and four Internationals on tour to South Africa.

The next decade was far more successful for the All Blacks, since they won both the 1950 and the 1959 Test series against the touring Lions, and also the 1956 series against the touring Springboks. In all, they lost a mere seven matches out of thirty during those ten years, two of which were against Wales and France on the 1953-54 Northern Hemisphere tour. The 1960s proved to be an amazing decade for New Zealand: in the period 1961 to 1969 they lost just two Internationals out of a total of thirty-eight played, and between 1961 and 1964 they achieved a run of seventeen games without defeat. Then from September 1965 to the end of 1969, the All Blacks remarkably topped their previous record with a sequence of seventeen wins in a row.

The start of the 1970s saw a dramatic reversal of form for the All Blacks when they lost an away series to South Africa 3-1, followed by a historic first-ever home series loss to the Lions, a year later, in 1971. Yet another 3-1 series loss to the Springboks in 1976 was a bitter pill to swallow and it wasn't until the following year that the All Blacks returned to their winning ways with a 3-1 home series win against the Lions. On their 1978 Northern Hemisphere tour they achieved a first-ever 'grand slam' of four wins against the four Home Nations. Home series wins against South Africa in 1981 and Australia in 1982 were followed by an incredible 4-0 series win against the touring Lions in 1983, and another 2-1 series win away to Australia in 1984. Just three defeats in eleven matches during 1985 and 1986 made New Zealand firm favourites to win the inaugural World Cup in 1987 and they did not disappoint their supporters: the team won all six games, which included a comprehensive 29 points to 9 win against France in the final in Auckland. Between May 1987 and August 1990, New Zealand were undefeated for twenty-three matches and from April 1995 to June 1998 they lost only three times in thirty-six games.

The All Blacks maintained their remarkable sequence of wins at the start of the new millennium with a run of eleven consecutive wins in 2003, fifteen in a row between August 2005 and August 2006 and a further fifteen in a row between September 2009 and September 2010. Another phenomenal run of sixteen wins began in September 2011, which extended to twenty matches without defeat but ended disappointingly for the All Blacks when they surprisingly lost to England at Twickenham in December 2012. However, within that run, they did win the 2011 World Cup, on home territory, after a gap of twenty-four years since their previous success in 1987. The final against France turned out to be much closer than expected, with only one point separating the teams at the end.

The New Zealanders dominated the Tri Nations Championship, launched in 1996. The competition was contested sixteen times to 2011 and during that period they won the title ten times, achieving a 100% record in four of the tournaments.

In 2012 Argentina finally entered the Tri Nations competition, which was renamed the Rugby Championship, and in the first two years of its existence the All Blacks won all twelve Internationals. In the calendar year 2013, New Zealand played fourteen Internationals and won every one of them. With a 3-0 series win against England in June 2014, they extended their run of wins to a world-record equalling sequence of seventeen matches. This came to an end, however, when they drew with Australia in August of that year.

The All Blacks' unbeaten sequence then reached twenty-two before they lost the final match of the 2014 Rugby Championship to South Africa in Johannesburg in October.

New Zealand still retained the title they had held for the first two years and this was followed by a successful autumn tour of the British Isles, as they recorded three wins against England, Scotland and Wales.

The Bledisloe Cup, awarded to the winner of a single game or a series of matches between New Zealand and Australia, has been contested fifty-four times between 1931 and 2014; the All Blacks have been title holders on forty-three occasions.

NEW ZEALAND

HEAD TO HEAD RESULTS TO 31 MARCH 2015

	P	W	D	L	%	F	A
v TIER 1 Teams							
v Argentina	20	19	1	0	97.5	816	260
v Australia	152	104	7	41	70.7	3066	2103
v England	40	32	1	7	81.3	969	560
v France	55	42	1	12	77.3	1345	713
v Ireland	28	27	1	0	98.2	812	310
v Italy	12	12	0	0	100.0	686	118
v Scotland	30	28	2	0	96.7	900	332
v South Africa	89	51	3	35	59.0	1718	1392
v Wales	30	27	0	3	90.0	916	307
v Lions	35	27	2	6	80.0	570	337
Sub-Total	**491**	**369**	**18**	**104**	**77.0**	**11798**	**6432**
v TIER 2/3 Group							
v Canada	5	5	0	0	100.0	313	54
v Fiji	5	5	0	0	100.0	364	50
v Japan	3	3	0	0	100.0	282	30
v Romania	2	2	0	0	100.0	99	14
v Samoa	5	5	0	0	100.0	308	56
v Tonga	4	4	0	0	100.0	279	26
v United States	3	3	0	0	100.0	171	15
v Georgia	0	0	0	0	0.0	0	0
v Namibia	0	0	0	0	0.0	0	0
v Russia	0	0	0	0	0.0	0	0
v Uruguay	0	0	0	0	0.0	0	0
Sub-Total	**27**	**27**	**0**	**0**	**100.0**	**1816**	**245**
v Other Teams							
v Anglo-Welsh	3	2	1	0	66.7	64	8
v Pacific Islanders	1	1	0	0	100.0	41	26
v Portugal	1	1	0	0	100.0	108	13
v World XV	3	2	0	1	66.7	94	69
Sub-Total	**8**	**6**	**1**	**1**	**81.3**	**307**	**116**
All Internationals	**526**	**402**	**19**	**105**	**78.2**	**13921**	**6793**

No	Date	Opponents	Tmt		Match Venue	Result	
1	15-Aug-03	Australia	Int-T	A	Cricket Ground, Sydney	W	22-3
2	13-Aug-04	Lions	Int	H	Athletic Park, Wellington	W	9-3
3	2-Sep-05	Australia	Int	H	Tahuna Park, Dunedin	W	14-3
4	18-Nov-05	Scotland	Int-T	A	Inverleith, Edinburgh	W	12-7
5	25-Nov-05	Ireland	Int-T	A	Lansdowne Road, Dublin	W	15-0
6	2-Dec-05	England	Int-T	A	Crystal Palace, London	W	15-0
7	16-Dec-05	Wales	Int-T	A	Arms Park, Cardiff	L	0-3
8	1-Jan-06	France	Int-T	A	Parc des Princess, Paris	W	38-8
9	20-Jul-07	Australia	Int-T	A	Cricket Ground, Sydney	W	26-6
10	3-Aug-07	Australia	Int-T	A	The Gabba Cricket Ground, Brisbane	W	14-5
11	10-Aug-07	Australia	Int-T	A	Cricket Ground, Sydney	D	5-5
12	6-Jun-08	Anglo-Welsh	Int	H	Carisbrook, Dunedin	W	32-5
13	27-Jun-08	Anglo-Welsh	Int	H	Athletic Park, Wellington	D	3-3
14	25-Jul-08	Anglo-Welsh	Int	H	Potter's Park, Auckland	W	29-0
15	25-Jun-10	Australia	Int-T	A	Cricket Ground, Sydney	W	6-0
16	27-Jun-10	Australia	Int-T	A	Cricket Ground, Sydney	L	0-11
17	2-Jul-10	Australia	Int-T	A	Cricket Ground, Sydney	W	28-13
18	6-Sep-13	Australia	Int	H	Athletic Park, Wellington	W	30-5
19	13-Sep-13	Australia	Int	H	Carisbrook, Dunedin	W	25-13
20	20-Sep-13	Australia	Int	H	Lancaster Park Oval, Christchurch	L	5-16
21	15-Nov-13	United States	Int-T	A	St Ignatius, California Field, Berkeley	W	51-3
22	18-Jul-14	Australia	Int-T	A	Sports Ground, Sydney	W	5-0
23	1-Aug-14	Australia	Int-T	A	The Gabba Cricket Ground, Brisbane	W	17-0
24	15-Aug-14	Australia	Int-T	A	Sports Ground, Sydney	W	22-7
25	13-Aug-21	South Africa	Int	H	Carisbrook, Dunedin	W	13-5
26	27-Aug-21	South Africa	Int	H	Eden Park, Auckland	L	5-9
27	17-Sep-21	South Africa	Int	H	Athletic Park, Wellington	D	0-0
28	1-Nov-24	Ireland	Int-T	A	Lansdowne Road, Dublin	W	6-0
29	29-Nov-24	Wales	Int-T	A	St Helen's, Swansea	W	19-0
30	3-Jan-25	England	Int-T	A	Twickenham, London	W	17-11
31	18-Jan-25	France	Int-T	A	Stade des Ponts, Jumeaux, Toulouse	W	30-6
32	30-Jun-28	South Africa	Int-T	A	Kingsmead Ground, Durban	L	0-17
33	21-Jul-28	South Africa	Int-T	A	Ellis Park, Johannesburg	W	7-6
34	18-Aug-28	South Africa	Int-T	A	Crusaders Ground, Port Elizabeth	L	6-11
35	1-Sep-28	South Africa	Int-T	A	Newlands Stadium, Cape Town	W	13-5
36	6-Jul-29	Australia	Int-T	A	Cricket Ground, Sydney	L	8-9
37	20-Jul-29	Australia	Int-T	A	Exhibition Ground, Brisbane	L	9-17
38	27-Jul-29	Australia	Int-T	A	Cricket Ground, Sydney	L	13-15
39	21-Jun-30	Lions	Int	H	Carisbrook, Dunedin	L	3-6
40	5-Jul-30	Lions	Int	H	Lancaster Park Oval, Christchurch	W	13-10

No	Date	Opponents	Tmt		Match Venue	Result	
41	26-Jul-30	Lions	Int	H	Eden Park, Auckland	W	15-10
42	9-Aug-30	Lions	Int	H	Athletic Park, Wellington	W	22-8
43	12-Sep-31	Australia	Bled	H	Eden Park, Auckland	W	20-13
44	2-Jul-32	Australia	Bled-T	A	Cricket Ground, Sydney	L	17-22
45	16-Jul-32	Australia	Bled-T	A	Exhibition Ground, Brisbane	W	21-3
46	23-Jul-32	Australia	Bled-T	A	Cricket Ground, Sydney	W	21-13
47	11-Aug-34	Australia	Bled-T	A	Cricket Ground, Sydney	L	11-25
48	25-Aug-34	Australia	Bled-T	A	Cricket Ground, Sydney	D	3-3
49	23-Nov-35	Scotland	Int-T	A	Murrayfield, Edinburgh	W	18-8
50	7-Dec-35	Ireland	Int-T	A	Lansdowne Road, Dublin	W	17-9
51	21-Dec-35	Wales	Int-T	A	Arms Park, Cardiff	L	12-13
52	4-Jan-36	England	Int-T	A	Twickenham, London	L	0-13
53	5-Sep-36	Australia	Bled	H	Athletic Park, Wellington	W	11-6
54	12-Sep-36	Australia	Bled	H	Carisbrook, Dunedin	W	38-13
55	14-Aug-37	South Africa	Int	H	Athletic Park, Wellington	W	13-7
56	4-Sep-37	South Africa	Int	H	Lancaster Park Oval, Christchurch	L	6-13
57	25-Sep-37	South Africa	Int	H	Eden Park, Auckland	L	6-17
58	23-Jul-38	Australia	Bled-T	A	Cricket Ground, Sydney	W	24-9
59	6-Aug-38	Australia	Bled-T	A	Exhibition Ground, Brisbane	W	20-14
60	13-Aug-38	Australia	Bled-T	A	Cricket Ground, Sydney	W	14-6
61	14-Sep-46	Australia	Bled	H	Carisbrook, Dunedin	W	31-8
62	28-Sep-46	Australia	Bled	H	Eden Park, Auckland	W	14-10
63	14-Jun-47	Australia	Bled-T	A	Exhibition Ground, Brisbane	W	13-5
64	28-Jun-47	Australia	Bled-T	A	Cricket Ground, Sydney	W	27-14
65	16-Jul-49	South Africa	Int-T	A	Newlands Stadium, Cape Town	L	11-15
66	13-Aug-49	South Africa	Int-T	A	Ellis Park, Johannesburg	L	6-12
67	3-Sep-49	Australia	Bled	H	Athletic Park, Wellington	L	6-11
68	3-Sep-49	South Africa	Int-T	A	Kingsmead Ground, Durban	L	3-9
69	17-Sep-49	South Africa	Int-T	A	Crusaders Ground, Port Elizabeth	L	8-11
70	24-Sep-49	Australia	Bled	H	Eden Park, Auckland	L	9-16
71	27-May-50	Lions	Int	H	Carisbrook, Dunedin	D	9-9
72	10-Jun-50	Lions	Int	H	Lancaster Park Oval, Christchurch	W	8-0
73	1-Jul-50	Lions	Int	H	Athletic Park, Wellington	W	6-3
74	29-Jul-50	Lions	Int	H	Eden Park, Auckland	W	11-8
75	23-Jun-51	Australia	Bled-T	A	Cricket Ground, Sydney	W	8-0
76	7-Jul-51	Australia	Bled-T	A	Cricket Ground, Sydney	W	17-11
77	21-Jul-51	Australia	Bled-T	A	The Gabba Cricket Ground, Brisbane	W	16-6
78	6-Sep-52	Australia	Bled	H	Lancaster Park Oval, Christchurch	L	9-14
79	13-Sep-52	Australia	Bled	H	Athletic Park, Wellington	W	15-8
80	19-Dec-53	Wales	Int-T	A	Arms Park, Cardiff	L	8-13

No	Date	Opponents	Tmt		Match Venue	Result	
81	9-Jan-54	Ireland	Int-T	A	Lansdowne Road, Dublin	W	14-3
82	30-Jan-54	England	Int-T	A	Twickenham, London	W	5-0
83	13-Feb-54	Scotland	Int-T	A	Murrayfield, Edinburgh	W	3-0
84	27-Feb-54	France	Int-T	A	Stade Colombes, Paris	L	0-3
85	20-Aug-55	Australia	Bled	H	Athletic Park, Wellington	W	16-8
86	3-Sep-55	Australia	Bled	H	Carisbrook, Dunedin	W	8-0
87	17-Sep-55	Australia	Bled	H	Eden Park, Auckland	L	3-8
88	14-Jul-56	South Africa	Int	H	Carisbrook, Dunedin	W	10-6
89	4-Aug-56	South Africa	Int	H	Athletic Park, Wellington	L	3-8
90	18-Aug-56	South Africa	Int	H	Lancaster Park Oval, Christchurch	W	17-10
91	1-Sep-56	South Africa	Int	H	Eden Park, Auckland	W	11-5
92	25-May-57	Australia	Bled-T	A	Cricket Ground, Sydney	W	25-11
93	1-Jun-57	Australia	Bled-T	A	Exhibition Ground, Brisbane	W	22-9
94	23-Aug-58	Australia	Bled	H	Athletic Park, Wellington	W	25-3
95	6-Sep-58	Australia	Bled	H	Lancaster Park Oval, Christchurch	L	3-6
96	20-Sep-58	Australia	Bled	H	Epsom Showgrounds, Auckland	W	17-8
97	18-Jul-59	Lions	Int	H	Carisbrook, Dunedin	W	18-17
98	15-Aug-59	Lions	Int	H	Athletic Park, Wellington	W	11-8
99	29-Aug-59	Lions	Int	H	Lancaster Park Oval, Christchurch	W	22-8
100	19-Sep-59	Lions	Int	H	Eden Park, Auckland	L	6-9
101	25-Jun-60	South Africa	Int-T	A	Ellis Park, Johannesburg	L	0-13
102	23-Jul-60	South Africa	Int-T	A	Newlands Stadium, Cape Town	W	11-3
103	13-Aug-60	South Africa	Int-T	A	Free State Stadium, Bloemfontein	D	11-11
104	27-Aug-60	South Africa	Int-T	A	Boet Erasmus Stadium, Port Elizabeth	L	3-8
105	22-Jul-61	France	Int	H	Eden Park, Auckland	W	13-6
106	5-Aug-61	France	Int	H	Athletic Park, Wellington	W	5-3
107	19-Aug-61	France	Int	H	Lancaster Park Oval, Christchurch	W	32-3
108	26-May-62	Australia	Bled-T	A	Exhibition Ground, Brisbane	W	20-6
109	4-Jun-62	Australia	Bled-T	A	Cricket Ground, Sydney	W	14-5
110	25-Aug-62	Australia	Bled	H	Athletic Park, Wellington	D	9-9
111	8-Sep-62	Australia	Bled	H	Carisbrook, Dunedin	W	3-0
112	22-Sep-62	Australia	Bled	H	Eden Park, Auckland	W	16-8
113	25-May-63	England	Int	H	Eden Park, Auckland	W	21-11
114	1-Jun-63	England	Int	H	Lancaster Park Oval, Christchurch	W	9-6
115	7-Dec-63	Ireland	Int-T	A	Lansdowne Road, Dublin	W	6-5
116	21-Dec-63	Wales	Int-T	A	Arms Park, Cardiff	W	6-0
117	4-Jan-64	England	Int-T	A	Twickenham, London	W	14-0
118	18-Jan-64	Scotland	Int-T	A	Murrayfield, Edinburgh	D	0-0
119	8-Feb-64	France	Int-T	A	Stade Colombes, Paris	W	12-3
120	15-Aug-64	Australia	Bled	H	Carisbrook, Dunedin	W	14-9

No	Date	Opponents	Tmt	Match Venue	Result	
121	22-Aug-64	Australia	Bled	H Lancaster Park Oval, Christchurch	W	18-3
122	29-Aug-64	Australia	Bled	H Athletic Park, Wellington	L	5-20
123	31-Jul-65	South Africa	Int	H Athletic Park, Wellington	W	6-3
124	21-Aug-65	South Africa	Int	H Carisbrook, Dunedin	W	13-0
125	4-Sep-65	South Africa	Int	H Lancaster Park Oval, Christchurch	L	16-19
126	18-Sep-65	South Africa	Int	H Eden Park, Auckland	W	20-3
127	16-Jul-66	Lions	Int	H Carisbrook, Dunedin	W	20-3
128	6-Aug-66	Lions	Int	H Athletic Park, Wellington	W	16-12
129	27-Aug-66	Lions	Int	H Lancaster Park Oval, Christchurch	W	19-6
130	10-Sep-66	Lions	Int	H Eden Park, Auckland	W	24-11
131	19-Aug-67	Australia	Bled	H Athletic Park, Wellington	W	29-9
132	4-Nov-67	England	Int-T	A Twickenham, London	W	23-11
133	11-Nov-67	Wales	Int-T	A Arms Park, Cardiff	W	13-6
134	25-Nov-67	France	Int-T	A Stade Colombes, Paris	W	21-15
135	2-Dec-67	Scotland	Int-T	A Murrayfield, Edinburgh	W	14-3
136	15-Jun-68	Australia	Bled-T	A Cricket Ground, Sydney	W	27-11
137	22-Jun-68	Australia	Bled-T	A Ballymore Oval, Brisbane	W	19-18
138	13-Jul-68	France	Int	H Lancaster Park Oval, Christchurch	W	12-9
139	27-Jul-68	France	Int	H Athletic Park, Wellington	W	9-3
140	10-Aug-68	France	Int	H Eden Park, Auckland	W	19-12
141	31-May-69	Wales	Int	H Lancaster Park Oval, Christchurch	W	19-0
142	14-Jun-69	Wales	Int	H Eden Park, Auckland	W	33-12
143	25-Jul-70	South Africa	Int-T	A Loftus Versfeld Stadium, Pretoria	L	6-17
144	8-Aug-70	South Africa	Int-T	A Newlands Stadium, Cape Town	W	9-8
145	29-Aug-70	South Africa	Int-T	A Boet Erasmus Stadium, Port Elizabeth	L	3-14
146	12-Sep-70	South Africa	Int-T	A Ellis Park, Johannesburg	L	17-20
147	26-Jun-71	Lions	Int	H Carisbrook, Dunedin	L	3-9
148	10-Jul-71	Lions	Int	H Lancaster Park Oval, Christchurch	W	22-12
149	31-Jul-71	Lions	Int	H Athletic Park, Wellington	L	3-13
150	14-Aug-71	Lions	Int	H Eden Park, Auckland	D	14-14
151	19-Aug-72	Australia	Bled	H Athletic Park, Wellington	W	29-6
152	2-Sep-72	Australia	Bled	H Lancaster Park Oval, Christchurch	W	30-17
153	16-Sep-72	Australia	Bled	H Eden Park, Auckland	W	38-3
154	2-Dec-72	Wales	Int-T	A National Stadium, Cardiff	W	19-16
155	16-Dec-72	Scotland	Int-T	A Murrayfield, Edinburgh	W	14-9
156	6-Jan-73	England	Int-T	A Twickenham, London	W	9-0
157	20-Jan-73	Ireland	Int-T	A Lansdowne Road, Dublin	D	10-10
158	10-Feb-73	France	Int-T	A Parc des Princess, Paris	L	6-13
159	15-Sep-73	England	Int	H Eden Park, Auckland	L	10-16
160	25-May-74	Australia	Bled-T	A Cricket Ground, Sydney	W	11-6

No	Date	Opponents	Tmt	Match Venue	Result	
161	1-Jun-74	Australia	Bled-T	A Ballymore Oval, Brisbane	D	16-16
162	8-Jun-74	Australia	Bled-T	A Cricket Ground, Sydney	W	16-6
163	23-Nov-74	Ireland	Int-T	A Lansdowne Road, Dublin	W	15-6
164	14-Jun-75	Scotland	Int	H Eden Park, Auckland	W	24-0
165	5-Jun-76	Ireland	Int	H Athletic Park, Wellington	W	11-3
166	24-Jul-76	South Africa	Int-T	A Kings Park Stadium, Durban	L	7-16
167	14-Aug-76	South Africa	Int-T	A Free State Stadium, Bloemfontein	W	15-9
168	4-Sep-76	South Africa	Int-T	A Newlands Stadium, Cape Town	L	10-15
169	18-Sep-76	South Africa	Int-T	A Ellis Park, Johannesburg	L	14-15
170	18-Jun-77	Lions	Int	H Athletic Park, Wellington	W	16-12
171	9-Jul-77	Lions	Int	H Lancaster Park Oval, Christchurch	L	9-13
172	30-Jul-77	Lions	Int	H Carisbrook, Dunedin	W	19-7
173	13-Aug-77	Lions	Int	H Eden Park, Auckland	W	10-9
174	11-Nov-77	France	Int-T	A Stade Municipal de Toulouse, Toulouse	L	13-18
175	19-Nov-77	France	Int-T	A Parc des Princess, Paris	W	15-3
176	19-Aug-78	Australia	Bled	H Athletic Park, Wellington	W	13-12
177	26-Aug-78	Australia	Bled	H Lancaster Park Oval, Christchurch	W	22-6
178	9-Sep-78	Australia	Bled	H Eden Park, Auckland	L	16-30
179	4-Nov-78	Ireland	Int-T	A Lansdowne Road, Dublin	W	10-6
180	11-Nov-78	Wales	Int-T	A National Stadium, Cardiff	W	13-12
181	25-Nov-78	England	Int-T	A Twickenham, London	W	16-6
182	9-Dec-78	Scotland	Int-T	A Murrayfield, Edinburgh	W	18-9
183	7-Jul-79	France	Int	H Lancaster Park Oval, Christchurch	W	23-9
184	14-Jul-79	France	Int	H Eden Park, Auckland	L	19-24
185	28-Jul-79	Australia	Bled-T	A Cricket Ground, Sydney	L	6-12
186	10-Nov-79	Scotland	Int-T	A Murrayfield, Edinburgh	W	20-6
187	24-Nov-79	England	Int-T	A Twickenham, London	W	10-9
188	21-Jun-80	Australia	Bled-T	A Cricket Ground, Sydney	L	9-13
189	28-Jun-80	Australia	Bled-T	A Ballymore Oval, Brisbane	W	12-9
190	12-Jul-80	Australia	Bled-T	A Cricket Ground, Sydney	L	10-26
191	1-Nov-81	Wales	Int-T	A National Stadium, Cardiff	W	23-3
192	13-Jun-81	Scotland	Int	H Carisbrook, Dunedin	W	11-4
193	20-Jun-81	Scotland	Int	H Eden Park, Auckland	W	40-15
194	15-Aug-81	South Africa	Int	H Lancaster Park Oval, Christchurch	W	14-9
195	29-Aug-81	South Africa	Int	H Athletic Park, Wellington	L	12-24
196	12-Sep-81	South Africa	Int	H Eden Park, Auckland	W	25-22
197	24-Oct-81	Romania	Int-T	A Stadionul 23 August, Bucharest	W	14-6
198	14-Nov-81	France	Int-T	A Stade Municipal de Toulouse, Toulouse	W	13-9
199	21-Nov-81	France	Int-T	A Parc des Princess, Paris	W	18-6
200	14-Aug-82	Australia	Bled	H Lancaster Park Oval, Christchurch	W	23-16

No	Date	Opponents	Tmt		Match Venue	Result	
201	28-Aug-82	Australia	Bled	H	Athletic Park, Wellington	L	16-19
202	11-Sep-82	Australia	Bled	H	Eden Park, Auckland	W	33-18
203	4-Jun-83	Lions	Int	H	Lancaster Park Oval, Christchurch	W	16-12
204	18-Jun-83	Lions	Int	H	Athletic Park, Wellington	W	9-0
205	2-Jul-83	Lions	Int	H	Carisbrook, Dunedin	W	15-8
206	16-Jul-83	Lions	Int	H	Eden Park, Auckland	W	38-6
207	20-Aug-83	Australia	Bled-T	A	Cricket Ground, Sydney	W	18-8
208	12-Nov-83	Scotland	Int-T	A	Murrayfield, Edinburgh	D	25-25
209	19-Nov-83	England	Int-T	A	Twickenham, London	L	9-15
210	16-Jun-84	France	Int	H	Lancaster Park Oval, Christchurch	W	10-9
211	23-Jun-84	France	Int	H	Eden Park, Auckland	W	31-18
212	21-Jul-84	Australia	Bled-T	A	Cricket Ground, Sydney	L	9-16
213	4-Aug-84	Australia	Bled-T	A	Ballymore Oval, Brisbane	W	19-15
214	18-Aug-84	Australia	Bled-T	A	Cricket Ground, Sydney	W	25-24
215	1-Jun-85	England	Int	H	Lancaster Park Oval, Christchurch	W	18-13
216	8-Jun-85	England	Int	H	Athletic Park, Wellington	W	42-15
217	29-Jun-85	Australia	Bled	H	Eden Park, Auckland	W	10-9
218	26-Oct-85	Argentina	Int-T	A	Ferro Carril Oeste Stadium, B Aires	W	33-20
219	2-Nov-85	Argentina	Int-T	A	Ferro Carril Oeste Stadium, B Aires	D	21-21
220	28-Jun-86	France	Int	H	Lancaster Park Oval, Christchurch	W	18-9
221	9-Aug-86	Australia	Bled	H	Athletic Park, Wellington	L	12-13
222	23-Aug-86	Australia	Bled	H	Carisbrook, Dunedin	W	13-12
223	6-Sep-86	Australia	Bled	H	Eden Park, Auckland	L	9-22
224	8-Nov-86	France	Int-T	A	Stade Municipal de Toulouse, Toulouse	W	19-7
225	15-Nov-86	France	Int-T	A	Stade de la Beaujoire, Nantes	L	3-16
226	22-May-87	Italy	WCp	H	Eden Park, Auckland	W	70-6
227	27-May-87	Fiji	WCp	H	Lancaster Park Oval, Christchurch	W	74-13
228	1-Jun-87	Argentina	WCp	H	Athletic Park, Wellington	W	46-15
229	6-Jun-87	Scotland	WCqf	H	Lancaster Park Oval, Christchurch	W	30-3
230	14-Jun-87	Wales	WCsf	N	Ballymore Oval, Brisbane	W	49-6
231	20-Jun-87	France	WCf	H	Eden Park, Auckland	W	29-9
232	25-Jul-87	Australia	Bled-T	A	Concord Oval, Sydney	W	30-16
233	23-May-88	Wales	Int	H	Lancaster Park Oval, Christchurch	W	52-3
234	11-Jun-88	Wales	Int	H	Eden Park, Auckland	W	54-9
235	3-Jul-88	Australia	Bled-T	A	Concord Oval, Sydney	W	32-7
236	16-Jul-88	Australia	Bled-T	A	Ballymore Oval, Brisbane	D	19-19
237	30-Jul-88	Australia	Bled-T	A	Concord Oval, Sydney	W	30-9
238	17-Jun-89	France	Int	H	Lancaster Park Oval, Christchurch	W	25-17
239	1-Jul-89	France	Int	H	Eden Park, Auckland	W	34-20
240	15-Jul-89	Argentina	Int	H	Carisbrook, Dunedin	W	60-9

No	Date	Opponents	Tmt		Match Venue	Result	
241	29-Jul-89	Argentina	Int	H	Athletic Park, Wellington	W	49-12
242	5-Aug-89	Australia	Bled	H	Eden Park, Auckland	W	24-12
243	4-Nov-89	Wales	Int-T	A	National Stadium, Cardiff	W	34-9
244	18-Nov-89	Ireland	Int-T	A	Lansdowne Road, Dublin	W	23-6
245	16-Jun-90	Scotland	Int	H	Carisbrook, Dunedin	W	31-16
246	23-Jun-90	Scotland	Int	H	Eden Park, Auckland	W	21-18
247	21-Jul-90	Australia	Bled	H	Lancaster Park Oval, Christchurch	W	21-6
248	4-Aug-90	Australia	Bled	H	Eden Park, Auckland	W	27-17
249	18-Aug-90	Australia	Bled	H	Athletic Park, Wellington	L	9-21
250	3-Nov-90	France	Int-T	A	Stade de la Beaujoire, Nantes	W	24-3
251	10-Nov-90	France	Int-T	A	Parc des Princess, Paris	W	30-12
252	6-Jul-91	Argentina	Int-T	A	Vélez Sarsfield Stadium, Buenos Aires	W	28-14
253	13-Jul-91	Argentina	Int-T	A	Vélez Sarsfield Stadium, Buenos Aires	W	36-6
254	10-Aug-91	Australia	Bled-T	A	Football Stadium, Sydney	L	12-21
255	24-Aug-91	Australia	Bled	H	Eden Park, Auckland	W	6-3
256	3-Oct-91	England	WCp	A	Twickenham, London	W	18-12
257	8-Oct-91	United States	WCp	N	Kingsholm, Gloucester	W	46-6
258	13-Oct-91	Italy	WCp	N	Welford Road, Leicester	W	31-21
259	20-Oct-91	Canada	WCqf	N	Stade Nord Lille Métropole	W	29-13
260	27-Oct-91	Australia	WCsf	N	Lansdowne Road, Dublin	L	6-16
261	30-Oct-91	Scotland	WC34	N	National Stadium, Cardiff	W	13-6
262	18-Apr-92	World XV	Int	H	Lancaster Park Oval, Christchurch	L	14-28
263	22-Apr-92	World XV	Int	H	Athletic Park, Wellington	W	54-26
264	25-Apr-92	World XV	Int	H	Eden Park, Auckland	W	26-15
265	30-May-92	Ireland	Int	H	Carisbrook, Dunedin	W	24-21
266	6-Jun-92	Ireland	Int	H	Athletic Park, Wellington	W	59-6
267	4-Jul-92	Australia	Bled-T	A	Football Stadium, Sydney	L	15-16
268	19-Jul-92	Australia	Bled-T	A	Ballymore Oval, Brisbane	L	17-19
269	25-Jul-92	Australia	Bled-T	A	Football Stadium, Sydney	W	26-23
270	15-Aug-92	South Africa	Int-T	A	Ellis Park, Johannesburg	W	27-24
271	12-Jun-93	Lions	Int	H	Lancaster Park Oval, Christchurch	W	20-18
272	26-Jun-93	Lions	Int	H	Athletic Park, Wellington	L	7-20
273	3-Jul-93	Lions	Int	H	Eden Park, Auckland	W	30-13
274	17-Jul-93	Australia	Bled	H	Carisbrook, Dunedin	W	25-10
275	31-Jul-93	Western Samoa	Int	H	Eden Park, Auckland	W	35-13
276	20-Nov-93	Scotland	Int-T	A	Murrayfield, Edinburgh	W	51-15
277	27-Nov-93	England	Int-T	A	Twickenham, London	L	9-15
278	26-Jun-94	France	Int	H	Lancaster Park Oval, Christchurch	L	8-22
279	3-Jul-94	France	Int	H	Eden Park, Auckland	L	20-23
280	9-Jul-94	South Africa	Int	H	Carisbrook, Dunedin	W	22-14

No	Date	Opponents	Tmt		Match Venue		Result	
281	23-Jul-94	South Africa	Int	H	Athletic Park, Wellington	W	13-9
282	6-Aug-94	South Africa	Int	H	Eden Park, Auckland	D	18-18
283	17-Aug-94	Australia	Bled-T	A	Football Stadium, Sydney	L	16-20
284	22-Apr-95	Canada	Int	H	Eden Park, Auckland	W	73-7
285	27-May-95	Ireland	WCp	N	Ellis Park, Johannesburg	W	43-19
286	31-May-95	Wales	WCp	N	Ellis Park, Johannesburg	W	34-9
287	4-Jun-95	Japan	WCp	N	Free State Stadium, Bloemfontein	W	145-17
288	11-Jun-95	Scotland	WCqf	N	Loftus Versfeld Stadium, Pretoria	W	48-30
289	18-Jun-95	England	WCsf	N	Newlands Stadium, Cape Town	W	45-29
290	24-Jun-95	South Africa	WCf	A	Ellis Park, Johannesburg (a-e-t)	L	12-15
291	22-Jul-95	Australia	Bled	H	Eden Park, Auckland	W	28-16
292	29-Jul-95	Australia	Bled-T	A	Football Stadium, Sydney	W	34-23
293	28-Oct-95	Italy	Int-T	A	Stadio Renato Dall'Ara, Bologna	W	70-6
294	11-Nov-95	France	Int-T	A	Stade Municipal de Toulouse, Toulouse	L	15-22
295	18-Nov-95	France	Int-T	A	Parc des Princess, Paris	W	37-12
296	7-Jun-96	Western Samoa	Int	H	McLean Park, Napier	W	51-10
297	15-Jun-96	Scotland	Int	H	Carisbrook, Dunedin	W	62-31
298	22-Jun-96	Scotland	Int	H	Eden Park, Auckland	W	36-12
299	6-Jul-96	Australia	TN-B	H	Athletic Park, Wellington	W	43-6
300	20-Jul-96	South Africa	TN	H	Lancaster Park Oval, Christchurch	W	15-11
301	27-Jul-96	Australia	TN-B	A	Suncorp Stadium, Brisbane	W	32-25
302	10-Aug-96	South Africa	TN	A	Norwich Park, Newlands, Cape Town	W	29-18
303	17-Aug-96	South Africa	Int-T	A	Kings Park Stadium, Durban	W	23-19
304	24-Aug-96	South Africa	Int-T	A	Loftus Versfeld Stadium, Pretoria	W	33-26
305	31-Aug-96	South Africa	Int-T	A	Ellis Park, Johannesburg	L	22-32
306	14-Jun-97	Fiji	Int	H	North Harbour Stadium, Albany	W	71-5
307	21-Jun-97	Argentina	Int	H	Athletic Park, Wellington	W	93-8
308	28-Jun-97	Argentina	Int	H	Rugby Park, Hamilton	W	62-10
309	5-Jul-97	Australia	Bled	H	Lancaster Park Oval, Christchurch	W	30-13
310	19-Jul-97	South Africa	TN	A	Ellis Park, Johannesburg	W	35-32
311	26-Jul-97	Australia	TN-B	A	Cricket Ground, Melbourne	W	33-18
312	9-Aug-97	South Africa	TN	H	Eden Park, Auckland	W	55-35
313	16-Aug-97	Australia	TN-B	H	Carisbrook, Dunedin	W	36-24
314	15-Nov-97	Ireland	Int-T	A	Lansdowne Road, Dublin	W	63-15
315	22-Nov-97	England	Int-T	A	Old Trafford, Manchester	W	25-8
316	29-Nov-97	Wales	Int-T	N	Wembley Stadium, London	W	42-7
317	6-Dec-97	England	Int-T	A	Twickenham, London	D	26-26
318	20-Jun-98	England	Int	H	Carisbrook, Dunedin	W	64-22
319	27-Jun-98	England	Int	H	Eden Park, Auckland	W	40-10
320	11-Jul-98	Australia	TN-B	A	Cricket Ground, Melbourne	L	16-24

No	Date	Opponents	Tmt		Match Venue	Result	
321	25-Jul-98	South Africa	TN	H	Athletic Park, Wellington	L	3-13
322	1-Aug-98	Australia	TN-B	H	Jade Stadium, Christchurch	L	23-27
323	15-Aug-98	South Africa	TN	A	Kings Park Stadium, Durban	L	23-24
324	29-Aug-98	Australia	Bled-T	A	Football Stadium, Sydney	L	14-19
325	18-Jun-99	Samoa	Int	H	North Harbour Stadium, Albany	W	71-13
326	26-Jun-99	France	Int	H	Athletic Park, Wellington	W	54-7
327	10-Jul-99	South Africa	TN	H	Carisbrook, Dunedin	W	28-0
328	24-Jul-99	Australia	TN-B	H	Eden Park, Auckland	W	34-15
329	7-Aug-99	South Africa	TN	A	Minolta Loftus Stadium, Pretoria	W	34-18
330	28-Aug-99	Australia	TN-B	A	Stadium Australia, Sydney	L	7-28
331	3-Oct-99	Tonga	WCp	N	Ashton Gate, Bristol	W	45-9
332	9-Oct-99	England	WCp	A	Twickenham, London	W	30-16
333	14-Oct-99	Italy	WCp	N	McAlpine Stadium, Huddersfield	W	101-3
334	24-Oct-99	Scotland	WCqf	A	Murrayfield, Edinburgh	W	30-18
335	31-Oct-99	France	WCsf	N	Twickenham, London	L	31-43
336	4-Nov-99	South Africa	WC34	N	Millennium Stadium, Cardiff	L	18-22
337	16-Jun-00	Tonga	Int	H	North Harbour Stadium, Albany	W	102-0
338	24-Jun-00	Scotland	Int	H	Carisbrook, Dunedin	W	69-20
339	1-Jul-00	Scotland	Int	H	Eden Park, Auckland	W	48-14
340	15-Jul-00	Australia	TN-B	A	Stadium Australia, Sydney	W	39-35
341	22-Jul-00	South Africa	TN	H	Jade Stadium, Christchurch	W	25-12
342	5-Aug-00	Australia	TN-B	H	Westpac Trust Stadium, Wellington	L	23-24
343	19-Aug-00	South Africa	TN	A	Ellis Park, Johannesburg	L	40-46
344	11-Nov-00	France	DGT-T	A	Stade de France, Paris	W	39-26
345	18-Nov-00	France	Int-T	A	Stade Vélodrome, Marseille	L	33-42
346	25-Nov-00	Italy	Int-T	A	Stadio Luigi Ferraris, Genova	W	56-19
347	16-Jun-01	Samoa	Int	H	North Harbour Stadium, Albany	W	50-6
348	23-Jun-01	Argentina	Int	H	Jade Stadium, Christchurch	W	67-19
349	30-Jun-01	France	DGT	H	Westpac Trust Stadium, Wellington	W	37-12
350	21-Jul-01	South Africa	TN	A	Fedsure Park, Newlands, Cape Town	W	12-3
351	11-Aug-01	Australia	TN-B	H	Carisbrook, Dunedin	L	15-23
352	25-Aug-01	South Africa	TN	H	Eden Park, Auckland	W	26-15
353	1-Sep-01	Australia	TN-B	A	Stadium Australia, Sydney	L	26-29
354	17-Nov-01	Ireland	Int-T	A	Lansdowne Road, Dublin	W	40-29
355	24-Nov-01	Scotland	Int-T	A	Murrayfield, Edinburgh	W	37-6
356	1-Dec-01	Argentina	Int-T	A	Estadio Monumental A V Liberti, B Aires	W	24-20
357	8-Jun-02	Italy	Int	H	Waikato Stadium, Hamilton	W	64-10
358	15-Jun-02	Ireland	Int	H	Carisbrook, Dunedin	W	15-6
359	22-Jun-02	Ireland	Int	H	Eden Park, Auckland	W	40-8
360	29-Jun-02	Fiji	Int	H	Westpac Trust Stadium, Wellington	W	68-18

No	Date	Opponents	Tmt		Match Venue	Result	
361	13-Jul-02	Australia	TN-B	H	Jade Stadium, Christchurch	W	12-6
362	20-Jul-02	South Africa	TN	H	Westpac Trust Stadium, Wellington	W	41-20
363	3-Aug-02	Australia	TN-B	A	Telstra Stadium, Sydney	L	14-16
364	10-Aug-02	South Africa	TN	A	ABSA Stadium, Durban	W	30-23
365	9-Nov-02	England	Int-T	A	Twickenham, London	L	28-31
366	16-Nov-02	France	DGT-T	A	Stade de France, Paris	D	20-20
367	23-Nov-02	Wales	Int-T	A	Millennium Stadium, Cardiff	W	43-17
368	14-Jun-03	England	Int	H	Westpac Trust Stadium, Wellington	L	13-15
369	21-Jun-03	Wales	Int	H	Waikato Stadium, Hamilton	W	55-3
370	28-Jun-03	France	DGT	H	Jade Stadium, Christchurch	W	31-23
371	19-Jul-03	South Africa	TN	A	Securicor Loftus Stadium, Pretoria	W	52-16
372	26-Jul-03	Australia	TN-B	A	Telstra Stadium, Sydney	W	50-21
373	9-Aug-03	South Africa	TN	H	Carisbrook, Dunedin	W	19-11
374	16-Aug-03	Australia	TN-B	H	Eden Park, Auckland	W	21-17
375	11-Oct-03	Italy	WCp	N	Telstra Dome, Melbourne	W	70-7
376	17-Oct-03	Canada	WCp	N	Telstra Dome, Melbourne	W	68-6
377	24-Oct-03	Tonga	WCp	N	Suncorp Stadium, Brisbane	W	91-7
378	2-Nov-03	Wales	WCp	N	Telstra Stadium, Sydney	W	53-37
379	8-Nov-03	South Africa	WCqf	N	Telstra Dome, Melbourne	W	29-9
380	15-Nov-03	Australia	WCsf	A	Telstra Stadium, Sydney	L	10-22
381	20-Nov-03	France	WC34	N	Telstra Stadium, Sydney	W	40-13
382	12-Jun-04	England	Int	H	Carisbrook, Dunedin	W	36-3
383	19-Jun-04	England	Int	H	Eden Park, Auckland	W	36-12
384	26-Jun-04	Argentina	Int	H	Waikato Stadium, Hamilton	W	41-7
385	10-Jul-04	Pacific Islands	Int	H	North Harbour Stadium, Albany	W	41-26
386	17-Jul-04	Australia	TN-B	H	Westpac Stadium, Wellington	W	16-7
387	24-Jul-04	South Africa	TN	H	Jade Stadium, Christchurch	W	23-21
388	7-Aug-04	Australia	TN-B	A	Telstra Stadium, Sydney	L	18-23
389	14-Aug-04	South Africa	TN-F	A	Ellis Park, Johannesburg	L	26-40
390	13-Nov-04	Italy	Int-T	A	Stadio Flaminio, Rome	W	59-10
391	20-Nov-04	Wales	Int-T	A	Millennium Stadium, Cardiff	W	26-25
392	27-Nov-04	France	DGT-T	A	Stade de France, Paris	W	45-6
393	10-Jun-05	Fiji	Int	H	North Harbour Stadium, Albany	W	91-0
394	25-Jun-05	Lions	Int	H	Jade Stadium, Christchurch	W	21-3
395	2-Jul-05	Lions	Int	H	Westpac Stadium, Wellington	W	48-18
396	9-Jul-05	Lions	Int	H	Eden Park, Auckland	W	38-19
397	6-Aug-05	South Africa	TN	A	Newlands Stadium, Cape Town	L	16-22
398	13-Aug-05	Australia	TN-B	A	Telstra Stadium, Sydney	W	30-13
399	27-Aug-05	South Africa	TN	H	Carisbrook, Dunedin	W	31-27
400	3-Sep-05	Australia	TN-B	H	Eden Park, Auckland	W	34-24

No	Date	Opponents	Tmt		Match Venue	Result	
481	2-Oct-11	Canada	WCp	H	Wellington Regional Stadium, Wellington	W	79-15
482	9-Oct-11	Argentina	WCqf	H	Eden Park, Auckland	W	33-10
483	16-Oct-11	Australia	WCsf	H	Eden Park, Auckland	W	20-6
484	23-Oct-11	France	WCf	H	Eden Park, Auckland	W	8-7
485	9-Jun-12	Ireland	Int	H	Eden Park, Auckland	W	42-10
486	16-Jun-12	Ireland	Int	H	Rugby League Park, Christchurch	W	22-19
487	23-Jun-12	Ireland	Int	H	Waikato Stadium, Hamilton	W	60-0
488	18-Aug-12	Australia	RC-B	A	ANZ Stadium, Sydney	W	27-19
489	25-Aug-12	Australia	RC-B	H	Eden Park, Auckland	W	22-0
490	8-Sep-12	Argentina	RC	H	Westpac Stadium, Wellington	W	21-5
491	15-Sep-12	South Africa	RC-F	H	Forsyth Barr Stadium, Dunedin	W	21-11
492	29-Sep-12	Argentina	RC	A	Estadio Ciudad de la Plata, La Plata	W	54-15
493	6-Oct-12	South Africa	RC-F	A	FNB Stadium, Soweto, Johannesburg	W	32-16
494	20-Oct-12	Australia	Bled-T	A	Suncorp Stadium, Brisbane	D	18-18
495	11-Nov-12	Scotland	Int-T	A	Murrayfield, Edinburgh	W	51-22
496	17-Nov-12	Italy	Int-T	A	Stadio Olimpico, Rome	W	42-10
497	24-Nov-12	Wales	Int-T	A	Millennium Stadium, Cardiff	W	33-10
498	1-Dec-12	England	EHS-T	A	Twickenham, London	L	21-38
499	8-Jun-13	France	DGT	H	Eden Park, Auckland	W	23-13
500	15-Jun-13	France	DGT	H	AMI Stadium, Addington	W	30-0
501	22-Jun-13	France	DGT	H	Yarrow Stadium, New Plymouth	W	24-9
502	17-Aug-13	Australia	RC-B	A	ANZ Stadium, Sydney	W	47-29
503	24-Aug-13	Australia	RC-B	H	Westpac Stadium, Wellington	W	27-16
504	7-Sep-13	Argentina	RC	H	Waikato Stadium, Hamilton	W	28-13
505	14-Sep-13	South Africa	RC-F	H	Eden Park, Auckland	W	29-15
506	28-Sep-13	Argentina	RC	A	Estadio Ciudad de la Plata, La Plata	W	33-15
507	5-Oct-13	South Africa	RC-F	A	Ellis Park, Johannesburg	W	38-27
508	19-Oct-13	Australia	Bled	H	Forsyth Barr Stadium, Dunedin	W	41-33
509	2-Nov-13	Japan	Int-T	A	Prince Chichibu Memorial Ground, Tokyo	W	54-6
510	9-Nov-13	France	DGT-T	A	Stade de France, Paris	W	26-19
511	16-Nov-13	England	EHS-T	A	Twickenham, London	W	30-22
512	24-Nov-13	Ireland	Int-T	A	Aviva Stadium, Dublin	W	24-22
513	7-Jun-14	England	EHS	H	Eden Park, Auckland	W	20-15
514	14-Jun-14	England	EHS	H	Forsyth Barr Stadium, Dunedin	W	28-27
515	21-Jun-14	England	EHS	H	Waikato Stadium, Hamilton	W	36-13
516	16-Aug-14	Australia	RC-B	A	ANZ Stadium, Sydney	D	12-12
517	23-Aug-14	Australia	RC-B	H	Eden Park, Auckland	W	51-20
518	6-Sep-14	Argentina	RC	H	McLean Park, Napier	W	28-9
519	13-Sep-14	South Africa	RC-F	H	Westpac Stadium, Wellington	W	14-10
520	27-Sep-14	Argentina	RC	A	Estadio Ciudad de la Plata, La Plata	W	34-13

No	Date	Opponents	Tmt		Match Venue	Result	
521	4-Oct-14	South Africa	RC-F	A	Ellis Park, Johannesburg	L	25-27
522	11-Oct-14	Australia	RC-B	A	Suncorp Stadium, Brisbane	W	29-28
523	1-Nov-14	United States	Int-T	A	Soldier Field, Chicago	W	74-6
524	8-Nov-14	England	EHS-T	A	Twickenham, London	W	24-21
525	15-Nov-14	Scotland	Int-T	A	Murrayfield, Edinburgh	W	24-16
526	22-Nov-14	Wales	Int-T	A	Millennium Stadium, Cardiff	W	34-16

SCOTLAND

On 25 March 1871, the *Glasgow Herald* reported that a rugby match would take place between Scotland and England. The newspaper noted that the rules of Rugby school would be used, with some minor alterations. With twenty players each side, the match was played at Raeburn Place in Edinburgh on a pitch measuring 120 yards by 55 yards. Two days later, the first rugby International took place and Scotland won by one goal and one try to one try. In 1883 Scotland finished runners-up in the inaugural Home Nations Championship, losing only to Triple Crown winners England.

Scotland finally won the Championship four years later, in 1887, in a three nations tournament that had excluded England because of their refusal to join the IRB in 1888. In the eleven-year period between 1882 and 1892 Scotland played 29 matches and lost just five times, but despite this fine run, they managed to win only one Triple Crown, in 1891. However, their record improved as they won four more Triple Crowns between 1895 and 1907 and, after a gap of eighteen years, they won a sixth Triple Crown in the 1925 Five Nations Championship. In addition, having beaten France earlier, they secured their first Grand Slam. The team's final match in that campaign was the inaugural game held at Murrayfield in Edinburgh.

The next Triple Crown success for Scotland came in 1933, but it was followed by a relatively uneventful period for the team between 1934 and 1937 as they won only three games out of thirteen, before finally winning the Triple Crown again in 1938.

The fortunes of the Scottish side were very disappointing in the four years after the Second World War and the team lost eleven games out of the first seventeen played. Their losing streak continued between February 1951 and February 1955, when Scotland suffered seventeen defeats in succession, including a 44 points to nil trouncing by the touring Springboks. There was a slight improvement from 1955 to 1963, but still no win against England.

That eventually came in 1964 when Scotland finally triumphed over the English side and, to the surprise of many, held New Zealand to a scoreless draw. The second half of the decade produced some stunning results for Scotland: not only did they defeat South Africa in 1965 and 1969 (thus ending five defeats in a row since their historic win in 1906), they also beat Australia in the two games played in 1966 and 1968. Unfortunately, Scotland failed to complete a hat-trick of wins over Southern Hemisphere opposition, losing to New Zealand in 1967.

The barren years of the 1970s and early 1980s came to an unexpected end in 1984, when Scotland achieved a second Grand Slam, a result that bridged a gap of fifty-nine years since their first Grand Slam in 1925. And there was more to come: six years later, in 1990, the Scots repeated their 1984 achievement when they gained a third Grand Slam at the expense of England (who were themselves seeking a Grand Slam).

Scotland's good form continued in the 1991 World Cup when they won their pool group and the quarter-final against Western Samoa by 28 points to 6, to reach the semi-final, only to lose by 9 points to 6 to England. Scottish success was not forthcoming in the next four World Cups when they lost each time at the quarter-final stage: to New Zealand in 1995 in a high-scoring match by 48 points to 30 and again to the All Blacks in 1999 by 30 points to 18; to hosts Australia in 2003 by 33 points to 16; and to Argentina by 19 points to 13 at the Stade de France in Paris in 2007.

With the advent of the Six Nations Championship in 2000,

the Scottish team failed to impress in the first twelve years of the competition: they performed so poorly that they were landed with the 'wooden spoon' (losing all five matches), in 2004 and again in 2007. Finishing in fifth place in each year from 2008 to 2011 wasn't much better. On the credit side, however, Scotland defeated Australia in Murrayfield in 2009, and Argentina twice on their 2010 Southern Hemisphere tour. They also beat South Africa in Murrayfield later that autumn.

The Scottish team failed to reach the quarter-final stage of a World Cup for the first time in 2011, losing to both Argentina and England in the pool matches. Things got even worse in the 2012 Six Nations Championship when Scotland lost all five matches again and with it gained a third wooden spoon in that tournament. This was followed, however, by a successful summer tour where Scotland defeated Australia away from home for the first time since 1982, winning by 9 points to 6 in a rain-lashed Newcastle to retain the Hopetoun Cup, before defeating Fiji by 37 points to 25 at Churchill Park, Lautoka, and concluding the tour with a victory over Samoa at Apia Park, Apia, by 17 points to 16.

There was a marked improvement in the 2013 Championship when the Scottish team won two home games against Italy and Ireland to finish in third place (a position they also held in 2001 and 2006).

A sole win in Rome in the 2014 Six Nations Championship, however, relegated Scotland back to fifth place in the table, before a stirring autumn where they defeated Argentina by 41 points to 31 and pushed New Zealand close in a 24 point to 16 loss at Murrayfield, before concluding the series with a 37 points to 12 win over Tonga at Rugby Park, Kilmarnock, which was notable as the first International to be played on an artificial surface.

However, five defeats in the 2015 Championship plunged the Scots to their fourth wooden spoon in sixteen years of the competition. In eighty Six Nations Championships, Scotland have won only nineteen games: a record of less than 25%.

SCOTLAND

HEAD TO HEAD RESULTS TO 31 MARCH 2015

	P	W	D	L	%	F	A
v TIER 1 Teams							
v Argentina	15	6	0	9	40.0	309	268
v Australia	28	9	0	19	32.1	330	671
v England *	133	42	18	73	38.3	1132	1547
v France	88	34	3	51	40.3	1057	1243
v Ireland * / **	130	65	5	59	52.3	1333	1412
v Italy	23	15	0	8	65.2	524	416
v New Zealand	30	0	2	28	3.3	332	900
v South Africa	25	5	0	20	20.0	270	652
v Wales *	120	48	3	69	41.2	1211	1584
Sub-Total	**592**	**224**	**31**	**336**	**40.5**	**6498**	**8693**
v TIER 2/3 Group							
v Canada	4	3	0	1	75.0	105	49
v Fiji	6	5	0	1	83.3	182	145
v Japan	4	4	0	0	100.0	221	45
v Romania	13	11	0	2	84.6	475	192
v Samoa	9	7	1	1	83.3	218	122
v Tonga	4	3	0	1	75.0	136	58
v United States	4	4	0	0	100.0	181	50
v Georgia	1	1	0	0	100.0	15	6
v Namibia	0	0	0	0	0.0	0.0	0
v Russia	0	0	0	0	0.0	0.0	0
v Uruguay	1	1	0	0	100.0	43	12
Sub-Total	**46**	**39**	**1**	**6**	**85.9**	**1576**	**679**
v Other Teams							
v Côte d'Ivoire	1	1	0	0	100.0	89	0
v Pacific Islanders	1	1	0	0	100.0	34	22
v Portugal	1	1	0	0	100.0	56	10
v President's XV	1	1	0	0	100.0	27	16
v Spain	1	1	0	0	100.0	48	0
v Zimbabwe	2	2	0	0	100.0	111	33
Sub-Total	**7**	**7**	**0**	**0**	**100.0**	**365**	**81**
All Internationals	**645**	**270**	**32**	**342**	**44.4**	**8439**	**9453**

* excludes points scored before the introduction of the modern points system
** excludes the abandoned match on 21 February 1885 (Ireland 0 Scotland 1)

No	Date	Opponents	Tmt		Match Venue	Result	
1	27-Mar-71	England	Int	H	Raeburn Place, Edinburgh	W	4-1
2	5-Feb-72	England	Int	A	Kennington Oval, London	L	3-8
3	3-Mar-73	England	Int	H	Hamilton Crescent, Glasgow	D	0-0
4	23-Feb-74	England	Int	A	Kennington Oval, London	L	1-3
5	8-Mar-75	England	Int	H	Raeburn Place, Edinburgh	D	0-0
6	6-Mar-76	England	Int	A	Kennington Oval, London	L	0-4
7	19-Feb-77	Ireland	Int	A	Ormeau, Belfast	W	20-0
8	5-Mar-77	England	Int	H	Raeburn Place, Edinburgh	W	3-0
9	4-Mar-78	England	Int	A	Kennington Oval, London	D	0-0
10	17-Feb-79	Ireland	Int	A	Ormeau, Belfast	W	7-0
11	10-Mar-79	England	CC	H	Raeburn Place, Edinburgh	D	3-3
12	14-Feb-80	Ireland	Int	H	Hamilton Crescent, Glasgow	W	11-0
13	28-Feb-80	England	CC	A	Whalley Range, Manchester	L	3-9
14	19-Feb-81	Ireland	Int	A	Ormeau, Belfast	L	1-3
15	19-Mar-81	England	CC	H	Raeburn Place, Edinburgh	D	4-4
16	18-Feb-82	Ireland	Int	H	Hamilton Crescent, Glasgow	W	2-0
17	4-Mar-82	England	CC	A	Whalley Range, Manchester	W	2-0
18	8-Jan-83	Wales	4N	H	Raeburn Place, Edinburgh	W	9-3
19	17-Feb-83	Ireland	Int	A	Ormeau, Belfast	W	4-0
20	3-Mar-83	England	4N-CC	H	Raeburn Place, Edinburgh	L	1-2
21	12-Jan-84	Wales	4N	A	Rodney Parade, Newport	W	4-0
22	16-Feb-84	Ireland	4N	H	Raeburn Place, Edinburgh	W	8-1
23	1-Mar-84	England	4N-CC	A	Rectory Field, Blackheath	L	1-3
24	10-Jan-85	Wales	4N	H	Hamilton Crescent, Glasgow	D	0-0
25	21-Feb-85	Ireland	4N	A	Ormeau, Belfast (abandoned)	a	1-0
26	7-Mar-85	Ireland	4N	H	Raeburn Place, Edinburgh	W	5-0
27	9-Jan-86	Wales	4N	A	Arms Park, Cardiff	W	7-0
28	20-Feb-86	Ireland	4N	H	Raeburn Place, Edinburgh	W	14-0
29	13-Mar-86	England	4N-CC	H	Raeburn Place, Edinburgh	D	0-0
30	19-Feb-87	Ireland	4N	A	Ormeau, Belfast	W	8-0
31	26-Feb-87	Wales	4N	H	Raeburn Place, Edinburgh	W	20-0
32	5-Mar-87	England	4N-CC	A	Whalley Range, Manchester	D	1-1
33	4-Feb-88	Wales	4N	A	Rodney Parade, Newport	L	0-1
34	10-Mar-88	Ireland	4N	H	Raeburn Place, Edinburgh	W	3-0
35	2-Feb-89	Wales	4N	H	Raeburn Place, Edinburgh	W	2-0
36	16-Feb-89	Ireland	4N	A	Ormeau, Belfast	W	3-0
37	1-Feb-90	Wales	4N	A	Arms Park, Cardiff	W	5-1
38	22-Feb-90	Ireland	4N	H	Raeburn Place, Edinburgh	W	5-0
39	1-Mar-90	England	4N-CC	H	Raeburn Place, Edinburgh	L	0-6
40	7-Feb-91	Wales	4N	H	Raeburn Place, Edinburgh	W	15-0

No	Date	Opponents	Tmt		Match Venue	Result	
41	21-Feb-91	Ireland	4N	A	Ballynafeigh, Belfast	W	14-0
42	7-Mar-91	England	4N-CC	A	Athletic Ground, Richmond	W	9-3
43	6-Feb-92	Wales	4N	A	St Helen's, Swansea	W	7-2
44	20-Feb-92	Ireland	4N	H	Raeburn Place, Edinburgh	W	2-0
45	5-Mar-92	England	4N-CC	H	Raeburn Place, Edinburgh	L	0-5
46	4-Feb-93	Wales	4N	H	Raeburn Place, Edinburgh	L	0-9
47	18-Feb-93	Ireland	4N	A	Ballynafeigh, Belfast	D	0-0
48	4-Mar-93	England	4N-CC	A	Headingley, Leeds	W	8-0
49	3-Feb-94	Wales	4N	A	Rodney Parade, Newport	L	0-7
50	24-Feb-94	Ireland	4N	A	Lansdowne Road, Dublin	L	0-5
51	17-Mar-94	England	4N-CC	H	Raeburn Place, Edinburgh	W	6-0
52	26-Jan-95	Wales	4N	H	Raeburn Place, Edinburgh	W	5-4
53	2-Mar-95	Ireland	4N	H	Raeburn Place, Edinburgh	W	6-0
54	9-Mar-95	England	4N-CC	A	Athletic Ground, Richmond	W	6-3
55	25-Jan-96	Wales	4N	A	Arms Park, Cardiff	L	0-6
56	15-Feb-96	Ireland	4N	A	Lansdowne Road, Dublin	D	0-0
57	14-Mar-96	England	4N-CC	H	Old Hampden Park, Glasgow	W	11-0
58	20-Feb-97	Ireland	4N	H	Powderhall, Edinburgh	W	8-3
59	13-Mar-97	England	4N-CC	A	Fallowfield, Manchester	L	3-12
60	19-Feb-98	Ireland	4N	A	Balmoral Showgrounds, Belfast	W	8-0
61	12-Mar-98	England	4N-CC	H	Powderhall, Edinburgh	D	3-3
62	18-Feb-99	Ireland	4N	H	Inverleith, Edinburgh	L	3-9
63	4-Mar-99	Wales	4N	H	Inverleith, Edinburgh	W	21-10
64	11-Mar-99	England	4N-CC	A	Rectory Field, Blackheath	W	5-0
65	27-Jan-00	Wales	4N	A	St Helen's, Swansea	L	3-12
66	24-Feb-00	Ireland	4N	A	Lansdowne Road, Dublin	D	0-0
67	10-Mar-00	England	4N-CC	H	Inverleith, Edinburgh	D	0-0
68	9-Feb-01	Wales	4N	H	Inverleith, Edinburgh	W	18-8
69	23-Feb-01	Ireland	4N	H	Inverleith, Edinburgh	W	9-5
70	9-Mar-01	England	4N-CC	A	Rectory Field, Blackheath	W	18-3
71	1-Feb-02	Wales	4N	A	Arms Park, Cardiff	L	5-14
72	22-Feb-02	Ireland	4N	A	Balmoral Showgrounds, Belfast	L	0-5
73	15-Mar-02	England	4N-CC	H	Inverleith, Edinburgh	L	3-6
74	7-Feb-03	Wales	4N	H	Inverleith, Edinburgh	W	6-0
75	28-Feb-03	Ireland	4N	H	Inverleith, Edinburgh	W	3-0
76	21-Mar-03	England	4N-CC	A	Athletic Ground, Richmond	W	10-6
77	6-Feb-04	Wales	4N	A	St Helen's, Swansea	L	3-21
78	27-Feb-04	Ireland	4N	A	Lansdowne Road, Dublin	W	19-3
79	19-Mar-04	England	4N-CC	H	Inverleith, Edinburgh	W	6-3
80	4-Feb-05	Wales	4N	H	Inverleith, Edinburgh	L	3-6

No	Date	Opponents	Tmt		Match Venue	Result	
81	25-Feb-05	Ireland	4N	H	Inverleith, Edinburgh	L	5-11
82	18-Mar-05	England	4N-CC	A	Athletic Ground, Richmond	W	8-0
83	18-Nov-05	New Zealand	Int	H	Inverleith, Edinburgh	L	7-12
84	3-Feb-06	Wales	4N	A	Arms Park, Cardiff,	L	3-9
85	24-Feb-06	Ireland	4N	A	Lansdowne Road, Dublin	W	13-6
86	17-Mar-06	England	4N-CC	H	Inverleith, Edinburgh	L	3-9
87	17-Nov-06	South Africa	Int	H	Hampden Park, Glasgow	W	6-0
88	2-Feb-07	Wales	4N	H	Inverleith, Edinburgh	W	6-3
89	23-Feb-07	Ireland	4N	H	Inverleith, Edinburgh	W	15-3
90	16-Mar-07	England	4N-CC	A	Rectory Field, Blackheath	W	8-3
91	1-Feb-08	Wales	4N	A	St Helen's, Swansea	L	5-6
92	29-Feb-08	Ireland	4N	A	Lansdowne Road, Dublin	L	11-16
93	21-Mar-08	England	4N-CC	H	Inverleith, Edinburgh	W	16-10
94	6-Feb-09	Wales	4N	H	Inverleith, Edinburgh	L	3-5
95	27-Feb-09	Ireland	4N	H	Inverleith, Edinburgh	W	9-3
96	20-Mar-09	England	4N-CC	A	Athletic Ground, Richmond	W	18-8
97	22-Jan-10	France	5N	H	Inverleith, Edinburgh	W	27-0
98	5-Feb-10	Wales	5N	A	Arms Park, Cardiff	L	0-14
99	26-Feb-10	Ireland	5N	A	Balmoral Showgrounds, Belfast	W	14-0
100	19-Mar-10	England	5N-CC	H	Inverleith, Edinburgh	L	5-14
101	2-Jan-11	France	5N	A	Stade Colombes, Paris	L	15-16
102	4-Feb-11	Wales	5N	H	Inverleith, Edinburgh	L	10-32
103	25-Feb-11	Ireland	5N	H	Inverleith, Edinburgh	L	10-16
104	18-Mar-11	England	5N-CC	A	Twickenham, London	L	8-13
105	20-Jan-12	France	5N	H	Inverleith, Edinburgh	W	31-3
106	3-Feb-12	Wales	5N	A	St Helen's, Swansea	L	6-21
107	24-Feb-12	Ireland	5N	A	Lansdowne Road, Dublin	L	8-10
108	16-Mar-12	England	5N-CC	H	Inverleith, Edinburgh	W	8-3
109	23-Nov-12	South Africa	Int	H	Inverleith, Edinburgh	L	0-16
110	1-Jan-13	France	5N	A	Parc des Princess, Paris	W	21-3
111	1-Feb-13	Wales	5N	H	Inverleith, Edinburgh	L	0-8
112	22-Feb-13	Ireland	5N	H	Inverleith, Edinburgh	W	29-14
113	15-Mar-13	England	5N-CC	A	Twickenham, London	L	0-3
114	7-Feb-14	Wales	5N	A	Arms Park, Cardiff	L	5-24
115	28-Feb-14	Ireland	5N	A	Lansdowne Road, Dublin	L	0-6
116	21-Mar-14	England	5N-CC	H	Inverleith, Edinburgh	L	15-16
117	1-Jan-20	France	5N	A	Parc des Princess, Paris	W	5-0
118	7-Feb-20	Wales	5N	H	Inverleith, Edinburgh	W	9-5
119	28-Feb-20	Ireland	5N	H	Inverleith, Edinburgh	W	19-0
120	20-Mar-20	England	5N-CC	A	Twickenham, London	L	4-13

No	Date	Opponents	Tmt		Match Venue	Result	
121	22-Jan-21	France	5N	H	Inverleith, Edinburgh	L	0-3
122	5-Feb-21	Wales	5N	A	St Helen's, Swansea	W	14-8
123	26-Feb-21	Ireland	5N	A	Lansdowne Road, Dublin	L	8-9
124	19-Mar-21	England	5N-CC	H	Inverleith, Edinburgh	L	0-18
125	2-Jan-22	France	5N	A	Stade Colombes, Paris	D	3-3
126	4-Feb-22	Wales	5N	H	Inverleith, Edinburgh	D	9-9
127	25-Feb-22	Ireland	5N	H	Inverleith, Edinburgh	W	6-3
128	18-Mar-22	England	5N-CC	A	Twickenham, London	L	5-11
129	20-Jan-23	France	5N	H	Inverleith, Edinburgh	W	16-3
130	3-Feb-23	Wales	5N	A	Arms Park, Cardiff	W	11-8
131	24-Feb-23	Ireland	5N	A	Lansdowne Road, Dublin	W	13-3
132	17-Mar-23	England	5N-CC	H	Inverleith, Edinburgh	L	6-8
133	1-Jan-24	France	5N	A	Stade Pershing, Vincennes, Paris	L	10-12
134	2-Feb-24	Wales	5N	H	Inverleith, Edinburgh	W	35-10
135	23-Feb-24	Ireland	5N	H	Inverleith, Edinburgh	W	13-8
136	15-Mar-24	England	5N-CC	A	Twickenham, London	L	0-19
137	24-Jan-25	France	5N	H	Inverleith, Edinburgh	W	25-4
138	7-Feb-25	Wales	5N	A	St Helen's, Swansea	W	24-14
139	28-Feb-25	Ireland	5N	A	Lansdowne Road, Dublin	W	14-8
140	21-Mar-25	England	5N-CC	H	Murrayfield, Edinburgh	W	14-11
141	2-Jan-26	France	5N	A	Stade Colombes, Paris	W	20-6
142	6-Feb-26	Wales	5N	H	Murrayfield, Edinburgh	W	8-5
143	27-Feb-26	Ireland	5N	H	Murrayfield, Edinburgh	L	0-3
144	20-Mar-26	England	5N-CC	A	Twickenham, London	W	17-9
145	22-Jan-27	France	5N	H	Murrayfield, Edinburgh	W	23-6
146	5-Feb-27	Wales	5N	A	Arms Park, Cardiff	W	5-0
147	26-Feb-27	Ireland	5N	A	Lansdowne Road, Dublin	L	0-6
148	19-Mar-27	England	5N-CC	H	Murrayfield, Edinburgh	W	21-13
149	17-Dec-27	Australia	Int	H	Murrayfield, Edinburgh	W	10-8
150	2-Jan-28	France	5N	A	Stade Colombes, Paris	W	15-6
151	4-Feb-28	Wales	5N	H	Murrayfield, Edinburgh	L	0-13
152	25-Feb-28	Ireland	5N	H	Murrayfield, Edinburgh	L	5-13
153	17-Mar-28	England	5N-CC	A	Twickenham, London	L	0-6
154	19-Jan-29	France	5N	H	Murrayfield, Edinburgh	W	6-3
155	2-Feb-29	Wales	5N	A	St Helen's, Swansea	L	7-14
156	23-Feb-29	Ireland	5N	A	Lansdowne Road, Dublin	W	16-7
157	16-Mar-29	England	5N-CC	H	Murrayfield, Edinburgh	W	12-6
158	1-Jan-30	France	5N	A	Stade Colombes, Paris	L	3-7
159	1-Feb-30	Wales	5N	H	Murrayfield, Edinburgh	W	12-9
160	22-Feb-30	Ireland	5N	H	Murrayfield, Edinburgh	L	11-14

No	Date	Opponents	Tmt		Match Venue	Result	
161	15-Mar-30	England	5N-CC	A	Twickenham, London	D	0-0
162	24-Jan-31	France	5N	H	Murrayfield, Edinburgh	W	6-4
163	7-Feb-31	Wales	5N	A	Arms Park, Cardiff	L	8-13
164	28-Feb-31	Ireland	5N	A	Lansdowne Road, Dublin	L	5-8
165	21-Mar-31	England	5N-CC	H	Murrayfield, Edinburgh	W	28-19
166	16-Jan-32	South Africa	Int	H	Murrayfield, Edinburgh	L	3-6
167	6-Feb-32	Wales	4N	H	Murrayfield, Edinburgh	L	0-6
168	27-Feb-32	Ireland	4N	H	Murrayfield, Edinburgh	L	8-20
169	19-Mar-32	England	4N-CC	A	Twickenham, London	L	3-16
170	4-Feb-33	Wales	4N	A	St Helen's, Swansea	W	11-3
171	18-Mar-33	England	4N-CC	H	Murrayfield, Edinburgh	W	3-0
172	1-Apr-33	Ireland	4N	A	Lansdowne Road, Dublin	W	8-6
173	3-Feb-34	Wales	4N	H	Murrayfield, Edinburgh	L	6-13
174	24-Feb-34	Ireland	4N	H	Murrayfield, Edinburgh	W	16-9
175	17-Mar-34	England	4N-CC	A	Twickenham, London	L	3-6
176	2-Feb-35	Wales	4N	A	Arms Park, Cardiff	L	6-10
177	23-Feb-35	Ireland	4N	A	Lansdowne Road, Dublin	L	5-12
178	16-Mar-35	England	4N-CC	H	Murrayfield, Edinburgh	W	10-7
179	23-Nov-35	New Zealand	Int	H	Murrayfield, Edinburgh	L	8-18
180	1-Feb-36	Wales	4N	H	Murrayfield, Edinburgh	L	3-13
181	22-Feb-36	Ireland	4N	H	Murrayfield, Edinburgh	L	4-10
182	21-Mar-36	England	4N-CC	A	Twickenham, London	L	8-9
183	6-Feb-37	Wales	4N	A	St Helen's, Swansea	W	13-6
184	27-Feb-37	Ireland	4N	A	Lansdowne Road, Dublin	L	4-11
185	20-Mar-37	England	4N-CC	H	Murrayfield, Edinburgh	L	3-6
186	5-Feb-38	Wales	4N	H	Murrayfield, Edinburgh	W	8-6
187	26-Feb-38	Ireland	4N	H	Murrayfield, Edinburgh	W	23-14
188	19-Mar-38	England	4N-CC	A	Twickenham, London	W	21-16
189	4-Feb-39	Wales	4N	A	Arms Park, Cardiff	L	3-11
190	25-Feb-39	Ireland	4N	A	Lansdowne Road, Dublin	L	3-12
191	18-Mar-39	England	4N-CC	H	Murrayfield, Edinburgh	L	6-9
192	1-Jan-47	France	5N	A	Stade Colombes, Paris	L	3-8
193	1-Feb-47	Wales	5N	H	Murrayfield, Edinburgh	L	8-22
194	22-Feb-47	Ireland	5N	H	Murrayfield, Edinburgh	L	0-3
195	15-Mar-47	England	5N-CC	A	Twickenham, London	L	5-24
196	22-Nov-47	Australia	Int	H	Murrayfield, Edinburgh	L	7-16
197	24-Jan-48	France	5N	H	Murrayfield, Edinburgh	W	9-8
198	7-Feb-48	Wales	5N	A	Arms Park, Cardiff	L	0-14
199	28-Feb-48	Ireland	5N	A	Lansdowne Road, Dublin	L	0-6
200	20-Mar-48	England	5N-CC	H	Murrayfield, Edinburgh	W	6-3

No	Date	Opponents	Tmt	Match Venue	Result	
201	15-Jan-49	France	5N	A	Stade Colombes, Paris	W 8-0
202	5-Feb-49	Wales	5N	H	Murrayfield, Edinburgh	W 6-5
203	26-Feb-49	Ireland	5N	H	Murrayfield, Edinburgh	L 3-13
204	19-Mar-49	England	5N-CC	A	Twickenham, London	L 3-19
205	14-Jan-50	France	5N	H	Murrayfield, Edinburgh	W 8-5
206	4-Feb-50	Wales	5N	A	St Helen's, Swansea	L 0-12
207	25-Feb-50	Ireland	5N	A	Lansdowne Road, Dublin	L 0-21
208	18-Mar-50	England	5N-CC	H	Murrayfield, Edinburgh	W 13-11
209	13-Jan-51	France	5N	A	Stade Colombes, Paris	L 12-14
210	3-Feb-51	Wales	5N	H	Murrayfield, Edinburgh	W 19-0
211	24-Feb-51	Ireland	5N	H	Murrayfield, Edinburgh	L 5-6
212	17-Mar-51	England	5N-CC	A	Twickenham, London	L 3-5
213	24-Nov-51	South Africa	Int	H	Murrayfield, Edinburgh	L 0-44
214	12-Jan-52	France	5N	H	Murrayfield, Edinburgh	L 11-13
215	2-Feb-52	Wales	5N	A	Arms Park, Cardiff	L 0-11
216	23-Feb-52	Ireland	5N	A	Lansdowne Road, Dublin	L 8-12
217	15-Mar-52	England	5N-CC	H	Murrayfield, Edinburgh	L 3-19
218	10-Jan-53	France	5N	A	Stade Colombes, Paris	L 5-11
219	7-Feb-53	Wales	5N	H	Murrayfield, Edinburgh	L 0-12
220	28-Feb-53	Ireland	5N	H	Murrayfield, Edinburgh	L 8-26
221	21-Mar-53	England	5N-CC	A	Twickenham, London	L 8-26
222	9-Jan-54	France	5N	H	Murrayfield, Edinburgh	L 0-3
223	13-Feb-54	New Zealand	Int	H	Murrayfield, Edinburgh	L 0-3
224	27-Feb-54	Ireland	5N	A	Ravenhill, Belfast	L 0-6
225	20-Mar-54	England	5N-CC	H	Murrayfield, Edinburgh	L 3-13
226	10-Apr-54	Wales	5N	A	St Helen's, Swansea	L 3-15
227	8-Jan-55	France	5N	A	Stade Colombes, Paris	L 0-15
228	5-Feb-55	Wales	5N	H	Murrayfield, Edinburgh	W 14-8
229	26-Feb-55	Ireland	5N	H	Murrayfield, Edinburgh	W 12-3
230	19-Mar-55	England	5N-CC	A	Twickenham, London	L 6-9
231	14-Jan-56	France	5N	H	Murrayfield, Edinburgh	W 12-0
232	4-Feb-56	Wales	5N	A	Arms Park, Cardiff	L 3-9
233	25-Feb-56	Ireland	5N	A	Lansdowne Road, Dublin	L 10-14
234	17-Mar-56	England	5N-CC	H	Murrayfield, Edinburgh	L 6-11
235	12-Jan-57	France	5N	A	Stade Colombes, Paris	W 6-0
236	2-Feb-57	Wales	5N	H	Murrayfield, Edinburgh	W 9-6
237	23-Feb-57	Ireland	5N	H	Murrayfield, Edinburgh	L 3-5
238	16-Mar-57	England	5N-CC	A	Twickenham, London	L 3-16
239	11-Jan-58	France	5N	H	Murrayfield, Edinburgh	W 11-9
240	1-Feb-58	Wales	5N	A	Arms Park, Cardiff	L 3-8

No	Date	Opponents	Tmt		Match Venue	Result	
241	15-Feb-58	Australia	Int	H	Murrayfield, Edinburgh	W	12-8
242	1-Mar-58	Ireland	5N	A	Lansdowne Road, Dublin	L	6-12
243	15-Mar-58	England	5N-CC	H	Murrayfield, Edinburgh	D	3-3
244	10-Jan-59	France	5N	A	Stade Colombes, Paris	L	0-9
245	7-Feb-59	Wales	5N	H	Murrayfield, Edinburgh	W	6-5
246	28-Feb-59	Ireland	5N	H	Murrayfield, Edinburgh	L	3-8
247	21-Mar-59	England	5N-CC	A	Twickenham, London	D	3-3
248	9-Jan-60	France	5N	H	Murrayfield, Edinburgh	L	11-13
249	6-Feb-60	Wales	5N	A	Arms Park, Cardiff	L	0-8
250	27-Feb-60	Ireland	5N	A	Lansdowne Road, Dublin	W	6-5
251	19-Mar-60	England	5N-CC	H	Murrayfield, Edinburgh	L	12-21
252	30-Apr-60	South Africa	Int-T	A	Boet Erasmus Stadium, Port Elizabeth	L	10-18
253	7-Jan-61	France	5N	A	Stade Colombes, Paris	L	0-11
254	21-Jan-61	South Africa	Int	H	Murrayfield, Edinburgh	L	5-12
255	11-Feb-61	Wales	5N	H	Murrayfield, Edinburgh	W	3-0
256	25-Feb-61	Ireland	5N	H	Murrayfield, Edinburgh	W	16-8
257	18-Mar-61	England	5N-CC	A	Twickenham, London	L	0-6
258	13-Jan-62	France	5N	H	Murrayfield, Edinburgh	L	3-11
259	3-Feb-62	Wales	5N	A	Arms Park, Cardiff	W	8-3
260	24-Feb-62	Ireland	5N	A	Lansdowne Road, Dublin	W	20-6
261	17-Mar-62	England	5N-CC	H	Murrayfield, Edinburgh	D	3-3
262	12-Jan-63	France	5N	A	Stade Colombes, Paris	W	11-6
263	2-Feb-63	Wales	5N	H	Murrayfield, Edinburgh	L	0-6
264	23-Feb-63	Ireland	5N	H	Murrayfield, Edinburgh	W	3-0
265	16-Mar-63	England	5N-CC	A	Twickenham, London	L	8-10
266	4-Jan-64	France	5N	H	Murrayfield, Edinburgh	W	10-0
267	18-Jan-64	New Zealand	Int	H	Murrayfield, Edinburgh	D	0-0
268	1-Feb-64	Wales	5N	A	Arms Park, Cardiff	L	3-11
269	22-Feb-64	Ireland	5N	A	Lansdowne Road, Dublin	W	6-3
270	21-Mar-64	England	5N-CC	H	Murrayfield, Edinburgh	W	15-6
271	9-Jan-65	France	5N	A	Stade Colombes, Paris	L	8-16
272	6-Feb-65	Wales	5N	H	Murrayfield, Edinburgh	L	12-14
273	27-Feb-65	Ireland	5N	H	Murrayfield, Edinburgh	L	6-16
274	20-Mar-65	England	5N-CC	A	Twickenham, London	D	3-3
275	17-Apr-65	South Africa	Int	H	Murrayfield, Edinburgh	W	8-5
276	15-Jan-66	France	5N	H	Murrayfield, Edinburgh	D	3-3
277	5-Feb-66	Wales	5N	A	Arms Park, Cardiff	L	3-8
278	26-Feb-66	Ireland	5N	A	Lansdowne Road, Dublin	W	11-3
279	19-Mar-66	England	5N-CC	H	Murrayfield, Edinburgh	W	6-3
280	17-Dec-66	Australia	Int	H	Murrayfield, Edinburgh	W	11-5

No	Date	Opponents	Tmt		Match Venue	Result	
281	14-Jan-67	France	5N	A	Stade Colombes, Paris	W	9-8
282	4-Feb-67	Wales	5N	H	Murrayfield, Edinburgh	W	11-5
283	25-Feb-67	Ireland	5N	H	Murrayfield, Edinburgh	L	3-5
284	18-Mar-67	England	5N-CC	A	Twickenham, London	L	14-27
285	2-Dec-67	New Zealand	Int	H	Murrayfield, Edinburgh	L	3-14
286	13-Jan-68	France	5N	H	Murrayfield, Edinburgh	L	6-8
287	3-Feb-68	Wales	5N	A	Arms Park, Cardiff	L	0-5
288	24-Feb-68	Ireland	5N	A	Lansdowne Road, Dublin	L	6-14
289	16-Mar-68	England	5N-CC	H	Murrayfield, Edinburgh	L	6-8
290	2-Nov-68	Australia	Int	H	Murrayfield, Edinburgh	W	9-3
291	11-Jan-69	France	5N	A	Stade Colombes, Paris	W	6-3
292	1-Feb-69	Wales	5N	H	Murrayfield, Edinburgh	L	3-17
293	22-Feb-69	Ireland	5N	H	Murrayfield, Edinburgh	L	0-16
294	15-Mar-69	England	5N-CC	A	Twickenham, London	L	3-8
295	6-Dec-69	South Africa	Int	H	Murrayfield, Edinburgh	W	6-3
296	10-Jan-70	France	5N	H	Murrayfield, Edinburgh	L	9-11
297	7-Feb-70	Wales	5N	A	National Stadium, Cardiff	L	9-18
298	28-Feb-70	Ireland	5N	A	Lansdowne Road, Dublin	L	11-16
299	21-Mar-70	England	5N-CC	H	Murrayfield, Edinburgh	W	14-5
300	6-Jun-70	Australia	Int-T	A	Cricket Ground, Sydney	L	3-23
301	16-Jan-71	France	5N	A	Stade Colombes, Paris	L	8-13
302	6-Feb-71	Wales	5N	H	Murrayfield, Edinburgh	L	18-19
303	27-Feb-71	Ireland	5N	H	Murrayfield, Edinburgh	L	5-17
304	20-Mar-71	England	5N-CC	A	Twickenham, London	W	16-15
305	27-Mar-71	England	Int-C	H	Murrayfield, Edinburgh	W	26-6
306	15-Jan-72	France	5N	H	Murrayfield, Edinburgh	W	20-9
307	5-Feb-72	Wales	5N	A	National Stadium, Cardiff	L	12-35
308	18-Mar-72	England	5N-CC	H	Murrayfield, Edinburgh	W	23-9
309	16-Dec-72	New Zealand	Int	H	Murrayfield, Edinburgh	L	9-14
310	13-Jan-73	France	5N	A	Parc des Princess, Paris	L	13-16
311	3-Feb-73	Wales	5N	H	Murrayfield, Edinburgh	W	10-9
312	24-Feb-73	Ireland	5N	H	Murrayfield, Edinburgh	W	19-14
313	17-Mar-73	England	5N-CC	A	Twickenham, London	L	13-20
314	31-Mar-73	President's XV	Int-C	H	Murrayfield, Edinburgh	W	27-16
315	19-Jan-74	Wales	5N	A	National Stadium, Cardiff	L	0-6
316	2-Feb-74	England	5N-CC	H	Murrayfield, Edinburgh	W	16-14
317	2-Mar-74	Ireland	5N	A	Lansdowne Road, Dublin	L	6-9
318	16-Mar-74	France	5N	H	Murrayfield, Edinburgh	W	19-6
319	1-Feb-75	Ireland	5N	H	Murrayfield, Edinburgh	W	20-13
320	15-Feb-75	France	5N	A	Parc des Princess, Paris	L	9-10

No	Date	Opponents	Tmt		Match Venue		Result	
321	1-Mar-75	Wales	5N	H	Murrayfield, Edinburgh		W	12-10
322	15-Mar-75	England	5N-CC	A	Twickenham, London		L	6-7
323	14-Jun-75	New Zealand	Int-T	A	Eden Park, Auckland		L	0-24
324	6-Dec-75	Australia	Int	H	Murrayfield, Edinburgh		W	10-3
325	10-Jan-76	France	5N	H	Murrayfield, Edinburgh		L	6-13
326	7-Feb-76	Wales	5N	A	National Stadium, Cardiff		L	6-28
327	21-Feb-76	England	5N-CC	H	Murrayfield, Edinburgh		W	22-12
328	20-Mar-76	Ireland	5N	A	Lansdowne Road, Dublin		W	15-6
329	15-Jan-77	England	5N-CC	A	Twickenham, London		L	6-26
330	19-Feb-77	Ireland	5N	H	Murrayfield, Edinburgh		W	21-18
331	5-Mar-77	France	5N	A	Parc des Princess, Paris		L	3-23
332	19-Mar-77	Wales	5N	H	Murrayfield, Edinburgh		L	9-18
333	21-Jan-78	Ireland	5N	A	Lansdowne Road, Dublin		L	9-12
334	4-Feb-78	France	5N	H	Murrayfield, Edinburgh		L	16-19
335	18-Feb-78	Wales	5N	A	National Stadium, Cardiff		L	14-22
336	4-Mar-78	England	5N-CC	H	Murrayfield, Edinburgh		L	0-15
337	9-Dec-78	New Zealand	Int	H	Murrayfield, Edinburgh		L	9-18
338	20-Jan-79	Wales	5N	H	Murrayfield, Edinburgh		L	13-19
339	3-Feb-79	England	5N-CC	A	Twickenham, London		D	7-7
340	3-Mar-79	Ireland	5N	H	Murrayfield, Edinburgh		D	11-11
341	17-Mar-79	France	5N	A	Parc des Princess, Paris		L	17-21
342	10-Nov-79	New Zealand	Int	H	Murrayfield, Edinburgh		L	6-20
343	2-Feb-80	Ireland	5N	A	Lansdowne Road, Dublin		L	15-22
344	16-Feb-80	France	5N	H	Murrayfield, Edinburgh		W	22-14
345	1-Mar-80	Wales	5N	A	National Stadium, Cardiff		L	6-17
346	15-Mar-80	England	5N-CC	H	Murrayfield, Edinburgh		L	18-30
347	17-Jan-81	France	5N	A	Parc des Princess, Paris		L	9-16
348	7-Feb-81	Wales	5N	H	Murrayfield, Edinburgh		W	15-6
349	21-Feb-81	England	5N-CC	A	Twickenham, London		L	17-23
350	21-Mar-81	Ireland	5N	H	Murrayfield, Edinburgh		W	10-9
351	13-Jun-81	New Zealand	Int-T	A	Carisbrook, Dunedin		L	4-11
352	20-Jun-81	New Zealand	Int-T	A	Eden Park, Auckland		L	15-40
353	26-Sep-81	Romania	Int	H	Murrayfield, Edinburgh		W	12-6
354	19-Dec-81	Australia	Int	H	Murrayfield, Edinburgh		W	24-15
355	16-Jan-82	England	5N-CC	H	Murrayfield, Edinburgh		D	9-9
356	20-Feb-82	Ireland	5N	A	Lansdowne Road, Dublin		L	12-21
357	6-Mar-82	France	5N	H	Murrayfield, Edinburgh		W	16-7
358	20-Mar-82	Wales	5N	A	National Stadium, Cardiff		W	34-18
359	4-Jul-82	Australia	Int-T	A	Ballymore Oval, Brisbane		W	12-7
360	10-Jul-82	Australia	Int-T	A	Cricket Ground, Sydney		L	9-33

No	Date	Opponents	Tmt		Match Venue	Result	
361	15-Jan-83	Ireland	5N	H	Murrayfield, Edinburgh	L	13-15
362	5-Feb-83	France	5N	A	Parc des Princess, Paris	L	15-19
363	19-Feb-83	Wales	5N	H	Murrayfield, Edinburgh	L	15-19
364	5-Mar-83	England	5N-CC	A	Twickenham, London	W	22-12
365	12-Nov-83	New Zealand	Int	H	Murrayfield, Edinburgh	D	25-25
366	21-Jan-84	Wales	5N	A	National Stadium, Cardiff	W	15-9
367	4-Feb-84	England	5N-CC	H	Murrayfield, Edinburgh	W	18-6
368	3-Mar-84	Ireland	5N	A	Lansdowne Road, Dublin	W	32-9
369	17-Mar-84	France	5N	H	Murrayfield, Edinburgh	W	21-12
370	12-May-84	Romania	Int	A	Stadionul 23 August, Bucharest	L	22-28
371	8-Dec-84	Australia	Int	H	Murrayfield, Edinburgh	L	12-37
372	2-Feb-85	Ireland	5N	H	Murrayfield, Edinburgh	L	15-18
373	16-Feb-85	France	5N	A	Parc des Princess, Paris	L	3-11
374	2-Mar-85	Wales	5N	H	Murrayfield, Edinburgh	L	21-25
375	16-Mar-85	England	5N-CC	A	Twickenham, London	L	7-10
376	18-Jan-86	France	5N	H	Murrayfield, Edinburgh	W	18-17
377	1-Feb-86	Wales	5N	A	National Stadium, Cardiff	L	15-22
378	15-Feb-86	England	5N-CC	H	Murrayfield, Edinburgh	W	33-6
379	15-Mar-86	Ireland	5N	A	Lansdowne Road, Dublin	W	10-9
380	29-Mar-86	Romania	Int	A	Stadionul 23 August, Bucharest	W	33-18
381	21-Feb-87	Ireland	5N	H	Murrayfield, Edinburgh	W	16-12
382	7-Mar-87	France	5N	A	Parc des Princess, Paris	L	22-28
383	21-Mar-87	Wales	5N	H	Murrayfield, Edinburgh	W	21-15
384	4-Apr-87	England	5N-CC	A	Twickenham, London	L	12-21
385	23-May-87	France	WCp	N	Lancaster Park Oval, Christchurch	D	20-20
386	30-May-87	Zimbabwe	WCp	N	Athletic Park, Wellington	W	60-21
387	2-Jun-87	Romania	WCp	N	Carisbrook, Dunedin	W	55-28
388	6-Jun-87	New Zealand	WCqf	A	Lancaster Park Oval, Christchurch	L	3-30
389	16-Jan-88	Ireland	5N	A	Lansdowne Road, Dublin	L	18-22
390	6-Feb-88	France	5N	H	Murrayfield, Edinburgh	W	23-12
391	20-Feb-88	Wales	5N	A	National Stadium, Cardiff	L	20-25
392	5-Mar-88	England	5N-CC	H	Murrayfield, Edinburgh	L	6-9
393	19-Nov-88	Australia	Int	H	Murrayfield, Edinburgh	L	13-32
394	21-Jan-89	Wales	5N	H	Murrayfield, Edinburgh	W	23-7
395	4-Feb-89	England	5N-CC	A	Twickenham, London	D	12-12
396	4-Mar-89	Ireland	5N-CQ	H	Murrayfield, Edinburgh	W	37-21
397	18-Mar-89	France	5N	A	Parc des Princess, Paris	L	3-19
398	28-Oct-89	Fiji	Int	H	Murrayfield, Edinburgh	W	38-17
399	9-Dec-89	Romania	Int	H	Murrayfield, Edinburgh	W	32-0
400	3-Feb-90	Ireland	5N-CQ	A	Lansdowne Road, Dublin	W	13-10

No	Date	Opponents	Tmt		Match Venue		Result	
401	17-Feb-90	France	5N	H	Murrayfield, Edinburgh		W	21-0
402	3-Mar-90	Wales	5N	A	National Stadium, Cardiff		W	13-9
403	17-Mar-90	England	5N-CC	H	Murrayfield, Edinburgh		W	13-7
404	16-Jun-90	New Zealand	Int-T	A	Carisbrook, Dunedin		L	16-31
405	23-Jun-90	New Zealand	Int-T	A	Eden Park, Auckland		L	18-21
406	10-Nov-90	Argentina	Int	H	Murrayfield, Edinburgh		W	49-3
407	19-Jan-91	France	5N	A	Parc des Princess, Paris		L	9-15
408	2-Feb-91	Wales	5N	H	Murrayfield, Edinburgh		W	32-12
409	16-Feb-91	England	5N-CC	A	Twickenham, London		L	12-21
410	16-Mar-91	Ireland	5N-CQ	H	Murrayfield, Edinburgh		W	28-25
411	31-Aug-91	Romania	Int	A	Stadionul 23 August, Bucharest		L	12-18
412	5-Oct-91	Japan	WCp	H	Murrayfield, Edinburgh		W	47-9
413	9-Oct-91	Zimbabwe	WCp	H	Murrayfield, Edinburgh		W	51-12
414	12-Oct-91	Ireland	WCp	H	Murrayfield, Edinburgh		W	24-15
415	19-Oct-91	Western Samoa	WCqf	H	Murrayfield, Edinburgh		W	28-6
416	26-Oct-91	England	WCsf	H	Murrayfield, Edinburgh		L	6-9
417	30-Oct-91	New Zealand	WC34	N	National Stadium, Cardiff		L	6-13
418	18-Jan-92	England	5N-CC	H	Murrayfield, Edinburgh		L	7-25
419	15-Feb-92	Ireland	5N-CQ	A	Lansdowne Road, Dublin		W	18-10
420	7-Mar-92	France	5N	H	Murrayfield, Edinburgh		W	10-6
421	21-Mar-92	Wales	5N	A	National Stadium, Cardiff		L	12-15
422	13-Jun-92	Australia	Int-T	A	Football Stadium, Sydney		L	12-27
423	21-Jun-92	Australia	Int-T	A	Ballymore Oval, Brisbane		L	13-37
424	16-Jan-93	Ireland	5N-CQ	H	Murrayfield, Edinburgh		W	15-3
425	6-Feb-93	France	5N	A	Parc des Princess, Paris		L	3-11
426	20-Feb-93	Wales	5N	H	Murrayfield, Edinburgh		W	20-0
427	6-Mar-93	England	5N-CC	A	Twickenham, London		L	12-26
428	20-Nov-93	New Zealand	Int	H	Murrayfield, Edinburgh		L	15-51
429	15-Jan-94	Wales	5N	A	National Stadium, Cardiff		L	6-29
430	5-Feb-94	England	5N-CC	H	Murrayfield, Edinburgh		L	14-15
431	5-Mar-94	Ireland	5N-CQ	A	Lansdowne Road, Dublin		D	6-6
432	19-Mar-94	France	5N	H	Murrayfield, Edinburgh		L	12-20
433	4-Jun-94	Argentina	Int-T	A	Ferro Carril Oeste Stadium, B Aires		L	15-16
434	11-Jun-94	Argentina	Int-T	A	Ferro Carril Oeste Stadium, B Aires		L	17-19
435	19-Nov-94	South Africa	Int	H	Murrayfield, Edinburgh		L	10-34
436	21-Jan-95	Canada	Int	H	Murrayfield, Edinburgh		W	22-6
437	4-Feb-95	Ireland	5N-CQ	H	Murrayfield, Edinburgh		W	26-13
438	18-Feb-95	France	5N	A	Parc des Princess, Paris		W	23-21
439	4-Mar-95	Wales	5N	H	Murrayfield, Edinburgh		W	26-13
440	18-Mar-95	England	5N-CC	A	Twickenham, London		L	12-24

No	Date	Opponents	Tmt	Match Venue	Result	
441	22-Apr-95	Romania	Int	H Murrayfield, Edinburgh	W	49-16
442	26-May-95	Côte d'Ivoire	WCp	N Olympia Park, Rustenburg	W	89-0
443	30-May-95	Tonga	WCp	N Loftus Versfeld Stadium, Pretoria	W	41-5
444	3-Jun-95	France	WCp	N Loftus Versfeld Stadium, Pretoria	L	19-22
445	11-Jun-95	New Zealand	WCqf	N Loftus Versfeld Stadium, Pretoria	L	30-48
446	18-Nov-95	Western Samoa	Int	H Murrayfield, Edinburgh	D	15-15
447	20-Jan-96	Ireland	5N-CQ	A Lansdowne Road, Dublin	W	16-10
448	3-Feb-96	France	5N	H Murrayfield, Edinburgh	W	19-14
449	17-Feb-96	Wales	5N	A National Stadium, Cardiff	W	16-14
450	2-Mar-96	England	5N-CC	H Murrayfield, Edinburgh	L	9-18
451	15-Jun-96	New Zealand	Int-T	A Carisbrook, Dunedin	L	31-62
452	22-Jun-96	New Zealand	Int-T	A Eden Park, Auckland	L	12-36
453	9-Nov-96	Australia	Int	H Murrayfield, Edinburgh	L	19-29
454	14-Dec-96	Italy	Int	H Murrayfield, Edinburgh	W	29-22
455	18-Jan-97	Wales	5N	H Murrayfield, Edinburgh	L	19-34
456	1-Feb-97	England	5N-CC	A Twickenham, London	L	13-41
457	1-Mar-97	Ireland	5N-CQ	H Murrayfield, Edinburgh	W	38-10
458	15-Mar-97	France	5N	A Parc des Princess, Paris	L	20-47
459	22-Nov-97	Australia	Int	H Murrayfield, Edinburgh	L	8-37
460	6-Dec-97	South Africa	Int	H Murrayfield, Edinburgh	L	10-68
461	24-Jan-98	Italy	Int	A Stadio Comunale di Monigo, Treviso	L	21-25
462	7-Feb-98	Ireland	5N-CQ	A Lansdowne Road, Dublin	W	17-16
463	21-Feb-98	France	5N	H Murrayfield, Edinburgh	L	16-51
464	7-Mar-98	Wales	5N	N Wembley Stadium, London	L	13-19
465	22-Mar-98	England	5N-CC	H Murrayfield, Edinburgh	L	20-34
466	26-May-98	Fiji	Int-T	A National Stadium, Suva	L	26-51
467	13-Jun-98	Australia	HT-T	A Football Stadium, Sydney	L	3-45
468	20-Jun-98	Australia	HT-T	A Ballymore Oval, Brisbane	L	11-33
469	21-Nov-98	South Africa	Int	H Murrayfield, Edinburgh	L	10-35
470	6-Feb-99	Wales	5N	H Murrayfield, Edinburgh	W	33-20
471	20-Feb-99	England	5N-CC	A Twickenham, London	L	21-24
472	6-Mar-99	Italy	Int	H Murrayfield, Edinburgh	W	30-12
473	20-Mar-99	Ireland	5N-CQ	H Murrayfield, Edinburgh	W	30-13
474	10-Apr-99	France	5N	A Stade de France, Paris	W	36-22
475	21-Aug-99	Argentina	Int	H Murrayfield, Edinburgh	L	22-31
476	28-Aug-99	Romania	Int	H Hampden Park, Glasgow	W	60-19
477	3-Oct-99	South Africa	WCp	H Murrayfield, Edinburgh	L	29-46
478	8-Oct-99	Uruguay	WCp	H Murrayfield, Edinburgh	W	43-12
479	16-Oct-99	Spain	WCp	H Murrayfield, Edinburgh	W	48-0
480	20-Oct-99	Samoa	QFpo	H Murrayfield, Edinburgh	W	35-20

No	Date	Opponents	Tmt		Match Venue		Result
481	24-Oct-99	New Zealand	WCqf	H	Murrayfield, Edinburgh	L	18-30
482	5-Feb-00	Italy	6N	A	Stadio Flaminio, Rome	L	20-34
483	19-Feb-00	Ireland	6N-CQ	A	Lansdowne Road, Dublin	L	22-44
484	4-Mar-00	France	6N	H	Murrayfield, Edinburgh	L	16-28
485	18-Mar-00	Wales	6N	A	Millennium Stadium, Cardiff	L	18-26
486	2-Apr-00	England	6N-CC	H	Murrayfield, Edinburgh	W	19-13
487	24-Jun-00	New Zealand	Int-T	A	Carisbrook, Dunedin	L	20-69
488	1-Jul-00	New Zealand	Int-T	A	Eden Park, Auckland	L	14-48
489	4-Nov-00	United States	Int	H	Murrayfield, Edinburgh	W	53-6
490	11-Nov-00	Australia	HT	H	Murrayfield, Edinburgh	L	9-30
491	18-Nov-00	Samoa	Int	H	Murrayfield, Edinburgh	W	31-8
492	4-Feb-01	France	6N	A	Stade de France, Paris	L	6-16
493	17-Feb-01	Wales	6N	H	Murrayfield, Edinburgh	D	28-28
494	3-Mar-01	England	6N-CC	A	Twickenham, London	L	3-43
495	17-Mar-01	Italy	6N	H	Murrayfield, Edinburgh	W	23-19
496	22-Sep-01	Ireland	6N-CQ	H	Murrayfield, Edinburgh	W	32-10
497	10-Nov-01	Tonga	Int	H	Murrayfield, Edinburgh	W	43-20
498	18-Nov-01	Argentina	Int	H	Murrayfield, Edinburgh	L	16-25
499	24-Nov-01	New Zealand	Int	H	Murrayfield, Edinburgh	L	6-37
500	2-Feb-02	England	6N-CC	H	Murrayfield, Edinburgh	L	3-29
501	16-Feb-02	Italy	6N	A	Stadio Flaminio, Rome	W	29-12
502	2-Mar-02	Ireland	6N-CQ	A	Lansdowne Road, Dublin	L	22-43
503	23-Mar-02	France	6N	H	Murrayfield, Edinburgh	L	10-22
504	6-Apr-02	Wales	6N	A	Millennium Stadium, Cardiff	W	27-22
505	15-Jun-02	Canada	Int-T	A	Thunderbird Stadium, Vancouver	L	23-26
506	22-Jun-02	United States	Int-T	A	Boxer Stadium, San Francisco	W	65-23
507	9-Nov-02	Romania	Int	H	Murrayfield, Edinburgh	W	37-10
508	16-Nov-02	South Africa	Int	H	Murrayfield, Edinburgh	W	21-6
509	24-Nov-02	Fiji	Int	H	Murrayfield, Edinburgh	W	36-22
510	16-Feb-03	Ireland	6N-CQ	H	Murrayfield, Edinburgh	L	6-36
511	23-Feb-03	France	6N	A	Stade de France, Paris	L	3-38
512	8-Mar-03	Wales	6N	H	Murrayfield, Edinburgh	W	30-22
513	22-Mar-03	England	6N-CC	A	Twickenham, London	L	9-40
514	29-Mar-03	Italy	6N	H	Murrayfield, Edinburgh	W	33-25
515	7-Jun-03	South Africa	Int-T	A	ABSA Stadium, Durban	L	25-29
516	14-Jun-03	South Africa	Int-T	A	Ellis Park, Johannesburg	L	19-28
517	23-Aug-03	Italy	Int	H	Murrayfield, Edinburgh	W	47-15
518	30-Aug-03	Wales	Int	A	Millennium Stadium, Cardiff	L	9-23
519	6-Sep-03	Ireland	Int	H	Murrayfield, Edinburgh	L	10-29
520	12-Oct-03	Japan	WCp	N	Dairy Farmers Stadium, Townsville	W	32-11

No	Date	Opponents	Tmt		Match Venue	Result	
521	20-Oct-03	United States	WCp	N	Suncorp Stadium, Brisbane	W	39-15
522	25-Oct-03	France	WCp	N	Telstra Stadium, Sydney	L	9-51
523	1-Nov-03	Fiji	WCp	N	Aussie Stadium, Sydney	W	22-20
524	8-Nov-03	Australia	WCqf	A	Suncorp Stadium, Brisbane	L	16-33
525	14-Feb-04	Wales	6N	A	Millennium Stadium, Cardiff	L	10-23
526	21-Feb-04	England	6N-CC	H	Murrayfield, Edinburgh	L	13-35
527	6-Mar-04	Italy	6N	A	Stadio Flaminio, Rome	L	14-20
528	21-Mar-04	France	6N	H	Murrayfield, Edinburgh	L	0-31
529	27-Mar-04	Ireland	6N-CQ	A	Lansdowne Road, Dublin	L	16-37
530	4-Jun-04	Samoa	Int-T	N	Westpac Trust Stadium, Wellington	W	38-3
531	13-Jun-04	Australia	HT-T	A	Telstra Dome, Melbourne	L	15-35
532	19-Jun-04	Australia	HT-T	A	Telstra Stadium, Sydney	L	13-34
533	6-Nov-04	Australia	HT	H	Murrayfield, Edinburgh	L	14-31
534	13-Nov-04	Japan	Int	H	McDiarmid Park, Perth	W	100-8
535	20-Nov-04	Australia	HT	H	Hampden Park, Glasgow	L	17-31
536	27-Nov-04	South Africa	Int	H	Murrayfield, Edinburgh	L	10-45
537	5-Feb-05	France	6N	A	Stade de France, Paris	L	9-16
538	12-Feb-05	Ireland	6N-CQ	H	Murrayfield, Edinburgh	L	13-40
539	26-Feb-05	Italy	6N	H	Murrayfield, Edinburgh	W	18-10
540	13-Mar-05	Wales	6N	H	Murrayfield, Edinburgh	L	22-46
541	19-Mar-05	England	6N-CC	A	Twickenham, London	L	22-43
542	5-Jun-05	Romania	Int	A	Stadionul Dinamo, Bucharest	W	39-19
543	12-Nov-05	Argentina	Int	H	Murrayfield, Edinburgh	L	19-23
544	20-Nov-05	Samoa	Int	H	Murrayfield, Edinburgh	W	18-11
545	26-Nov-05	New Zealand	Int	H	Murrayfield, Edinburgh	L	10-29
546	5-Feb-06	France	6N	H	Murrayfield, Edinburgh	W	20-16
547	12-Feb-06	Wales	6N	A	Millennium Stadium, Cardiff	L	18-28
548	25-Feb-06	England	6N-CC	H	Murrayfield, Edinburgh	W	18-12
549	11-Mar-06	Ireland	6N-CQ	A	Lansdowne Road, Dublin	L	9-15
550	18-Mar-06	Italy	6N	A	Stadio Flaminio, Rome	W	13-10
551	10-Jun-06	South Africa	Int-T	A	The ABSA Stadium, Durban	L	16-36
552	17-Jun-06	South Africa	Int-T	A	EPRFU Stadium, Port Elizabeth	L	15-29
553	11-Nov-06	Romania	Int	H	Murrayfield, Edinburgh	W	48-6
554	18-Nov-06	Pacific Islands	Int	H	Murrayfield, Edinburgh	W	34-22
555	25-Nov-06	Australia	HT	H	Murrayfield, Edinburgh	L	15-44
556	3-Feb-07	England	6N-CC	A	Twickenham, London	L	20-42
557	10-Feb-07	Wales	6N	H	Murrayfield, Edinburgh	W	21-9
558	24-Feb-07	Italy	6N	H	Murrayfield, Edinburgh	L	17-37
559	10-Mar-07	Ireland	6N-CQ	H	Murrayfield, Edinburgh	L	18-19
560	17-Mar-07	France	6N	A	Stade de France, Paris	L	19-46

No	Date	Opponents	Tmt		Match Venue		Result	
561	11-Aug-07	Ireland	Int	H	Murrayfield, Edinburgh		W	31-21
562	25-Aug-07	South Africa	Int	H	Murrayfield, Edinburgh		L	3-27
563	9-Sep-07	Portugal	WCp	N	Stade Geoffroy Guichard, Saint Étienne		W	56-10
564	18-Sep-07	Romania	WCp	H	Murrayfield, Edinburgh		W	42-0
565	23-Sep-07	New Zealand	WCp	H	Murrayfield, Edinburgh		L	0-40
566	29-Sep-07	Italy	WCp	N	Stade Geoffroy Guichard, Saint Étienne		W	18-16
567	7-Oct-07	Argentina	WCqf	N	Stade de France, Paris		L	13-19
568	3-Feb-08	France	6N	H	Murrayfield, Edinburgh		L	6-27
569	9-Feb-08	Wales	6N	A	Millennium Stadium, Cardiff		L	15-30
570	23-Feb-08	Ireland	6N-CQ	A	Croke Park, Dublin		L	13-34
571	8-Mar-08	England	6N-CC	H	Murrayfield, Edinburgh		W	15-9
572	15-Mar-08	Italy	6N	A	Stadio Flaminio, Rome		L	20-23
573	7-Jun-08	Argentina	Int-T	A	Stadio Gigante de Arroyito, Rosario		L	15-21
574	14-Jun-08	Argentina	Int-T	A	Vélez Sarsfield Stadium, Buenos Aires		W	26-14
575	8-Nov-08	New Zealand	Int	H	Murrayfield, Edinburgh		L	6-32
576	15-Nov-08	South Africa	Int	H	Murrayfield, Edinburgh		L	10-14
577	22-Nov-08	Canada	DHT	H	Pittodrie Stadium, Aberdeen		W	41-0
578	8-Feb-09	Wales	6N	H	Murrayfield, Edinburgh		L	13-26
579	14-Feb-09	France	6N	A	Stade de France, Paris		L	13-22
580	28-Feb-09	Italy	6N	H	Murrayfield, Edinburgh		W	26-6
581	14-Mar-09	Ireland	6N-CQ	H	Murrayfield, Edinburgh		L	15-22
582	21-Mar-09	England	6N-CC	A	Twickenham, London		L	12-26
583	14-Nov-09	Fiji	Int	H	Murrayfield, Edinburgh		W	23-10
584	21-Nov-09	Australia	HT	H	Murrayfield, Edinburgh		W	9-8
585	28-Nov-09	Argentina	Int	H	Murrayfield, Edinburgh		L	6-9
586	7-Feb-10	France	6N	H	Murrayfield, Edinburgh		L	9-18
587	13-Feb-10	Wales	6N	A	Millennium Stadium, Cardiff		L	24-31
588	27-Feb-10	Italy	6N	A	Stadio Flaminio, Rome		L	12-16
589	13-Mar-10	England	6N-CC	H	Murrayfield, Edinburgh		D	15-15
590	20-Mar-10	Ireland	6N-CQ	A	Croke Park, Dublin		W	23-20
591	12-Jun-10	Argentina	Int-T	A	Estadio Monumental José Fierro, Tucumán		W	24-16
592	19-Jun-10	Argentina	Int-T	A	Estadio José Maria Minella, Mar del Plata		W	13-9
593	13-Nov-10	New Zealand	Int	H	Murrayfield, Edinburgh		L	3-49
594	20-Nov-10	South Africa	Int	H	Murrayfield, Edinburgh		W	21-17
595	27-Nov-10	Samoa	Int	H	Pittodrie Stadium, Aberdeen		W	19-16
596	5-Feb-11	France	6N	A	Stade de France, Paris		L	21-34
597	12-Feb-11	Wales	6N	H	Murrayfield, Edinburgh		L	6-24
598	27-Feb-11	Ireland	6N-CQ	H	Murrayfield, Edinburgh		L	18-21
599	13-Mar-11	England	6N-CC	A	Twickenham, London		L	16-22
600	19-Mar-11	Italy	6N	H	Murrayfield, Edinburgh		W	21-8

No	Date	Opponents	Tmt	Match Venue	Result	
601	6-Aug-11	Ireland	Int	H Murrayfield, Edinburgh	W	10-6
602	20-Aug-11	Italy	Int	H Murrayfield, Edinburgh	W	23-12
603	10-Sep-11	Romania	WCp	N Rugby Park Stadium, Invercargill	W	34-24
604	14-Sep-11	Georgia	WCp	N Rugby Park Stadium, Invercargill	W	15-6
605	25-Sep-11	Argentina	WCp	N Wellington Regional Stadium, Wellington	L	12-13
606	1-Oct-11	England	WCp	N Eden Park, Auckland	L	12-16
607	4-Feb-12	England	6N-CC	H Murrayfield, Edinburgh	L	6-13
608	12-Feb-12	Wales	6N	A Millennium Stadium, Cardiff	L	13-27
609	25-Feb-12	France	6N	H Murrayfield, Edinburgh	L	17-23
610	10-Mar-12	Ireland	6N-CQ	A Aviva Stadium, Dublin	L	14-32
611	17-Mar-12	Italy	6N	A Stadio Olimpico, Rome	L	6-13
612	5-Jun-12	Australia	HT-T	A Ausgrid Stadium, Newcastle, NSW	W	9-6
613	16-Jun-12	Fiji	Int-T	A Churchill Park, Lautoka	W	37-25
614	23-Jun-12	Samoa	Int-T	A Apia Park, Apia	W	17-16
615	11-Nov-12	New Zealand	Int	H Murrayfield, Edinburgh	L	22-51
616	17-Nov-12	South Africa	Int	H Murrayfield, Edinburgh	L	10-21
617	24-Nov-12	Tonga	Int	H Murrayfield, Edinburgh	L	15-21
618	2-Feb-13	England	6N-CC	A Twickenham, London	L	18-38
619	9-Feb-13	Italy	6N	H Murrayfield, Edinburgh	W	34-10
620	24-Feb-13	Ireland	6N-CQ	H Murrayfield, Edinburgh	W	12-8
621	9-Mar-13	Wales	6N	H Murrayfield, Edinburgh	L	18-28
622	16-Mar-13	France	6N	A Stade de France, Paris	L	16-23
623	8-Jun-13	Samoa	quad	N Kings Park Stadium, Durban	L	17-27
624	15-Jun-13	South Africa	quad	A Mbombela Stadium, Nelspruit	L	17-30
625	22-Jun-13	Italy	quad	N Loftus Versfeld Stadium, Pretoria	W	30-29
626	9-Nov-13	Japan	Int	H Murrayfield, Edinburgh	W	42-17
627	16-Nov-13	South Africa	Int	H Murrayfield, Edinburgh	L	0-28
628	23-Nov-13	Australia	HT	A Murrayfield, Edinburgh	L	15-21
629	2-Feb-14	Ireland	6N-CQ	A Aviva Stadium, Dublin	L	6-28
630	8-Feb-14	England	6N-CC	H Murrayfield, Edinburgh	L	0-20
631	22-Feb-14	Italy	6N	A Stadio Olimpico, Rome	W	21-20
632	8-Mar-14	France	6N	H Murrayfield, Edinburgh	L	17-19
633	15-Mar-14	Wales	6N	A Millennium Stadium, Cardiff	L	3-51
634	7-Jun-14	United States	Int-T	A BBVA Compass Stadium, Houston	W	24-6
635	14-Jun-14	Canada	DHT-T	A BMO Stadium, Toronto	W	19-17
636	21-Jun-14	Argentina	Int-T	A Estadio Olimpico Ch. Carreras, Córdoba	W	21-19
637	28-Jun-14	South Africa	Int-T	A Nelson Mandela Bay Stad, Port Elizabeth	L	6-55
638	8-Nov-14	Argentina	Int	H Murrayfield, Edinburgh	W	41-31
639	15-Nov-14	New Zealand	Int	H Murrayfield, Edinburgh	L	16-24
640	22-Nov-14	Tonga	Int	H Rugby Park, Kilmarnock	W	37-12

No	Date	Opponents	Tmt		Match Venue	Result	
641	7-Feb-15	France	6N	A	Stade de France, Paris	L	8-15
642	15-Feb-15	Wales	6N	H	Murrayfield, Edinburgh	L	23-26
643	28-Feb-15	Italy	6N	H	Murrayfield, Edinburgh	L	19-22
644	14-Mar-15	England	6N-CC	A	Twickenham, London	L	13-25
645	21-Mar-15	Ireland	6N-CQ	H	Murrayfield, Edinburgh	L	10-40

SOUTH AFRICA

The South African Rugby Union was formed in Kimberley in 1889. Two years later, a team drawn from the four Home Nations, known at the time as 'Great Britain' but later as the Lions, toured South Africa and won all three Internationals. A second tour followed in 1896 and on that occasion the South Africans won their very first International in the fourth match of the series. In 1903 they were even more successful, winning the third match against the touring Great Britain team after drawing the first two. A tour of Britain and Ireland was arranged in 1906, and the team, now known as the Springboks, lost their first International to Scotland, before beating Ireland and Wales and drawing with England. The Great Britain tour of South Africa in 1910 brought more success for the Springboks as they won the three-match series, 2-1. The second South African tour of the Northern Hemisphere in 1912-13 was an outstanding one for the Springboks, because they won all five International matches against the Home Nations and France.

In 1921 South Africa toured New Zealand for the first time and shared the three-match series with a win apiece and a drawn third match. The Lions name was adopted by the 1924 British and Irish touring team, and on that tour the Lions lost the four-match series 3-0, with one test drawn. The Springboks squared up against the visiting New Zealand team in 1928 and the result was a closely contested series that ended in two wins apiece. Three years later, on a 1931-32 tour of Britain and Ireland, the third Springboks won all four Internationals against the Home Nations.

In 1933, Australia faced the Springboks on their first visit to South Africa and lost a five-match series 3-2. Four years later, in 1937, the South Africans toured Australia and New Zealand and won 2-1 in a three match series against the All Blacks. They also triumphed 2-0 in the series against the Wallabies. The Springboks' winning streak continued the following year as they won a three-match series against the touring Lions, 3-1.

After the Second World War the Springboks hit a purple patch, winning ten games in a row, including a 4-0 clean sweep against New Zealand in the 1949 home series and ultimately achieving a 'grand slam' of five victories over the Home Nations and France on their 1951-52 tour. Next came a home series win over Australia in 1953 and a drawn series against the touring Lions in 1955. The sequence was finally broken when the All Blacks gained their revenge and won the 1956 series 3-1. However, the Springboks came back again with a series win against the touring All Blacks in 1960, four wins against the Home Nations on their 1960-61 tour, and a series win against the touring Lions in 1962. In another twist, the Springboks hit their most mediocre run to date as they lost seven games in a row between 1964 and 1965. The South Africans soon recovered and recorded a 3-0 series win against the touring Lions in 1968, a 2-0 series win in France, also in 1968, and a 4-0 series win against Australia in 1969. However, this success was soon followed by a disastrous four match mini-tour of Britain and Ireland, when they lost to both Scotland and England in December 1969 and could muster only draws against Ireland and Wales in the following month.

Although massive anti-apartheid demonstrations dominated the 1970s, South Africa rode the storm with two 3-1 home series wins against New Zealand in 1970 and 1976, a 3-0 away series win against Australia in 1971, and four wins in a row against France in 1974-75. Indeed the only blemish on that decade of success was the series loss to the unbeaten Lions on tour in 1974, which was later avenged with a 3-1 home series win against the Lions in 1980.

The Springboks played very few matches against the major

nations during the 1980s, but when the apartheid system was dismantled, the team was finally readmitted to international rugby in 1992. And what a comeback it was: having missed the 1987 and the 1991 World Cup competitions, the South Africans stormed back, triumphing in extra time with a 15 points to 12 win over the All Blacks in the final of the 1995 World Cup. It was a victory that was even sweeter since it took place on home ground in Johannesburg. Despite this success, the Springboks' performance level over the next two years slipped a little, but by August 1997 they were back on track, and during the next fifteen months they won seventeen Internationals in a row, an impressive record that they currently share with New Zealand. The South African performance in the next two World Cup tournaments was, by their standard, less stellar, as they lost to Australia in the semi-final in 1999 and to the All Blacks in the quarter-final in 2003, before finally turning it around and securing the coveted trophy for a second time in 2007.

South Africa entered the 2011 World Cup as title holders and, despite strong resistance from both Wales and Samoa, they topped the pool. However, they were eventually forced to relinquish the title in the quarter-final when they lost to Australia by 11 points to 9.

The Springboks have not fared so well in the Tri Nations Championship, launched in 1996 and contested annually with Australia and New Zealand: in sixteen years of the competition, the All Blacks have dominated, with ten title wins to South Africa's three (1998, 2004 and 2009). With the admission of Argentina in 2012, the tournament was replaced by a new competition known as the Rugby Championship. The Springboks have encountered mixed results in that tournament: they finished in third place in 2012, before registering a slight improvement in 2013 when they moved up to second place. As before, it was New Zealand, title winners in both those years, which dominated: the All Blacks won all twelve matches, compared to South Africa's six.

The Springboks were much more successful on both their 2012 and 2013 Northern Hemisphere autumn tours. In 2012 they defeated Ireland, Scotland and England, and in 2013 they overcame Wales, Scotland and France. In the 2014 summer Internationals they recorded a 2-0 series win against the touring Welsh team and a thumping 55 points to 6 win at home to Scotland. The South African team also finished runners-up in the 2014 Rugby Championship, defeating New Zealand in the final match. However, South Africa's performance in the 2014 autumn series of games was, by their high standards, very disappointing: they lost to both Ireland and Wales and managed only a narrow win, by 31 points to 28, against England.

SOUTH AFRICA

HEAD TO HEAD RESULTS TO 31 MARCH 2015

	P	W	D	L	%	F	A
v TIER 1 Teams							
v Argentina	19	18	1	0	97.4	728	361
v Australia	80	45	1	34	56.9	1552	1391
v England	37	23	2	12	64.9	780	592
v France	39	22	6	11	64.1	783	578
v Ireland	22	16	1	5	75.0	432	277
v Italy	12	12	0	0	100.0	599	145
v New Zealand	89	35	3	51	41.0	1392	1718
v Scotland	25	20	0	5	80.0	652	270
v Wales	30	27	1	2	91.7	814	440
v Lions	46	23	6	17	56.5	600	516
Sub-Total	**399**	**241**	**21**	**137**	**63.0**	**8332**	**6288**
v TIER 2/3 Group							
v Canada	2	2	0	0	100.0	71	18
v Fiji	3	3	0	0	100.0	129	41
v Japan	0	0	0	0	0.0	0	0
v Romania	1	1	0	0	100.0	21	8
v Samoa	8	8	0	0	100.0	385	93
v Tonga	2	2	0	0	100.0	104	35
v United States	3	3	0	0	100.0	145	42
v Georgia	1	1	0	0	100.0	46	19
v Namibia	2	2	0	0	100.0	192	13
v Russia	0	0	0	0	0.0	0	0
v Uruguay	3	3	0	0	100.0	245	12
Sub-Total	**25**	**25**	**0**	**0**	**100.0**	**1338**	**281**
v Other Teams							
v N Z Cavaliers	4	3	0	1	75.0	96	62
v Pacific Islanders	1	1	0	0	100.0	38	24
v South America	8	7	0	1	87.5	210	114
v Spain	1	1	0	0	100.0	47	3
v World XV	3	3	0	0	100.0	87	59
Sub-Total	**17**	**15**	**0**	**2**	**88.2**	**478**	**262**
All Internationals	**441**	**281**	**21**	**139**	**66.1**	**10148**	**6831**

No	Date	Opponents	Tmt		Match Venue	Result	
1	30-Jul-91	Lions	Int	H	Crusaders Ground, Port Elizabeth	L	0-4
2	29-Aug-91	Lions	Int	H	Eclectic Cricket Ground, Kimberley	L	0-3
3	5-Sep-91	Lions	Int	H	Newlands Stadium, Cape Town	L	0-4
4	30-Jul-96	Lions	Int	H	Crusaders Ground, Port Elizabeth	L	0-8
5	22-Aug-96	Lions	Int	H	The Wanderers Ground, Johannesburg	L	8-17
6	29-Aug-96	Lions	Int	H	The Kimberley Athletics Club, Kimberley	L	3-9
7	5-Sep-96	Lions	Int	H	Newlands Stadium, Cape Town	W	5-0
8	26-Aug-03	Lions	Int	H	The Wanderers Ground, Johannesburg	D	10-10
9	5-Sep-03	Lions	Int	H	The Kimberley Athletics Club, Kimberley	D	0-0
10	12-Sep-03	Lions	Int	H	Newlands Stadium, Cape Town	W	8-0
11	17-Nov-06	Scotland	Int-T	A	Hampden Park, Glasgow	L	0-6
12	24-Nov-06	Ireland	Int-T	A	Balmoral Showgrounds, Belfast	W	15-12
13	1-Dec-06	Wales	Int-T	A	St Helen's, Swansea	W	11-0
14	8-Dec-06	England	Int-T	A	Crystal Palace, London	D	3-3
15	6-Aug-10	Lions	Int	H	The Wanderers Ground, Johannesburg	W	14-10
16	27-Aug-10	Lions	Int	H	Crusaders Ground, Port Elizabeth	L	3-8
17	3-Sep-10	Lions	Int	H	Newlands Stadium, Cape Town	W	21-5
18	23-Nov-12	Scotland	Int-T	A	Inverleith, Edinburgh	W	16-0
19	30-Nov-12	Ireland	Int-T	A	Lansdowne Road, Dublin	W	38-0
20	14-Dec-12	Wales	Int-T	A	Arms Park, Cardiff	W	3-0
21	4-Jan-13	England	Int-T	A	Twickenham, London	W	9-3
22	11-Jan-13	France	Int-T	A	Route du Médoc, Le Bouscat, Bordeaux	W	38-5
23	13-Aug-21	New Zealand	Int-T	A	Carisbrook, Dunedin	L	5-13
24	27-Aug-21	New Zealand	Int-T	A	Eden Park, Auckland	W	9-5
25	17-Sep-21	New Zealand	Int-T	A	Athletic Park, Wellington	D	0-0
26	16-Aug-24	Lions	Int	H	Kingsmead Ground, Durban	W	7-3
27	23-Aug-24	Lions	Int	H	The Wanderers Ground, Johannesburg	W	17-0
28	13-Sep-24	Lions	Int	H	Crusaders Ground, Port Elizabeth	D	3-3
29	20-Sep-24	Lions	Int	H	Newlands Stadium, Cape Town	W	16-9
30	30-Jun-28	New Zealand	Int	H	Kingsmead Ground, Durban	W	17-0
31	21-Jul-28	New Zealand	Int	H	Ellis Park, Johannesburg	L	6-7
32	18-Aug-28	New Zealand	Int	H	Crusaders Ground, Port Elizabeth	W	11-6
33	1-Sep-28	New Zealand	Int	H	Newlands Stadium, Cape Town	L	5-13
34	5-Dec-31	Wales	Int-T	A	St Helen's, Swansea	W	8-3
35	19-Dec-31	Ireland	Int-T	A	Lansdowne Road, Dublin	W	8-3
36	2-Jan-32	England	Int-T	A	Twickenham, London	W	7-0
37	16-Jan-32	Scotland	Int-T	A	Murrayfield, Edinburgh	W	6-3
38	8-Jul-33	Australia	Int	H	Newlands Stadium, Cape Town	W	17-3
39	22-Jul-33	Australia	Int	H	Kingsmead Ground, Durban	L	6-21
40	12-Aug-33	Australia	Int	H	Ellis Park, Johannesburg	W	12-3

No	Date	Opponents	Tmt	Match Venue	Result	
41	26-Aug-33	Australia	Int	H Crusaders Ground, Port Elizabeth	W	11-0
42	2-Sep-33	Australia	Int	H Springbok Park, Bloemfontein	L	4-15
43	26-Jun-37	Australia	Int-T	A Cricket Ground, Sydney	W	9-5
44	17-Jul-37	Australia	Int-T	A Cricket Ground, Sydney	W	26-17
45	14-Aug-37	New Zealand	Int-T	A Athletic Park, Wellington	L	7-13
46	4-Sep-37	New Zealand	Int-T	A Lancaster Park Oval, Christchurch	W	13-6
47	25-Sep-37	New Zealand	Int-T	A Eden Park, Auckland	W	17-6
48	6-Aug-38	Lions	Int	H Ellis Park, Johannesburg	W	26-12
49	3-Sep-38	Lions	Int	H Crusaders Ground, Port Elizabeth	W	19-3
50	10-Sep-38	Lions	Int	H Newlands Stadium, Cape Town	L	16-21
51	16-Jul-49	New Zealand	Int	H Newlands Stadium, Cape Town	W	15-11
52	13-Aug-49	New Zealand	Int	H Ellis Park, Johannesburg	W	12-6
53	3-Sep-49	New Zealand	Int	H Kingsmead Ground, Durban	W	9-3
54	17-Sep-49	New Zealand	Int	H Crusaders Ground, Port Elizabeth	W	11-8
55	24-Nov-51	Scotland	Int-T	A Murrayfield, Edinburgh	W	44-0
56	8-Dec-51	Ireland	Int-T	A Lansdowne Road, Dublin	W	17-5
57	22-Dec-51	Wales	Int-T	A Arms Park, Cardiff	W	6-3
58	5-Jan-52	England	Int-T	A Twickenham, London	W	8-3
59	16-Feb-52	France	Int-T	A Stade Colombes, Paris	W	25-3
60	22-Aug-53	Australia	Int	H Ellis Park, Johannesburg	W	25-3
61	5-Sep-53	Australia	Int	H Newlands Stadium, Cape Town	L	14-18
62	19-Sep-53	Australia	Int	H Kingsmead Ground, Durban	W	18-8
63	26-Sep-53	Australia	Int	H Crusaders Ground, Port Elizabeth	W	22-9
64	6-Aug-55	Lions	Int	H Ellis Park, Johannesburg	L	22-23
65	20-Aug-55	Lions	Int	H Newlands Stadium, Cape Town	W	25-9
66	3-Sep-55	Lions	Int	H Loftus Versfeld Stadium, Pretoria	L	6-9
67	24-Sep-55	Lions	Int	H Crusaders Ground, Port Elizabeth	W	22-8
68	26-May-56	Australia	Int-T	A Cricket Ground, Sydney	W	9-0
69	2-Jun-56	Australia	Int-T	A Exhibition Ground, Brisbane	W	9-0
70	14-Jul-56	New Zealand	Int-T	A Carisbrook, Dunedin	L	6-10
71	4-Aug-56	New Zealand	Int-T	A Athletic Park, Wellington	W	8-3
72	18-Aug-56	New Zealand	Int-T	A Lancaster Park Oval, Christchurch	L	10-17
73	1-Sep-56	New Zealand	Int-T	A Eden Park, Auckland	L	5-11
74	26-Jul-58	France	Int	H Newlands Stadium, Cape Town	D	3-3
75	16-Aug-58	France	Int	H Ellis Park, Johannesburg	L	5-9
76	30-Apr-60	Scotland	Int	H Boet Erasmus Stadium, Port Elizabeth	W	18-10
77	25-Jun-60	New Zealand	Int	H Ellis Park, Johannesburg	W	13-0
78	23-Jul-60	New Zealand	Int	H Newlands Stadium, Cape Town	L	3-11
79	13-Aug-60	New Zealand	Int	H Free State Stadium, Bloemfontein	D	11-11
80	27-Aug-60	New Zealand	Int	H Boet Erasmus Stadium, Port Elizabeth	W	8-3

No	Date	Opponents	Tmt		Match Venue		Result
81	3-Dec-60	Wales	Int-T	A	Arms Park, Cardiff	W	3-0
82	17-Dec-60	Ireland	Int-T	A	Lansdowne Road, Dublin	W	8-3
83	7-Jan-61	England	Int-T	A	Twickenham, London	W	5-0
84	21-Jan-61	Scotland	Int-T	A	Murrayfield, Edinburgh	W	12-5
85	18-Feb-61	France	Int-T	A	Stade Colombes, Paris	D	0-0
86	13-May-61	Ireland	Int	H	Newlands Stadium, Cape Town	W	24-8
87	5-Aug-61	Australia	Int	H	Ellis Park, Johannesburg	W	28-3
88	12-Aug-61	Australia	Int	H	Boet Erasmus Stadium, Port Elizabeth	W	23-11
89	23-Jun-62	Lions	Int	H	Ellis Park, Johannesburg	D	3-3
90	21-Jul-62	Lions	Int	H	Kings Park Stadium, Durban	W	3-0
91	4-Aug-62	Lions	Int	H	Newlands Stadium, Cape Town	W	8-3
92	25-Aug-62	Lions	Int	H	Free State Stadium, Bloemfontein	W	34-14
93	13-Jul-63	Australia	Int	H	Loftus Versfeld Stadium, Pretoria	W	14-3
94	10-Aug-63	Australia	Int	H	Newlands Stadium, Cape Town	L	5-9
95	24-Aug-63	Australia	Int	H	Ellis Park, Johannesburg	L	9-11
96	7-Sep-63	Australia	Int	H	Boet Erasmus Stadium, Port Elizabeth	W	22-6
97	23-May-64	Wales	Int	H	Kings Park Stadium, Durban	W	24-3
98	25-Jul-64	France	Int	H	P A M Brink Stadium, Springs	L	6-8
99	10-Apr-65	Ireland	Int-T	A	Lansdowne Road, Dublin	L	6-9
100	17-Apr-65	Scotland	Int-T	A	Murrayfield, Edinburgh	L	5-8
101	19-Jun-65	Australia	Int-T	A	Cricket Ground, Sydney	L	11-18
102	26-Jun-65	Australia	Int-T	A	Lang Park, Brisbane	L	8-12
103	31-Jul-65	New Zealand	Int-T	A	Athletic Park, Wellington	L	3-6
104	21-Aug-65	New Zealand	Int-T	A	Carisbrook, Dunedin	L	0-13
105	4-Sep-65	New Zealand	Int-T	A	Lancaster Park Oval, Christchurch	W	19-16
106	18-Sep-65	New Zealand	Int-T	A	Eden Park, Auckland	L	3-20
107	15-Jul-67	France	Int	H	Kings Park Stadium, Durban	W	26-3
108	22-Jul-67	France	Int	H	Free State Stadium, Bloemfontein	W	16-3
109	29-Jul-67	France	Int	H	Ellis Park, Johannesburg	L	14-19
110	12-Aug-67	France	Int	H	Newlands Stadium, Cape Town	D	6-6
111	8-Jun-68	Lions	Int	H	Loftus Versfeld Stadium, Pretoria	W	25-20
112	22-Jun-68	Lions	Int	H	Boet Erasmus Stadium, Port Elizabeth	D	6-6
113	13-Jul-68	Lions	Int	H	Newlands Stadium, Cape Town	W	11-6
114	27-Jul-68	Lions	Int	H	Ellis Park, Johannesburg	W	19-6
115	9-Nov-68	France	Int-T	A	Stade du Parc Lescure, Bordeaux	W	12-9
116	16-Nov-68	France	Int-T	A	Stade Colombes, Paris	W	16-11
117	2-Aug-69	Australia	Int	H	Ellis Park, Johannesburg	W	30-11
118	16-Aug-69	Australia	Int	H	Kings Park Stadium, Durban	W	16-9
119	6-Sep-69	Australia	Int	H	Newlands Stadium, Cape Town	W	11-3
120	20-Sep-69	Australia	Int	H	Free State Stadium, Bloemfontein	W	19-8

No	Date	Opponents	Tmt		Match Venue	Result	
121	6-Dec-69	Scotland	Int-T	A	Murrayfield, Edinburgh	L	3-6
122	20-Dec-69	England	Int-T	A	Twickenham, London	L	8-11
123	10-Jan-70	Ireland	Int-T	A	Lansdowne Road, Dublin	D	8-8
124	24-Jan-70	Wales	Int-T	A	National Stadium, Cardiff	D	6-6
125	25-Jul-70	New Zealand	Int	H	Loftus Versfeld Stadium, Pretoria	W	17-6
126	8-Aug-70	New Zealand	Int	H	Newlands Stadium, Cape Town	L	8-9
127	29-Aug-70	New Zealand	Int	H	Boet Erasmus Stadium, Port Elizabeth	W	14-3
128	12-Sep-70	New Zealand	Int	H	Ellis Park, Johannesburg	W	20-17
129	12-Jun-71	France	Int	H	Free State Stadium, Bloemfontein	W	22-9
130	19-Jun-71	France	Int	H	Kings Park Stadium, Durban	D	8-8
131	17-Jul-71	Australia	Int-T	A	Cricket Ground, Sydney	W	19-11
132	31-Jul-71	Australia	Int-T	A	Exhibition Ground, Brisbane	W	14-6
133	7-Aug-71	Australia	Int-T	A	Cricket Ground, Sydney	W	18-6
134	3-Jun-72	England	Int	H	Ellis Park, Johannesburg	L	9-18
135	8-Jun-74	Lions	Int	H	Newlands Stadium, Cape Town	L	3-12
136	22-Jun-74	Lions	Int	H	Loftus Versfeld Stadium, Pretoria	L	9-28
137	13-Jul-74	Lions	Int	H	Boet Erasmus Stadium, Port Elizabeth	L	9-26
138	27-Jul-74	Lions	Int	H	Ellis Park, Johannesburg	D	13-13
139	23-Nov-74	France	Int-T	A	Stade Municipal de Toulouse, Toulouse	W	13-4
140	30-Nov-74	France	Int-T	A	Parc de Princes, Paris	W	10-8
141	21-Jun-75	France	Int	H	Free State Stadium, Bloemfontein	W	38-25
142	28-Jun-75	France	Int	H	Loftus Versfeld Stadium, Pretoria	W	33-18
143	24-Jul-76	New Zealand	Int	H	Kings Park Stadium, Durban	W	16-7
144	14-Aug-76	New Zealand	Int	H	Free State Stadium, Bloemfontein	L	9-15
145	4-Sep-76	New Zealand	Int	H	Newlands Stadium, Cape Town	W	15-10
146	18-Sep-76	New Zealand	Int	H	Ellis Park, Johannesburg	W	15-14
147	27-Aug-77	World XV	Int	H	Loftus Versfeld Stadium, Pretoria	W	45-24
148	26-Apr-80	South America	Int	H	The Wanderers Ground, Johannesburg	W	24-9
149	3-May-80	South America	Int	H	Kings Park Stadium, Durban	W	18-9
150	31-May-80	Lions	Int	H	Newlands Stadium, Cape Town	W	26-22
151	14-Jun-80	Lions	Int	H	Free State Stadium, Bloemfontein	W	26-19
152	28-Jun-80	Lions	Int	H	Boet Erasmus Stadium, Port Elizabeth	W	12-10
153	12-Jul-80	Lions	Int	H	Loftus Versfeld Stadium, Pretoria	L	13-17
154	18-Oct-80	South America	Int-T	A	Wanderers Club Ground, Montevideo	W	22-13
155	25-Oct-80	South America	Int-T	A	Prince of Wales Country Club, Santiago	W	30-16
156	8-Nov-80	France	Tmt	H	Loftus Versfeld Stadium, Pretoria	W	37-15
157	30-May-81	Ireland	Int	H	Newlands Stadium, Cape Town	W	23-15
158	6-Jun-81	Ireland	Int	H	Kings Park Stadium, Durban	W	12-10
159	15-Aug-81	New Zealand	Int-T	A	Lancaster Park Oval, Christchurch	L	9-14
160	29-Aug-81	New Zealand	Int-T	A	Athletic Park, Wellington	W	24-12

No	Date	Opponents	Tmt		Match Venue	Result	
161	12-Sep-81	New Zealand	Int-T	A	Eden Park, Auckland	L	22-25
162	25-Sep-81	United States	Int-T	A	Owl Creek Polo Field, Glenville, New York	W	38-7
163	27-Mar-82	South America	Int	H	Loftus Versfeld Stadium, Pretoria	W	50-18
164	3-Apr-82	South America	Int	H	Free State Stadium, Bloemfontein	L	12-21
165	2-Jun-84	England	Int	H	Boet Erasmus Stadium, Port Elizabeth	W	33-15
166	9-Jun-84	England	Int	H	Ellis Park, Johannesburg	W	35-9
167	20-Oct-84	South America	Int	H	Loftus Versfeld Stadium, Pretoria	W	32-15
168	27-Oct-84	South America	Int	H	Newlands Stadium, Cape Town	W	22-13
169	10-May-86	NZ Cavaliers	Int	H	Newlands Stadium, Cape Town	W	21-15
170	17-May-86	NZ Cavaliers	Int	H	Kings Park Stadium, Durban	L	18-19
171	24-May-86	NZ Cavaliers	Int	H	Loftus Versfeld Stadium, Pretoria	W	33-18
172	31-May-86	NZ Cavaliers	Int	H	Ellis Park, Johannesburg	W	24-10
173	26-Aug-89	World XV	Int	H	Newlands Stadium, Cape Town	W	20-19
174	2-Sep-89	World XV	Int	H	Ellis Park, Johannesburg	W	22-16
175	15-Aug-92	New Zealand	Int	H	Ellis Park, Johannesburg	L	24-27
176	22-Aug-92	Australia	Int	H	Newlands Stadium, Cape Town	L	3-26
177	17-Oct-92	France	Int-T	A	Stade de Gerland, Lyon	W	20-15
178	24-Oct-92	France	Int-T	A	Parc de Princes, Paris	L	16-29
179	14-Nov-92	England	Int-T	A	Twickenham, London	L	16-33
180	26-Jun-93	France	Int	H	Kings Park Stadium, Durban	D	20-20
181	3-Jul-93	France	Int	H	Ellis Park, Johannesburg	L	17-18
182	31-Jul-93	Australia	Int-T	A	Football Stadium, Sydney	W	19-12
183	14-Aug-93	Australia	Int-T	A	Ballymore Oval, Brisbane	L	20-28
184	21-Aug-93	Australia	Int-T	A	Football Stadium, Sydney	L	12-19
185	6-Nov-93	Argentina	Int-T	A	Ferro Carril Oeste Stadium, B Aires	W	29-26
186	13-Nov-93	Argentina	Int-T	A	Ferro Carril Oeste Stadium, B Aires	W	52-23
187	4-Jun-94	England	Int	H	Loftus Versfeld Stadium, Pretoria	L	15-32
188	11-Jun-94	England	Int	H	Newlands Stadium, Cape Town	W	27-9
189	9-Jul-94	New Zealand	Int-T	A	Carisbrook, Dunedin	L	14-22
190	23-Jul-94	New Zealand	Int-T	A	Athletic Park, Wellington	L	9-13
191	6-Aug-94	New Zealand	Int-T	A	Eden Park, Auckland	D	18-18
192	8-Oct-94	Argentina	Int	H	Boet Erasmus Stadium, Port Elizabeth	W	42-22
193	15-Oct-94	Argentina	Int	H	Ellis Park, Johannesburg	W	46-26
194	19-Nov-94	Scotland	Int-T	A	Murrayfield, Edinburgh	W	34-10
195	26-Nov-94	Wales	Int-T	A	National Stadium, Cardiff	W	20-12
196	13-Apr-95	Western Samoa	Int	H	Ellis Park, Johannesburg	W	60-8
197	25-May-95	Australia	WCp	H	Newlands Stadium, Cape Town	W	27-18
198	30-May-95	Romania	WCp	H	Newlands Stadium, Cape Town	W	21-8
199	3-Jun-95	Canada	WCp	H	Boet Erasmus Stadium, Port Elizabeth	W	20-0
200	10-Jun-95	Western Samoa	WCqf	H	Ellis Park, Johannesburg	W	42-14

No	Date	Opponents	Tmt		Match Venue	Result	
201	17-Jun-95	France	WCsf	H	Kings Park Stadium, Durban	W	19-15
202	24-Jun-95	New Zealand	WCf	H	Ellis Park, Johannesburg (a-e-t)	W	15-12
203	2-Sep-95	Wales	Int	H	Ellis Park, Johannesburg	W	40-11
204	12-Nov-95	Italy	Int-T	A	Stadio Olimpico, Rome	W	40-21
205	18-Nov-95	England	Int-T	A	Twickenham, London	W	24-14
206	2-Jul-96	Fiji	Int	H	Loftus Versfeld Stadium, Pretoria	W	43-18
207	13-Jul-96	Australia	TN	A	Football Stadium, Sydney	L	16-21
208	20-Jul-96	New Zealand	TN	A	Lancaster Park Oval, Christchurch	L	11-15
209	3-Aug-96	Australia	TN	H	Free State Stadium, Bloemfontein	W	25-19
210	10-Aug-96	New Zealand	TN	H	Norwich Park, Newlands, Cape Town	L	18-29
211	17-Aug-96	New Zealand	Int	H	Kings Park Stadium, Durban	L	19-23
212	24-Aug-96	New Zealand	Int	H	Loftus Versfeld Stadium, Pretoria	L	26-33
213	31-Aug-96	New Zealand	Int	H	Ellis Park, Johannesburg	W	32-22
214	9-Nov-96	Argentina	Int-T	A	Ferro Carril Oeste Stadium, B Aires	W	46-15
215	16-Nov-96	Argentina	Int-T	A	Ferro Carril Oeste Stadium, B Aires	W	44-21
216	30-Nov-96	France	Int-T	A	Stade du Parc Lescure, Bordeaux	W	22-12
217	7-Dec-96	France	Int-T	A	Parc de Princes, Paris	W	13-12
218	15-Dec-96	Wales	Int-T	A	National Stadium, Cardiff	W	37-20
219	10-Jun-97	Tonga	Int	H	Norwich Park, Newlands, Cape Town	W	74-10
220	21-Jun-97	Lions	Int	H	Norwich Park, Newlands, Cape Town	L	16-25
221	28-Jun-97	Lions	Int	H	Kings Park Stadium, Durban	L	15-18
222	5-Jul-97	Lions	Int	H	Ellis Park, Johannesburg	W	35-16
223	19-Jul-97	New Zealand	TN	H	Ellis Park, Johannesburg	L	32-35
224	2-Aug-97	Australia	TN	A	Suncorp Stadium, Lang Park, Brisbane	L	20-32
225	9-Aug-97	New Zealand	TN	A	Eden Park, Auckland	L	35-55
226	23-Aug-97	Australia	TN	H	Loftus Versfeld Stadium, Pretoria	W	61-22
227	8-Nov-97	Italy	Int-T	A	Stadio Renato Dall'Ara, Bologna	W	62-31
228	15-Nov-97	France	Int-T	A	Stade de Gerland, Lyon	W	36-32
229	22-Nov-97	France	Int-T	A	Parc de Princes, Paris	W	52-10
230	29-Nov-97	England	Int-T	A	Twickenham, London	W	29-11
231	6-Dec-97	Scotland	Int-T	A	Murrayfield, Edinburgh	W	68-10
232	13-Jun-98	Ireland	Int	H	Free State Stadium, Bloemfontein	W	37-13
233	20-Jun-98	Ireland	Int	H	Minolta Loftus Stadium, Pretoria	W	33-0
234	27-Jun-98	Wales	Int	H	Minolta Loftus Stadium, Pretoria	W	96-13
235	4-Jul-98	England	Int	H	Norwich Park, Newlands, Cape Town	W	18-0
236	18-Jul-98	Australia	TN	A	Subiaco Oval, Perth	W	14-13
237	25-Jul-98	New Zealand	TN	A	Athletic Park, Wellington	W	13-3
238	15-Aug-98	New Zealand	TN	H	Kings Park Stadium, Durban	W	24-23
239	22-Aug-98	Australia	TN	H	Ellis Park, Johannesburg	W	29-15
240	14-Nov-98	Wales	Int-T	N	Wembley Stadium, London	W	28-20

No	Date	Opponents	Tmt		Match Venue	Result	
241	21-Nov-98	Scotland	Int-T	A	Murrayfield, Edinburgh	W	35-10
242	28-Nov-98	Ireland	Int-T	A	Lansdowne Road, Dublin	W	27-13
243	5-Dec-98	England	Int-T	A	Twickenham, London	L	7-13
244	12-Jun-99	Italy	Int	H	Telkom Park Stadium, Port Elizabeth	W	74-3
245	19-Jun-99	Italy	Int	H	Kings Park Stadium, Durban	W	101-0
246	26-Jun-99	Wales	Int-T	A	Millennium Stadium, Cardiff	L	19-29
247	10-Jul-99	New Zealand	TN	A	Carisbrook, Dunedin	L	0-28
248	17-Jul-99	Australia	TN	A	Suncorp Stadium, Brisbane	L	6-32
249	7-Aug-99	New Zealand	TN	H	Minolta Loftus Stadium, Pretoria	L	18-34
250	14-Aug-99	Australia	TN	H	Norwich Park, Newlands, Cape Town	W	10-9
251	3-Oct-99	Scotland	WCp	A	Murrayfield, Edinburgh	W	46-29
252	10-Oct-99	Spain	WCp	N	Murrayfield, Edinburgh	W	47-3
253	15-Oct-99	Uruguay	WCp	N	Hampden Park, Glasgow	W	39-3
254	24-Oct-99	England	WCqf	N	Stade de France, Paris	W	44-21
255	30-Oct-99	Australia	WCsf	N	Twickenham, London	L	21-27
256	4-Nov-99	New Zealand	WC34	N	Millennium Stadium, Cardiff	W	22-18
257	10-Jun-00	Canada	Int	H	Waverley Park, East London	W	51-18
258	17-Jun-00	England	Int	H	Minolta Loftus Stadium, Pretoria	W	18-13
259	24-Jun-00	England	Int	H	Free State Stadium, Bloemfontein	L	22-27
260	8-Jul-00	Australia	MCP T	A	Colonial Stadium, Melbourne	L	23-44
261	22-Jul-00	New Zealand	TN	A	Jade Stadium, Christchurch	L	12-25
262	29-Jul-00	Australia	TN	A	Stadium Australia, Sydney	L	6-26
263	19-Aug-00	New Zealand	TN	H	Ellis Park, Johannesburg	W	46-40
264	26-Aug-00	Australia	TN	H	ABSA Stadium, Durban	L	18-19
265	12-Nov-00	Argentina	Int-T	A	Estadio Monumental A V Liberti, B Aires	W	37-33
266	19-Nov-00	Ireland	Int-T	A	Lansdowne Road, Dublin	W	28-18
267	26-Nov-00	Wales	Int-T	A	Millennium Stadium, Cardiff	W	23-13
268	2-Dec-00	England	Int-T	A	Twickenham, London	L	17-25
269	16-Jun-01	France	Int	H	Ellis Park, Johannesburg	L	23-32
270	23-Jun-01	France	Int	H	ABSA Stadium, Durban	W	20-15
271	30-Jun-01	Italy	Int	H	Telkom Park Stadium, Port Elizabeth	W	60-14
272	21-Jul-01	New Zealand	TN	H	Fedsure Park, Newlands, Cape Town	L	3-12
273	28-Jul-01	Australia	TN	H	Minolta Loftus Stadium, Pretoria	W	20-15
274	18-Aug-01	Australia	TN	A	Subiaco Oval, Perth	D	14-14
275	25-Aug-01	New Zealand	TN	A	Eden Park, Auckland	L	15-26
276	10-Nov-01	France	Int-T	A	Stade de France, Paris	L	10-20
277	17-Nov-01	Italy	Int-T	A	Stadio Luigi Ferraris, Genova	W	54-26
278	24-Nov-01	England	Int-T	A	Twickenham, London	L	9-29
279	1-Dec-01	United States	Int-T	A	Robertson Stadium, Houston	W	43-20
280	8-Jun-02	Wales	Int	H	Vodacom Park Stadium, Bloemfontein	W	34-19

No	Date	Opponents	Tmt	Match Venue	Result
281	15-Jun-02	Wales	Int	H Newlands Stadium, Cape Town	W 19-8
282	29-Jun-02	Argentina	Int	H P A M Brink Stadium, Springs	W 49-29
283	6-Jul-02	Samoa	Int	H Minolta Loftus Stadium, Pretoria	W 60-18
284	20-Jul-02	New Zealand	TN	A Westpac Trust Stadium, Wellington	L 20-41
285	27-Jul-02	Australia	TN	A The Gabba Cricket Ground, Brisbane	L 27-38
286	10-Aug-02	New Zealand	TN	H ABSA Stadium, Durban	L 23-30
287	17-Aug-02	Australia	TN-M	H Ellis Park, Johannesburg	W 33-31
288	9-Nov-02	France	Int-T	A Stade Vélodrome, Marseille	L 10-30
289	16-Nov-02	Scotland	Int-T	A Murrayfield, Edinburgh	L 6-21
290	23-Nov-02	England	Int-T	A Twickenham, London	L 3-53
291	7-Jun-03	Scotland	Int	H ABSA Stadium, Durban	W 29-25
292	14-Jun-03	Scotland	Int	H Ellis Park, Johannesburg	W 28-19
293	28-Jun-03	Argentina	Int	H EPRFU Stadium, Port Elizabeth	W 26-25
294	12-Jul-03	Australia	TN	H Newlands Stadium, Cape Town	W 26-22
295	19-Jul-03	New Zealand	TN	H Securicor Loftus Stadium, Pretoria	L 16-52
296	2-Aug-03	Australia	TN	A Suncorp Stadium, Brisbane	L 9-29
297	9-Aug-03	New Zealand	TN	A Carisbrook, Dunedin	L 11-19
298	11-Oct-03	Uruguay	WCp	N Subiaco Oval, Perth	W 72-6
299	18-Oct-03	England	WCp	N Subiaco Oval, Perth	L 6-25
300	24-Oct-03	Georgia	WCp	N Aussie Stadium, Sydney	W 46-19
301	1-Nov-03	Samoa	WCp	N Suncorp Stadium, Brisbane	W 60-10
302	8-Nov-03	New Zealand	WCq	N Telstra Dome, Melbourne	L 9-29
303	12-Jun-04	Ireland	Int	H Vodacom Park Stadium, Bloemfontein	W 31-17
304	19-Jun-04	Ireland	Int	H Newlands Stadium, Cape Town	W 26-17
305	26-Jun-04	Wales	Int	H Securicor Loftus Stadium, Pretoria	W 53-18
306	17-Jul-04	Pacific Islands	Int	N Express Advocate Stadium, Gosford, NSW	W 38-24
307	24-Jul-04	New Zealand	TN	A Jade Stadium, Christchurch	L 21-23
308	31-Jul-04	Australia	TN	A Subiaco Oval, Perth	L 26-30
309	14-Aug-04	New Zealand	TN-F	H Ellis Park, Johannesburg	W 40-26
310	21-Aug-04	Australia	TN	H ABSA Stadium, Durban	W 23-19
311	6-Nov-04	Wales	Int-T	A Millennium Stadium, Cardiff	W 38-36
312	13-Nov-04	Ireland	Int-T	A Lansdowne Road, Dublin	L 12-17
313	20-Nov-04	England	Int-T	A Twickenham, London	L 16-32
314	27-Nov-04	Scotland	Int-T	A Murrayfield, Edinburgh	W 45-10
315	4-Dec-04	Argentina	Int-T	A Velez Sarsfield Stadium, Buenos Aires	W 39-7
316	11-Jun-05	Uruguay	Int	H ABSA Stadium, East London	W 134-3
317	18-Jun-05	France	Int	H The ABSA Stadium, Durban	D 30-30
318	25-Jun-05	France	Int	H EPRFU Stadium, Port Elizabeth	W 27-13
319	9-Jul-05	Australia	MCP-T	A Telstra Stadium, Sydney	L 12-30
320	23-Jul-05	Australia	MCP	H Ellis Park, Johannesburg	W 33-20

No	Date	Opponents	Tmt		Match Venue	Result	
321	30-Jul-05	Australia	TN	H	Securicor Loftus Stadium, Pretoria	W	22-16
322	6-Aug-05	New Zealand	TN	H	Newlands Stadium, Cape Town	W	22-16
323	20-Aug-05	Australia	TN	A	Subiaco Oval, Perth	W	22-19
324	27-Aug-05	New Zealand	TN	A	Carisbrook, Dunedin	L	27-31
325	5-Nov-05	Argentina	Int-T	A	Vélez Sarsfield Stadium, Buenos Aires	W	34-23
326	19-Nov-05	Wales	Int-T	A	Millennium Stadium, Cardiff	W	33-16
327	26-Nov-05	France	Int-T	A	Stade de France, Paris	L	20-26
328	10-Jun-06	Scotland	Int	H	The ABSA Stadium, Durban	W	36-16
329	17-Jun-06	Scotland	Int	H	EPRFU Stadium, Port Elizabeth	W	29-15
330	24-Jun-06	France	Int	H	Newlands Stadium, Cape Town	L	26-36
331	15-Jul-06	Australia	TN-M	A	Suncorp Stadium, Brisbane	L	0-49
332	22-Jul-06	New Zealand	TN-F	A	Westpac Stadium, Wellington	L	17-35
333	5-Aug-06	Australia	TN-M	A	Telstra Stadium, Sydney	L	18-20
334	26-Aug-06	New Zealand	TN-F	H	Loftus Versfeld Stadium, Pretoria	L	26-45
335	2-Sep-06	New Zealand	TN-F	H	Royal Bafokeng Sports Palace, Rustenburg	W	21-20
336	9-Sep-06	Australia	TN-M	H	Ellis Park, Johannesburg	W	24-16
337	11-Nov-06	Ireland	Int-T	A	Lansdowne Road, Dublin	L	15-32
338	18-Nov-06	England	Int-T	A	Twickenham, London	L	21-23
339	25-Nov-06	England	Int-T	A	Twickenham, London	W	25-14
340	26-May-07	England	Int	H	Vodacom Park Stadium, Bloemfontein	W	58-10
341	2-Jun-07	England	Int	H	Loftus Versfeld Stadium, Pretoria	W	55-22
342	9-Jun-07	Samoa	Int	H	Royal Bafokeng Sports Palace, Rustenburg	W	35-8
343	16-Jun-07	Australia	TN-M	H	Ellis Park, Johannesburg	W	22-19
344	23-Jun-07	New Zealand	TNa-F	H	The ABSA Stadium, Durban	L	21-26
345	7-Jul-07	Australia	TN-M	A	Telstra Stadium, Sydney	L	17-25
346	14-Jul-07	New Zealand	TN-F	A	Jade Stadium, Christchurch	L	6-33
347	15-Aug-07	Namibia	Int	H	Newlands Stadium, Cape Town	W	105-13
348	25-Aug-07	Scotland	Int-T	A	Murrayfield, Edinburgh	W	27-3
349	9-Sep-07	Samoa	WCp	N	Parc de Princes, Paris	W	59-7
350	14-Sep-07	England	WCp	N	Stade de France, Paris	W	36-0
351	22-Sep-07	Tonga	WCp	N	Stade Félix Bolleart, Lens	W	30-25
352	30-Sep-07	United States	WCp	N	Stade de la Mosson, Montpellier	W	64-15
353	7-Oct-07	Fiji	WCqf	N	Stade Vélodrome, Marseille	W	37-20
354	14-Oct-07	Argentina	WCsf	N	Stade de France, Paris	W	37-13
355	20-Oct-07	England	WCf	N	Stade de France, Paris	W	15-6
356	24-Nov-07	Wales	PWC-T	A	Millennium Stadium, Cardiff	W	34-12
357	7-Jun-08	Wales	PWC	H	Vodacom Park Stadium, Bloemfontein	W	43-17
358	14-Jun-08	Wales	PWC	H	Loftus Versfeld Stadium, Pretoria	W	37-21
359	21-Jun-08	Italy	Int	H	Newlands Stadium, Cape Town	W	26-0
360	5-Jul-08	New Zealand	TN-F	A	Westpac Stadium, Wellington	L	8-19

No	Date	Opponents	Tmt		Match Venue	Result	
361	12-Jul-08	New Zealand	TN-F	A	Carisbrook, Dunedin	W	30-28
362	19-Jul-08	Australia	TN-M	A	Subiaco Oval, Perth	L	9-16
363	9-Aug-08	Argentina	Int	H	Coca Cola Park, Johannesburg	W	63-9
364	16-Aug-08	New Zealand	TN-F	H	Newlands Stadium, Cape Town	L	0-19
365	23-Aug-08	Australia	TN-M	H	The ABSA Stadium, Durban	L	15-27
366	30-Aug-08	Australia	TN-M	H	Coca Cola Park, Johannesburg	W	53-8
367	8-Nov-08	Wales	PWC-T	A	Millennium Stadium, Cardiff	W	20-15
368	15-Nov-08	Scotland	Int-T	A	Murrayfield, Edinburgh	W	14-10
369	22-Nov-08	England	Int-T	A	Twickenham, London	W	42-6
370	20-Jun-09	Lions	LSA	H	The ABSA Stadium, Durban	W	26-21
371	27-Jun-09	Lions	LSA	H	Loftus Versfeld Stadium, Pretoria	W	28-25
372	4-Jul-09	Lions	LSA	H	Coca Cola Park, Johannesburg	L	9-28
373	25-Jul-09	New Zealand	TN-F	H	Vodacom Park Stadium, Bloemfontein	W	28-19
374	1-Aug-09	New Zealand	TN-F	H	The ABSA Stadium, Durban	W	31-19
375	8-Aug-09	Australia	TN-M	H	Newlands Stadium, Cape Town	W	29-17
376	29-Aug-09	Australia	TN-M	A	Subiaco Oval, Perth	W	32-25
377	5-Sep-09	Australia	TN-M	A	Suncorp Stadium, Brisbane	L	6-21
378	12-Sep-09	New Zealand	TN-F	A	Waikato Stadium, Hamilton	W	32-29
379	13-Nov-09	France	Int-T	A	Stade Municipal de Toulouse, Toulouse	L	13-20
380	21-Nov-09	Italy	Int-T	A	Stadio Friuli, Udine	W	32-10
381	28-Nov-09	Ireland	Int-T	A	Croke Park, Dublin	L	10-15
382	5-Jun-10	Wales	PWC-T	A	Millennium Stadium, Cardiff	W	34-31
383	12-Jun-10	France	Int	H	Newlands Stadium, Cape Town	W	42-17
384	19-Jun-10	Italy	Int	H	Johann van Riebeeck Stadium, Witbank	W	29-13
385	26-Jun-10	Italy	Int	H	Buffalo City Stadium, East London	W	55-11
386	10-Jul-10	New Zealand	TN-F	A	Eden Park, Auckland	L	12-32
387	17-Jul-10	New Zealand	TN-F	A	Westpac Stadium, Wellngton	L	17-31
388	24-Jul-10	Australia	TN-M	A	Suncorp Stadium, Brisbane	L	13-30
389	21-Aug-10	New Zealand	TN-F	H	FNB Stadium, Soweto, Johannesburg	L	22-29
390	28-Aug-10	Australia	TN-M	H	Loftus Versfeld Stadium, Pretoria	W	44-31
391	4-Sep-10	Australia	TN-M	H	Vodacom Park Stadium, Bloemfontein	L	39-41
392	6-Nov-10	Ireland	Int-T	A	Aviva Stadium, Dublin	W	23-21
393	13-Nov-10	Wales	PWC-T	A	Millennium Stadium, Cardiff	W	29-25
394	20-Nov-10	Scotland	Int-T	A	Murrayfield, Edinburgh	L	17-21
395	27-Nov-10	England	Int-T	A	Twickenham, London	W	21-11
396	23-Jul-11	Australia	TN-M	A	ANZ Stadium, Sydney	L	20-39
397	30-Jul-11	New Zealand	TN-F	A	Westpac Stadium, Wellngton	L	7-40
398	13-Aug-11	Australia	TN-M	H	Kings Park Stadium, Durban	L	9-14
399	20-Aug-11	New Zealand	TN-F	H	Nelson Mandela Bay Stad., Port Elizabeth	W	18-5
400	11-Sep-11	Wales	WCp	N	Wellington Regional Stadium, Wellington	W	17-16

No	Date	Opponents	Tmt	Match Venue		Result
401	17-Sep-11	Fiji	WCp	N Wellington Regional Stadium, Wellington	W	49-3
402	22-Sep-11	Namibia	WCp	N North Harbour Stadium, Albany	W	87-0
403	30-Sep-11	Samoa	WCp	N North Harbour Stadium, Albany	W	13-5
404	9-Oct-11	Australia	WCqf	N Wellington Regional Stadium, Wellington	L	9-11
405	9-Jun-12	England	Int	H Kings Park Stadium, Durban	W	22-17
406	16-Jun-12	England	Int	H Ellis Park, Johannesburg	W	36-27
407	23-Jun-12	England	Int	H Nelson Mandela Bay Stad., Port Elizabeth	D	14-14
408	18-Aug-12	Argentina	RC	H Newlands Stadium, Cape Town	W	27-6
409	25-Aug-12	Argentina	RC	A Estadio Malvinas Argentinas, Mendoza	D	16-16
410	8-Sep-12	Australia	RC-M	A Patersons Stadium, Perth	L	19-26
411	15-Sep-12	New Zealand	RC-F	A Forsyth Barr Stadium, Dunedin	L	11-21
412	29-Sep-12	Australia	RC-M	H Loftus Versfeld Stadium, Pretoria	W	31-8
413	6-Oct-12	New Zealand	RC-F	H FNB Stadium, Soweto, Johannesburg	L	16-32
414	10-Nov-12	Ireland	Int-T	A Aviva Stadium, Dublin	W	16-12
415	17-Nov-12	Scotland	Int-T	A Murrayfield, Edinburgh	W	21-10
416	24-Nov-12	England	Int-T	A Twickenham, London	W	16-15
417	8-Jun-13	Italy	quad	H Growthpoint Kings Park, Durban	W	44-10
418	15-Jun-13	Scotland	quad	H Mbombela Stadium, Nelspruit	W	30-17
419	22-Jun-13	Samoa	quad	H Loftus Versfeld Stadium, Pretoria	W	56-23
420	17-Aug-13	Argentina	RC	H FNB Stadium, Soweto, Johannesburg	W	73-13
421	24-Aug-13	Argentina	RC	A Estadio Malvinas Argentinas, Mendoza	W	22-17
422	7-Sep-13	Australia	RC-M	A Suncorp Stadium, Brisbane	W	38-12
423	14-Sep-13	New Zealand	RC-F	A Eden Park, Auckland	L	15-29
424	28-Sep-13	Australia	RC-M	H Newlands Stadium, Cape Town	W	28-8
425	5-Oct-13	New Zealand	RC-F	H Ellis Park, Johannesburg	L	27-38
426	9-Nov-13	Wales	PWC-T	A Millennium Stadium, Cardiff	W	24-15
427	16-Nov-13	Scotland	Int-T	A Murrayfield, Edinburgh	W	28-0
428	23-Nov-13	France	Int-T	A Stade de France, Paris	W	19-10
429	14-Jun-14	Wales	PWC	H Kings Park Stadium, Durban	W	38-16
430	21-Jun-14	Wales	PWC	H Mbombela Stadium, Nelspruit	W	31-30
431	28-Jun-14	Scotland	Int	H Nelson Mandela Bay Stad., Port Elizabeth	W	55-6
432	16-Aug-14	Argentina	RC	H Loftus Versfeld Stadium, Pretoria	W	13-6
433	23-Aug-14	Argentina	RC	A Estadio Padre Ernesto Martearena, Salta	W	33-31
434	6-Sep-14	Australia	RC-M	A Patersons Stadium, Perth	L	23-24
435	13-Sep-14	New Zealand	RC-F	A Westpac Stadium, Wellngton	L	10-14
436	27-Sep-14	Australia	RC-M	H Newlands Stadium, Cape Town	W	28-10
437	4-Oct-14	New Zealand	RC-F	H Ellis Park, Johannesburg	W	27-25
438	8-Nov-14	Ireland	Int-T	A Aviva Stadium, Dublin	L	15-29
439	15-Nov-14	England	Int-T	A Twickenham, London	W	31-28
440	22-Nov-14	Italy	Int-T	A Stadio Euganeo, Padova	W	22-6

No	Date	Opponents	Tmt		Match Venue	Result	
441	29-Nov-14	Wales	PWC-T	A	Millennium Stadium, Cardiff	L	6-12

WALES

The first International played by Wales, which ended in a defeat to England, was held at Mr. Richardson's Field, Blackheath on 18 February 1881. Three weeks later, on 12 March 1881, delegates representing eleven rugby clubs met at the Castle Hotel in Neath and the Welsh Rugby Union was formed. The first Home Nations Championship was staged in 1883. Wales lost both games, and another decade passed before the Welsh team finally won the Championship and with it the first of twenty Triple Crowns. The start of the twentieth century heralded a 'Welsh Golden Era'. Between 1900 and 1911, Wales played forty-three matches, won thirty-five, drew one, and lost only seven. They also won six Triple Crowns and three Grand Slams during that period, and recorded twenty-two consecutive home wins against the Home Nations and France (who had entered the Championship in 1910). Wales also defeated New Zealand in 1905 and Australia in 1908, but lost to South Africa in 1906. In 1911 Wales won the first Five Nations Grand Slam, but it took them another thirty-nine years to repeat that feat, when they won the Grand Slam for a second time in 1950.

After the First World War, Welsh rugby declined somewhat but there was a significant resurgence during the 1930s and Wales had some famous victories (defeating New Zealand for a second time in 1935), but also some disappointing defeats (a third loss to South Africa in 1931). Between 1950 and 1956 Wales played thirty matches and won twenty-two; these included two Grand Slams and a third victory over New Zealand in 1953.

With the exception of a Triple Crown victory in 1965, the 1960s proved to be a mediocre decade for the team, in comparison with the previous decade. However, the years 1969 to 1979 ushered in a 'Second Golden Era' for Wales, when the team won the Championship outright six times, including six Triple Crowns, four of which were won in consecutive years between 1976 and 1979, and three Grand Slams. During that memorable period Wales played forty-three Five Nations Championship games, winning thirty-three, drawing three and losing only seven. This winning streak also included a sequence of twenty-two home Championship games without defeat, which was extended to twenty-seven in 1982.

In contrast, Wales fared poorly against the Southern Hemisphere major nations, losing four times to the All Blacks, drawing against the Springboks, and winning three of five games against Australia.

The 1980s again proved to be a disappointing anti-climax for the Welsh team as they suffered twenty defeats out of forty matches up to the beginning of the World Cup in 1987. The team did, however, derive some comfort in that 1987 World Cup by securing third place, and followed it with a Triple Crown in 1988. The next three years leading up to the second World Cup in 1991, would be witness to the worse sequence of results in Welsh rugby history. In twenty-three matches played between late March 1988 and early October 1991, Wales recorded only four wins, two of which were against Namibia, an emerging rugby nation. Those wins were of little consolation as the Welsh suffered three heavy defeats: two to the All Blacks on their summer tour of New Zealand in 1988, and one to the Wallabies in Brisbane in 1991. Worse was to follow when Wales, beaten by Western Samoa in Cardiff at the pool stage, failed to qualify for the quarter-final of the 1991 World Cup.

Mixed fortunes continued for the Welsh team when, after winning the 1994 Five Nations Championship, they failed to reach the quarter-final of the 1995 World Cup in South Africa, losing by one point to Ireland at the pool stage. In 1999, the year that Wales hosted the fourth World Cup, the home team strung together ten straight victories, including a first-ever win over South Africa in the opening match at the newly built Millennium Stadium in Cardiff. The Welsh qualified for the quarter-final after a gap of twelve long years, but were well beaten at that stage by Australia, the eventual winners of the trophy. Wales also qualified for the quarter-final of the 2003 World Cup, losing to England the eventual winners of the competition.

A roller-coaster of results occurred during the first decade of the new millennium. After finishing in fourth place in both the inaugural year of the Six Nations Championship in 2000 and also in 2001, Wales finished fifth in 2002, then hit rock bottom by finishing in sixth place in 2003, fourth again in 2004, only to amazingly win the Grand Slam in 2005. In both the 2006 and 2007 competition Wales finished back in fifth place yet again, before bouncing back and gaining their tenth Grand Slam in 2008. However, a year before that 2008 Grand Slam there had been further disappointment for the Welsh team in the 2007 World Cup held in France, when they failed to qualify for the quarter-final for the third time in a World Cup competition after losing to Fiji at the pool stage.

The 2008 success did not continue and in each of the three seasons, 2009 to 2011, Wales finished in fourth place in the Six Nations Championship, with only Scotland and Italy below them in the table. Things looked bleak as the 2011 World Cup loomed. The Welsh performance in that tournament surprised everyone when they reached the semi-final, only to lose by one point to France. Although they had lost that game, there was a sense that there was a renewed energy on the Welsh side: and they went on to win an eleventh Grand Slam in 2012. Three Grand Slams in the space of eight years (between 2005 and 2012) recalled the great Welsh team of the 1970s, which had also won three Grand Slams in eight years (between 1971 and 1978).

In 2013, Wales again topped the Six Nations table with four wins, denying England a Grand Slam in the final Championship match, but they failed in their bid to win three titles in succession when they lost both their away matches in the 2014 Six Nations campaign to finish in third place. On tour in June 2014, the Welsh team lost both Internationals to South Africa, but gained revenge in the November series when they defeated the Springboks (for only the second time) by 12 points to 6.

Despite the recent success against Northern Hemisphere opponents, the Welsh team has fared very badly against Australia, New Zealand and South Africa. Since the start of the new millennium, the Welsh team has lost forty-four times in forty-eight matches against the three Southern Hemisphere giants. In the 2015 Six Nations Championship, despite winning four matches, Wales finished in third place again when the team lost on points difference to both England and the title winners, Ireland.

WALES

HEAD TO HEAD RESULTS TO 31 MARCH 2015

	P	W	D	L	%	F	A
v TIER 1 Teams							
v Argentina	15	10	0	5	66.7	428	350
v Australia	38	10	1	27	27.6	590	897
v England *	126	56	12	58	49.2	1456	1596
v France	93	47	3	43	52.1	1384	1338
v Ireland *	121	66	6	49	57.0	1424	1320
v Italy	22	19	1	2	88.6	725	367
v New Zealand	30	3	0	27	10.0	307	916
v Scotland *	120	69	3	48	58.8	1584	1211
v South Africa	30	2	1	27	8.3	440	814
Sub-Total	595	282	27	286	49.7	8338	8809
v TIER 2/3 Group							
v Canada	12	11	0	1	91.7	460	207
v Fiji	10	8	1	1	85.0	306	132
v Japan	9	8	0	1	88.9	493	129
v Romania	8	6	0	2	75.0	342	96
v Samoa	9	5	0	4	55.6	216	163
v Tonga	7	7	0	0	100.0	203	78
v United States	7	7	0	0	100.0	305	86
v Georgia	0	0	0	0	0.0	0	0
v Namibia	4	4	0	0	100.0	171	69
v Russia	0	0	0	0	0.0	0	0
Sub-Total	66	56	1	9	85.6	2496	960
v Other Teams							
v Barbarians	4	2	0	2	50.0	113	93
v N Z Services	1	0	0	1	0.0	3	6
v New Zealand Natives*	1	1	0	0	100.0	-	-
v Pacific Islanders	1	1	0	0	100.0	38	20
v Portugal	1	1	0	0	100.0	102	11
v Spain	1	1	0	0	100.0	54	0
v Zimbabwe	3	3	0	0	100.0	126	38
Sub-Total	12	9	0	3	75.0	436	168
All Internationals	673	347	28	298	53.6	11270	9937

* excludes points scored before the introduction of the modern points system

No	Date	Opponents	Tmt		Match Venue		Result
1	19-Feb-81	England	Int	A	Richardson's Field, Blackheath	L	0-30
2	28-Jan-82	Ireland	Int	A	Lansdowne Road, Dublin	W	8-0
3	16-Dec-82	England	4N	H	St Helen's, Swansea	L	0-10
4	8-Jan-83	Scotland	4N	A	Raeburn Place, Edinburgh	L	3-9
5	5-Jan-84	England	4N	A	Cardigan Fields, Leeds	L	3-5
6	12-Jan-84	Scotland	4N	H	Rodney Parade, Newport	L	0-4
7	12-Apr-84	Ireland	4N	H	Arms Park, Cardiff	W	5-0
8	3-Jan-85	England	4N	H	St Helen's, Swansea	L	4-7
9	10-Jan-85	Scotland	4N	A	Hamilton Crescent, Glasgow	D	0-0
10	2-Jan-86	England	4N	A	Rectory Field, Blackheath	L	3-5
11	9-Jan-86	Scotland	4N	H	Arms Park, Cardiff	L	0-7
12	8-Jan-87	England	4N	H	Stradey Park, Llanelli	D	0-0
13	26-Feb-87	Scotland	4N	A	Raeburn Place, Edinburgh	L	0-20
14	12-Mar-87	Ireland	4N	N	Upper Park, Birkenhead Park	W	4-3
15	4-Feb-88	Scotland	4N	H	Rodney Parade, Newport	W	1-0
16	3-Mar-88	Ireland	4N	A	Lansdowne Road, Dublin	L	0-7
17	22 Dec 88	N Z Natives	Int	H	St Helen's, Swansea	W	5-0
18	2-Feb-89	Scotland	4N	A	Raeburn Place, Edinburgh	L	0-2
19	2-Mar-89	Ireland	4N	H	St Helen's, Swansea	L	0-2
20	1-Feb-90	Scotland	4N	H	Arms Park, Cardiff	L	1-5
21	15-Feb-90	England	4N	A	Crown Flatt, Dewsbury	W	1-0
22	1-Mar-90	Ireland	4N	A	Lansdowne Road, Dublin	D	3-3
23	3-Jan-91	England	4N	H	Rodney Parade, Newport	L	3-7
24	7-Feb-91	Scotland	4N	A	Raeburn Place, Edinburgh	L	0-15
25	7-Mar-91	Ireland	4N	H	Stradey Park, Llanelli	W	6-4
26	2-Jan-92	England	4N	A	Rectory Field, Blackheath	L	0-17
27	6-Feb-92	Scotland	4N	H	St Helen's, Swansea	L	2-7
28	5-Mar-92	Ireland	4N	A	Lansdowne Road, Dublin	L	0-9
29	7-Jan-93	England	4N	H	Arms Park, Cardiff	W	12-11
30	4-Feb-93	Scotland	4N	A	Raeburn Place, Edinburgh	W	9-0
31	11-Mar-93	Ireland	4N	H	Stradey Park, Llanelli	W	2-0
32	6-Jan-94	England	4N	A	Upper Park, Birkenhead Park	L	3-24
33	3-Feb-94	Scotland	4N	H	Rodney Parade, Newport	W	7-0
34	10-Mar-94	Ireland	4N	A	Ballynafeigh, Belfast	L	0-3
35	5-Jan-95	England	4N	H	St Helen's, Swansea	L	6-14
36	26-Jan-95	Scotland	4N	A	Raeburn Place, Edinburgh	L	4-5
37	16-Mar-95	Ireland	4N	H	Arms Park, Cardiff	W	5-3
38	4-Jan-96	England	4N	A	Rectory Field, Blackheath	L	0-25
39	25-Jan-96	Scotland	4N	H	Arms Park, Cardiff	W	6-0
40	14-Mar-96	Ireland	4N	A	Lansdowne Road, Dublin	L	4-8

No	Date	Opponents	Tmt	Match Venue	Result	
41	9-Jan-97	England	4N	H Rodney Parade, Newport	W	11-0
42	19-Mar-98	Ireland	4N	A Thomond Park, Limerick	W	11-3
43	2-Apr-98	England	4N	A Rectory Field, Blackheath	L	7-14
44	7-Jan-99	England	4N	H St Helen's, Swansea	W	26-3
45	4-Mar-99	Scotland	4N	A Inverleith, Edinburgh	L	10-21
46	18-Mar-99	Ireland	4N	H Arms Park, Cardiff	L	0-3
47	6-Jan-00	England	4N	A Kingsholm, Gloucester	W	13-3
48	27-Jan-00	Scotland	4N	H St Helen's, Swansea	W	12-3
49	17-Mar-00	Ireland	4N	A Balmoral Showgrounds, Belfast	W	3-0
50	5-Jan-01	England	4N	H Arms Park, Cardiff	W	13-0
51	9-Feb-01	Scotland	4N	A Inverleith, Edinburgh	L	8-18
52	16-Mar-01	Ireland	4N	H St Helen's, Swansea	W	10-9
53	11-Jan-02	England	4N	A Rectory Field, Blackheath	W	9-8
54	1-Feb-02	Scotland	4N	H Arms Park, Cardiff	W	14-5
55	8-Mar-02	Ireland	4N	A Lansdowne Road, Dublin	W	15-0
56	10-Jan-03	England	4N	H St Helen's, Swansea	W	21-5
57	7-Feb-03	Scotland	4N	A Inverleith, Edinburgh	L	0-6
58	14-Mar-03	Ireland	4N	H Arms Park, Cardiff	W	18-0
59	9-Jan-04	England	4N	A Welford Road, Leicester	D	14-14
60	6-Feb-04	Scotland	4N	H St Helen's, Swansea	W	21-3
61	12-Mar-04	Ireland	4N	A Balmoral Showgrounds, Belfast	L	12-14
62	14-Jan-05	England	4N	H Arms Park, Cardiff	W	25-0
63	4-Feb-05	Scotland	4N	A Inverleith, Edinburgh	W	6-3
64	11-Mar-05	Ireland	4N	H St Helen's, Swansea	W	10-3
65	16-Dec-05	New Zealand	Int	H Arms Park, Cardiff	W	3-0
66	13-Jan-06	England	4N	A Athletic Ground, Richmond	W	16-3
67	3-Feb-06	Scotland	4N	H Arms Park, Cardiff	W	9-3
68	10-Mar-06	Ireland	4N	A Balmoral Showgrounds, Belfast	L	6-11
69	1-Dec-06	South Africa	Int	H St Helen's, Swansea	L	0-11
70	12-Jan-07	England	4N	H St Helen's, Swansea	W	22-0
71	2-Feb-07	Scotland	4N	A Inverleith, Edinburgh	L	3-6
72	9-Mar-07	Ireland	4N	H Arms Park, Cardiff	W	29-0
73	18-Jan-08	England	4N	A Ashton Gate, Bristol	W	28-18
74	1-Feb-08	Scotland	4N	H St Helen's, Swansea	W	6-5
75	2-Mar-08	France	Int	H Arms Park, Cardiff	W	36-4
76	14-Mar-08	Ireland	4N	A Balmoral Showgrounds, Belfast	W	11-5
77	12-Dec-08	Australia	Int	H Arms Park, Cardiff	W	9-6
78	16-Jan-09	England	4N	H Arms Park, Cardiff	W	8-0
79	6-Feb-09	Scotland	4N	A Inverleith, Edinburgh	W	5-3
80	23-Feb-09	France	Int	A Stade Colombes, Paris	W	47-5

No	Date	Opponents	Tmt		Match Venue		Result	
81	13-Mar-09	Ireland	4N	H	St Helen's, Swansea		W	18-5
82	1-Jan-10	France	5N	H	St Helen's, Swansea		W	49-14
83	15-Jan-10	England	5N	A	Twickenham, London		L	6-11
84	5-Feb-10	Scotland	5N	H	Arms Park, Cardiff		W	14-0
85	12-Mar-10	Ireland	5N	A	Lansdowne Road, Dublin		W	19-3
86	21-Jan-11	England	5N	H	St Helen's, Swansea		W	15-11
87	4-Feb-11	Scotland	5N	A	Inverleith, Edinburgh		W	32-10
88	28-Feb-11	France	5N	A	Parc des Princess, Paris		W	15-0
89	11-Mar-11	Ireland	5N	H	Arms Park, Cardiff		W	16-0
90	20-Jan-12	England	5N	A	Twickenham, London		L	0-8
91	3-Feb-12	Scotland	5N	H	St Helen's, Swansea		W	21-6
92	9-Mar-12	Ireland	5N	A	Balmoral Showgrounds, Belfast		L	5-12
93	25-Mar-12	France	5N	H	Rodney Parade, Newport		W	14-8
94	14-Dec-12	South Africa	Int	H	Arms Park, Cardiff		L	0-3
95	18-Jan-13	England	5N	H	Arms Park, Cardiff		L	0-12
96	1-Feb-13	Scotland	5N	A	Inverleith, Edinburgh		W	8-0
97	27-Feb-13	France	5N	A	Parc des Princess, Paris		W	11-8
98	8-Mar-13	Ireland	5N	H	St Helen's, Swansea		W	16-13
99	17-Jan-14	England	5N	A	Twickenham, London		L	9-10
100	7-Feb-14	Scotland	5N	H	Arms Park, Cardiff		W	24-5
101	2-Mar-14	France	5N	H	St Helen's, Swansea		W	31-0
102	14-Mar-14	Ireland	5N	A	Balmoral Showgrounds, Belfast		W	11-3
103	21-Apr-19	NZ Army	Int	H	St Helen's, Swansea		L	3-6
104	17-Jan-20	England	5N	H	St Helen's, Swansea		W	19-5
105	7-Feb-20	Scotland	5N	A	Inverleith, Edinburgh		L	5-9
106	17-Feb-20	France	5N	A	Stade Colombes, Paris		W	6-5
107	13-Mar-20	Ireland	5N	H	Arms Park, Cardiff		W	28-4
108	15-Jan-21	England	5N	A	Twickenham, London		L	3-18
109	5-Feb-21	Scotland	5N	H	St Helen's, Swansea		L	8-14
110	26-Feb-21	France	5N	H	Arms Park, Cardiff		W	12-4
111	12-Mar-21	Ireland	5N	A	Balmoral Showgrounds, Belfast		W	6-0
112	21-Jan-22	England	5N	H	Arms Park, Cardiff		W	28-6
113	4-Feb-22	Scotland	5N	A	Inverleith, Edinburgh		D	9-9
114	11-Mar-22	Ireland	5N	H	St Helen's, Swansea		W	11-5
115	23-Mar-22	France	5N	A	Stade Colombes, Paris		W	11-3
116	20-Jan-23	England	5N	A	Twickenham, London		L	3-7
117	3-Feb-23	Scotland	5N	H	Arms Park, Cardiff		L	8-11
118	24-Feb-23	France	5N	H	St Helen's, Swansea		W	16-8
119	10-Mar-23	Ireland	5N	A	Lansdowne Road, Dublin		L	4-5
120	19-Jan-24	England	5N	H	St Helen's, Swansea		L	9-17

No	Date	Opponents	Tmt		Match Venue		Result	
121	2-Feb-24	Scotland	5N	A	Inverleith, Edinburgh		L	10-35
122	8-Mar-24	Ireland	5N	H	Arms Park, Cardiff		L	10-13
123	27-Mar-24	France	5N	A	Stade Colombes, Paris		W	10-6
124	29-Nov-24	New Zealand	Int	H	St Helen's, Swansea		L	0-19
125	17-Jan-25	England	5N	A	Twickenham, London		L	6-12
126	7-Feb-25	Scotland	5N	H	St Helen's, Swansea		L	14-24
127	28-Feb-25	France	5N	H	Arms Park, Cardiff		W	11-5
128	14-Mar-25	Ireland	5N	A	Ravenhill, Belfast		L	3-19
129	16-Jan-26	England	5N	H	Arms Park, Cardiff		D	3-3
130	6-Feb-26	Scotland	5N	A	Murrayfield, Edinburgh		L	5-8
131	13-Mar-26	Ireland	5N	H	St Helen's, Swansea		W	11-8
132	5-Apr-26	France	5N	A	Stade Colombes, Paris		W	7-5
133	15-Jan-27	England	5N	A	Twickenham, London		L	9-11
134	5-Feb-27	Scotland	5N	H	Arms Park, Cardiff		L	0-5
135	26-Feb-27	France	5N	H	St Helen's, Swansea		W	25-7
136	12-Mar-27	Ireland	5N	A	Lansdowne Road, Dublin		L	9-19
137	26-Nov-27	Australia	Int	H	Arms Park, Cardiff		L	8-18
138	21-Jan-28	England	5N	H	St Helen's, Swansea		L	8-10
139	4-Feb-28	Scotland	5N	A	Murrayfield, Edinburgh		W	13-0
140	10-Mar-28	Ireland	5N	H	Arms Park, Cardiff		L	10-13
141	9-Apr-28	France	5N	A	Stade Colombes, Paris		L	3-8
142	19-Jan-29	England	5N	A	Twickenham, London		L	3-8
143	2-Feb-29	Scotland	5N	H	St Helen's, Swansea		W	14-7
144	23-Feb-29	France	5N	H	Arms Park, Cardiff		W	8-3
145	9-Mar-29	Ireland	5N	A	Ravenhill, Belfast		D	5-5
146	18-Jan-30	England	5N	H	Arms Park, Cardiff		L	3-11
147	1-Feb-30	Scotland	5N	A	Murrayfield, Edinburgh		L	9-12
148	8-Mar-30	Ireland	5N	H	St Helen's, Swansea		W	12-7
149	21-Apr-30	France	5N	A	Stade Colombes, Paris		W	11-0
150	17-Jan-31	England	5N	A	Twickenham, London		D	11-11
151	7-Feb-31	Scotland	5N	H	Arms Park, Cardiff		W	13-8
152	28-Feb-31	France	5N	H	St Helen's, Swansea		W	35-3
153	14-Mar-31	Ireland	5N	A	Ravenhill, Belfast		W	15-3
154	5-Dec-31	South Africa	Int	H	St Helen's, Swansea		L	3-8
155	16-Jan-32	England	4N	H	St Helen's, Swansea		W	12-5
156	6-Feb-32	Scotland	4N	A	Murrayfield, Edinburgh		W	6-0
157	12-Mar-32	Ireland	4N	H	Arms Park, Cardiff		L	10-12
158	21-Jan-33	England	4N	A	Twickenham, London		W	7-3
159	4-Feb-33	Scotland	4N	H	St Helen's, Swansea		L	3-11
160	11-Mar-33	Ireland	4N	A	Ravenhill, Belfast		L	5-10

No	Date	Opponents	Tmt		Match Venue		Result	
161	20-Jan-34	England	4N	H	Arms Park, Cardiff		L	0-9
162	3-Feb-34	Scotland	4N	A	Murrayfield, Edinburgh		W	13-6
163	10-Mar-34	Ireland	4N	H	St Helen's, Swansea		W	13-0
164	19-Jan-35	England	4N	A	Twickenham, London		D	3-3
165	2-Feb-35	Scotland	4N	H	Arms Park, Cardiff		W	10-6
166	9-Mar-35	Ireland	4N	A	Ravenhill, Belfast		L	3-9
167	21-Dec-35	New Zealand	Int	H	Arms Park, Cardiff		W	13-12
168	18-Jan-36	England	4N	H	St Helen's, Swansea		D	0-0
169	1-Feb-36	Scotland	4N	A	Murrayfield, Edinburgh		W	13-3
170	14-Mar-36	Ireland	4N	H	Arms Park, Cardiff		W	3-0
171	16-Jan-37	England	4N	A	Twickenham, London		L	3-4
172	6-Feb-37	Scotland	4N	H	St Helen's, Swansea		L	6-13
173	3-Apr-37	Ireland	4N	A	Ravenhill, Belfast		L	3-5
174	15-Jan-38	England	4N	H	Arms Park, Cardiff		W	14-8
175	5-Feb-38	Scotland	4N	A	Murrayfield, Edinburgh		L	6-8
176	12-Mar-38	Ireland	4N	H	St Helen's, Swansea		W	11-5
177	21-Jan-39	England	4N	A	Twickenham, London		L	0-3
178	4-Feb-39	Scotland	4N	H	Arms Park, Cardiff		W	11-3
179	11-Mar-39	Ireland	4N	A	Ravenhill, Belfast		W	7-0
180	18-Jan-47	England	5N	H	Arms Park, Cardiff		L	6-9
181	1-Feb-47	Scotland	5N	A	Murrayfield, Edinburgh		W	22-8
182	22-Mar-47	France	5N	A	Stade Colombes, Paris		W	3-0
183	29-Mar-47	Ireland	5N	H	St Helen's, Swansea		W	6-0
184	20-Dec-47	Australia	Int	H	Arms Park, Cardiff		W	6-0
185	17-Jan-48	England	5N	A	Twickenham, London		D	3-3
186	7-Feb-48	Scotland	5N	H	Arms Park, Cardiff		W	14-0
187	21-Feb-48	France	5N	H	St Helen's, Swansea		L	3-11
188	13-Mar-48	Ireland	5N	A	Ravenhill, Belfast		L	3-6
189	15-Jan-49	England	5N	H	Arms Park, Cardiff		W	9-3
190	5-Feb-49	Scotland	5N	A	Murrayfield, Edinburgh		L	5-6
191	12-Mar-49	Ireland	5N	H	St Helen's, Swansea		L	0-5
192	26-Mar-49	France	5N	A	Stade Colombes, Paris		L	3-5
193	21-Jan-50	England	5N	A	Twickenham, London		W	11-5
194	4-Feb-50	Scotland	5N	H	St Helen's, Swansea		W	12-0
195	11-Mar-50	Ireland	5N	A	Ravenhill, Belfast		W	6-3
196	25-Mar-50	France	5N	H	Arms Park, Cardiff		W	21-0
197	20-Jan-51	England	5N	H	St Helen's, Swansea		W	23-5
198	3-Feb-51	Scotland	5N	A	Murrayfield, Edinburgh		L	0-19
199	10-Mar-51	Ireland	5N	H	Arms Park, Cardiff		D	3-3
200	7-Apr-51	France	5N	A	Stade Colombes, Paris		L	3-8

No	Date	Opponents	Tmt		Match Venue	Result	
201	22-Dec-51	South Africa	Int	H	Arms Park, Cardiff	L	3-6
202	19-Jan-52	England	5N	A	Twickenham, London	W	8-6
203	2-Feb-52	Scotland	5N	H	Arms Park, Cardiff	W	11-0
204	8-Mar-52	Ireland	5N	A	Lansdowne Road, Dublin	W	14-3
205	22-Mar-52	France	5N	H	St Helen's, Swansea	W	9-5
206	17-Jan-53	England	5N	H	Arms Park, Cardiff	L	3-8
207	7-Feb-53	Scotland	5N	A	Murrayfield, Edinburgh	W	12-0
208	14-Mar-53	Ireland	5N	H	St Helen's, Swansea	W	5-3
209	28-Mar-53	France	5N	A	Stade Colombes, Paris	W	6-3
210	19-Dec-53	New Zealand	Int	H	Arms Park, Cardiff	W	13-8
211	16-Jan-54	England	5N	A	Twickenham, London	L	6-9
212	13-Mar-54	Ireland	5N	A	Lansdowne Road, Dublin	W	12-9
213	27-Mar-54	France	5N	H	Arms Park, Cardiff	W	19-13
214	10-Apr-54	Scotland	5N	H	St Helen's, Swansea	W	15-3
215	22-Jan-55	England	5N	H	Arms Park, Cardiff	W	3-0
216	5-Feb-55	Scotland	5N	A	Murrayfield, Edinburgh	L	8-14
217	12-Mar-55	Ireland	5N	H	Arms Park, Cardiff	W	21-3
218	26-Mar-55	France	5N	A	Stade Colombes, Paris	W	16-11
219	21-Jan-56	England	5N	A	Twickenham, London	W	8-3
220	4-Feb-56	Scotland	5N	H	Arms Park, Cardiff	W	9-3
221	10-Mar-56	Ireland	5N	A	Lansdowne Road, Dublin	L	3-11
222	24-Mar-56	France	5N	H	Arms Park, Cardiff	W	5-3
223	19-Jan-57	England	5N	H	Arms Park, Cardiff	L	0-3
224	2-Feb-57	Scotland	5N	A	Murrayfield, Edinburgh	L	6-9
225	9-Mar-57	Ireland	5N	H	Arms Park, Cardiff	W	6-5
226	23-Mar-57	France	5N	A	Stade Colombes, Paris	W	19-13
227	4-Jan-58	Australia	Int	H	Arms Park, Cardiff	W	9-3
228	18-Jan-58	England	5N	A	Twickenham, London	D	3-3
229	1-Feb-58	Scotland	5N	H	Arms Park, Cardiff	W	8-3
230	15-Mar-58	Ireland	5N	A	Lansdowne Road, Dublin	W	9-6
231	29-Mar-58	France	5N	H	Arms Park, Cardiff	L	6-16
232	17-Jan-59	England	5N	H	Arms Park, Cardiff	W	5-0
233	7-Feb-59	Scotland	5N	A	Murrayfield, Edinburgh	L	5-6
234	14-Mar-59	Ireland	5N	H	Arms Park, Cardiff	W	8-6
235	4-Apr-59	France	5N	A	Stade Colombes, Paris	L	3-11
236	16-Jan-60	England	5N	A	Twickenham, London	L	6-14
237	6-Feb-60	Scotland	5N	H	Arms Park, Cardiff	W	8-0
238	12-Mar-60	Ireland	5N	A	Lansdowne Road, Dublin	W	10-9
239	26-Mar-60	France	5N	H	Arms Park, Cardiff	L	8-16
240	3-Dec-60	South Africa	Int	H	Arms Park, Cardiff	L	0-3

No	Date	Opponents	Tmt		Match Venue		Result
241	21-Jan-61	England	5N	H	Arms Park, Cardiff	W	6-3
242	11-Feb-61	Scotland	5N	A	Murrayfield, Edinburgh	L	0-3
243	11-Mar-61	Ireland	5N	H	Arms Park, Cardiff	W	9-0
244	25-Mar-61	France	5N	A	Stade Colombes, Paris	L	6-8
245	20-Jan-62	England	5N	A	Twickenham, London	D	0-0
246	3-Feb-62	Scotland	5N	H	Arms Park, Cardiff	L	3-8
247	24-Mar-62	France	5N	H	Arms Park, Cardiff	W	3-0
248	17-Nov-62	Ireland	5N	A	Lansdowne Road, Dublin	D	3-3
249	19-Jan-63	England	5N	H	Arms Park, Cardiff	L	6-13
250	2-Feb-63	Scotland	5N	A	Murrayfield, Edinburgh	W	6-0
251	9-Mar-63	Ireland	5N	H	Arms Park, Cardiff	L	6-14
252	23-Mar-63	France	5N	A	Stade Colombes, Paris	L	3-5
253	21-Dec-63	New Zealand	Int	H	Arms Park, Cardiff	L	0-6
254	18-Jan-64	England	5N	A	Twickenham, London	D	6-6
255	1-Feb-64	Scotland	5N	H	Arms Park, Cardiff	W	11-3
256	7-Mar-64	Ireland	5N	A	Lansdowne Road, Dublin	W	15-6
257	21-Mar-64	France	5N	H	Arms Park, Cardiff	D	11-11
258	23-May-64	South Africa	Int-T	A	Kings Park Stadium, Durban	L	3-24
259	16-Jan-65	England	5N	H	Arms Park, Cardiff	W	14-3
260	6-Feb-65	Scotland	5N	A	Murrayfield, Edinburgh	W	14-12
261	13-Mar-65	Ireland	5N	H	Arms Park, Cardiff	W	14-8
262	27-Mar-65	France	5N	A	Stade Colombes, Paris	L	13-22
263	15-Jan-66	England	5N	A	Twickenham, London	W	11-6
264	5-Feb-66	Scotland	5N	H	Arms Park, Cardiff	W	8-3
265	12-Mar-66	Ireland	5N	A	Lansdowne Road, Dublin	L	6-9
266	26-Mar-66	France	5N	H	Arms Park, Cardiff	W	9-8
267	3-Dec-66	Australia	Int	H	Arms Park, Cardiff	L	11-14
268	4-Feb-67	Scotland	5N	A	Murrayfield, Edinburgh	L	5-11
269	11-Mar-67	Ireland	5N	H	Arms Park, Cardiff	L	0-3
270	1-Apr-67	France	5N	A	Stade Colombes, Paris	L	14-20
271	15-Apr-67	England	5N	H	Arms Park, Cardiff	W	34-21
272	11-Nov-67	New Zealand	Int	H	Arms Park, Cardiff	L	6-13
273	20-Jan-68	England	5N	A	Twickenham, London	D	11-11
274	3-Feb-68	Scotland	5N	H	Arms Park, Cardiff	W	5-0
275	9-Mar-68	Ireland	5N	A	Lansdowne Road, Dublin	L	6-9
276	23-Mar-68	France	5N	H	Arms Park, Cardiff	L	9-14
277	1-Feb-69	Scotland	5N	A	Murrayfield, Edinburgh	W	17-3
278	8-Mar-69	Ireland	5N	H	National Stadium, Cardiff	W	24-11
279	22-Mar-69	France	5N	A	Stade Colombes, Paris	D	8-8
280	12-Apr-69	England	5N	H	National Stadium, Cardiff	W	30-9

No	Date	Opponents	Tmt		Match Venue	Result	
281	31-May-69	New Zealand	Int-T	A	Lancaster Park Oval, Christchurch	L	0-19
282	14-Jun-69	New Zealand	Int-T	A	Eden Park, Auckland	L	12-33
283	21-Jun-69	Australia	Int-T	A	Cricket Ground, Sydney	W	19-16
284	24-Jan-70	South Africa	Int	H	National Stadium, Cardiff	D	6-6
285	7-Feb-70	Scotland	5N	H	National Stadium, Cardiff	W	18-9
286	28-Feb-70	England	5N	A	Twickenham, London	W	17-13
287	14-Mar-70	Ireland	5N	A	Lansdowne Road, Dublin	L	0-14
288	4-Apr-70	France	5N	H	National Stadium, Cardiff	W	11-6
289	16-Jan-71	England	5N	H	National Stadium, Cardiff	W	22-6
290	6-Feb-71	Scotland	5N	A	Murrayfield, Edinburgh	W	19-18
291	13-Mar-71	Ireland	5N	H	National Stadium, Cardiff	W	23-9
292	27-Mar-71	France	5N	A	Stade Colombes, Paris	W	9-5
293	15-Jan-72	England	5N	A	Twickenham, London	W	12-3
294	5-Feb-72	Scotland	5N	H	National Stadium, Cardiff	W	35-12
295	25-Mar-72	France	5N	H	National Stadium, Cardiff	W	20-6
296	2-Dec-72	New Zealand	Int	H	National Stadium, Cardiff	L	16-19
297	20-Jan-73	England	5N	H	National Stadium, Cardiff	W	25-9
298	3-Feb-73	Scotland	5N	A	Murrayfield, Edinburgh	L	9-10
299	10-Mar-73	Ireland	5N	H	National Stadium, Cardiff	W	16-12
300	24-Mar-73	France	5N	A	Parc des Princess, Paris	L	3-12
301	10-Nov-73	Australia	Int	H	National Stadium, Cardiff	W	24-0
302	19-Jan-74	Scotland	5N	H	National Stadium, Cardiff	W	6-0
303	2-Feb-74	Ireland	5N	A	Lansdowne Road, Dublin	D	9-9
304	16-Feb-74	France	5N	H	National Stadium, Cardiff	D	16-16
305	16-Mar-74	England	5N	A	Twickenham, London	L	12-16
306	18-Jan-75	France	5N	A	Parc des Princess, Paris	W	25-10
307	15-Feb-75	England	5N	H	National Stadium, Cardiff	W	20-4
308	1-Mar-75	Scotland	5N	A	Murrayfield, Edinburgh	L	10-12
309	15-Mar-75	Ireland	5N	H	National Stadium, Cardiff	W	32-4
310	20-Dec-75	Australia	Int	H	National Stadium, Cardiff	W	28-3
311	17-Jan-76	England	5N	A	Twickenham, London	W	21-9
312	7-Feb-76	Scotland	5N	H	National Stadium, Cardiff	W	28-6
313	21-Feb-76	Ireland	5N	A	Lansdowne Road, Dublin	W	34-9
314	6-Mar-76	France	5N	H	National Stadium, Cardiff	W	19-13
315	15-Jan-77	Ireland	5N	H	National Stadium, Cardiff	W	25-9
316	5-Feb-77	France	5N	A	Parc des Princess, Paris	L	9-16
317	5-Mar-77	England	5N	H	National Stadium, Cardiff	W	14-9
318	19-Mar-77	Scotland	5N	A	Murrayfield, Edinburgh	W	18-9
319	4-Feb-78	England	5N	A	Twickenham, London	W	9-6
320	18-Feb-78	Scotland	5N	H	National Stadium, Cardiff	W	22-14

No	Date	Opponents	Tmt		Match Venue		Result
321	4-Mar-78	Ireland	5N	A	Lansdowne Road, Dublin	W	20-16
322	18-Mar-78	France	5N	H	National Stadium, Cardiff	W	16-7
323	11-Jun-78	Australia	Int-T	A	Ballymore Oval, Brisbane	L	8-18
324	17-Jun-78	Australia	Int-T	A	Cricket Ground, Sydney	L	17-19
325	11-Nov-78	New Zealand	Int	H	National Stadium, Cardiff	L	12-13
326	20-Jan-79	Scotland	5N	A	Murrayfield, Edinburgh	W	19-13
327	3-Feb-79	Ireland	5N	H	National Stadium, Cardiff	W	24-21
328	17-Feb-79	France	5N	A	Parc des Princess, Paris	L	13-14
329	17-Mar-79	England	5N	H	National Stadium, Cardiff	W	27-3
330	19-Jan-80	France	5N	H	National Stadium, Cardiff	W	18-9
331	16-Feb-80	England	5N	A	Twickenham, London	L	8-9
332	1-Mar-80	Scotland	5N	H	National Stadium, Cardiff	W	17-6
333	15-Mar-80	Ireland	5N	A	Lansdowne Road, Dublin	L	7-21
334	1-Nov-80	New Zealand	Int	H	National Stadium, Cardiff	L	3-23
335	17-Jan-81	England	5N	H	National Stadium, Cardiff	W	21-19
336	7-Feb-81	Scotland	5N	A	Murrayfield, Edinburgh	L	6-15
337	21-Feb-81	Ireland	5N	H	National Stadium, Cardiff	W	9-8
338	7-Mar-81	France	5N	A	Parc des Princess, Paris	L	15-19
339	5-Dec-81	Australia	Int	H	National Stadium, Cardiff	W	18-13
340	23-Jan-82	Ireland	5N	A	Lansdowne Road, Dublin	L	12-20
341	6-Feb-82	France	5N	H	National Stadium, Cardiff	W	22-12
342	6-Mar-82	England	5N	A	Twickenham, London	L	7-17
343	20-Mar-82	Scotland	5N	H	National Stadium, Cardiff	L	18-34
344	5-Feb-83	England	5N	H	National Stadium, Cardiff	D	13-13
345	19-Feb-83	Scotland	5N	A	Murrayfield, Edinburgh	W	19-15
346	5-Mar-83	Ireland	5N	H	National Stadium, Cardiff	W	23-9
347	19-Mar-83	France	5N	A	Parc des Princess, Paris	L	9-16
348	12-Nov-83	Romania	Int	A	Stadionul 23 August, Bucharest	L	6-24
349	21-Jan-84	Scotland	5N	H	National Stadium, Cardiff	L	9-15
350	4-Feb-84	Ireland	5N	A	Lansdowne Road, Dublin	W	18-9
351	18-Feb-84	France	5N	H	National Stadium, Cardiff	L	16-21
352	17-Mar-84	England	5N	A	Twickenham, London	W	24-15
353	24-Nov-84	Australia	Int	H	National Stadium, Cardiff	L	9-28
354	2-Mar-85	Scotland	5N	A	Murrayfield, Edinburgh	W	25-21
355	16-Mar-85	Ireland	5N	H	National Stadium, Cardiff	L	9-21
356	30-Mar-85	France	5N	A	Parc des Princess, Paris	L	3-14
357	20-Apr-85	England	5N	H	National Stadium, Cardiff	W	24-15
358	9-Nov-85	Fiji	Int	H	National Stadium, Cardiff	W	40-3
359	18-Jan-86	England	5N	A	Twickenham, London	L	18-21
360	1-Feb-86	Scotland	5N	H	National Stadium, Cardiff	W	22-15

No	Date	Opponents	Tmt		Match Venue	Result	
361	15-Feb-86	Ireland	5N	A	Lansdowne Road, Dublin	W	19-12
362	1-Mar-86	France	5N	H	National Stadium, Cardiff	L	15-23
363	31-May-86	Fiji	Int-T	A	National Stadium, Suva	W	22-15
364	12-Jun-86	Tonga	Int-T	A	Teufaiva Sport Stadium, Nuku'alofa	W	15-7
365	14-Jun-86	Western Samoa	Int-T	A	Apia Park, Apia	W	32-14
366	7-Feb-87	France	5N	A	Parc des Princess, Paris	L	9-16
367	7-Mar-87	England	5N	H	National Stadium, Cardiff	W	19-12
368	21-Mar-87	Scotland	5N	A	Murrayfield, Edinburgh	L	15-21
369	4-Apr-87	Ireland	5N	H	National Stadium, Cardiff	L	11-15
370	25-May-87	Ireland	WCp	N	Athletic Park, Wellington	W	13-6
371	29-May-87	Tonga	WCp	N	Showgrounds Oval, Palmerston North	W	29-16
372	3-Jun-87	Canada	WCp	N	Rugby Park Stadium, Invercargill	W	40-9
373	8-Jun-87	England	WCqf	N	Ballymore Oval, Brisbane	W	16-3
374	14-Jun-87	New Zealand	WCsf	N	Ballymore Oval, Brisbane	L	6-49
375	18-Jun-87	Australia	WC34	N	Rotorua International Stadium, Rotorua	W	22-21
376	7-Nov-87	United States	Int	H	National Stadium, Cardiff	W	46-0
377	6-Feb-88	England	5N	A	Twickenham, London	W	11-3
378	20-Feb-88	Scotland	5N	H	National Stadium, Cardiff	W	25-20
379	5-Mar-88	Ireland	5N	A	Lansdowne Road, Dublin	W	12-9
380	19-Mar-88	France	5N	H	National Stadium, Cardiff	L	9-10
381	28-May-88	New Zealand	Int-T	A	Lancaster Park Oval, Christchurch	L	3-52
382	11-Jun-88	New Zealand	Int-T	A	Eden Park, Auckland	L	9-54
383	12-Nov-88	Western Samoa	Int	H	National Stadium, Cardiff	W	28-6
384	10-Dec-88	Romania	Int	H	National Stadium, Cardiff	L	9-15
385	21-Jan-89	Scotland	5N	A	Murrayfield, Edinburgh	L	7-23
386	4-Feb-89	Ireland	5N	H	National Stadium, Cardiff	L	13-19
387	18-Feb-89	France	5N	A	Parc des Princess, Paris	L	12-31
388	18-Mar-89	England	5N	H	National Stadium, Cardiff	W	12-9
389	4-Nov-89	New Zealand	Int	H	National Stadium, Cardiff	L	9-34
390	20-Jan-90	France	5N	H	National Stadium, Cardiff	L	19-29
391	17-Feb-90	England	5N	A	Twickenham, London	L	6-34
392	3-Mar-90	Scotland	5N	H	National Stadium, Cardiff	L	9-13
393	24-Mar-90	Ireland	5N	A	Lansdowne Road, Dublin	L	8-14
394	2-Jun-90	Namibia	Int-T	A	South-West Stadium, Windhoek	W	18-9
395	9-Jun-90	Namibia	Int-T	A	South-West Stadium, Windhoek	W	34-30
396	6-Oct-90	Barbarians	Int	H	National Stadium, Cardiff	L	24-31
397	19-Jan-91	England	5N	H	National Stadium, Cardiff	L	6-25
398	2-Feb-91	Scotland	5N	A	Murrayfield, Edinburgh	L	12-32
399	16-Feb-91	Ireland	5N	H	National Stadium, Cardiff	D	21-21
400	2-Mar-91	France	5N	A	Parc des Princess, Paris	L	3-36

No	Date	Opponents	Tmt		Match Venue		Result	
401	22-Jul-91	Australia	Int-T	A	Ballymore Oval, Brisbane	L	6-63
402	4-Sep-91	France	Int	H	National Stadium, Cardiff	L	9-22
403	6-Oct-91	Western Samoa	WCp	H	National Stadium, Cardiff	L	13-16
404	9-Oct-91	Argentina	WCp	H	National Stadium, Cardiff	W	16-7
405	12-Oct-91	Australia	WCp	H	National Stadium, Cardiff	L	3-38
406	18-Jan-92	Ireland	5N	A	Lansdowne Road, Dublin	W	16-15
407	1-Feb-92	France	5N	H	National Stadium, Cardiff	L	9-12
408	7-Mar-92	England	5N	A	Twickenham, London	L	0-24
409	21-Mar-92	Scotland	5N	H	National Stadium, Cardiff	W	15-12
410	21-Nov-92	Australia	Int	H	National Stadium, Cardiff	L	6-23
411	6-Feb-93	England	5N	H	National Stadium, Cardiff	W	10-9
412	20-Feb-93	Scotland	5N	A	Murrayfield, Edinburgh	L	0-20
413	6-Mar-93	Ireland	5N	H	National Stadium, Cardiff	L	14-19
414	20-Mar-93	France	5N	A	Parc des Princess, Paris	L	10-26
415	22-May-93	Zimbabwe	Int-T	A	Hartsfield Rugby Ground, Bulawayo	W	35-14
416	29-May-93	Zimbabwe	Int-T	A	Police Ground, Harare	W	42-13
417	5-Jun-93	Namibia	Int-T	A	South West Stadium, Windhoek	W	38-23
418	16-Oct-93	Japan	Int	H	National Stadium, Cardiff	W	55-5
419	10-Nov-93	Canada	Int	H	National Stadium, Cardiff	L	24-26
420	15-Jan-94	Scotland	5N	H	National Stadium, Cardiff	W	29-6
421	5-Feb-94	Ireland	5N	A	Lansdowne Road, Dublin	W	17-15
422	19-Feb-94	France	5N	H	National Stadium, Cardiff	W	24-15
423	19-Mar-94	England	5N	A	Twickenham, London	L	8-15
424	18-May-94	Portugal	WCQ	A	Estádio Universitário de Lisboa, Lisbon	W	102-11
425	21-May-94	Spain	WCQ	A	Campo Ciudad Universitaria, Madrid	W	54-0
426	11-Jun-94	Canada	Int-T	A	Fletcher's Field, Markham, Toronto	W	33-15
427	18-Jun-94	Fiji	Int-T	A	National Stadium, Suva	W	23-8
428	22-Jun-94	Tonga	Int-T	A	Teufaiva Sport Stadium, Nuku'alofa	W	18-9
429	25-Jun-94	Western Samoa	Int-T	A	Chanel College, Moamoa, Apia	L	9-34
430	17-Sep-94	Romania	WCQ	A	Stadionul 23 August, Bucharest	W	16-9
431	12-Oct-94	Italy	WCQ	H	National Stadium, Cardiff	W	29-19
432	26-Nov-94	South Africa	Int	H	National Stadium, Cardiff	L	12-20
433	21-Jan-95	France	5N	A	Parc des Princess, Paris	L	9-21
434	18-Feb-95	England	5N	H	National Stadium, Cardiff	L	9-23
435	4-Mar-95	Scotland	5N	A	Murrayfield, Edinburgh	L	13-26
436	18-Mar-95	Ireland	5N	H	National Stadium, Cardiff	L	12-16
437	27-May-95	Japan	WCp	N	Free State Stadium, Bloemfontein	W	57-10
438	31-May-95	New Zealand	WCp	N	Ellis Park, Johannesburg	L	9-34
439	4-Jun-95	Ireland	WCp	N	Ellis Park, Johannesburg	L	23-24
440	2-Sep-95	South Africa	Int-T	A	Ellis Park, Johannesburg	L	11-40

No	Date	Opponents	Tmt	Match Venue	Result	
441	11-Nov-95	Fiji	Int	H National Stadium, Cardiff	W	19-15
442	16-Jan-96	Italy	Int	H National Stadium, Cardiff	W	31-26
443	3-Feb-96	England	5N	A Twickenham, London	L	15-21
444	17-Feb-96	Scotland	5N	H National Stadium, Cardiff	L	14-16
445	2-Mar-96	Ireland	5N	A Lansdowne Road, Dublin	L	17-30
446	16-Mar-96	France	5N	H National Stadium, Cardiff	W	16-15
447	9-Jun-96	Australia	Int-T	A Ballymore Oval, Brisbane	L	25-56
448	22-Jun-96	Australia	Int-T	A Football Stadium, Sydney	L	3-42
449	24-Aug-96	Barbarians	Int	H National Stadium, Cardiff	W	31-10
450	25-Sep-96	France	Int	H National Stadium, Cardiff	L	33-40
451	5-Oct-96	Italy	Int	A Stadio Olimpico, Rome	W	31-22
452	1-Dec-96	Australia	Int	H National Stadium, Cardiff	L	19-28
453	15-Dec-96	South Africa	Int	H National Stadium, Cardiff	L	20-37
454	11-Jan-97	United States	Int	H National Stadium, Cardiff	W	34-14
455	18-Jan-97	Scotland	5N	A Murrayfield, Edinburgh	W	34-19
456	1-Feb-97	Ireland	5N	H National Stadium, Cardiff	L	25-26
457	15-Feb-97	France	5N	A Parc des Princess, Paris	L	22-27
458	15-Mar-97	England	5N	H National Stadium, Cardiff	L	13-34
459	5-Jul-97	United States	Int-T	A Brook's Field, Wilmington, North Carolina	W	30-20
460	12-Jul-97	United States	Int-T	A Boxer Stadium, San Francisco	W	28-23
461	19-Jul-97	Canada	Int-T	A Fletcher's Field, Markham, Toronto	W	28-25
462	30-Aug-97	Romania	Int	H The Racecourse, Wrexham	W	70-21
463	16-Nov-97	Tonga	Int	H St Helen's, Swansea	W	46-12
464	29-Nov-97	New Zealand	Int	N Wembley Stadium, London	L	7-42
465	7-Feb-98	Italy	Int	H Stradey Park, Llanelli	W	23-20
466	21-Feb-98	England	5N	A Twickenham, London	L	26-60
467	7-Mar-98	Scotland	5N	N Wembley Stadium, London	W	19-13
468	21-Mar-98	Ireland	5N	A Lansdowne Road, Dublin	W	30-21
469	5-Apr-98	France	5N	N Wembley Stadium, London	L	0-51
470	6-Jun-98	Zimbabwe	Int-T	A National Sports Stadium, Harare	W	49-11
471	27-Jun-98	South Africa	Int-T	A Minolta Loftus Stadium, Pretoria	L	13-96
472	14-Nov-98	South Africa	Int	N Wembley Stadium, London	L	20-28
473	21-Nov-98	Argentina	Int	H Stradey Park, Llanelli	W	43-30
474	6-Feb-99	Scotland	5N	A Murrayfield, Edinburgh	L	20-33
475	20-Feb-99	Ireland	5N	N Wembley Stadium, London	L	23-29
476	6-Mar-99	France	5N	A Stade de France, Paris	W	34-33
477	20-Mar-99	Italy	Int	A Stadio Comunale di Monigo, Treviso	W	60-21
478	11-Apr-99	England	5N	N Wembley Stadium, London	W	32-31
479	5-Jun-99	Argentina	Int-T	A Ferro Carril Oeste Stadium, B Aires	W	36-26
480	12-Jun-99	Argentina	Int-T	A Ferro Carril Oeste Stadium, B Aires	W	23-16

No	Date	Opponents	Tmt		Match Venue	Result	
481	26-Jun-99	South Africa	Int	H	Millennium Stadium, Cardiff	W	29-19
482	21-Aug-99	Canada	Int	H	Millennium Stadium, Cardiff	W	33-19
483	28-Aug-99	France	Int	H	Millennium Stadium, Cardiff	W	34-23
484	1-Oct-99	Argentina	WCp	H	Millennium Stadium, Cardiff	W	23-18
485	9-Oct-99	Japan	WCp	H	Millennium Stadium, Cardiff	W	64-15
486	14-Oct-99	Samoa	WCp	H	Millennium Stadium, Cardiff	L	31-38
487	23-Oct-99	Australia	WCqf	H	Millennium Stadium, Cardiff	L	9-24
488	5-Feb-00	France	6N	H	Millennium Stadium, Cardiff	L	3-36
489	19-Feb-00	Italy	6N	H	Millennium Stadium, Cardiff	W	47-16
490	4-Mar-00	England	6N	A	Twickenham, London	L	12-46
491	18-Mar-00	Scotland	6N	H	Millennium Stadium, Cardiff	W	26-18
492	1-Apr-00	Ireland	6N	A	Lansdowne Road, Dublin	W	23-19
493	11-Nov-00	Samoa	Int	H	Millennium Stadium, Cardiff	W	50-6
494	18-Nov-00	United States	Int	H	Millennium Stadium, Cardiff	W	42-11
495	26-Nov-00	South Africa	Int	H	Millennium Stadium, Cardiff	L	13-23
496	3-Feb-01	England	6N	H	Millennium Stadium, Cardiff	L	15-44
497	17-Feb-01	Scotland	6N	A	Murrayfield, Edinburgh	D	28-28
498	17-Mar-01	France	6N	A	Stade de France, Paris	W	43-35
499	8-Apr-01	Italy	6N	A	Stadio Flaminio, Rome	W	33-23
500	10-Jun-01	Japan	Int-T	A	Hanazono Stadium, Osaka	W	64-10
501	17-Jun-01	Japan	Int-T	A	Prince Chichibu Memorial Ground, Tokyo	W	53-30
502	19-Sep-01	Romania	Int	H	Millennium Stadium, Cardiff	W	81-9
503	13-Oct-01	Ireland	6N	H	Millennium Stadium, Cardiff	L	6-36
504	10-Nov-01	Argentina	Int	H	Millennium Stadium, Cardiff	L	16-30
505	17-Nov-01	Tonga	Int	H	Millennium Stadium, Cardiff	W	51-7
506	25-Nov-01	Australia	Int	H	Millennium Stadium, Cardiff	L	13-21
507	3-Feb-02	Ireland	6N	A	Lansdowne Road, Dublin	L	10-54
508	16-Feb-02	France	6N	H	Millennium Stadium, Cardiff	L	33-37
509	2-Mar-02	Italy	6N	H	Millennium Stadium, Cardiff	W	44-20
510	23-Mar-02	England	6N	A	Twickenham, London	L	10-50
511	6-Apr-02	Scotland	6N	H	Millennium Stadium, Cardiff	L	22-27
512	8-Jun-02	South Africa	Int-T	A	Vodacom Park Stadium, Bloemfontein	L	19-34
513	15-Jun-02	South Africa	Int-T	A	Newlands Stadium, Cape Town	L	8-19
514	1-Nov-02	Romania	Int	H	The Racecourse, Wrexham	W	40-3
515	9-Nov-02	Fiji	Int	H	Millennium Stadium, Cardiff	W	58-14
516	16-Nov-02	Canada	Int	H	Millennium Stadium, Cardiff	W	32-21
517	23-Nov-02	New Zealand	Int	H	Millennium Stadium, Cardiff	L	17-43
518	15-Feb-03	Italy	6N	A	Stadio Flaminio, Rome	L	22-30
519	22-Feb-03	England	6N	H	Millennium Stadium, Cardiff	L	9-26
520	8-Mar-03	Scotland	6N	A	Murrayfield, Edinburgh	L	22-30

No	Date	Opponents	Tmt	Match Venue	Result	
521	22-Mar-03	Ireland	6N	H Millennium Stadium, Cardiff	L	24-25
522	29-Mar-03	France	6N	A Stade de France, Paris	L	5-33
523	14-Jun-03	Australia	Int-T	A Telstra Stadium, Sydney	L	10-30
524	21-Jun-03	New Zealand	Int-T	A Waikato Stadium, Hamilton	L	3-55
525	16-Aug-03	Ireland	Int	A Lansdowne Road, Dublin	L	12-35
526	23-Aug-03	England	Int	H Millennium Stadium, Cardiff	L	9-43
527	27-Aug-03	Romania	Int	H The Racecourse, Wrexham	W	54-8
528	30-Aug-03	Scotland	Int	H Millennium Stadium, Cardiff	W	23-9
529	12-Oct-03	Canada	WCp	N Telstra Dome, Melbourne	W	41-10
530	19-Oct-03	Tonga	WCp	N Canberra Stadium, Canberra	W	27-20
531	25-Oct-03	Italy	WCp	N Canberra Stadium, Canberra	W	27-15
532	2-Nov-03	New Zealand	WCp	N Telstra Stadium, Sydney	L	37-53
533	9-Nov-03	England	WCqf	N Suncorp Stadium, Brisbane	L	17-28
534	14-Feb-04	Scotland	6N	H Millennium Stadium, Cardiff	W	23-10
535	22-Feb-04	Ireland	6N	A Lansdowne Road, Dublin	L	15-36
536	7-Mar-04	France	6N	H Millennium Stadium, Cardiff	L	22-29
537	20-Mar-04	England	6N	A Twickenham, London	L	21-31
538	27-Mar-04	Italy	6N	H Millennium Stadium, Cardiff	W	44-10
539	12-Jun-04	Argentina	Int-T	A Estadio Monumental José Fierro, Tucumán	L	44-50
540	19-Jun-04	Argentina	Int-T	A Vélez Sarsfield Stadium, Buenos Aires	W	35-20
541	26-Jun-04	South Africa	Int-T	A Securicor Loftus Stadium, Pretoria	L	18-53
542	6-Nov-04	South Africa	Int	H Millennium Stadium, Cardiff	L	36-38
543	12-Nov-04	Romania	Int	H Millennium Stadium, Cardiff	W	66-7
544	20-Nov-04	New Zealand	Int	H Millennium Stadium, Cardiff	L	25-26
545	26-Nov-04	Japan	Int	H Millennium Stadium, Cardiff	W	98-0
546	5-Feb-05	England	6N	H Millennium Stadium, Cardiff	W	11-9
547	12-Feb-05	Italy	6N	A Stadio Flaminio, Rome	W	38-8
548	26-Feb-05	France	6N	A Stade de France, Paris	W	24-18
549	13-Mar-05	Scotland	6N	A Murrayfield, Edinburgh	W	46-22
550	19-Mar-05	Ireland	6N	H Millennium Stadium, Cardiff	W	32-20
551	4-Jun-05	United States	Int-T	A Rentschler Field, Hartford, Connecticut	W	77-3
552	11-Jun-05	Canada	Int-T	A York Stadium, Toronto	W	60-3
553	5-Nov-05	New Zealand	Int	H Millennium Stadium, Cardiff	L	3-41
554	9-Nov-05	Fiji	Int	H Millennium Stadium, Cardiff	W	11-10
555	19-Nov-05	South Africa	Int	H Millennium Stadium, Cardiff	L	16-33
556	26-Nov-05	Australia	Int	H Millennium Stadium, Cardiff	W	24-22
557	4-Feb-06	England	6N	A Twickenham, London	L	13-47
558	12-Feb-06	Scotland	6N	H Millennium Stadium, Cardiff	W	28-18
559	26-Feb-06	Ireland	6N	A Lansdowne Road, Dublin	L	5-31
560	11-Mar-06	Italy	6N	H Millennium Stadium, Cardiff	D	18-18

No	Date	Opponents	Tmt		Match Venue	Result	
561	18-Mar-06	France	6N	H	Millennium Stadium, Cardiff	L	16-21
562	11-Jun-06	Argentina	Int-T	A	Estadio Raúl Conti, Puerto Madryn	L	25-27
563	17-Jun-06	Argentina	Int-T	A	Vélez Sarsfield Stadium, Buenos Aires	L	27-45
564	4-Nov-06	Australia	Int	H	Millennium Stadium, Cardiff	D	29-29
565	11-Nov-06	Pacific Islands	Int	H	Millennium Stadium, Cardiff	W	38-20
566	17-Nov-06	Canada	Int	H	Millennium Stadium, Cardiff	W	61-26
567	25-Nov-06	New Zealand	Int	H	Millennium Stadium, Cardiff	L	10-45
568	4-Feb-07	Ireland	6N	H	Millennium Stadium, Cardiff	L	9-19
569	10-Feb-07	Scotland	6N	A	Murrayfield, Edinburgh	L	9-21
570	24-Feb-07	France	6N	A	Stade de France, Paris	L	21-32
571	10-Mar-07	Italy	6N	A	Stadio Flaminio, Rome	L	20-23
572	17-Mar-07	England	6N	H	Millennium Stadium, Cardiff	W	27-18
573	26-May-07	Australia	JBT-T	A	Telstra Stadium, Sydney	L	23-29
574	2-Jun-07	Australia	JBT-T	A	Suncorp Stadium, Brisbane	L	0-31
575	4-Aug-07	England	Int	A	Twickenham, London	L	5-62
576	18-Aug-07	Argentina	Int	H	Millennium Stadium, Cardiff	W	27-20
577	26-Aug-07	France	Int	H	Millennium Stadium, Cardiff	L	7-34
578	9-Sep-07	Canada	WCp	N	Stade de la Beaujoire, Nantes	W	42-17
579	15-Sep-07	Australia	WCp	H	Millennium Stadium, Cardiff	L	20-32
580	20-Sep-07	Japan	WCp	H	Millennium Stadium, Cardiff	W	72-18
581	29-Sep-07	Fiji	WCp	N	Stade de la Beaujoire, Nantes	L	34-38
582	24-Nov-07	South Africa	PWC	H	Millennium Stadium, Cardiff	L	12-34
583	2-Feb-08	England	6N	A	Twickenham, London	W	26-19
584	9-Feb-08	Scotland	6N	H	Millennium Stadium, Cardiff	W	30-15
585	23-Feb-08	Italy	6N	H	Millennium Stadium, Cardiff	W	47-8
586	8-Mar-08	Ireland	6N	A	Croke Park, Dublin	W	16-12
587	15-Mar-08	France	6N	H	Millennium Stadium, Cardiff	W	29-12
588	7-Jun-08	South Africa	PWC-T	A	Vodacom Park Stadium, Bloemfontein	L	17-43
589	14-Jun-08	South Africa	PWC-T	A	Loftus Versfeld Stadium, Pretoria	L	21-37
590	8-Nov-08	South Africa	PWC	H	Millennium Stadium, Cardiff	L	15-20
591	14-Nov-08	Canada	Int	H	Millennium Stadium, Cardiff	W	34-13
592	22-Nov-08	New Zealand	Int	H	Millennium Stadium, Cardiff	L	9-29
593	29-Nov-08	Australia	JBT	H	Millennium Stadium, Cardiff	W	21-18
594	8-Feb-09	Scotland	6N	A	Murrayfield, Edinburgh	W	26-13
595	14-Feb-09	England	6N	H	Millennium Stadium, Cardiff	W	23-15
596	27-Feb-09	France	6N	A	Stade de France, Paris	L	16-21
597	14-Mar-09	Italy	6N	A	Stadio Flaminio, Rome	W	20-15
598	21-Mar-09	Ireland	6N	H	Millennium Stadium, Cardiff	L	15-17
599	30-May-09	Canada	Int-T	A	York Stadium, Toronto	W	32-23
600	6-Jun-09	United States	Int-T	A	Toyota Park Stadium, Chicago	W	48-15

No	Date	Opponents	Tmt		Match Venue	Result	
601	7-Nov-09	New Zealand	Int	H	Millennium Stadium, Cardiff	L	12-19
602	13-Nov-09	Samoa	Int	H	Millennium Stadium, Cardiff	W	17-13
603	21-Nov-09	Argentina	Int	H	Millennium Stadium, Cardiff	W	33-16
604	28-Nov-09	Australia	JBT	H	Millennium Stadium, Cardiff	L	12-33
605	6-Feb-10	England	6N	A	Twickenham, London	L	17-30
606	13-Feb-10	Scotland	6N	H	Millennium Stadium, Cardiff	W	31-24
607	26-Feb-10	France	6N	H	Millennium Stadium, Cardiff	L	20-26
608	13-Mar-10	Ireland	6N	A	Croke Park, Dublin	L	12-27
609	20-Mar-10	Italy	6N	H	Millennium Stadium, Cardiff	W	33-10
610	5-Jun-10	South Africa	PWC	H	Millennium Stadium, Cardiff	L	31-34
611	19-Jun-10	New Zealand	Int-T	A	Carisbrook, Dunedin	L	9-42
612	26-Jun-10	New Zealand	Int-T	A	Waikato Stadium, Hamilton	L	10-29
613	6-Nov-10	Australia	JBT	H	Millennium Stadium, Cardiff	L	16-25
614	13-Nov-10	South Africa	PWC	H	Millennium Stadium, Cardiff	L	25-29
615	19-Nov-10	Fiji	Int	H	Millennium Stadium, Cardiff	D	16-16
616	27-Nov-10	New Zealand	Int	H	Millennium Stadium, Cardiff	L	25-37
617	4-Feb-11	England	6N	H	Millennium Stadium, Cardiff	L	19-26
618	12-Feb-11	Scotland	6N	A	Murrayfield, Edinburgh	W	24-6
619	26-Feb-11	Italy	6N	A	Stadio Flaminio, Rome	W	24-16
620	12-Mar-11	Ireland	6N	H	Millennium Stadium, Cardiff	W	19-13
621	19-Mar-11	France	6N	A	Stade de France, Paris	L	9-28
622	4-Jun-11	Barbarians	Int	H	Millennium Stadium, Cardiff	L	28-31
623	6-Aug-11	England	Int	A	Twickenham, London	L	19-23
624	13-Aug-11	England	Int	H	Millennium Stadium, Cardiff	W	19-9
625	20-Aug-11	Argentina	Int	H	Millennium Stadium, Cardiff	W	28-13
626	11-Sep-11	South Africa	WCp	N	Wellington Regional Stadium, Wellington	L	16-17
627	18-Sep-11	Samoa	WCp	N	Waikato Stadium, Hamilton	W	17-10
628	26-Sep-11	Namibia	WCp	N	Stadium Taranaki, New Plymouth	W	81-7
629	2-Oct-11	Fiji	WCp	N	Waikato Stadium, Hamilton	W	66-0
630	8-Oct-11	Ireland	WCqf	N	Wellington Regional Stadium, Wellington	W	22-10
631	15-Oct-11	France	WCsf	N	Eden Park, Auckland	L	8-9
632	21-Oct-11	Australia	WC34	N	Eden Park, Auckland	L	18-21
633	3-Dec-11	Australia	JBT	H	Millennium Stadium, Cardiff	L	18-24
634	5-Feb-12	Ireland	6N	A	Aviva Stadium, Dublin	W	23-21
635	12-Feb-12	Scotland	6N	H	Millennium Stadium, Cardiff	W	27-13
636	25-Feb-12	England	6N	A	Twickenham, London	W	19-12
637	10-Mar-12	Italy	6N	H	Millennium Stadium, Cardiff	W	24-3
638	17-Mar-12	France	6N	H	Millennium Stadium, Cardiff	W	16-9
639	2-Jun-12	Barbarians	Int	H	Millennium Stadium, Cardiff	W	30-21
640	9-Jun-12	Australia	JBT-T	A	Suncorp Stadium, Brisbane	L	19-27

No	Date	Opponents	Tmt		Match Venue	Result	
641	16-Jun-12	Australia	JBT-T	A	Etihad Stadium, Docklands, Melbourne	L	23-25
642	23-Jun-12	Australia	JBT-T	A	Football Stadium, Sydney	L	19-20
643	10-Nov-12	Argentina	Int	H	Millennium Stadium, Cardiff	L	12-26
644	16-Nov-12	Samoa	Int	H	Millennium Stadium, Cardiff	L	19-26
645	24-Nov-12	New Zealand	Int	H	Millennium Stadium, Cardiff	L	10-33
646	1-Dec-12	Australia	JBT	H	Millennium Stadium, Cardiff	L	12-14
647	2-Feb-13	Ireland	6N	H	Millennium Stadium, Cardiff	L	22-30
648	9-Feb-13	France	6N	A	Stade de France, Paris	W	16-6
649	23-Feb-13	Italy	6N	A	Stadio Olimpico, Rome	W	26-9
650	9-Mar-13	Scotland	6N	A	Murrayfield, Edinburgh	W	28-18
651	16-Mar-13	England	6N	H	Millennium Stadium, Cardiff	W	30-3
652	8-Jun-13	Japan	Int-T	A	Hanazono Stadium, Osaka	W	22-18
653	15-Jun-13	Japan	Int-T	A	Prince Chichibu Memorial Ground, Tokyo	L	8-23
654	9-Nov-13	South Africa	PWC	H	Millennium Stadium, Cardiff	L	15-24
655	16-Nov-13	Argentina	Int	H	Millennium Stadium, Cardiff	W	40-6
656	22-Nov-13	Tonga	Int	H	Millennium Stadium, Cardiff	W	17-7
657	30-Nov-13	Australia	JBT	H	Millennium Stadium, Cardiff	L	26-30
658	1-Feb-14	Italy	6N	H	Millennium Stadium, Cardiff	W	23-15
659	8-Feb-14	Ireland	6N	A	Aviva Stadium, Dublin	L	3-26
660	21-Feb-14	France	6N	H	Millennium Stadium, Cardiff	W	27-6
661	9-Mar-14	England	6N	A	Twickenham, London	L	18-29
662	15-Mar-14	Scotland	6N	H	Millennium Stadium, Cardiff	W	51-3
663	14-Jun-14	South Africa	PWC-T	A	Kings Park Stadium, Durban	L	16-38
664	21-Jun-14	South Africa	PWC-T	A	Mbombela Stadium, Nelspruit	L	30-31
665	8-Nov-14	Australia	JBT	H	Millennium Stadium, Cardiff	L	28-33
666	15-Nov-14	Fiji	Int	H	Millennium Stadium, Cardiff	W	17-13
667	22-Nov-14	New Zealand	Int	H	Millennium Stadium, Cardiff	L	16-34
668	29-Nov-14	South Africa	PWC	H	Millennium Stadium, Cardiff	W	12-6
669	6-Feb-15	England	6N	H	Millennium Stadium, Cardiff	L	16-21
670	15-Feb-15	Scotland	6N	A	Murrayfield, Edinburgh	W	26-23
671	28-Feb-15	France	6N	A	Stade de France, Paris	W	20-13
672	14-Mar-15	Ireland	6N	H	Millennium Stadium, Cardiff	W	23-16
673	21-Mar-15	Italy	6N	A	Stadio Olimpico, Rome	W	61-20

THE MINOR NATIONS

TIER 2,3 TEAMS

CANADA

The Canadian Rugby Football Union (CRU) was established in 1884, but was disbanded just before the First World War. The Rugby Union of Canada was then formed in 1929 and was followed by a tour of Japan in 1932. Most of the players on this tour were from British Columbia and the team lost both Internationals, the first in Osaka, by 9 points to 8, and the second in Tokyo, by 38 points to 5.

In the years that followed, the Canadian team seldom toured internationally, but they did visit the UK in 1962 with a team that was again made up of many players from British Columbia. During that tour, they drew with the Barbarians 3 points all, before losing by 8 points to nil to a Welsh under-23 side. In 1965, the Rugby Union of Canada was renamed the Canadian Rugby Union, and a year later the team, nicknamed the 'Canucks', lost by 19 points to 8 to the Lions who were returning from their tour of Australia and New Zealand.

Canada, along with fifteen other countries, was invited to compete in the 1987 World Cup. The team finished in third place in their pool behind Wales and Ireland. They performed better in the 1991 tournament and qualified for the quarter-finals by beating Fiji and Romania and finishing in second place to France in the pool. Two years later, the Canadians scored a famous victory against Wales in Cardiff in November 1993, and this was followed by an equally impressive home win over France the following year, in June 1994.

To date Canada has been successful on seven occasions in sixty-four matches against Tier 1 teams, having beaten Italy twice in 1983 and in 2000, Argentina twice in 1990 and Scotland once in

2002, in addition to the two wins against Wales and France. As quarter-finalists in the World Cup in 1991, Canada automatically qualified for the 1995 competition, but finished only in third place in a tough pool that contained holders Australia, and hosts and eventual winners, South Africa. Canada had to qualify for the next four World Cup tournaments and on each occasion failed to make it to the quarter-final stage.

The Canucks were very successful in the Pacific Rim tournament held between 1996 and 2001, having won three titles in succession: in 1996, 1997 and 1998. They also performed well in the Pan American Championship by finishing runners-up to Argentina in four of the five competitions held between 1995 and 2003. Canada also competed in all nine Churchill Cup tournaments held between 2003 and 2011.

The Canadians have a good record against their main Tier 2 and 3 group rivals and have won 70 out of the 117 matches played to date. To the end of March 2015, the Canadians have played a total of 223 International matches, and of these have won 94, drawn 5, and lost 124. They have defeated nearest rivals, the United States, 38 times in 52 games played, and are currently in 17th place in the World Rugby rankings table.

CANADA

HEAD TO HEAD RESULTS TO 31 MARCH 2015

	P	W	D	L	%	F	A
v TIER 1 Teams							
v Argentina	8	2	0	6	25.0	137	262
v Australia	6	0	0	6	0.0	60	283
v England	6	0	0	6	0.0	73	273
v France	8	1	0	7	12.5	101	274
v Ireland	6	0	1	5	8.3	77	226
v Italy	7	2	0	5	28.6	92	203
v New Zealand	5	0	0	5	0.0	54	313
v Scotland	4	1	0	3	25.0	49	105
v South Africa	2	0	0	2	0.0	18	71
v Wales	12	1	0	11	8.3	207	460
Sub-Total	**64**	**7**	**1**	**56**	**11.7**	**868**	**2470**
v TIER 2/3 Group							
v Fiji	9	3	0	6	33.3	173	267
v Japan	23	8	2	13	39.1	553	566
v Romania	5	2	0	3	40.0	102	75
v Samoa	4	0	0	4	0.0	60	123
v Tonga	7	5	0	2	71.4	175	127
v United States	52	38	1	13	74.0	1226	754
v Georgia	4	2	0	2	50.0	103	63
v Namibia	2	2	0	0	100.0	89	24
v Russia	3	3	0	0	100.0	91	27
v Uruguay	8	7	0	1	87.5	247	108
Sub-Total	**117**	**70**	**3**	**44**	**61.1**	**2819**	**2134**
v Tier 3 Selection							
v Hong Kong	6	5	0	1	83.3	182	99
v Portugal	4	4	0	0	100.0	138	53
v Spain	1	1	0	0	100.0	60	22
Sub-Total	**11**	**10**	**0**	**1**	**90.9**	**380**	**174**
v Tier 1 XV teams	14	3	0	11	21.4	163	422
v Other Teams	17	4	1	12	26.4	307	422
All Internationals	**223**	**94**	**5**	**124**	**43.3**	**4537**	**5622**

FIJI

Although rugby was first played on Viti Levu island in 1884, the Fiji Rugby Football Union was not officially formed until 1913. Two years later, the Fiji Native Rugby Union was established, and later on that year became affiliated to the Fiji RFU.

On 18 August 1924, the Fijians played their first International match against Western Samoa in Apia, which they won by six points to nil. They continued their tour by visiting Tonga to play three Internationals against the home side. A win, a draw and a defeat in Nuku'alofa meant that the series was shared. They returned via Apia to play the final match against Western Samoa on 19 September 1924, which they lost by 9 points to 3.

The Fijian team toured Australia in 1952 and 1954 and on each occasion shared the two-Test series, 1-1. In 1963 the Fiji RFU was renamed Fiji Rugby Union and a year later the Fijians, on their first European tour, lost by 21 points to 3 to France and by 28 points to 22 to a Wales XV.

The Fijians have contested six of the seven World Cup competitions held to date, the only exception being the 1995 tournament when they failed to qualify. In the first World Cup in 1987 they reached the quarter-final before bowing out to France, and in 1999, in a sudden death play-off for a quarter-final place, Fiji lost a high-scoring game against England by 45 points to 24. In 2003, a narrow 22 points to 20 defeat to Scotland in the final pool game deprived them of a quarter-final place, but in 2007 they finally reached the quarter-final for the second time by beating Wales by 38 points to 34 in a pulsating match. South Africa, the eventual champions, won the quarter-final encounter by 37 points to 20.

In 1982 the South Pacific Tri Nations series was established and held annually until 1997 (except on one occasion, in 1989). The Fijians won three titles out of the fifteen tournaments staged. They also won three titles in the South Pacific Tri Nations series renamed the Pacific Tri Nations Championship in 1998.

Other successes include the Pacific Rim Championship, which Fiji won in 2001, and the IRB Pacific Nations Cup competition which they won in 2013.

The Fijians have beaten Tier 1 teams ten times: their victories include five wins against Italy, a home win against Scotland in 1998, and two away wins against Australia in 1952 and 1954. The remaining two victories occurred in the 1987 World Cup game against Argentina, and in the aforementioned 2007 World Cup match against Wales.

Fiji has played 171 matches against Tier 2 and 3 group rivals and has won 112 of them. To the end of March 2015, the Fijians have played 308 International matches and of these have won 148, drawn 9, and lost 151. They have beaten their great rivals Samoa 25 times in 47 games and Tonga 58 times in 87 games. Fiji is currently ranked 12th in the World Rugby rankings table.

FIJI

HEAD TO HEAD RESULTS TO 31 MARCH 2015

	P	W	D	L	%	F	A
v TIER 1 Teams							
v Argentina	4	1	0	3	25.0	96	130
v Australia	19	2	1	16	13.2	221	546
v England	5	0	0	5	0.0	83	210
v France	9	0	0	9	0.0	111	359
v Ireland	3	0	0	3	0.0	31	149
v Italy	10	5	0	5	50.0	243	244
v New Zealand	5	0	0	5	0.00	50	364
v Scotland	6	1	0	5	16.7	145	182
v South Africa	3	0	0	3	0.00	41	129
v Wales	10	1	1	8	15.0	132	306
Sub-Total	**74**	**10**	**2**	**62**	**14.9**	**1153**	**2619**
v TIER 2/3 Group							
v Canada	9	6	0	3	66.7	267	173
v Japan	15	12	0	3	80.0	402	265
v Romania	3	2	0	1	66.7	70	42
v Samoa	47	25	2	20	55.3	882	805
v Tonga	87	58	3	26	68.4	1694	1141
v United States	6	5	0	1	83.3	143	97
v Georgia	1	1	0	0	100.0	24	19
v Namibia	2	2	0	0	100.0	116	43
v Russia	0	0	0	0	0.0	0	0
v Uruguay	1	1	0	0	100.0	39	24
Sub-Total	**171**	**112**	**5**	**54**	**67.0**	**3637**	**2609**
v Tier 3 Selection							
v Portugal	2	2	0	0	100.0	62	30
v Spain	1	1	0	0	100.0	39	20
Sub-Total	**3**	**3**	**0**	**0**	**100.0**	**101**	**50**
v New Zealand Maori	28	7	2	19	28.6	357	490
v Tier 1 XV teams	16	0	0	16	0.0	137	449
v Other Teams	16	16	0	0	100.0	1076	120
All Internationals	**308**	**148**	**9**	**151**	**49.5**	**6461**	**6337**

GEORGIA

The first rugby session in Georgia was held at Tblisi in 1959 and five years later, in 1964, the Georgia Rugby Union was founded and became part of the Soviet Union's rugby federation. During that Soviet period, Georgia regularly supplied players to the USSR national side, until May 1991, when the Independent Georgian Rugby Union was established. On achieving independence in 1992, they became an official affiliate of the International Rugby Board (IRB).

Georgia's first International, against Zimbabwe, took place in Kutaisi, the country's second largest city, on 12 September 1989, and the home team won it by 16 points to 3. The following year, the Georgians made a return visit to Zimbabwe and drew the two Test series. Throughout the 1990s all their games were played against European opposition, until March 1999 when they faced Tonga in a match over two legs to decide who would gain entry to the 1999 World Cup in Wales. They lost the first game in Nuku'alofa by 37 points to 6, but, despite winning the return leg by 28 points to 27, it was not enough to qualify for the finals. However, the Georgians did contest the next three World Cup tournaments. In Australia in 2003, they lost all four pool games, but fared slightly better in both the 2007 and the 2011 World Cup competitions, winning one of their four pool games on each occasion.

The Georgian team's performance in European competition has been more impressive: in their first season in the 1992-94 FIRA Trophy competition they won the Division 3 Pool 'A' title and followed it with a second place in Division 2 Pool 1 in the 1995-97 season. In 2000 the tournament was revamped and renamed the European Nations Cup (ENC), and Georgia, now in Division 1, continued to improve by finishing as runners-up to Romania in that first year and went on to win the title in 2001. Known as the 'Lelos', they won two further titles in the 2006-08 and 2008-10 seasons.

Georgia also won the ENC Division 1 competition, renamed Six Nations 'B' Championship, in its first two seasons, 2011-12, and 2013-14. The Georgians competed in four IRB Nations Cup competitions between 2007 and 2011, finishing in second place in 2008 and in 2011. They also competed in the first two Tbilisi Cup competitions held in 2013 and 2014.

Georgia's best sequence of eight wins, which started on 20 November 2010, was finally ended by the South African Kings in the IRB Nations Cup on 10 June 2011, and their worst run of seven losses occurred between March 2003 and February 2004. They also had another sequence of seven wins between November 2013 and June 2014.

In 63 Internationals against Tier 2 and 3 group rivals, the Georgians have won 38 times. They have played thirteen times against Tier 1 teams, but have yet to win. To the end of March 2015, the Lelos have played 175 International matches, and of these have won 107, drawn 6, and lost 62. They are currently in 14th place in the World Rugby rankings table.

GEORGIA

HEAD TO HEAD RESULTS TO 31 MARCH 2015

	P	W	D	L	%	F	A
v TIER 1 Teams							
v Argentina	3	0	0	3	0.0	28	87
v Australia	0	0	0	0	0.0	0	0
v England	2	0	0	2	0.0	16	125
v France	1	0	0	1	0.0	7	64
v Ireland	4	0	0	4	0.0	31	196
v Italy	1	0	0	1	0.0	22	31
v New Zealand	0	0	0	0	0.0	0	0
v Scotland	1	0	0	1	0.0	6	15
v South Africa	1	0	0	1	0.0	19	46
v Wales	0	0	0	0	0.0	0	0
Sub-Total	**13**	**0**	**0**	**13**	**0.0**	**129**	**564**
v TIER 2/3 Group							
v Canada	4	2	0	2	50.0	63	103
v Fiji	1	0	0	1	0.0	19	24
v Japan	3	1	0	2	33.3	64	81
v Romania	19	10	1	8	55.3	347	339
v Samoa	2	1	0	1	50.0	25	61
v Tonga	3	1	0	2	33.3	43	87
v United States	4	1	0	3	25.0	75	109
v Namibia	4	3	0	1	75.0	95	57
v Russia	19	17	1	1	92.1	476	224
v Uruguay	4	2	0	2	50.0	66	62
Sub-Total	**63**	**38**	**2**	**23**	**61.9**	**1273**	**1147**
v Tier 3 Selection							
v Czech Republic	8	8	0	0	100.0	310	58
v Germany	4	4	0	0	100.0	193	19
v Netherlands	4	3	0	1	75.0	164	64
v Portugal	19	13	2	4	73.7	440	265
v Spain	16	12	1	3	78.1	509	253
v Ukraine	9	9	0	0	100.0	281	63
Sub-Total	**60**	**49**	**3**	**8**	**84.2**	**1897**	**722**
v Other Teams	**39**	**20**	**1**	**18**	**52.6**	**768**	**742**
All Internationals	**175**	**107**	**6**	**62**	**62.9**	**4067**	**3175**

JAPAN

Rugby was introduced to Japan at Keio University in Minato, Tokyo, in 1899, and in 1926 the Japanese Rugby Football Union (JRFU) was founded. In 1930, in their first match, a touring Japanese team drew 3 points all with British Columbia in Vancouver, and two years later, on 31 January 1932, they played their first International against Canada in Osaka, which they won by 9 points to 8. They also won the second match in Tokyo eleven days later, by 38 points to 5.

Nicknamed the 'Cherry Blossoms', they had to wait until the 1970s before meeting Tier 1 teams. They met France twice in 1973, Australia twice in 1975, and Italy once in 1976, all away from home, and on each occasion it resulted in a defeat for the touring team.

The Japanese have competed in all seven World Cup competitions, but have yet to qualify for the quarter-finals. In twenty-four matches played, their only win was in 1991, when they defeated Zimbabwe by 52 points to 8. Japan's next best performances in the World Cup were their two drawn games, both against Canada, in 2007 and 2011. The heaviest defeat came in the 1995 World Cup when they were soundly beaten by 145 points to 17 by a strong New Zealand team.

The Japanese have won only three times in forty Internationals against Tier 1 teams. Their first win was achieved in Tokyo in September 1998 when they beat Argentina by 44 points to 29. The second success came in June 2013 when they triumphed over Wales in Osaka by 23 points to 8, and the third victory came in June 2014, when they defeated Italy in Tokyo by 26 points to 23. The Cherry Blossoms have faced nine Tier 1 countries over the years, with South Africa remaining the only team they have yet to play.

While the Japanese team's record in Internationals has been rather poor, they have a more impressive record in Asian competitions. In nineteen Asian Championships held between 1969 and 2004, the Japanese have won the title fourteen times, and have been runners-up to South Korea the remaining five times. They also won the Asia Nations Series in 2007, and have been crowned champions in all seven of the current Asia Five Nations Championships staged between 2008 and 2014.

The Japanese have played in all nine IRB Pacific Cup competitions held between 2006 to 2014, winning the title in 2011 and the North American section of the competition in 2014. Between 15 November 2013, and 15 November 2014, Japan recorded eleven successive wins before losing to Georgia in the final match of the year on 23 November 2014.

To the end of March 2015, the Cherry Blossoms have played 306 International matches and of these have won 125, drawn 9, and lost 172. The team has played Tier 2 and 3 group rivals 102 times and has won on 44 occasions. Japan is currently in 11th place in the World Rugby rankings table.

JAPAN

HEAD TO HEAD RESULTS TO 31 MARCH 2015

	P	W	D	L	%	F	A
v TIER 1 Teams							
v Argentina	5	1	0	4	20.0	139	205
v Australia	4	0	0	4	0.0	58	220
v England	1	0	0	1	0.0	7	60
v France	3	0	0	3	0.0	68	128
v Ireland	5	0	0	5	0.0	83	251
v Italy	6	1	0	5	16.7	90	199
v New Zealand	3	0	0	3	0.0	30	282
v Scotland	4	0	0	4	0.0	45	221
v South Africa	0	0	0	0	0.0	0	0
v Wales	9	1	0	8	11.1	129	493
Sub-Total	**40**	**3**	**0**	**37**	**7.5**	**649**	**2059**
v TIER 2/3 Group							
v Canada	23	13	2	8	60.9	566	553
v Fiji	15	3	0	12	20.0	265	402
v Romania	5	4	0	1	80.0	119	98
v Samoa	14	3	0	11	21.4	247	477
v Tonga	15	7	0	8	46.7	359	409
v United States	21	8	1	12	40.5	480	614
v Georgia	3	2	0	1	66.7	81	64
v Namibia	0	0	0	0	0.0	0	0
v Russia	5	4	0	1	80.0	237	90
v Uruguay	1	0	0	1	0.0	18	24
Sub-Total	**102**	**44**	**3**	**55**	**44.6**	**2372**	**2731**
v Tier 3 Selection							
v Hong Kong	23	19	0	4	82.6	989	333
v Kazakhstan	5	5	0	0	100.0	418	23
v South Korea	30	23	1	6	78.3	1220	435
v Spain	3	3	0	0	100.0	114	43
Sub-Total	**61**	**50**	**1**	**10**	**82.8**	**2741**	**834**
v Tier 1 XV teams	23	1	0	22	4.3	254	1058
v Other Teams	80	27	5	48	36.9	2466	2107
All Internationals	**306**	**125**	**9**	**172**	**42.3**	**8482**	**8789**

NAMIBIA

Rugby was first played in Namibia, then known as South-West Africa, in 1916, having been introduced to the game by South African soldiers who had invaded the German-run colony during the First World War.

Namibia gained its independence in 1990 and the Namibia Rugby Union was formed in March of that year. The Namibians joined the IRB in the same month and played their first International against Zimbabwe in Windhoek on 24 March. They won that match comfortably by 33 points to 18, and followed it with a resounding 86 points to 9 win against Portugal on 21 April 1990. However, the team lost the next two matches to the touring Welsh side in June of that year – but bounced back with an amazing period of fourteen straight wins in a sequence stretching from July 1990 to June 1993. During that incredible run, the Namibians had home wins against Italy (twice) in June 1991, and Ireland (twice) in July 1991.The team's winning streak was brought to an end when they lost to Wales by 38 points to 23 in June 1993.

The Namibians have competed in each World Cup tournament since 1999 but have struggled against the opposition, losing all fifteen matches played in the four tournaments, including eight games by more than fifty points. Their heaviest defeat came in 2003 when they lost by 142 points to nil to host nation, Australia.

Nicknamed the 'Welwitschias', they have been successful in competitions on the African continent, winning the Confederation of African Rugby Championship (CAR), held between 2000 and 2005, in both 2002 and 2004. The tournament was renamed the Africa Cup in 2006 and the Namibian team won the title for the third time in the 2008-09 season. Namibia withdrew from that competition the following year to concentrate on the much more demanding IRB Nations Cup, which was first held in 2006. The team first entered that tournament in 2007, but had to wait until 2010 before their second invitation, and on that occasion they won the cup, defeating both Georgia and the then tournament hosts, Romania, en route to the final. Those two wins remain their only victories against Tier 2 and 3 group rivals. They finished a disappointing fourth out of six the following year.

Namibia's four wins against Tier 1 countries are confined to the ones achieved against Italy and Ireland in 1991. In July 2014, the Namibians qualified for the 2015 World Cup when they won the Africa Cup for the fourth time on points difference from Zimbabwe and Kenya.

To the end of March 2015, the Namibians had played 118 Internationals and of these have won 68, drawn 2, and lost 46. They are currently in 22nd place in the World Rugby ratings table.

NAMIBIA

HEAD TO HEAD RESULTS TO 31 MARCH 2015

v TIER 1 Teams	P	W	D	L	%	F	A
v Argentina	2	0	0	2	0.0	17	130
v Australia	1	0	0	1	0.0	0	142
v England	0	0	0	0	0.0	0	0
v France	2	0	0	2	0.0	23	134
v Ireland	4	2	0	2	50.0	65	117
v Italy	3	2	0	1	66.7	74	75
v New Zealand	0	0	0	0	0.0	0	0
v Scotland	0	0	0	0	0.0	0	0
v South Africa	2	0	0	2	0.0	13	192
v Wales	4	0	0	4	0.0	69	171
Sub-Total	**18**	**4**	**0**	**14**	**22.2**	**261**	**961**
v TIER 2/3 Group							
v Canada	2	0	0	2	0.0	24	89
v Fiji	2	0	0	2	0.0	43	116
v Japan	0	0	0	0	0.0	0	0
v Romania	4	1	0	3	25.0	55	95
v Samoa	2	0	0	2	0.0	25	89
v Tonga	1	0	0	1	0.0	14	20
v United States	0	0	0	0	0.0	0	0
v Georgia	4	1	0	3	25.0	57	95
v Russia	2	0	0	2	0.0	27	61
v Uruguay	1	0	0	1	0.0	12	23
Sub-Total	**18**	**2**	**0**	**16**	**11.1**	**257**	**588**
v Tier 3 Selection							
v Côte d'Ivoire	4	2	1	1	62.5	101	50
v Kenya	8	6	0	2	75.0	382	142
v Madagascar	4	3	0	1	75.0	310	84
v Morocco	7	4	1	2	64.3	133	137
v Portugal	7	5	0	2	71.4	229	125
v Tunisia	8	5	0	3	62.5	175	138
v Zimbabwe	27	25	0	2	92.6	943	551
Sub-Total	**65**	**50**	**2**	**13**	**78.5**	**2273**	**1227**
v Other Teams	**17**	**12**	**0**	**5**	**70.6**	**702**	**291**
All Internationals	**118**	**68**	**2**	**48**	**58.5**	**3493**	**3067**

ROMANIA

Rugby was first brought to Romania when students, returning from their studies in Paris, formed Stadiul Roman, in addition to seventeen other clubs in Bucharest, in 1913. Although the Romanian Rugby Championship was contested in 1914, it was five years before the national side played its first International – against the United States in Stade Colombes, Paris, in June 1919. They lost that match by 20 points to nil.

In 1931, the governing body for rugby union in Romania, Federația Română de Rugby (FRR), was formed and a year later Romania became one of the nine founder members of the Fédération Internationale de Rugby Amateur (FIRA).

During the period 1919 to 1936, the Romanians played their opening eleven matches away from home, and it wasn't until 25 April 1937 that they finally played a home International against Italy in Bucharest, which ended scoreless. The Romanians were one of three teams to enter both the 1920 Antwerp Olympic Games and the 1924 Paris Olympic Games. They lost heavily to both a France XV and to the United States respectively.

The team, nicknamed the 'Oaks', first entered the FIRA tournament in 1935 and are the only team to have played in all the competitions ever since. Of the eight FIRA Nations Cups held between 1965 and 1973, they won the title in 1968-69 and were runners-up to France on six occasions.

The Romanians were also four-time winners in the FIRA Trophy competition, held between 1974 and 1996, and runners-up to France on six occasions. During that time, the Oaks were arguably the top team in Europe, outside the Five Nations sides.

Romania won the European Nations Cup three times between 2000 and 2010 and finished in second place twice. The Romanians were also runners-up to Georgia in both the 2010-11 and the 2012-13 season of the ENC competition (which is now known as the Six Nations 'B' Championship).

Except for the 2006 tournament, Romania played in eight of the nine IRB Nations Cup competitions held between 2006 and 2014, winning in both 2012 and 2013, and gaining second place in 2010 and 2014.

The Oaks have played in all seven World Cup competitions since their invitation to the 1987 tournament, the same year they joined the IRB. Unfortunately, they failed to progress further than the pool stage on each occasion. Their World Cup record currently stands at five wins in twenty-four games played. They have played 70 matches against Tier 2 and 3 group rivals, winning on 36 occasions. They have beaten Tier 1 teams 28 times in 138 games, which includes 16 wins against Italy, 8 wins against France, and two each against Wales and Scotland. The away wins against Wales in 1988 and against France in 1990 remain their most memorable victories.

To the end of March 2015, the Oaks have played 409 International matches and of these have won 230, drawn 12, and lost 167; 105 of these defeats were against Tier 1 teams. Romania is currently in 18th place in the World Rugby rankings table.

ROMANIA

HEAD TO HEAD RESULTS TO 31 MARCH 2015

	P	W	D	L	%	F	A
v TIER 1 Teams							
v Argentina	8	0	0	8	0.0	97	317
v Australia	3	0	0	3	0.0	20	189
v England	5	0	0	5	0.0	24	335
v France	49	8	2	39	18.4	451	1277
v Ireland	8	0	0	8	0.0	92	346
v Italy	41	16	3	22	42.7	612	577
v New Zealand	2	0	0	2	0.0	14	99
v Scotland	13	2	0	11	15.4	192	475
v South Africa	1	0	0	1	0.0	8	21
v Wales	8	2	0	6	25.0	96	342
Sub-Total	**138**	**28**	**5**	**105**	**22.1**	**1606**	**3978**
v TIER 2/3 Group							
v Canada	5	3	0	2	60.0	75	102
v Fiji	3	1	0	2	33.3	42	70
v Japan	5	1	0	4	20.0	98	119
v Samoa	1	1	0	0	100.0	32	24
v Tonga	1	1	0	0	100.0	19	18
v United States	7	1	0	6	14.3	76	189
v Georgia	19	8	1	10	44.7	339	347
v Namibia	4	3	0	1	75.0	95	55
v Russia	19	12	1	6	65.8	460	284
v Uruguay	6	5	1	0	91.7	150	75
Sub-Total	**70**	**36**	**3**	**31**	**53.6**	**1386**	**1283**
v Tier 3 Selection							
v Netherlands	7	7	0	0	100.0	296	46
v Poland	16	14	0	2	87.5	514	143
v Portugal	22	19	0	3	86.4	683	213
v Spain	32	30	0	2	93.8	962	311
v Ukraine	7	7	0	0	100.0	400	43
v USSR *	15	12	0	3	80.0	251	153
Sub-Total	**99**	**89**	**0**	**10**	**89.9**	**3106**	**909**
v Other Teams	**102**	**77**	**4**	**21**	**77.5**	**2887**	**1235**
All Internationals	**409**	**230**	**12**	**167**	**57.7**	**8985**	**7405**

* 1976-90

RUSSIA

The first official rugby match in the USSR took place in Moscow in 1923, but the Rugby Union of the Soviet Union was founded much later, in 1936. The national side did not play its first International until 1974, and all subsequent matches over the next two years were against eastern European teams. In 1977, the USSR was invited to play in Division 2 of the Fédération Internationale de Amateur (FIRA) tournament. By winning the title at the first attempt, the team was then promoted to Division 1. The Soviets performed reasonably well at the top level for the next six years and excelled in the 1985-87 season when they finished runners-up to France, ahead of both Romania and Italy. They also repeated that feat the following two seasons, in 1987-88 and 1989-90.

With the break up of the USSR in 1991, the Russian national team was born. It was administered by the Rugby Union of Russia (RUR), which subsequently became affiliated to the IRB. The Russians played their first match against Belgium on 11 October 1992, in the FIRA 1992-94 tournament, and although the team was depleted owing to the loss of a large number of players (who, following the break up of USSR, were now playing for the independent states), they still won that match by 17 points to 11. However, this loss of experienced players had a longer term effect on the team's performance and Russia was placed in Division 2 of the newly structured European Nations Cup in 2000.

Despite this, as immediate champions of that division the Russians were promoted to Division 1 in 2001, and were placed more or less in mid-table for the next six years. Success returned in 2006-08 and 2008-10 when they finished in second place to Georgia in both seasons. The Russians competed in ENC Division 1, renamed Six Nations 'B' in the 2011-12 and 2013-14 seasons.

They also competed in the IRB Nations Cup in 2006, 2008, 2009, 2012, 2013 and 2014, and by invitation in the Churchill Cup in 2010 and 2011. The then-USSR was invited to play in the first World Cup in 1987, but declined to take part on political grounds, not least the continued IRB membership of apartheid South Africa. In both the 1995 and 1999 World Cups, the Russian team failed to qualify, and was expelled from qualifying for the 2003 tournament for fielding ineligible players.

A loss to Portugal in the European qualifying rounds deprived them of a place in the 2007 World Cup, but they finally made it to the next World Cup in New Zealand in 2011. Disappointingly, they lost all four matches and finished bottom in a tough pool that consisted of Australia, Italy, Ireland and the United States.

The Russians have never beaten a Tier 1 team in all seven of their attempts, but they have defeated Tier 2 and 3 group rivals on 14 occasions in 61 matches. They failed to qualify for the 2015 World Cup when they lost on aggregate to Uruguay in a two-match play-off.

To the end of March 2015, the Russians have played 170 International matches, and of these have won 86, drawn 3, and lost 81. Russia is currently in 19th place in the World Rugby rankings table.

RUSSIA

HEAD TO HEAD RESULTS TO 31 MARCH 2015

	P	W	D	L	%	F	A
v TIER 1 Teams							
v Australia	1	0	0	1	0.0	22	68
v Ireland	2	0	0	2	0.0	15	97
v Italy	4	0	0	4	0.0	61	198
Sub-Total	**7**	**0**	**0**	**7**	**0.0**	**98**	**363**
v TIER 2/3 Group							
v Canada	3	0	0	3	0.0	27	91
v Fiji	0	0	0	0	0.0	0	0
v Japan	5	1	0	4	20.0	90	237
v Romania	19	6	1	12	34.2	284	460
v Samoa	0	0	0	0	0.0	0	0
v Tonga	0	0	0	0	0.0	0	0
v United States	6	0	0	6	0.0	97	193
v Georgia	19	1	1	17	7.9	224	476
v Namibia	2	2	0	0	100.0	61	27
v Uruguay	7	4	0	3	57.1	160	151
Sub-Total	**61**	**14**	**2**	**45**	**24.6**	**943**	**1635**
v Tier 3 Selection							
v Belgium	4	4	0	0	100.0	126	78
v Czech Republic	8	6	0	2	75.0	309	104
v Denmark	3	3	0	0	100.0	191	28
v Germany	7	7	0	0	100.0	352	79
v Hong Kong	2	2	0	0	100.0	70	37
v Morocco	3	2	0	1	66.7	44	46
v Netherlands	4	4	0	0	100.0	208	39
v Poland	4	4	0	0	100.0	201	59
v Portugal	17	11	1	5	67.7	442	329
v Spain	18	15	0	3	83.3	572	415
v Tunisia	2	2	0	0	100.0	57	41
v Ukraine	9	9	0	0	100.0	439	115
Sub-Total	**81**	**69**	**1**	**11**	**85.8**	**3011**	**1370**
v Other Teams	**21**	**3**	**0**	**18**	**14.3**	**353**	**719**
All Internationals	**170**	**86**	**3**	**81**	**51.5**	**4405**	**4087**

SAMOA

The Marist Brothers religious order brought rugby to Western Samoa in 1920 and the Western Samoa Rugby Union was formed in 1924. Later that year, on 18 August, they lost their first International to Fiji on home ground in Apia, by 6 points to nil. A month later, on 19 September, Western Samoa gained revenge by defeating Fiji by 9 points to 3. In their third game at home, again against Fiji in 1928, they lost by 9 points to 8. The next match, in Apia in 1932, was against Tonga, and the Western Samoan team lost by 15 points to 9. However, they defeated Tonga in their next match in 1947, by 5 points to 3.

Nearly forty years elapsed before Western Samoans finally faced opponents from outside the South Pacific islands, in a match against Wales on 14 June 1986, which the Welsh won by 32 points to 4. This led to a return visit to Wales in 1988. Western Samoa lost the two Internationals on that tour: the first to Ireland by 49 points to 22, and the second to their hosts, Wales, by 24 points to 6.

The three Pacific Island teams met so regularly during the 1950s, 1960s and 1970s that in 1982 the South Pacific Tri Nations Series was formed. Western Samoa won the inaugural competition, and also triumphed in 1985, but unlike Fiji and Tonga, the team was not invited to compete in the first World Cup in 1987. However, they have subsequently competed in all six of the other World Cup tournaments.

Western Samoa caused a sensation in the 1991 World Cup when the team reached the quarter-final stage by eliminating both Wales and Argentina in the pool games. They repeated that feat in the 1995 World Cup when they beat Italy and Argentina again at the pool stage, only to lose to eventual winners South Africa in the last eight. The team, renamed Samoa in 1997, defeated hosts Wales yet again in the Millennium Stadium in the 1999 World Cup, but lost to Scotland in the play-off, required to secure a place in the quarter-final. The Samoans have not emerged from the pool stage in subsequent World Cup competitions.

Samoa have beaten Tier 1 teams 15 times in 63 games played, and Tier 2 and 3 group rivals 72 times in 125 games played. On the domestic front, the Samoans has been very successful, winning ten titles in the South Pacific Tri Nations Series held between 1982 and 1997, and four titles in the Pacific Tri Nations Championship staged between 1998 and 2005. Samoa also won the Pacific Rim tournament in 2000-01, the IRB Pacific Nations Cup in 2010 and 2012, and the Pacific section of that tournament in 2014, by defeating Fiji and drawing with Tonga.

To the end of March 2015, the Samoans have played 201 Internationals, and of these have won 97, drawn 6 and lost 98. They have beaten local rivals Tonga 30 times out of 51 games played, and Fiji 20 times in 47 Internationals. Samoa is currently in 9th place in the World Rugby rankings table.

SAMOA

HEAD TO HEAD RESULTS TO 31 MARCH 2015

v TIER 1 Teams	P	W	D	L	%	F	A
v Argentina	4	3	0	1	75.0	111	82
v Australia	5	1	0	4	20.0	58	204
v England	7	0	0	7	0.0	100	244
v France	3	0	0	3	0.0	41	104
v Ireland	6	1	0	5	16.7	103	209
v Italy	7	5	0	2	71.4	175	109
v New Zealand	5	0	0	5	0.0	56	308
v Scotland	9	1	1	7	16.7	122	218
v South Africa	8	0	0	8	0.0	93	385
v Wales	9	4	0	5	44.4	163	216
Sub-Total	**63**	**15**	**1**	**47**	**24.6**	**1022**	**2079**
v TIER 2/3 Group							
v Canada	4	4	0	0	100.0	123	60
v Fiji	47	20	2	25	44.7	805	882
v Japan	14	11	0	3	78.6	477	247
v Romania	1	0	0	1	0.0	24	32
v Tonga	51	30	3	18	61.8	935	742
v United States	3	3	0	0	100.0	71	53
v Georgia	2	1	0	1	50.0	61	25
v Namibia	2	2	0	0	100.0	89	25
v Russia	0	0	0	0	0.0	0	0
v Uruguay	1	1	0	0	100.0	60	13
Sub-Total	**125**	**72**	**5**	**48**	**59.6**	**2645**	**2079**
v Tier 3 Selection							
v Belgium	1	1	0	0	100.0	37	8
v Cook Islands	3	3	0	0	100.0	102	31
v Papua New Guinea	2	2	0	0	100.0	188	19
Sub-Total	**6**	**6**	**0**	**0**	**100.0**	**327**	**58**
v Other Teams	**7**	**4**	**0**	**3**	**57.1**	**209**	**91**
All Internationals	**201**	**97**	**6**	**98**	**49.8**	**4203**	**4307**

TONGA

Rugby was introduced to Tonga in the early part of the twentieth century. Following the formation of the Tonga Rugby Football Union in late 1923, the team (nicknamed 'The Sea Eagles') won their first match at home, in Nuku'alofa, in August 1924 by defeating neighbours Fiji by 9 points to 6. With the exception of one match against Western Samoa in 1932, Tonga's only opponent was Fiji, whom they played a further sixteen times between September 1924 and July 1947, before facing Western Samoa again in August 1947.

Most of the Sea Eagles' games in the 1960s were against old rivals Fiji and Western Samoa, but in 1973 they toured Australia and gained a memorable 16 points to 11 win against their hosts in the second International. The Tongans lost heavily to a Scottish XV and to a Welsh XV on their first tour to the Northern Hemisphere, but redeemed themselves admirably by beating Canada by 40 points to 14 on their return journey home.

Tonga has contested six of the seven World Cup competitions held to date, the only exception being the 1991 tournament when the team failed to qualify. Despite their involvement, they have never progressed beyond the pool stages, winning only six matches out of twenty-one played. The Sea Eagles' most notable victory came in the 2011 World Cup when they defeated France by 19 points to 14, recalling an earlier home win against the French in June 1999. A previous World Cup win against Italy, also in 1999, meant that their 2011 triumph was the fourth against Tier 1 teams. This record was increased to five when the Tongans defeated Scotland in Edinburgh in November 2012.

When it comes to wins, Tonga has never had more than four in a row, but sequences of losses have been rather more commonplace: twelve consecutive defeats between October 2003 and November 2005 probably represents the lowest point in their history. Tonga has also been less successful than both Fiji and Samoa in the domestic tournaments, winning only two titles out of fifteen in the South Pacific Tri Nations series held between 1982 and 1997, and registering no victories at all in the renamed Pacific Tri Nations Championship staged between 1998 and 2005. The Sea Eagles did achieve some success when they beat both their South Sea rivals in the IRB Pacific Nations Cup in 2011.

The Tongans have played 172 Internationals against Tier 2 and 3 group rivals, and of these have won 63, drawn 6, and lost 103. Their record against Tier 1 countries remains at 5 wins in 34 matches played.

To the end of March 2015, the Sea Eagles played 240 International matches and of these won 87, drawn 6, and lost 147. Against their Pacific rivals, they have beaten Fiji only 26 times in 87 matches played, and Samoa only 18 times in 51 matches. Tonga is currently in 13th place in the World Rugby rankings table.

TONGA

HEAD TO HEAD RESULTS TO 31 MARCH 2015

	P	W	D	L	%	F	A
v TIER 1 Teams							
v Argentina	0	0	0	0	0.0	0	0
v Australia	4	1	0	3	25.0	42	167
v England	2	0	0	2	0.0	30	137
v France	5	2	0	3	40.0	75	149
v Ireland	2	0	0	2	0.0	28	72
v Italy	4	1	0	3	25.0	63	137
v New Zealand	4	0	0	4	0.0	26	279
v Scotland	4	1	0	3	25.0	58	136
v South Africa	2	0	0	2	0.0	35	104
v Wales	7	0	0	7	0.0	78	203
Sub-Total	**34**	**5**	**0**	**29**	**14.7**	**435**	**1384**
v TIER 2/3 Group							
v Canada	7	2	0	5	28.6	127	175
v Fiji	87	26	3	58	31.6	1141	1694
v Japan	15	8	0	7	53.3	409	359
v Romania	1	0	0	1	0.0	18	19
v Samoa	51	18	3	30	38.2	742	935
v United States	7	6	0	1	85.7	188	98
v Georgia	3	2	0	1	66.7	87	43
v Namibia	1	1	0	0	100.0	20	14
v Russia	0	0	0	0	0.0	0	0
v Uruguay	0	0	0	0	0.0	0	0
Sub-Total	**172**	**63**	**6**	**103**	**38.4**	**2732**	**3337**
v Tier 3 Selection							
v Cook Islands	3	3	0	0	100.0	235	22
v South Korea	6	6	0	0	100.0	464	66
v New Zealand Maori	12	4	0	8	33.3	165	319
v Papua New Guinea	2	2	0	0	100.0	131	26
Sub-Total	**23**	**15**	**0**	**8**	**65.2**	**995**	**433**
v Other Teams	**11**	**4**	**0**	**7**	**57.1**	**202**	**340**
All Internationals	**240**	**87**	**6**	**147**	**37.5**	**4364**	**5494**

UNITED STATES

The first rugby match recorded in the United States occurred on 14 May 1874, when Harvard University hosted a team from McGill University, Montreal. The national team then played its first International in 1912, losing by 12 points to 8 against Australia.

The United States' first International win was against Romania in 1919, and a year later, at the Antwerp Olympics, the US team won the rugby Gold Medal. Nicknamed 'The Eagles', the team surprised the world at the next Olympic Games, held in Paris in 1924, when they defeated the host nation, France, in the final and won a second Gold Medal. Because Rugby has not featured in subsequent Olympics, the USA remains the holders.

The Eagles have competed in six of the seven World Cup competitions held to date, the only exception being the 1995 tournament when they failed to qualify for the finals. In twenty-one matches played in the World Cup, the USA has won only three times: twice against Japan in 1987 and 2003, and once against Russia in 2011.

There were also few triumphs for the Eagles in the five Pacific Rim championships, held annually between 1996 and 2000. However, some success came their way in 2003 when they finished runners-up to Argentina, ahead of both Canada and Uruguay, in the Pan American Championships, which was staged five times between 1995 and 2003. It was also in 2003 that the Eagles won four International matches in a row, for the first and only time to date, when they defeated Japan, Canada, and Spain (twice). On the other side of the coin, the US team suffered a run of ten consecutive losses between May 2007 and June 2008. Four of those losses, to England, Tonga, Samoa and South Africa, occurred in the 2007 World Cup in France.

The Eagles have also competed in all nine Churchill Cup tournaments, held between 2003 and 2011. Their best result in that competition was in 2005 when they won the plate competition as runners-up to England 'A'. In March 2014, the United States qualified for the 2015 World Cup by holding Uruguay to a draw in Montevideo and defeating them in Atlanta a week later.

With the exception of their win against France in 1924, the United States has never beaten any of the Tier 1 teams in the 56 matches played, and has won only 54 times in the 120 Internationals played against Tier 2 and 3 group rivals.

To the end of March 2015, the Eagles have played 211 Internationals, and of these have won 68 games, drawn 3, and lost 140. They are currently in 16th place in the World Rugby rankings table.

UNITED STATES

HEAD TO HEAD RESULTS TO 31 MARCH 2015

	P	W	D	L	%	F	A
v TIER 1 Teams							
v Argentina	8	0	0	8	0.0	119	247
v Australia	7	0	0	7	0.0	68	321
v England	5	0	0	5	0.0	52	253
v France	7	1	0	6	14.3	93	181
v Ireland	8	0	0	8	0.0	82	306
v Italy	4	0	0	4	0.0	54	130
v New Zealand	3	0	0	3	0.0	15	171
v Scotland	4	0	0	4	0.0	50	181
v South Africa	3	0	0	3	0.0	42	145
v Wales	7	0	0	7	0.0	86	305
Sub-Total	**56**	**1**	**0**	**55**	**1.8**	**661**	**2240**
v TIER 2/3 Group							
v Canada	52	13	1	38	26.0	754	1226
v Fiji	6	1	0	5	16.7	97	143
v Japan	21	12	1	8	59.5	614	480
v Romania	7	6	0	1	85.7	189	76
v Samoa	3	0	0	3	0.0	53	71
v Tonga	7	1	0	6	14.3	98	188
v Georgia	4	3	0	1	75.0	109	75
v Namibia	0	0	0	0	0.0	0	0
v Russia	6	6	0	0	100.0	193	97
v Uruguay	14	12	1	1	89.3	438	211
Sub-Total	**120**	**54**	**3**	**63**	**46.2**	**2545**	**2567**
v Tier 3 Selection							
v Hong Kong	7	3	0	4	42.9	152	191
v Portugal	2	2	0	0	100.0	83	22
v Spain	3	3	0	0	100.0	169	29
Sub-Total	**12**	**8**	**0**	**4**	**66.7**	**404**	**242**
v Tier 1 XV teams	**8**	**1**	**0**	**7**	**12.5**	**84**	**272**
v Other Teams	**15**	**4**	**0**	**11**	**26.7**	**358**	**479**
All Internationals	**211**	**68**	**3**	**140**	**32.9**	**4052**	**5800**

URUGUAY

It is generally accepted that rugby was introduced to Uruguay in the early twentieth century through the network of schools run by the Christian Brothers religious order. The Uruguayan Rugby Union, known as Unión de Rugby del Uruguay, was then formed in January 1951. Nine months later, the first South American Championship was staged: Uruguay lost heavily to the Argentinians but defeated both Chile and Brazil and finished as runners-up. In the second Championship, held in 1958, Uruguay lost to both Argentina and Chile and finished in third place ahead of Peru, who lost all three of their matches. In August 1960, the Uruguayan team played a France XV, their first match against a Northern Hemisphere side, and lost by 59 points to nil.

Throughout the 1960s all Uruguay's matches were against fellow South American sides, and only once during the 1970s, when they lost to a touring New Zealand XV in 1976, did they face a nation outside the continent. The Uruguayans played only two matches against non-South American teams during the 1980s, losing to a France XV in 1985 and to the United States in 1989. It was in 1989 that the Uruguayan Union joined the IRB. This development opened up opportunities to play against teams outside South America.

A loss to Canada and a win against Spain in 1995 paved the way for Uruguay's first fixtures overseas, with a visit to North America in 1996. Nicknamed 'Los Teros' (the Lapwings), they lost on two occasions on that tour: first to Canada and then to the USA. They hosted both countries in return matches in 1998, only to lose both games again. On the domestic front, however, Uruguay has come second only to Argentina as the dominant team in South America.

The highlight of the 1990s occurred when Uruguay qualified for the 1999 World Cup in Wales and by defeating Spain, Los Teros finished third in a pool of four teams. In 2003, they again qualified for the World Cup and finished fourth in a pool of five after defeating Georgia. Uruguay failed to qualify for either the 2007 World Cup or the 2011 World Cup, but qualified for the 2015 World Cup by winning, on aggregate, a two-legged play-off against Russia in October 2014.

Throughout the 2000s, Uruguay has been involved in many tournaments, such as the Pan American Championship, the Intercontinental Cup, the IRB Nations Cup (in 2008, 2009, 2012 and 2014), and the Tblisi Cup in 2013.

The Uruguayans have an excellent record in the South American Championship. In thirty-five tournaments, they have been runners-up on twenty-six occasions and won the tournament in 1981 and again in 2014 (on both occasions, Argentina did not enter the competition).

In their 56 attempts, most of which have been against Argentina, they have failed to beat a Tier 1 team and have had only 9 wins in 44 International matches against Tier 2 and 3 group rivals.

To the end of March 2015, Los Teros have played 218 Internationals and of these have won 100, drawn 4, and lost 114. They are currently in 20th place in the World Rugby rankings table.

URUGUAY

HEAD TO HEAD RESULTS TO 31 MARCH 2015

	P	W	D	L	%	F	A
v TIER 1 Teams							
v Argentina	39	0	0	39	0.0	391	1666
v Argentina XV	7	0	0	7	0.0	72	342
v England	1	0	0	1	0.0	13	111
v France 'A'	2	0	0	2	0.0	6	93
v Italy	3	0	0	3	0.0	25	92
v New Zealand XV	1	0	0	1	0.0	3	64
v Scotland	1	0	0	1	0.0	12	43
v South Africa	3	0	0	3	0.0	12	245
Sub-Total	**56**	**0**	**0**	**56**	**0.0**	**513**	**2629**
v TIER 2/3 Group							
v Canada	8	1	0	7	12.5	108	247
v Fiji	1	0	0	1	0.0	24	39
v Fiji XV	1	0	0	1	0.0	3	24
v Japan	1	1	0	0	100.0	24	18
v Romania	6	0	1	5	8.3	75	150
v Samoa	1	0	0	1	0.0	13	60
v United States	14	1	1	12	10.7	211	438
v Georgia	4	2	0	2	50.0	62	66
v Namibia	1	1	0	0	100.0	23	12
v Russia	7	3	0	4	42.9	151	160
Sub-Total	**44**	**9**	**2**	**33**	**22.7**	**694**	**1214**
v Tier 3 Selection							
v Belgium	1	1	0	0	100.0	39	13
v Brazil	21	18	0	3	85.7	717	175
v Chile	45	34	1	10	76.7	1045	679
v Morocco	2	1	0	1	50.0	36	24
v Paraguay	23	22	1	0	97.8	1139	201
v Portugal	10	7	0	3	70.0	234	142
v Spain	8	4	0	4	50.0	155	109
v Venezuela	1	1	0	0	100.0	92	8
Sub-Total	**111**	**88**	**2**	**21**	**80.2**	**3457**	**1351**
v Other Teams	**7**	**3**	**0**	**4**	**42.9**	**134**	**209**
All Internationals	**218**	**100**	**4**	**114**	**46.8**	**4798**	**5403**

RUGBY WORLD CUPS

1987-2015

1987	NEW ZEALAND & AUSTRALIA
1991	ENGLAND
1995	SOUTH AFRICA
1999	WALES
2003	AUSTRALIA
2007	FRANCE
2011	NEW ZEALAND
2015	ENGLAND

POOL STAGES

Pool

3	22 May	New Zealand	70	Italy	6	Eden Park, Auckland
4	23 May	Scotland	20	France	20	Lancaster Park Oval, Christchurch
4	23 May	Romania	21	Zimbabwe	20	Eden Park, Auckland
1	23 May	Australia	19	England	6	Concord Oval, Sydney
2	24 May	Canada	37	Tonga	4	McLean Park, Napier
3	24 May	Fiji	28	Argentina	9	Rugby Park, Hamilton
1	24 May	United States	21	Japan	18	Ballymore Oval, Brisbane
2	25 May	Wales	13	Ireland	6	Athletic Park, Wellington
3	27 May	New Zealand	74	Fiji	13	Lancaster Park Oval, Christchurch
3	28 May	Argentina	25	Italy	16	Lancaster Park Oval, Christchurch
4	28 May	France	55	Romania	12	Athletic Park, Wellington
2	29 May	Wales	29	Tonga	16	Showgrounds Oval, Palmerston N.
2	30 May	Ireland	46	Canada	19	Carisbrook, Dunedin
4	30 May	Scotland	60	Zimbabwe	21	Athletic Park, Wellington
1	30 May	England	60	Japan	7	Concord Oval, Sydney
3	31 May	Italy	18	Fiji	15	Carisbrook, Dunedin
1	31 May	Australia	47	United States	12	Ballymore Oval, Brisbane
3	1 June	New Zealand	46	Argentina	15	Athletic Park, Wellington
4	2 June	Scotland	55	Romania	28	Carisbrook, Dunedin
4	2 June	France	70	Zimbabwe	12	Eden Park, Auckland
2	3 June	Wales	40	Canada	9	Rugby Park Stadium, Invercargill
2	3 June	Ireland	32	Tonga	9	Ballymore Oval, Brisbane
1	3 June	Australia	42	Japan	23	Concord Oval, Sydney
1	3 June	England	34	United States	6	Concord Oval, Sydney

QUARTER-FINALS

6 June	New Zealand	30	Scotland	3	Lancaster Park Oval, Christchurch
7 June	France	31	Fiji	16	Eden Park, Auckland
7 June	Australia	33	Ireland	15	Concord Oval, Sydney
8 June	Wales	16	England	3	Ballymore Oval, Brisbane

SEMI-FINALS

13 June	Australia	24	France	30	Concord Oval, Sydney
14 June	New Zealand	49	Wales	6	Ballymore Oval, Brisbane

BRONZE

18 June	Wales	22	Australia	21	Rotorua Internat. Stadium, Rotorua

FINAL

20 June	New Zealand	29	France	9	Eden Park, Auckland

POOL STAGES

POOL 1

	P	W	D	L	For	Against	PTS
Australia	3	3	0	0	108	41	6
England	3	2	0	1	100	32	4
United States	3	1	0	2	39	99	2
Japan	3	0	0	3	48	123	0

POOL 2

	P	W	D	L	For	Against	PTS
Wales	3	3	0	0	82	31	6
Ireland	3	2	0	1	84	41	4
Canada	3	1	0	2	65	90	2
Tonga	3	0	0	3	29	98	0

POOL 3

	P	W	D	L	For	Against	PTS
New Zealand	3	3	0	0	190	34	6
Fiji	3	1	0	2	56	101	2
Argentina	3	1	0	2	49	90	2
Italy	3	1	0	2	40	110	2

POOL 4

	P	W	D	L	For	Against	PTS
France	3	2	1	0	145	44	5
Scotland	3	2	1	0	135	69	5
Romania	3	1	0	2	61	130	2
Zimbabwe	3	0	0	3	53	151	0

POOL STAGES
Pool

A	3 Oct.	England	12	New Zealand	18	Twickenham, London
C	4 Oct.	Australia	32	Argentina	19	Stradey Park, Llanelli
D	4 Oct.	France	30	Romania	3	Stade de la Méditerranée, Béziers
A	5 Oct.	Italy	30	United States	9	Cross Green, Otley
B	5 Oct.	Scotland	47	Japan	9	Murrayfield, Edinburgh
D	5 Oct.	Canada	13	Fiji	3	Stade Jean Dauger, Bayonne
C	6 Oct.	Wales	13	W. Samoa	16	National Stadium, Cardiff
B	6 Oct.	Ireland	55	Zimbabwe	11	Lansdowne Road, Dublin
A	8 Oct.	New Zealand	46	United States	6	Kingsholm, Gloucester
A	8 Oct.	England	36	Italy	6	Twickenham, London
D	8 Oct.	France	33	Fiji	9	Stade Lesdiguières, Grenoble
C	9 Oct.	Australia	9	W. Samoa	3	Pontypool Park, Pontypool
B	9 Oct.	Ireland	32	Japan	16	Lansdowne Road, Dublin
B	9 Oct.	Scotland	51	Zimbabwe	12	Murrayfield, Edinburgh
D	9 Oct.	Canada	19	Romania	11	Stade Ernest-Wallon, Toulouse
C	9 Oct.	Wales	16	Argentina	7	National Stadium, Cardiff
A	11 Oct.	England	37	United States	9	Twickenham, London
B	12 Oct.	Scotland	24	Ireland	15	Murrayfield, Edinburgh
C	12 Oct.	Wales	3	Australia	38	National Stadium, Cardiff
D	12 Oct.	Romania	17	Fiji	15	Parc Municipal des Sports, Brive
C	13 Oct.	W Samoa	35	Argentina	12	Sardis Road, Pontypridd
A	13 Oct.	New Zealand	31	Italy	21	Welford Road, Leicester
D	13 Oct.	France	19	Canada	13	Stade Armandie, Agen
B	14 Oct.	Japan	52	Zimbabwe	6	Ravenhill, Belfast

QUARTER-FINALS

19 Oct.	Scotland	28	W. Samoa	6	Murrayfield, Edinburgh
19 Oct.	France	10	England	19	Parc des Princess, Paris
20 Oct.	New Zealand	29	Canada	13	Stade Lille-Métropole, Villeneuve
20 Oct.	Ireland	18	Australia	19	Lansdowne Road, Dublin

SEMI-FINALS

26 Oct.	Scotland	6	England	9	Murrayfield, Edinburgh
27 Oct.	Australia	16	New Zealand	6	Lansdowne Road, Dublin

BRONZE

30 Oct.	New Zealand	13	Scotland	6	National Stadium, Cardiff

FINAL

2 Nov.	England	6	Australia	12	Twickenham, London

POOL STAGES

POOL A

	P	W	D	L	For	Against	PTS
New Zealand	3	3	0	0	95	39	9
England	3	2	0	1	85	33	7
Italy	3	1	0	2	57	76	5
United States	3	0	0	3	24	113	3

POOL B

	P	W	D	L	For	Against	PTS
Scotland	3	3	0	0	122	36	9
Ireland	3	2	0	1	102	51	7
Japan	3	1	0	2	77	87	5
Zimbabwe	3	0	0	3	31	158	3

POOL C

	P	W	D	L	For	Against	PTS
Australia	3	3	0	0	79	25	9
W. Samoa	3	2	0	1	54	34	7
Wales	3	1	0	2	32	61	5
Argentina	3	0	0	3	38	83	3

POOL D

	P	W	D	L	For	Against	PTS
France	3	3	0	0	82	25	9
Canada	3	2	0	1	45	33	7
Romania	3	1	0	2	31	64	5
Fiji	3	0	0	3	27	63	3

POOL STAGES
Pool

A	25 May	South Africa	27	Australia	18	Newlands Stadium, Cape Town
D	26 May	Scotland	89	Côte d'Ivoire	0	Olympia Park, Rustenburg
D	26 May	France	38	Tonga	10	Loftus Versfeld Stadium, Pretoria
A	26 May	Canada	34	Romania	3	Boet Erasmus Stadium, Port Elizabeth
B	27 May	W Samoa	42	Italy	18	Basil Kenyon Stadium, East London
C	27 May	Wales	57	Japan	10	Free State Stadium, Bloemfontein
B	27 May	England	24	Argentina	18	Kings Park Stadium, Durban
C	27 May	New Zealand	43	Ireland	19	Ellis Park, Johannesburg
B	30 May	W Samoa	32	Argentina	26	Basil Kenyon Stadium, East London
A	30 May	South Africa	21	Romania	8	Newlands Stadium, Cape Town
D	30 May	France	54	Côte d'Ivoire	18	Olympia Park, Rustenburg
D	30 May	Scotland	41	Tonga	5	Loftus Versfeld Stadium, Pretoria
A	31 May	Australia	27	Canada	11	Boet Erasmus Stadium, Port Elizabeth
C	31 May	Ireland	50	Japan	28	Free State Stadium, Bloemfontein
B	31 May	England	27	Italy	20	Kings Park Stadium, Durban
C	31 May	New Zealand	34	Wales	9	Ellis Park, Johannesburg
D	3 June	Tonga	29	Côte d'Ivoire	11	Olympia Park, Rustenburg
A	3 June	Australia	42	Romania	3	Danie Craven Stadium, Stellenbosch
D	3 June	France	22	Scotland	19	Loftus Versfeld Stadium, Pretoria
A	3 June	South Africa	20	Canada	0	Boet Erasmus Stadium, Port Elizabeth
B	4 June	Italy	31	Argentina	25	Basil Kenyon Stadium, East London
C	4 June	New Zealand	145	Japan	17	Free State Stadium, Bloemfontein
C	4 June	Ireland	24	Wales	23	Ellis Park, Johannesburg
B	4 June	England	44	W Samoa	22	Kings Park Stadium, Durban

QUARTER-FINALS

10 June	South Africa	42	W. Samoa	14	Ellis Park, Johannesburg
10 June	France	36	Ireland	12	Kings Park Stadium, Durban
11 June	England	25	Australia	22	Newlands Stadium, Cape Town
11 June	New Zealand	48	Scotland	30	Loftus Versfeld, Pretoria

SEMI-FINALS

17 June	South Africa	19	France	15	Kings Park Stadium, Durban
18 June	New Zealand	45	England	29	Newlands Stadium, Cape Town

BRONZE

22 June	France	19	England	9	Loftus Versfeld Stadium, Pretoria

FINAL

24 June	South Africa	15	New Zealand	12	Ellis Park, Johannesburg (a e t)

POOL STAGES

POOL A

	P	W	D	L	For	Against	PTS
South Africa	3	3	0	0	68	26	9
Australia	3	2	0	1	87	41	7
Canada	3	1	0	2	45	50	5
Romania	3	0	0	3	14	97	3

POOL B

	P	W	D	L	For	Against	PTS
England	3	3	0	0	95	60	9
W. Samoa	3	2	0	1	96	88	7
Italy	3	1	0	2	69	94	5
Argentina	3	0	0	3	69	87	3

POOL C

	P	W	D	L	For	Against	PTS
New Zealand	3	3	0	0	222	45	9
Ireland	3	2	0	1	93	94	7
Wales	3	1	0	2	89	68	5
Japan	3	0	0	3	55	252	3

POOL D

	P	W	D	L	For	Against	PTS
France	3	3	0	0	114	47	9
Scotland	3	2	0	1	149	27	7
Tonga	3	1	0	2	44	90	5
Côte d'Ivoire	3	0	0	3	29	172	3

RUGBY WORLD CUP RESULTS 1999

POOL STAGES

Pool

4	1 Oct.	Wales	23	Argentina	18	Millennium Stadium, Cardiff
3	1 Oct.	Fiji	67	Namibia	18	Stade de la Méditerranée, Béziers
3	2 Oct.	France	33	Canada	20	Stade de la Méditerranée, Béziers
1	2 Oct.	Uruguay	27	Spain	15	Netherdale, Galashiels
2	2 Oct.	England	67	Italy	7	Twickenham, London
5	2 Oct.	Ireland	53	United States	8	Lansdowne Road, Dublin
4	3 Oct.	Samoa	43	Japan	9	Racecourse Ground, Wrexham
2	3 Oct.	New Zealand	45	Tonga	9	Ashdon Gate, Bristol
1	3 Oct.	Scotland	29	South Africa	46	Murrayfield, Edinburgh
5	3 Oct.	Australia	57	Romania	9	Ravenhill, Belfast
1	8 Oct.	Scotland	43	Uruguay	12	Murrayfield, Edinburgh
3	8 Oct.	France	47	Namibia	13	Stade Municipal du Parc Lescure, Bordeaux
3	9 Oct.	Fiji	38	Canada	22	Stade Municipal du Parc Lescure, Bordeaux
4	9 Oct.	Wales	64	Japan	15	Millennium Stadium, Cardiff
2	9 Oct.	England	16	New Zealand	30	Twickenham, London
5	9 Oct.	Romania	27	United States	25	Lansdowne Road, Dublin
4	10 Oct.	Argentina	32	Samoa	16	Stradey Park, Llanelli
5	10 Oct.	Ireland	3	Australia	23	Lansdowne Road, Dublin
1	10 Oct.	South Africa	47	Spain	3	Murrayfield, Edinburgh
2	10 Oct.	Tonga	28	Italy	25	Welford Road, Leicester
2	14 Oct.	New Zealand	101	Italy	3	McAlpine Stadium, Huddersfield
4	14 Oct.	Wales	31	Samoa	38	Millennium Stadium, Cardiff
5	14 Oct.	Australia	55	United States	19	Thomond Park, Limerick
3	14 Oct.	Canada	72	Namibia	11	Stade Municipal de Toulouse, Toulouse
2	15 Oct.	England	101	Tonga	10	Twickenham, London
1	15 Oct.	South Africa	39	Uruguay	3	Hampden Park, Glasgow
5	15 Oct.	Ireland	44	Romania	14	Lansdowne Road, Dublin
3	16 Oct.	France	28	Fiji	19	Stade Municipal de Toulouse, Toulouse
1	16 Oct.	Scotland	48	Spain	0	Murrayfield, Edinburgh
4	16 Oct.	Argentina	33	Japan	12	Millennium Stadium, Cardiff

QUARTER-FINAL PLAY-OFFS

20 Oct.	England	45	Fiji	24	Twickenham, London
20 Oct.	Scotland	35	Samoa	20	Murrayfield, Edinburgh
20 Oct.	Argentina	28	Ireland	24	Stade Félix Bollaert, Lens

QUARTER-FINALS

23 Oct.	Wales	9	Australia	24	Millennium Stadium, Cardiff
24 Oct.	South Africa	44	England	21	Stade de France, Paris
24 Oct.	Scotland	18	New Zealand	30	Murrayfield, Edinburgh
24 Oct.	France	47	Argentina	26	Lansdowne Road, Dublin

SEMI-FINALS

30 Oct.	Australia	27	South Africa	21	Twickenham, London (a e t)
31 Oct.	France	43	New Zealand	31	Twickenham, London

BRONZE

4 Nov.	South Africa	22	New Zealand	18	Millennium Stadium, Cardiff

FINAL

6 Nov.	Australia	35	France	12	Millennium Stadium, Cardiff

POOL STAGES

POOL 1

	P	W	D	L	For	Against	PTS
South Africa	3	3	0	0	132	35	6
Scotland	3	2	0	1	120	58	4
Uruguay	3	1	0	2	42	97	2
Spain	3	0	0	3	18	122	0

POOL 2

	P	W	D	L	For	Against	PTS
New Zealand	3	3	0	0	176	28	6
England	3	2	0	1	184	47	4
Tonga	3	1	0	2	47	171	2
Italy	3	0	0	3	35	196	0

POOL 3

	P	W	D	L	For	Against	PTS
France	3	3	0	0	108	52	6
Fiji	3	2	0	1	124	68	4
Canada	3	1	0	2	114	82	2
Namibia	3	0	0	3	42	186	4

POOL 4

	P	W	D	L	For	Against	PTS
Wales	3	2	0	1	118	71	4
Samoa	3	2	0	1	97	72	4
Argentina	3	2	0	1	83	51	4
Japan	3	0	0	3	36	140	0

POOL 5

	P	W	D	L	For	Against	PTS
Australia	3	3	0	0	135	31	6
Ireland	3	2	0	1	100	45	4
Romania	3	1	0	2	50	126	2
United States	3	0	0	3	52	135	0

POOL STAGES

A	10 Oct.	Australia	24	Argentina	8	Telstra Stadium, Sydney
D	11 Oct.	New Zealand	70	Italy	7	Telstra Dome, Melbourne
A	11 Oct.	Ireland	45	Romania	17	Central Coast Stadium, Gosford, NSW
B	11 Oct.	France	61	Fiji	18	Suncorp Stadium, Brisbane
C	11 Oct.	South Africa	72	Uruguay	6	Subiaco Oval, Perth
D	12 Oct.	Wales	41	Canada	10	Telstra Dome, Melbourne
B	12 Oct.	Scotland	32	Japan	11	Dairy Farmers Stadium, Townsville
C	12 Oct.	England	84	Georgia	6	Subiaco Oval, Perth
A	14 Oct.	Argentina	67	Namibia	14	Central Coast Stadium, Gosford, NSW
B	14 Oct.	Fiji	19	United States	18	Suncorp Stadium, Brisbane
D	15 Oct.	Italy	36	Tonga	12	Canberra Stadium, Canberra
C	15 Oct.	Samoa	60	Uruguay	13	Subiaco Oval, Perth
D	17 Oct.	New Zealand	68	Canada	6	Telstra Dome, Melbourne
A	18 Oct.	Australia	90	Romania	8	Suncorp Stadium, Brisbane
B	18 Oct.	France	51	Japan	29	Dairy Farmers Stadium, Townsville
C	18 Oct.	England	25	South Africa	6	Subiaco Oval, Perth
D	19 Oct.	Wales	27	Tonga	20	Canberra Stadium, Canberra
A	19 Oct.	Ireland	64	Namibia	7	Aussie Stadium, Sydney
C	19 Oct.	Samoa	48	Georgia	9	Subiaco Oval, Perth
B	20 Oct.	Scotland	39	United States	15	Suncorp Stadium, Brisbane
D	21 Oct.	Italy	19	Canada	14	Canberra Stadium, Canberra
A	22 Oct.	Argentina	50	Romania	3	Aussie Stadium, Sydney
B	23 Oct.	Fiji	41	Japan	13	Dairy Farmers Stadium, Townsville
D	24 Oct.	New Zealand	91	Tonga	7	Suncorp Stadium, Brisbane
C	24 Oct.	South Africa	46	Georgia	19	Aussie Stadium, Sydney
A	25 Oct.	Australia	142	Namibia	0	Adelaide Oval, Adelaide
D	25 Oct.	Wales	27	Italy	15	Canberra Stadium, Canberra
B	25 Oct.	France	51	Scotland	9	Telstra Stadium, Sydney
A	26 Oct.	Ireland	16	Argentina	15	Adelaide Oval, Adelaide
C	26 Oct.	England	35	Samoa	22	Telstra Dome, Melbourne
B	27 Oct.	United States	39	Japan	26	Central Coast Stadium, Gosford, NSW
C	28 Oct.	Uruguay	24	Georgia	12	Aussie Stadium, Sydney
D	29 Oct.	Canada	24	Tonga	7	WIN Stadium, Wollongong
A	30 Oct.	Romania	37	Namibia	7	Aurora Stadium, Launceston
B	31 Oct.	France	41	United States	14	WIN Stadium, Wollongong
B	1 Nov.	Scotland	22	Fiji	20	Aussie Stadium, Sydney
C	1 Nov.	South Africa	60	Samoa	10	Suncorp Stadium, Brisbane
A	1 Nov.	Australia	17	Ireland	16	Telstra Dome, Melbourne
C	2 Nov.	England	111	Uruguay	13	Suncorp Stadium, Brisbane
D	2 Nov.	New Zealand	53	Wales	37	Telstra Stadium, Sydney

POOL STAGES

POOL A

	P	W	D	L	For	Against	Bonus	PTS
Australia	4	4	0	0	273	32	2	18
Ireland	4	3	0	1	141	56	3	15
Argentina	4	2	0	2	140	57	3	11
Romania	4	1	0	3	65	192	1	5
Namibia	4	0	0	4	28	310	0	0

POOL B

	P	W	D	L	For	Against	Bonus	PTS
France	4	4	0	0	204	70	4	20
Scotland	4	3	0	1	102	97	2	14
Fiji	4	2	0	2	98	114	2	10
United States	4	1	0	3	86	125	2	6
Japan	4	0	0	4	79	163	0	0

POOL C

	P	W	D	L	For	Against	Bonus	PTS
England	4	4	0	0	255	47	3	19
South Africa	4	3	0	1	184	60	3	15
Samoa	4	2	0	2	138	117	2	10
Uruguay	4	1	0	3	56	255	0	4
Georgia	4	0	0	4	46	200	0	0

POOL D

	P	W	D	L	For	Against	Bonus	PTS
New Zealand	4	4	0	0	282	57	4	20
Wales	4	3	0	1	132	98	2	14
Italy	4	2	0	2	77	123	0	8
Canada	4	1	0	3	54	135	1	5
Tonga	4	0	0	4	46	178	1	1

QUARTER-FINALS

8 Nov.	New Zealand	29	South Africa	9	Telstra Dome, Melbourne
8 Nov.	Australia	33	Scotland	16	Suncorp Stadium, Sydney
9 Nov.	France	43	Ireland	21	Telstra Dome, Melbourne
9 Nov.	England	28	Wales	17	Suncorp Stadium, Sydney

SEMI-FINALS

15 Nov.	Australia	22	New Zealand	10	Telstra Stadium, Sydney
16 Nov.	England	24	France	7	Telstra Stadium, Sydney

BRONZE

20 Nov.	New Zealand	40	France	13	Telstra Stadium, Sydney

FINAL

22 Nov.	Australia	17	England	20	Telstra Stadium, Sydney (a e t)

POOL STAGES

D	7 Sep.	France	12	Argentina	17	Stade de France, Paris
C	8 Sep.	New Zealand	76	Italy	14	Stade Vélodrome, Marseille
B	8 Sep.	Australia	91	Japan	3	Stade de Gerland, Lyon
A	8 Sep.	England	28	United States	10	Stade Félix Bollaert, Lens
B	9 Sep.	Wales	42	Canada	17	Stade de la Beaujoire, Nantes
A	9 Sep.	South Africa	59	Samoa	7	Parc des Princess, Paris
C	9 Sep.	Scotland	56	Portugal	10	Stade Geoffroy-Guichard, Saint Étienne
D	9 Sep.	Ireland	32	Namibia	17	Stade Chaban-Delmas, Bordeaux
D	11 Sep.	Argentina	33	Georgia	3	Stade de Gerland, Lyon
A	12 Sep.	Tonga	25	United States	15	Stade de la Mosson, Montpellier
B	12 Sep.	Fiji	35	Japan	31	Stade Municipal de Toulouse, Toulouse
C	12 Sep.	Italy	24	Romania	18	Stade Vélodrome, Marseille
A	14 Sep.	South Africa	36	England	0	Stade de France, Paris
C	15 Sep.	New Zealand	108	Portugal	13	Stade de Gerland, Lyon
B	15 Sep.	Wales	20	Australia	32	Millennium Stadium, Cardiff
D	15 Sep.	Ireland	14	Georgia	10	Stade Chaban-Delmas, Bordeaux
B	16 Sep.	Fiji	29	Canada	16	Millennium Stadium, Cardiff
A	16 Sep.	Tonga	19	Samoa	15	Stade de la Mosson, Montpelier
D	16 Sep.	France	87	Namibia	10	Stade Municipal de Toulouse, Toulouse
C	18 Sep.	Scotland	42	Romania	0	Murrayfield, Edinburgh
C	19 Sep.	Italy	31	Portugal	5	Parc des Princess, Paris
B	20 Sep.	Wales	72	Japan	18	Millennium Stadium, Cardiff
D	21 Sep.	France	25	Ireland	3	Stade de France, Paris
A	22 Sep.	South Africa	30	Tonga	25	Stade Félix Bollaert, Lens
A	22 Sep.	England	44	Samoa	22	Stade de la Beaujoire, Nantes
D	22 Sep.	Argentina	63	Namibia	3	Stade Vélodrome, Marseille
B	23 Sep.	Australia	55	Fiji	12	Stade de la Mosson, Montpelier
C	23 Sep.	Scotland	0	New Zealand	40	Murrayfield, Edinburgh
B	25 Sep.	Canada	12	Japan	12	Stade Chaban-Delmas, Bordeaux
C	25 Sep.	Romania	14	Portugal	10	Stade Municipal de Toulouse, Toulouse
D	26 Sep.	Georgia	30	Namibia	0	Stade Félix Bollaert, Lens
A	26 Sep.	Samoa	25	United States	21	Stade Geoffroy-Guichard, Saint Étienne
A	28 Sep.	England	36	Tonga	20	Parc des Princess, Paris
C	29 Sep.	New Zealand	85	Romania	8	Stade Municipal de Toulouse, Toulouse
B	29 Sep.	Australia	37	Canada	6	Stade Chaban-Delmas, Bordeaux
B	29 Sep.	Fiji	38	Wales	34	Stade de la Beaujoire, Nantes
C	29 Sep.	Scotland	18	Italy	16	Stade Geoffroy-Guichard, Saint Étienne
D	30 Sep.	France	64	Georgia	7	Stade Vélodrome, Marseille
D	30 Sep.	Argentina	30	Ireland	15	Parc des Princess, Paris
A	30 Sep.	South Africa	64	United States	15	Stade de la Mosson, Montpellier

POOL STAGES

POOL A

	P	W	D	L	For	Against	Bonus	PTS
South Africa	4	4	0	0	189	47	3	19
England	4	3	0	1	108	88	2	14
Tonga	4	2	0	2	89	96	1	9
Samoa	4	1	0	3	69	143	1	5
United States	4	0	0	4	61	142	1	1

POOL B

	P	W	D	L	For	Against	Bonus	PTS
Australia	4	4	0	0	215	41	4	20
Fiji	4	3	0	1	114	136	3	15
Wales	4	2	0	2	168	105	4	12
Japan	4	0	1	3	64	210	1	3
Canada	4	0	1	3	51	120	0	2

POOL C

	P	W	D	L	For	Against	Bonus	PTS
New Zealand	4	4	0	0	309	35	4	20
Scotland	4	3	0	1	116	66	2	14
Italy	4	2	0	2	85	117	1	9
Romania	4	1	0	3	40	161	1	5
Portugal	4	0	0	4	38	209	1	1

POOL D

	P	W	D	L	For	Against	Bonus	PTS
Argentina	4	4	0	0	143	33	2	18
France	4	3	0	1	188	37	3	15
Ireland	4	2	0	2	64	82	1	9
Georgia	4	1	0	3	50	111	1	5
Namibia	4	0	0	4	30	212	0	0

QUARTER-FINALS

6 Oct.	England	12	Australia	10	Stade Vélodrome, Marseille
6 Oct.	France	20	New Zealand	18	Millennium Stadium, Cardiff
7 Oct.	South Africa	37	Fiji	20	Stade Vélodrome, Marseille
7 Oct.	Argentina	19	Scotland	13	Stade de France, Paris

SEMI-FINALS

13 Oct.	France	9	England	14	Stade de France, Paris
14 Oct.	South Africa	37	Argentina	13	Stade de France, Paris

BRONZE

19 Oct.	France	10	Argentina	34	Parc des Princes, Paris

FINAL

20 Oct.	South Africa	15	England	6	Stade de France, Paris

POOL STAGES

A	9 Sep.	New Zealand	41	Tonga	10	Eden Park, Auckland
B	10 Sep.	Scotland	34	Romania	24	Rugby Park Stadium, Invercargill
D	10 Sep.	Fiji	49	Namibia	25	Rotorua International Stadium, Rotorua
A	10 Sep.	France	47	Japan	21	North Harbour Stadium, Albany
B	10 Sep.	Argentina	9	England	13	Otago Stadium, Dunedin
C	11 Sep.	Australia	32	Italy	6	North Harbour Stadium, Albany
C	11 Sep.	Ireland	22	United States	10	Stadium Taranaki, New Plymouth
D	11 Sep.	South Africa	17	Wales	16	Wellington Regional Stadium, Wellington
D	14 Sep.	Samoa	49	Namibia	12	Rotorua International Stadium, Rotorua
A	14 Sep.	Tonga	20	Canada	25	Northland Events Centre, Whangarei
B	14 Sep.	Scotland	15	Georgia	6	Rugby Park Stadium, Invercargill
C	15 Sep.	Russia	6	United States	13	Stadium Taranaki, New Plymouth
A	16 Sep.	New Zealand	83	Japan	7	Waikato Stadium, Hamilton
B	17 Sep.	Argentina	43	Romania	8	Rugby Park Stadium, Invercargill
D	17 Sep.	South Africa	49	Fiji	3	Wellington Regional Stadium, Wellington
C	17 Sep.	Australia	6	Ireland	15	Eden Park, Auckland
D	18 Sep.	Wales	17	Samoa	10	Waikato Stadium, Hamilton
B	18 Sep.	England	41	Georgia	10	Otago Stadium, Dunedin
A	18 Sep.	France	46	Canada	19	McLean Park, Napier
C	20 Sep.	Italy	53	Russia	17	Trafalgar Park, Nelson
A	21 Sep.	Tonga	31	Japan	18	Northland Events Centre, Whangarei
D	22 Sep.	South Africa	87	Namibia	0	North Harbour Stadium, Albany
C	23 Sep.	Australia	67	United States	5	Wellington Regional Stadium, Wellington
B	24 Sep.	England	67	Romania	3	Otago Stadium, Dunedin
A	24 Sep.	New Zealand	37	France	17	Eden Park, Auckland
D	25 Sep.	Fiji	7	Samoa	27	Eden Park, Auckland
C	25 Sep.	Ireland	62	Russia	12	Rotorua International Stadium, Rotorua
B	25 Sep.	Argentina	13	Scotland	12	Wellington Regional Stadium, Wellington
D	26 Sep.	Wales	81	Namibia	7	Stadium Taranaki, New Plymouth
A	27 Sep.	Canada	23	Japan	23	McLean Park, Napier
C	27 Sep.	Italy	27	United States	10	Trafalgar Park, Nelson
B	28 Sep.	Georgia	25	Romania	9	Arena Manawatu, Palmerston North
D	30 Sep.	South Africa	13	Samoa	5	North Harbour Stadium, Albany
C	1 Oct.	Australia	68	Russia	22	Trafalgar Park, Nelson
A	1 Oct.	France	14	Tonga	19	Wellington Regional Stadium, Wellington
B	1 Oct.	England	16	Scotland	12	Eden Park, Auckland
B	2 Oct.	Argentina	25	Georgia	7	Arena Manawatu, Palmerston North
A	2 Oct.	New Zealand	79	Canada	15	Wellington Regional Stadium, Wellington
D	2 Oct.	Wales	66	Fiji	0	Waikato Stadium, Hamilton
C	2 Oct.	Ireland	36	Italy	6	Otago Stadium, Dunedin

POOL STAGES

POOL A

	P	W	D	L	For	Against	Bonus	PTS
New Zealand	4	4	0	0	240	49	4	20
France	4	2	0	2	124	96	3	11
Tonga	4	2	0	2	80	98	1	9
Canada	4	1	1	2	82	168	0	6
Japan	4	0	1	3	69	184	0	2

POOL B

	P	W	D	L	For	Against	Bonus	PTS
England	4	4	0	0	137	34	2	18
Argentina	4	3	0	1	90	40	2	14
Scotland	4	2	0	2	73	59	3	11
Georgia	4	1	0	3	48	90	0	4
Romania	4	0	0	4	44	189	0	0

POOL C

	P	W	D	L	For	Against	Bonus	PTS
Ireland	4	4	0	0	135	34	1	17
Australia	4	3	0	1	173	48	3	15
Italy	4	2	0	2	92	95	2	10
United States	4	1	0	3	38	122	0	4
Russia	4	0	0	4	57	196	1	1

POOL D

	P	W	D	L	For	Against	Bonus	PTS
South Africa	4	4	0	0	166	24	2	18
Wales	4	3	0	1	180	34	3	15
Samoa	4	2	0	2	91	49	2	10
Fiji	4	1	0	3	59	167	1	5
Namibia	4	0	0	4	44	266	0	0

QUARTER-FINALS

8 Oct.	Ireland	10	Wales	22	Wellington Reg'l Stadium, Wellington
8 Oct.	England	12	France	19	Eden Park, Auckland
9 Oct.	South Africa	9	Australia	11	Wellington Reg'l Stadium, Wellington
9 Oct.	New Zealand	33	Argentina	10	Eden Park, Auckland

SEMI-FINALS

15 Oct.	Wales	8	France	9	Eden Park, Auckland
16 Oct.	New Zealand	20	Australia	6	Eden Park, Auckland

BRONZE

21 Oct.	Wales	18	Australia	21	Eden Park, Auckland

FINAL

23 Oct.	New Zealand	8	France	7	Eden Park, Auckland

POOL STAGES

A	18 Sep.	England	Fiji	Twickenham, London
C	19 Sep.	Tonga	Georgia	Kingsholm, Gloucester
D	19 Sep.	Ireland	Canada	Millennium Stadium, Cardiff
D	19 Sep.	France	Italy	Twickenham, London
B	19 Sep.	South Africa	Japan	Brighton Community Stadium
B	20 Sep.	Samoa	United States	Brighton Community Stadium
A	20 Sep.	Wales	Uruguay	Millennium Stadium, Cardiff
C	20 Sep.	New Zealand	Argentina	Wembley Stadium, London
B	23 Sep.	Scotland	Japan	Kingsholm, Gloucester
A	23 Sep.	Australia	Fiji	Millennium Stadium, Cardiff
D	23 Sep.	France	Romania	Olympic Stadium, London
C	24 Sep.	New Zealand	Namibia	Olympic Stadium, London
C	25 Sep.	Argentina	Georgia	Kingsholm, Gloucester
D	26 Sep.	Italy	Canada	Elland Road, Leeds
B	26 Sep.	South Africa	Samoa	Villa Park, Birmingham
A	26 Sep.	England	Wales	Twickenham, London
A	27 Sep.	Australia	Uruguay	Villa Park, Birmingham
B	27 Sep.	Scotland	United States	Elland Road, Leeds
D	27 Sep.	Ireland	Romania	Wembley Stadium, London
C	29 Sep.	Tonga	Namibia	Sandy Park, Exeter
D	1 Oct.	France	Canada	Stadium MK, Milton Keynes
A	1 Oct.	Wales	Fiji	Millennium Stadium, Cardiff
C	2 Oct.	New Zealand	Georgia	Millennium Stadium, Cardiff
B	3 Oct.	Samoa	Japan	Stadium MK, Milton Keynes
B	3 Oct.	South Africa	Scotland	St James' Park, Newcastle
A	3 Oct.	England	Australia	Twickenham, London
C	4 Oct.	Argentina	Tonga	Leicester City Stadium, Leicester
D	4 Oct.	Ireland	Italy	Olympic Stadium, London
D	6 Oct.	Canada	Romania	Leicester City Stadium, Leicester
A	6 Oct.	Fiji	Uruguay	Stadium MK, Milton Keynes
B	7 Oct.	South Africa	United States	Olympic Stadium, London
C	7 Oct.	Namibia	Georgia	Sandy Park, Exeter
C	9 Oct.	New Zealand	Tonga	St James' Park, Newcastle
B	10 Oct.	Samoa	Scotland	St James' Park, Newcastle
A	10 Oct.	Australia	Wales	Twickenham, London
A	10 Oct.	England	Uruguay	Manchester City Stadium, Manchester
C	11 Oct.	Argentina	Namibia	Leicester City Stadium, Leicester
D	11 Oct.	Italy	Romania	Sandy Park, Exeter
B	11 Oct.	United States	Japan	Kingsholm, Gloucester
D	11 Oct.	Ireland	France	Millennium Stadium, Cardiff

POOL STAGES

POOL A

	P	W	D	L	For	Against	Bonus	PTS
Australia								
England								
Wales								
Fiji								
Uruguay								

POOL B

	P	W	D	L	For	Against	Bonus	PTS
South Africa								
Scotland								
Samoa								
Japan								
United States								

POOL C

	P	W	D	L	For	Against	Bonus	PTS
New Zealand								
Argentina								
Tonga								
Georgia								
Namibia								

POOL D

	P	W	D	L	For	Against	Bonus	PTS
Ireland								
France								
Italy								
Canada								
Romania								

QUARTER-FINALS

17 Oct.	Winner Pool 'C'	R-Up Pool 'D'	Millennium Stadium, Cardiff
17 Oct.	Winner Pool 'B'	R-Up Pool 'A'	Twickenham, London
18 Oct.	Winner Pool 'D'	R-Up Pool 'C'	Millennium Stadium, Cardiff
18 Oct.	Winner Pool 'A'	R-Up Pool 'B'	Twickenham, London

SEMI-FINALS

24 Oct.	Winner QF 1	Winner QF 2	Twickenham, London
25 Oct.	Winner QF 3	Winner QF 4	Twickenham, London

BRONZE

30 Oct.	R-Up SF 1	R-Up SF 2	Olympic Stadium, London

FINAL

31 Oct.	Winner SF 1	Winner SF 2	Twickenham, London

RUGBY TRIVIA

RUGBY TRIVIA

IN THE BEGINNING

When William Webb Ellis decided to pick up the ball in a football match at Rugby school in 1823, the sport of rugby was born. In those early days there were many interpretations of the rules, and even the dimensions of the ball varied enormously in shape and size. That was until Richard Linden, an apprentice working for shoemaker William Gilbert, hit upon the idea of creating a standard leather ball that could be inflated with a pig's bladder. Gilbert displayed his ball in 1851 at the Great Exhibition in London and, amazingly, the Gilbert manufactured ball is still used to this day.

THE EARLY DAYS IN THE NORTHERN HEMISPHERE

The rules of rugby in the first half of the nineteenth century were anything but uniform and were adopted to reflect local influences. In fact, Rugby school started to discuss the standardisation of rules with university students from other schools during the 1830s and the 1840s. The basic rules of rugby, therefore, developed gradually by word of mouth. The main feature of those early rules was that by taking the ball across the opposing team's line, your team earned a try at goal, hence the word 'try'. Points were awarded only for a successful kick at goal.

The first set of rules actually written down was in 1845. These defined the concept of off-side and also confirmed the definition of the try, which would be followed by a kick at goal. Hacking was permitted, as was kicking an opposing player nearest the ball or within a scrummage. During the mid-1850s, rugby was rapidly spreading from the schools and universities to the towns. A

Liverpool team played its first match in 1857, and the Manchester club was born three years later, in 1860. Richmond football club, founded in 1861, took up rugby a year later but declined to become a founder member of the Football Association (FA) in 1863. Blackheath was another staunch English rugby club, founded in 1858.

The rugby tradition was also taken up in the Edinburgh and Glasgow areas in the 1850s. It is generally accepted that the game arrived at the Edinburgh Academy in 1854 via the Crombie brothers, and within three years it had reached Merchiston Castle School and the Royal Academy in Edinburgh. Soon after, in 1858, fixtures were being arranged by these schools. Rugby football soon spread to Wales, when students at Lampeter College, played the game in 1850. University connections also helped to spread the word across the Irish Sea, when rugby was introduced to students in Trinity College, Dublin in 1854. The Trinity Club, nowadays known as Dublin University, claims to be the oldest existing rugby club in the world. In France, the first rugby club was Le Havre, formed in 1872 by a group of British wine merchants who worked in the area surrounding the port.

THE EARLY DAYS IN THE SOUTHERN HEMISPHERE

Canon George Ogilvie emigrated from England to South Africa in 1858 and three years later, in 1861, he became headmaster at a leading private school and introduced rugby football to his pupils. The rules adopted were the ones then used at Winchester public school, the Canon's alma mater.

Rugby was introduced to New Zealand in 1870 by Charles John Monro who learnt the sport whilst studying at Christ's College Finchley in north London. At the age of 19, he returned home to Nelson on the South Island, and was successful in persuading the local club to switch from football to rugby. He then arranged a match between the converted Nelson club and Nelson College on 14 May 1870, and on 12 September 1870, he organised a match between the Nelson club and Wellington on the North Island (by bringing the home team by steamer across the Cook Straits). Nelson won the game.

Sydney University Football Club, believed to have been founded in 1863, began playing rugby matches in 1865. The first officially recorded game was between Sydney University and its near neighbours, Sydney Football Club. The match took place on 19 August 1865.

Rugby Union also reached South America in the 1870s when the first match was played in Argentina in 1873.

RUGBY UNION AT THE OLYMPIC GAMES

Rugby was played at four Olympic Games between 1900 and 1924. Three teams participated at the Paris Games in 1900. France was represented by a team from Paris, Great Britain by Moseley Wanderers, and Germany by Eintracht Frankfurt. Host nation France won the Gold Medal by defeating Great Britain by 27 points to 8 and then Germany by 27 points to 17 in the final.

Only two teams turned up for the 1908 Games held in London. Great Britain, the host nation, nominated Cornwall as County champions to compete against Australia, who were touring Britain at the time. Australia won the Gold Medal by beating Cornwall by 32 points to 3, but it was not recognised as a full International match. The Wallabies, however, did play two Internationals on that tour, beating England but losing to Wales. They also lost to three Welsh clubs: Llanelli, Swansea and Cardiff.

Only two teams entered the 1920 Olympics in Antwerp, with the United States taking the Gold Medal by defeating France by 8 point to nil. As was the case in 1908, this match was again not classified as a rugby International. Three teams entered the 1924

Olympics, held in Paris again, and this time they did represent their country. In the opening match France defeated Romania by 61 points to 3, followed by a victory for the United States team when they beat Romania by 37 points to nil a week later. The United States then went on to win the Gold Medal by defeating France by 17 points to 3 at Stade Colombes in Paris in the final. All three matches are recognised as full Internationals. Rugby Union has not been represented at the Olympic Games since, although a Pre-Olympic tournament involving France, Germany, Romania and Italy was held prior to the 1936 Berlin Olympics. The United States are therefore the reigning rugby union Olympic champions.

THE EVOLUTION OF THE TRY

In the early days gaining a try was the only way a team could score a goal and gain points. The number of goals resulting from successful kicks was used to determine the winner of the match.

In 1886, the value of the try was set at one point and a successful conversion would add a further two points to the total. Five years later, in 1891, the try was increased to two points and the conversion was simultaneously increased to three points. However, in 1893 there was yet another change with the try increased again to three points and the conversion reduced to two points, thus retaining the value of a converted try to five points.

The try remained at three points for nearly seventy years before it was increased to four points on 1 September 1971. Two months later, Jean-Claude Skrela became the first man to score a four-point try in an International match whilst playing for France against Australia in Toulouse on 20 November 1971.

When the try was increased again, to five points on 1 July 1992, David Sole of Scotland became the last man to score a four-point try in an International when playing against Australia in Brisbane on 26 June 1992. Eight days later on 4 July 1992, the Samoan, Va'aiga Tuigamala scored the first five-point try in an International match whilst playing for New Zealand against Australia in Sydney. Curiously, all three milestones have been achieved in matches involving Australia.

THE DEVELOPMENT OF
THE INTERNATIONAL RUGBY BOARD (IRB)

The IRB was founded in 1886 at a meeting in Dublin of the Irish, Scottish and Welsh rugby unions as a result of dissatisfaction with the English RFU's interpretation of the rules At that meeting of the Celtic nations it was agreed that the creation of an International Rugby Football Board (IRFB), as it was then known, would be the appropriate body to govern the rules of rugby union. The first formal meeting of the Board took place in Manchester on 5 December 1887, at which broad terms of reference were drawn up. The English RFU could not agree with the IRFB's role as lawmaker, so the dispute went to arbitration.

An agreement was finally reached in 1890, and England was allocated six seats on the Board, compared with two to each of the three Celtic nations. The IRFB's first set of rules was drawn up later that year. The RFU's allocation of seats on the IRFB Board in 1890 did, in fact, give the English an effective veto on law changes, so, in 1911, the RFU agreed to reduce its allocation to four seats.

In 1948, Australia, New Zealand and South Africa, known as the SANZAR nations, were each allocated one seat on the Board, and England's allocation was simultaneously reduced to two seats. Then, in 1958, the SANZAR countries were allocated two seats each, thus achieving parity with the four Home Nations. France was finally invited to the Board in 1978 and also given an allocation of two seats.

Despite rejecting the concept of a Rugby World Cup as far

back as 1957, the IRFB finally yielded to pressure from Australia and New Zealand, and a motion to initiate such a competition was put to a vote at the 1985 AGM. The motion was carried by 10 votes to 6.

In 1991, Argentina, Canada, Japan and Italy were given seats on the IRFB council and allocated one vote each. In 1998, the IRFB was renamed the International Rugby Board or IRB, and on 19 November 2014, the Board was further renamed 'World Rugby'.

THE LAWS OF RUGBY – GENESIS

On 26 January 1871, a meeting of twenty-one English rugby-playing clubs was held at a restaurant in London's Pall Mall. The meeting was called to form a code of practice in order to standardise the rules of the game. Shortly afterwards, the Rugby Football Union, known as the RFU, was founded and the first laws of rugby football were drawn up and approved in June 1871. It is interesting to note that the very first International between Scotland and England was played before that date, on 27 March 1871. In 1877, a new rule stated that the ball must be released after a tackle. It was an immediate success and removed the congregation of a large number of players in the tackle area and furthermore encouraged the art of dribbling.

As stated earlier, the four Home Nations provisionally agreed a set of rules drawn up by the newly formed IRFB in 1890, but it took another 40 years before it was finally agreed, in 1930, that all matches between members would be played under the laws of the International Football Board.

THE LAWS OF RUGBY – EVOLUTION

Prior to 1958, it was necessary for a player to play the ball with his foot before picking up the ball after a tackle. The removal of this rule greatly increased the flow of play. In the 1968-69 season a ban on kicking directly to touch outside the then 22-metre line came into experimental law. Known as 'The Australian Dispensation', on account of years of canvassing by the Australians, it was made permanent in 1990. Injury replacements were allowed for the first time in the Five Nations tournament at the beginning of the 1969 campaign. Jean-Pierre Salut became the first player to be replaced when he fell and twisted his ankle in the dressing room at the start of the France versus Scotland match on 11 January 1969. Three tactical substitutions were allowed in 1996, irrespective of whether the replaced player was injured or not. This measure went a long way towards eliminating faked injuries. Over the years, the number of substitutions has gradually increased to the present-day level of eight. There have also been many other rule changes, such as supporting a player at the line-out and the issuing of yellow and red cards to players for various rule offences.

PROFESSIONALISM

In late 1894, Yorkshire clubs declared that the RFU view on professionalism was unreasonable, so in January 1895 eighteen of them proposed forming a society called the Northern Union. On 12 August, the RFU reissued its code on professionalism, which prompted the Yorkshire clubs to meet again on 27 August. Two days they later, they had a further meeting with their Lancashire counterparts, at the George Hotel in Huddersfield, and formed the Northern Rugby Union on the basis of 'payment for broken time only'. Twenty-two clubs were represented, and in 1922 the 'Union' was given the new title, the Rugby League.

Amateurism was again put to the test in 1896 when the Welsh Rugby Union decided to honour Arthur Gould, one of Wales' greatest players of that era, with a retirement gift. The Welsh RFU decided to buy his house and offer it to him as a present for services rendered. This kind gesture was immediately seen by the other three nations as a professional act. The Irish and Scottish RFUs were so incensed that their national teams refused to play Wales in the 1897 Home Nations tournament and Scotland further declined to play Wales in the 1898 competition.

In 1905, US President Theodore Roosevelt, appalled by the violence he had witnessed in a university match, threatened to ban that form of rugby as being too dangerous. This ultimately led to the development of the professional game we now know as American Football, in which the players wear padding protection.

In the late 1920s there was an uneasy situation in France whereby certain clubs were being subsidised. This put them at odds with their own Union, and also caused disquiet in the four Home Unions. The situation worsened in 1931 when twelve clubs broke away from the French Federation to form their own alliance. The Home Unions acted promptly and on 12 February, 1931, at a meeting in Twickenham, a resolution was passed that International matches would not be resumed with France until the French had resolved the professional stance of some of their clubs. France was ejected from the Five Nations Championship at the end of the tournament on 6 April, and the competition became the Home Nations Championship again between 1932 and 1939. France were then reinstated to the Championship in September 1939, which allowed them to compete in 1940. The Second World War intervened and they were finally readmitted in 1947.

At a special meeting of the RFU on 19 September 1985, professionalism in any form was outlawed and strict new by-laws were adopted to 'govern the structure of the amateur rugby union game'.

SANZAR, short for South Africa, New Zealand, Australia Rugby, was formed in 1995 with an objective of creating a provincial competition between teams from the three nations and an International tournament between the three Southern

Hemisphere teams. During the 1995 World Cup in South Africa, on the eve of the third place match between France and England, SANZAR leaders announced that they had signed a contract with Rupert Murdoch who had offered the organisation $550 million for the sole rights to screen the newly proposed annual Super 12 Rugby competition for the provincial teams and a Tri Nations tournament for the SANZAR International teams, on a home and away basis. The matches would be screened on his News Corporation network for a period of ten years. As a result of this deal, the IRB met in Paris on 26 August 1995, and declared rugby union as an open game, thus lifting restrictions on all form of payments to both players and clubs. The amateur days of rugby were well and truly over and the professional era had arrived.

FAMOUS STADIUMS – THE FIRST INTERNATIONAL

The first match played at Lansdowne Road was between Ireland and England on 11 March 1878. It was Ireland's third home International, the first two having been played at the Leinster Cricket Ground in Rathmines in Dublin and at the Ormeau Ground in Belfast.

Wales' first International match at Cardiff Arms Park was against Ireland on 12 April 1884. It was also their third home game, the previous two having taken place at St Helen's Ground in Swansea and Rodney Parade in Newport.

On 15 January 1910, England first played Wales at Twickenham, thirty-eight years after their first home game at the Kennington Oval in London in 1872, while Scotland's first International at Murrayfield was on 21 March 1925, when they faced England. Their previous seventy home matches had been played at various venues in Edinburgh and Glasgow.

New Zealand played their first home game at Athletic Park in Wellington against the touring Lions on 13 August 1904, a match they won by 9 points to 3. Seventeen years later, on 27 August 1921, the All Blacks lost to South Africa in their first game at Eden Park, Auckland by 9 points to 5. The Australians played their very first match at the Cricket Ground, Sydney against the Lions on 24 June 1899, and continued to play at that venue until 1986. The Sydney Football Stadium was then built in 1988 and the Wallabies played their opening game, at that ground, again against the Lions, on 1 July 1989. Australia's second International match was against the same touring Lions at the Exhibition Ground, Brisbane on 22 July 1899. After nearly seventy years, Test matches in Brisbane were switched to the new stadium built in 1966 and named Ballymore Oval. Then on 22 June 1968, Australia played the first match at that stadium, against the All Blacks, which they lost by 19 points to 18.

South Africa's first International at Newlands Stadium in Cape Town took place on 5 September 1891. That match, only the team's third game, was against the 1891 touring Lions.

The Springboks' first match at Ellis Park, Johannesburg came much later, on 21 July 1928, when they were narrowly defeated by New Zealand by 7 points to 6.

France played their first International match at Parc des Princes in Paris on 1 January 1906, against New Zealand, who were on their first major tour of the Northern Hemisphere. Exactly two years later, on 1 January 1908, the French played their first game at Paris' Stade Colombes, against England. France's opening match at the Stade de France in Saint Denis, north of Paris, was played ninety years later on 7 February 1998, against England.

Italy's first International match at Stadio Flaminio in Rome, which took place on 22 April 1935, was against a France XV selection. This was Italy's first real test against strong opposition in eight Internationals and, as expected, they lost the game by 44 points to 6. With the increased interest in rugby, after Italy's admission to the Six Nations Championship in 2000, the venue was moved to the larger Stadio Olimpico in Rome on 11 February 2012. The Italians lost the first game, against England, at the new venue, by 19 points to 15.

Argentina's first recognised International match at the Ferro Carril Oeste Stadium in Buenos Aires was played on 16 July 1932, against a touring South African team known as the Junior Springboks, and the Pumas' first International at the Velez Sarsfield Stadium also in Buenos Aires, took place on 31 May 1986, when they defeated France by 15 points to 13.

SOME AMAZING COMEBACKS

On 15 August 1998, in a Tri Nations match against the All Blacks in Durban, the Springboks came back from 3-23 down to beat New Zealand by 24 points to 23.

The Welsh tour of Argentina in June 1999 looked like being an utter disaster, when in the first match in Buenos Aires the Pumas raced into a 20-0 lead in the first half hour. However, Wales struck back strongly but were still 10-23 down at half-time. They staged a tremendous comeback in the second half, and eventually ran out winners by 36 points to 26.

Arguably the most remarkable comeback of them all occurred in the semi-final of the World Cup match between France and New Zealand at Twickenham on 31 October 1999. With the score standing at New Zealand 24, France 10, ten minutes into the second half the French suddenly sprang into life and, displaying their famous Gallic flare, scored thirty-three unanswered points in the space of twenty-seven minutes. Suddenly the scoreboard read: New Zealand 24, France 43. The match ended a few minutes later with France victors by 43 points to 31 following a late converted try by the All Blacks.

Four years later, at the 2003 World Cup tournament, New

Zealand were very nearly victims of an amazing Welsh comeback. Drawn in the same pool as Wales, the All Blacks entered the final match of the pool having beaten Italy by 70 points to 7, Canada by 68 points to 6, and Tonga by 91 points to 7. The Welsh had struggled somewhat against the same three opponents, so the All Blacks were expected to sweep them aside in a one sided match at the Telstra Stadium in Sydney on 2 November. Indeed things did look ominous for the Welsh when New Zealand raced to a 28 points to 10 lead after only 32 minutes. Then suddenly Wales discovered some magic and at half-time had clawed themselves back into the game, but were still four points behind at 24 points to 28. Six minutes into the second half, Wales were actually leading by 34 points to 28: they had scored twenty-four points in just fourteen minutes. There the Welsh luck ended. New Zealand soon regained their composure and eventually ran out winners by 53 points to 37.

INTERESTING ANECDOTES

- The final split between the soccer form of football and rugby football came in 1863 and later that year the Football Association (FA) was formed.

- The first ever rugby union international match, which was between Scotland and England, took place in Edinburgh on 27 March 1871, with each team fielding twenty players. Scotland's line up comprised of fourteen forwards, three full-backs and three half- backs, and England lined up with thirteen forwards three full-backs, three half-backs and one three-quarter-back.

- The selection of the Irish team for their very first International match against England at Kennington Oval on 15 February 1875, was rather more unorthodox. The selectors decided on the less contentious option of picking ten players from the Republic and ten players from Northern Ireland, rather than choosing the best possible combination of players. Most of them were unknown to each other and many played out of position and so, given these unusual circumstances, it is quite amazing that Ireland only lost by 7 points to nil.

Two years later on 5 February 1877, in the match between England and Ireland, the number of players each side was reduced to fifteen, with both teams fielding nine forwards, two full-backs, two half-backs and two three-quarter-backs.

The Calcutta Cup, a trophy awarded to the winner of the annual England v Scotland match, has an interesting history. In 1878 the Calcutta Rugby Football Club, which had been formed in 1873, disbanded owing to lack of support, so the members decided to melt down the funds, which were in silver rupees, and create a cup that was subsequently presented to the RFU by G. A. J. Rothney. The first match, which ended 3-3, took place on 10 March 1879.

Twickenham is located on a piece of land that was originally the site of a market garden. In 1907, committee member William Williams recommended that the RFU purchase the land so that the England rugby team could have a permanent home. A price of £5,572 was agreed, and to this day the so-called 'RFU Headquarters' is affectionately known as the 'Cabbage Patch'.

The first five nations match after the First World War was between France and Scotland at Parc des Princess in Paris on 1 January 1920, and it featured a most amusing incident involving Jock Wemyss, the Scottish prop forward, who played for his country before and after the War. In those days players were given jerseys on their International debut but were expected to retain them for use in subsequent International matches. So, when the Scottish baggage man started handing out jerseys to the players, he skipped Jock because he had been capped before the war in 1914. The baggage man told him he should have brought his jersey with him and even Wemyss' explanation, that he had swapped his jersey with an opponent six years earlier, was ignored. It was only when he lined up to enter the pitch bare-chested that he was finally handed a jersey. That match also produced an unusual coincidence, since both Wemyss and the French prop, Marcel Lubin-Lebrere, had each lost an eye in the Great War.

Internationals between the Southern Hemisphere nations resumed after the First World War in 1921 when South Africa toured New Zealand. After a long seven-year wait, the first Test on 13 August must have been a disappointment for the Dunedin spectators when 114 line-outs were awarded during the match. The count even beats the infamous 111 line-outs recorded during the Scotland v Wales game in Murrayfield on 2 February 1963, when the Welsh captain decided that gaining ground by kicking to touch as much as possible was the best tactic in such muddy conditions (the tactic paid off as Wales won the match by six points to nil).

On 18 August 1924, Western Samoa played a touring Fijian side in Apia. Both teams played this, their very first International, barefooted. The game kicked off at 7am to allow the Samoans to go to work after the match and also to give the Fijians sufficient time to catch the boat to Tonga, to continue their tour. The other unusual feature about the match was that there was a tree on the halfway line. Fiji won the game by 6 points to nil.

Vivian Jenkins became the first player to score a try from the full-back position in the International Championship. It occurred on 10 March 1934, in the match between Wales and Ireland in Swansea.

On 28 September 1935, Swansea became the first club team to beat all three SANZAR countries when they triumphed over New Zealand by 11 points to 3. This was also the first match that the All Blacks had lost to a club side. That win followed the club's 6 points to nil win against Australia on 26 December 1908, and the 26 December 1912, win against South Africa by 3 points to nil.

The Lions tour to New Zealand in 1950 was the last tour on which players travelled by ship. The route carried them through the Panama Canal on the outward journey, and via the Suez Canal on the return leg, more or less a journey around the world. On that tour, nineteen year old Lewis Jones was summoned to join the Lions as an injury replacement and became the first Lion to fly from the UK on a rugby tour.

The term Grand Slam, which means a side winning all four matches in the Five Nations series, was first coined in the press in 1957, when England achieved that distinction.

The legendary Colin Meads became only the second player in International history to be sent off by a referee. The man in charge, Ken Kelleher, gave Meads his marching orders on 2 December 1967, in the Murrayfield game between Scotland and New Zealand.

The Irish tour of New Zealand in 1976 included one Test against the All Blacks and a final game against Fiji on 9 June. The team arrived in Fiji only to find that owing to a scheduling error the Fijian team was on tour in Australia. The Fiji Rugby Union had to put together what was basically a reserve side, and the Irish team had to play a non-cap International as Ireland XV.

Upon his retirement in 1978, Welsh International Gareth Edwards had achieved the unique distinction of gaining fifty-three International caps in succession without missing a single match through injury or non-selection since his debut in 1967.

The International between the United States and South Africa, which took place on 25 September 1981, is often referred to as the 'Secret International'. It was scheduled at the height of anti-apartheid protests that followed the Springboks wherever they went. The venue was kept secret until the very last minute and the match went ahead at the Owl Creek Polo Field in Glenville, New York, in front of an estimated thirty spectators. This was the first International between the two countries and, after a brave performance from the US Eagles in the first half, when they trailed a full strength South African side by only two points, they eventually lost this historic match by 38 points to 7.

Dick (Red) Conway was so keen to tour South Africa with Wilson Whineray's All Blacks in 1960, that he took the extraordinary step of having an injured finger, which had been badly set, amputated. He was duly selected for the tour and played in three of the four Tests as a number eight forward.

An extremely unusual scoring sequence occurred in the Tri Nations match between New Zealand and Australia at the Carisbrook ground in Dunedin on 16 August 1997. The All Blacks were unstoppable in the first half and raced into a 36 points to nil lead at the end of that half. However, the tide changed in the second half and the Wallabies staged a remarkable recovery, scoring 24 points without reply. Unfortunately it was a matter of 'too little too late', and the home team eventually won by 36 points to 24.

The remarkable thing about that game was that all sixty points had been scored at the same end of the ground.

The match between Scotland and Wales at Murrayfield on 6 February 1999, will be remembered by both Scottish and Welsh fans for years to come. Fly half Duncan Hodge changed the direction of his kick-off and caught the Welsh defence napping. Confusion between the Welsh wing Matthew Robinson, in his debut International, and the full-back Shane Howarth, allowed Scottish centre John Leslie to snatch the ball from Howarth's grasp and race to the line for a try. Many re-runs of the move clocked the try at 9 seconds, making it the fastest in International history, surely unlikely to be beaten in the future. Scotland went on to win the match by 33 points to 20.

Another record, which is unlikely to be broken, is the one set by prolific Welsh kicker Neil Jenkins. During the 2003-04 season, playing for club side Celtic Warriors, he was successful with forty-four consecutive kicks.

Wales versus South Africa at the Millennium Stadium on 6 November 2004, featured six players in the Welsh team with the surname Jones. The front row, Duncan, Steve and Adam, wing forward Dafydd and, number eight Ryan, and, to complete the sextet, Stephen, who played at outside half. South Africa scraped home that day by 38 points to 36.

SELECTED RUGBY MILESTONES

1877: On 5 February at Kennington Oval, the first XV-a-side International match took place between England and Ireland. The home team won by 8 points to nil.

1883: The first season when all four Home Nations played against each other.

1910: The first Five Nations match between Wales and France was played at St Helen's in Swansea on New Year's Day. Wales overwhelmed France by 49 points to 14.

1920: On 17 January, when Wales defeated England in Swansea by 19 points to 5, Gerry O'Shea became the first player to perform the so-called 'full house' by scoring a try, kicking the conversion, kicking a penalty goal, and dropping a goal. Thirty years would elapse before the feat was repeated by Lewis Jones, playing for the Lions, in 1950.

1922: Numbers appeared on the back of rugby shirts for the first time in the Five Nations Championship in the match between Wales and England in Cardiff on 21 January. Wales won by 28 points to 6.

1925: New Zealand faced England at Twickenham on 3 January, having won all twenty-seven matches between September and December 1924. The game was so ferocious that the referee Albert Freethy had to warn both teams three times in the first six minutes about dangerous play, stating that the next transgressor would be dismissed. After ten minutes, following a line out fracas, he blew his whistle and Cyril Brownlie of New Zealand became the first player to be sent off in an International. Even with just fourteen men, the All Blacks emerged triumphant, winning by 17 points to 11.

1927: The first BBC radio commentary on the match between England and Wales was transmitted live on 15 January. England won the Twickenham game by 11 points to 9.

1938: On 19 March, BBC television broadcasted the match between England and Scotland at Twickenham live to an audience in the London area. Scotland won the game by 21 points to 16 and with it the Triple Crown.

1953-54: This was the year when New Zealand became the first International rugby team to travel by air when they toured Britain, Ireland, France, Canada and the United States between October and March.

1955: The Lions travelled by air for the first time on their tour to South Africa, in a flight that took thirty-six hours.

1987: The year of the inaugural Rugby World Cup when host nation New Zealand won the first match of the tournament, played on 22 May, at Eden Park, Auckland by beating Italy 70 points to 6.

1992: On 23 March, the non-racial South African Rugby Union (SARU) and the South African Rugby Board (SARB) merged to form the South African Rugby Football Union (SARFU). The unification was signed at the Sun Hotel, Kimberley, which led to the readmission of South Africa to International rugby. On 15 August, the Springboks played New Zealand at Ellis Park, Johannesburg in their first game for eight years. They only narrowly lost by 27 points to 24.

1993: In January, with the Springboks now competing internationally, it was decided to award South Africa the hosting of the 1995 Rugby World Cup. Unfortunately, Dr Danie Craven, an iconic figure in South African rugby for decades, and the first co-president of the newly formed SARFU, died on 4 January, shortly before the award was made public.

1994: On 26 June, Philippe Sella became the first player to reach 100 caps when he led France on to the field against New Zealand at Lancaster Park Oval in Christchurch. The team celebrated the occasion in style, defeating the All Blacks by 22 points to 8. A week later on 3 July, they won again at Eden Park in Auckland by 23 points to 20, thus achieving a first ever series win in New Zealand.

1996: As a result of negotiations with Rupert Murdoch the previous year, the Tri Nations tournament, involving the SANZAR members, was launched. The inaugural match took place at the Athletic Park ground in Wellington on 6 July. New Zealand ran out easy winners when they beat old rivals Australia by 43 points to 6.

2000: The year when the Five Nations tournament was expanded to the Six Nations with the introduction of Italy to the competition. All three matches in the first round were played on Saturday 5 February. Italy played Scotland in Rome at 1pm, England faced Ireland in Twickenham at 2.30pm, and Wales took on France in Cardiff at 4pm.

With the dawn of the new millennium, video replay technology was introduced to rugby union to ascertain whether a try had been scored. The video referee or the Television Match Official (TMO), was called upon for the first time during New Zealand's match with Tonga in Albany on 16 June, when English referee Steve Lander requested the televised replay of a disputed try by the All Blacks forward and captain, Todd Blackadder. The melee that had developed on the Tongan line had made it virtually impossible for the referee to make a correct decision. After some discussion between Lander and TMO Steve Walsh, the score was eventually allowed and New Zealand went on to win the match by 102 points to nil.

2001: On 3 February, Welshman Neil Jenkins became the first rugby union player to score over 1,000 points. It was appropriate that this remarkable achievement occurred at the Millennium Stadium in Cardiff with Wales facing rivals, England. Included in the total was the 41 points Jenkins had scored for the Lions whilst on tour in South Africa in 1997. Yet another milestone was reached six weeks later when he reached 1,000 points for Wales in the International match against France at Stade de France in Paris on 17 March. It was fitting that his 28 point haul in that match, which Wales won by 43 points to 35, included the unique 'full house' of scores.

2012: Argentina was finally invited to participate in an expanded Tri Nations tournament, which was renamed 'The Rugby Championship'. The first two games, played on 18 August, featured a victory for New Zealand against Australia at the ANZ Stadium, Sydney and a South African win against newcomers Argentina at Newlands Stadium, Cape Town.

APPENDIX I

THE RUGBY TROPHIES
AND COMPETITIONS

TOURNAMENTS	COMPETITION	DATE	CODE	OPPONENT(S)
	WEBB ELLIS WORLD CUP	1987	WC	ALL NATIONS
CHAMPIONSHIPS				
	TRI NATIONS	1996	TN	Aus, NZ and SA
	FIVE NATIONS TROPHY	1993	5NT	E, F, Ir, S & W
	SIX NATIONS TROPHY	2000	6NT	E, F, Ir, It, S & W
	TRIPLE CROWN TROPHY	2006	TCT	E, Ir, S, & W
	RUGBY CHAMPIONSHIP	2012	RC	Arg, Aus, NZ and SA
AUSTRALIA	BLEDISLOE CUP	1931	Bled	NEW ZEALAND
	TROPHEE DES BICENTENAIRES	1989	BIC	FRANCE
	COOK CUP	1997	CKC	ENGLAND
	HOPETOUN CUP	1998	HC	SCOTLAND
	LANSDOWNE CUP	1999	LC	IRELAND
	MANDELA CHALLENGE PLATE	2000	MCP	SOUTH AFRCA
	PUMA TROPHY	2000	PT	ARGENTINA
	TOM RICHARDS TROPHY	2001	TRT	B & I LIONS
	JAMES BEVAN TROPHY	2007	JBT	WALES
NEW ZEALAND	DAVE GALLAHER TROPHY	2000	DGT	FRANCE
	FREEDOM CUP	2004	FC	SOUTH AFRICA
	SIR EDMUND HILLARY SHIELD	2008	EHS	ENGLAND
SOUTH AFRICA	PRINCE WILLIAM CUP	2007	PWC	WALES
	LIONS / SOUTH AFRICA SERIES	2009	LSA	B & I LIONS
ENGLAND	CALCUTTA CUP	1879	CC	SCOTLAND
	MILLENNIUM TROPHY	1988	MT	IRELAND
	INVESTEC CHALLENGE CUP	2013	ICC	ARGENTINA
IRELAND	CENTENARY QUAICH TROPHY	1989	CQT	SCOTLAND
	ADMIRAL WILLIAM BROWN CUP	2012	ABC	ARGENTINA
SCOTLAND	DOUGLAS HORN TROPHY	2008	DHT	CANADA
FRANCE	GIUSEPPE GARIBALDI TROPHY	2007	GGT	ITALY
BARBARIANS	CORNWALL CUP	2008	CWC	AUSTRALIA
	MASTERCARD TROPHY	2010	MCT	SOUTH AFRICA

APPENDIX I

COMPETITION	CODE
AFRICA CUP (2000 on)	AFC
AMERICAS RUGBY CHAMPIONSHIP (2009 on)	AMC
ANTIM CUP (2002) - ROMANIA v GEORGIA	AC
ASIA FIVE NATIONS CHAMPIONSHIP (2008 on)	A5N
ASIA GAMES (1998 & 2002)	AG
ASIA NATIONS SERIES (2007)	ANS
ASIAN (ARFU) CHAMPIONSHIP (1969-2004)	ASC
BALTIC CUP (1994,1995)	BC
CHURCHILL CUP (2003 - 2011)	CHC
CONFEDERATION OF AFRICAN RUGBY CHAMPIONSHIP	CAR
CONSUR CUP (2014 on)	CSC
CORNWALL CUP (2008)	CWC
EUROPEAN NATIONS CUP (2000 on)	ENC
FIRA CHAMPIONSHIP (1966-1997)	FIRA
INTERCONTINENTAL CUP (2005)	IC
IRB NATIONS CUP (2006 on)	INC
IRB PACIFIC NATIONS CUP (2006 on)	PNC
IRB TBILISI CUP (2013 on)	ITC
MASTERCARD TROPHY	MCT
MEMORIAL CUP (1997)	MC
PACIFIC RIM CHAMPIONSHIP (1996-2001)	PRC
PACIFIC TRI NATIONS SERIES (1998-2005)	PTN
PAN AMERICAN CHAMPIONSHIP (1995-2003)	PAC
SIX NATIONS 'B' CHAMPIONSHIP (2011 on)	6NB
SOUTH AMERICAN CHAMPIONSHIP (1951 on)	SAC
SOUTH PACIFIC CHAMPIONSHIP (1982-1997)	SPC
SOUTH PACIFIC GAMES (1963-1983)	SPG
SUNSHINE COAST CUP (1976)	SCC
VICTORY CUP (1959)	VC

APPENDIX II

THE RUGBY TOURNAMENTS

NORTHERN HEMISPHERE
SOUTHERN HEMISPHERE

THE RUGBY TOURNAMENTS

THE RUGBY WORLD CUP
(WILLIAM WEBB ELLIS TROPHY)

This is the premier competition in world rugby and has been staged every four years since 1987. The first tournament, co-hosted by Australia and New Zealand, was won by the All Blacks and featured sixteen teams who received special invitations from the International Rugby Board (IRB). However, subsequent tournaments required qualifying matches to determine the final list of contestants.

World Cup venues / Winners:

1987 New Zealand and Australia – *New Zealand*
1991 England – *Australia*
1995 South Africa – *South Africa*
1999 Wales – *Australia*
2003 Australia – *England*
2007 France – *South Africa*
2011 New Zealand – *New Zealand*

THE SIX NATIONS CHAMPIONSHIP

The Six Nations Championship started as a four-nations competition between England, Scotland, Ireland and Wales in 1883. It was expanded to a five-nations competition in 1910, when France was invited to participate. In 1931, when France was expelled from the competition for not abiding by the strict amateur rules of rugby union football, the Championship became a four-Home Nations competition once again. It remained so until 1939 and the outbreak of the Second World War. In 1947, France was reinstated and the revived Five Nations Championship continued uninterrupted until 1999.

In 1993 it was decided to present 'The Championship Trophy' to the winning nation and in 1994 a tie-break system was introduced for the first time to decide the champion if two or more teams ended with equal match points: the victor was then deemed to be the one with the greatest difference between total points scored and total points conceded over the whole tournament. In the event that the teams were also equal on points difference, the team who had scored the greater number of tries during the campaign was deemed to be the trophy winners. With the entry of Italy in 2000, rugby's oldest International tournament became known as the Six Nations Championship.

Outright winners of the Five/Six Nations Championship between 1883 and 2015:
England (26 times)
Wales (26 times)
France (17 times)
Scotland (14 times)
Ireland (13 times)
Italy (none).

THE TRI NATIONS CHAMPIONSHIP

The Tri Nations Championship was contested each year from 1996 to 2011 by the three major Southern Hemisphere nations. During that time the tournament was dominated by New Zealand, who won the competition on ten occasions. Australia and South Africa both won three titles.

THE RUGBY CHAMPIONSHIP

In 2012 the Tri Nations Championship was expanded to a four-nations tournament with the addition of Argentina, who had finished in third place in the 2007 World Cup. This new Southern Hemisphere competition was named The Rugby Championship. New Zealand have been champions in all three years, 2012, 2013 and 2014.

THE FIRA CHAMPIONSHIP

The expulsion of France from the Five Nations Championship in 1931 led to the formation of FIRA, the Fédération Internationale de Rugby Amateur on 2 January 1934. The ten founding members were: Italy, Germany, Belgium, Spain, France, Holland, Portugal, Romania, Sweden and Czechoslovakia. In 1966 FIRA organised a second string European competition as an alternative to the Five Nations Championship.

France won the tournament on twenty occasions between 1966 and 1997, and they were the only team from the Five Nations tournament to compete in the FIRA league. In most instances France fielded an 'A' side. The Romanian team won the competition five times between 1968 and 1983, and Italy won the title once, in 1997.

THE EUROPEAN NATIONS CUP

The FIRA Championship was renamed the European Nations Cup (ENC) in 2000. The ENC consists of three divisions, with the first division known as the Six Nations 'B' Championship. Romania became the first Six Nations 'B' champions, followed by Georgia in 2001. From 2002 the tournament became biennial, with the winners declared every two years when each team had played the other five teams twice on a home and away basis. Georgia, Romania, Spain, Russia, Portugal and Belgium competed in the 2013-14 Championship. In the nine tournaments played between 2000 and 2014, Georgia has won the title five times, Romania has had three title wins, and Portugal has won the title once, in the

2003-04 season. Belgium was replaced by Germany in the 2015 campaign.

THE PAN AMERICAN CHAMPIONSHIP

Argentina won all five tournaments held irregularly in the Americas between 1995 and 2003. Except for 1995, when the United States did not enter, the four competing teams have been Argentina, Uruguay, Canada and the United States.

THE IRB NATIONS CUP

The Nations Cup was first held in Lisbon in 2006 and has been staged annually at Bucharest ever since. The aim of this particular tournament is to provide competition between Tier 2 teams, Tier 3 teams and the 'A' sides representing Tier 1 teams. In 2014, the four competing teams were: Romania, Russia, Uruguay and Emerging Ireland (who won the title). Namibia, who won in 2010, and Romania, who won in 2012 and 2013, are the only cup winners outside the Tier 1 'A' sides.

THE SOUTH AMERICAN CHAMPIONSHIP / CONSUR CUP

The first South American Championship was held in Buenos Aires in 1951, involved four teams: Argentina, Chile, Uruguay and Brazil. The next three competitions were held in 1958, 1961 and 1964. In 1967, it became a biennial event and this continued until 1997; in 2000, it was agreed to run the competition annually. Over the years, the Championship has been expanded from one division to two divisions and, from 2012, to three divisions.

In 2014 a new competition called the Consur Cup was launched, with the top two teams from Division One of the South American Championship competing with Argentina (who were seeded) for the title. Argentina, winners of the Championship thirty-four times between 1951 and 2013, did not enter the competition in 1981 and 2014. Uruguay won in both those years. Argentina won the inaugural Consur Cup in 2014.

THE SOUTH PACIFIC CHAMPIONSHIP

The South Pacific Championship contested by Fiji, Western Samoa and Tonga, was held between 1982 and 1997. Western Samoa were title winners ten times, followed by Fiji, who won three times and Tonga, who won the title twice. There was no competition in 1989. The Championship was renamed the Pacific Tri Nations Series in 1998.

THE PACIFIC RIM CHAMPIONSHIP

Between 1996 and 1998, the tournament comprised four teams: Canada, Hong Kong, Japan and the United States. Canada won on all three occasions. In 1999-2000, six teams were in competition when Fiji, Samoa and Tonga joined the Championship and Hong Kong dropped out. Samoa won the title that year, and in 2001, the final year of the tournament, the United States dropped out and Fiji won the title.

THE PACIFIC TRI NATIONS SERIES

The series, a continuation of the South Pacific Championship, ran from 1998 to 2005. The same three nations, Fiji, Tonga and the renamed Samoa, were in competition.

The tournament was suspended in 2003 owing to the Rugby World Cup in Australia. In the seven years of competition Samoa has won four titles to Fiji's three.

THE IRB PACIFIC NATIONS CUP

The IRB Pacific Nations Cup was originally known as the IRB Pacific Five Nations in 2006, the first year of the competition. The five nations competing for the title then were: Japan, Samoa, Tonga, Fiji and the Junior All Blacks, who won the inaugural tournament. They retained the trophy in 2007 when the tournament was renamed the IRB Pacific Nations Cup, and triumphed a third time in 2009. The New Zealand Maori team won in 2008. During the years 2010 to 2012, the Pacific Nations competition was reduced from five International teams to four: Samoa, Fiji, Tonga and Japan. Samoa were the Cup winners in 2010 and 2012, and Japan won in 2011. The five nations competing in 2013 were Tonga, Japan, Canada, the United States, and Fiji, the winners.

In 2014, the tournament was revamped and split into two separate competitions. The six competing teams were divided into two groups of three: Fiji, Tonga and winners Samoa formed one group, and the United States, Canada and winners Japan, the other.

THE AFRICA CUP

The Africa Cup is an annual tournament first held in 2000, run by the Confederation of African Rugby. Originally known as the CAR top9 / top10, the competition was renamed in 2006. There are twenty-nine nations playing in three divisions of the Africa Cup at present and the most successful team since its inception has been Namibia, who has won the title four times in 2002, 2004, the 2008-09 season and in 2014.

THE ASIA FIVE NATIONS CHAMPIONSHIP

The Asian Rugby Championship was held between 1969 and 2004. In that period Japan won the Championship fourteen times to South Korea's five wins. Japan also won the title in the Asian Rugby Series held between 2005 and 2007, which was then replaced by the current Asian Five Nations Championship. This round-robin tournament was first held in 2008, and the competing sides over the years have been Japan, Kazakhstan, Hong Kong, Singapore, South Korea, the Arabian Gulf, the United Arab Emirates, Sri Lanka and the Philippines. Japan won all seven titles between 2008 and 2014, winning all twenty-eight matches in the process. The tournament will revert back to its original name 'The Asian Rugby Championship' in 2015.

THE IRB TBILISI CUP

The Tblisi Cup, with similar terms of reference as the IRB Nations Cup, was launched in 2013 when the hosts Georgia were joined by Uruguay, Emerging Ireland and the South African President's XV, who became inaugural champions after they won all three matches. Argentina Jaguars, who were invited to participate in 2014, emerged as cup winners that year.

THE CHURCHILL CUP

The Churchill Cup was held annually between 2003 and 2011. The competition was mainly between Canada, the United States and, in various years, representative teams from England, Ireland, France, Italy, Argentina, Scotland and the New Zealand Maori. In recent years, Georgia, Uruguay, Tonga and Russia were also invited to participate in the competition.

Past winners of the tournament are: New Zealand Maoris in 2004 and 2006; Ireland 'A' in 2009; and England 'A' on the other six occasions.

APPENDIX III

THE MAJOR STADIUMS

NORTHERN HEMISPHERE

SOUTHERN HEMISPHERE

MAJOR STADIUMS IN ARGENTINA

1 BELGRANO STADIUM, BUENOS AIRES

A multi-purpose Stadium and home ground of Belgrano Athletic Club.

2 CLUB ATLÉTICO SAN ISIDRO GROUND, BUENOS AIRES

The club was founded on 24 October 1902, and rugby was first played at the ground in 1907.

3 CRICKET AND RUGBY CLUB GROUND, BUENOS AIRES

The club was founded on 8 December 1864.

4 ESTADIO DON LEON KOLBOVSKI, BUENOS AIRES

A multi-purpose stadium, mainly used for football matches, was opened on 5 May 1960, and renovated in 2009.

5 ESTADIO MONUMENTAL, RIVER PLATE, BUENOS AIRES

The stadium, also known as 'Estadio Antonio Vespucio Liberti', was opened on 25 May 1938, and renovated in 1978.

6 FERRO CARRIL OESTE STADIUM, BUENOS AIRES

The stadium was opened on 2 January 1905, and was given the often used name of 'Estadio Arquitecto Ricardo Etcheverry' in 1995.

7 GIMNASIA y ESGRIMA de BUENOS AIRES

The stadium, known in short as 'Estadio GEBA', and also as 'Jorge Newbery Gimnasia', was established on 11 November 1880.

8 VÉLEZ SARSFIELD STADIUM, BUENOS AIRES

Also known as 'Estadio José Amalfitani', the stadium was opened on 11 April 1943, renovated in 1951, and expanded in 1978.

9 ESTADIO OLIMPICO CHÂTEAU CARRERAS, CÓRDOBA

Opened on 16 May 1978 as a football stadium, it is also known as 'Estadio Mario Alberto Kempes' or just 'Estadio Córdoba'.

10 ESTADIO CIUDAD de LA PLATA, LA PLATA

The stadium, also known as 'Estadio Unico', was opened on 7 June 2003.

11 ESTADIO JOSÉ MARIA MINELLA, MAR DEL PLATA

This football stadium was opened on May 21, 1978, in time for the 1978 Football World Cup.

12 ESTADIO BAUTISTA GARGANTINI, MENDOZA

The stadium was opened on 5 April 1925, and is the home ground of Club Sportivo Independiente Rivadavia.

MAJOR STADIUMS IN ARGENTINA

13 ESTADIO MALVINAS ARGENTINAS, MENDOZA

The stadium was opened in 1978 to coincide with the 1978 Football World Cup, and is also known as 'Estadio Mundialista Malvinas'.

14 RUGBY CLUB CATARATAS, PUERTO IGUAZU, MISIONES

The home ground of Cataratas Rugby Club.

15 TACURU SOCIAL CLUB, POSADAS, MISIONES

The Tacuru Social Club ground is also known as 'Estadio Posadas' in Posadas, the capital city of the province of Misiones.

16 ESTADIO RAÚL CONTI, PUERTO MADRYN

This mainly rugby stadium was opened on 25 May 1967. It is situated in the Chubut region of Argentina.

17 ESTADIO GABINO SOSA, ROSARIO

The home ground of Club Atlético Central Córdoba in Rosario in the province of Santa Fe.

18 ESTADIO GIGANTE de ARROYITO, ROSARIO

The stadium was opened on 27 October 1929, renovated in 1957, 1963 and 1968 and also between 1974 and 1978.

19 ESTADIO PADRE ERNESTO MARTEARENA, SALTA

A multi-purpose stadium opened in 2001.

20 ESTADIO SAN MARTIN de SAN JUAN, SAN JUAN

The home ground of Club Atlético San Martin.

21 ESTADIO SAN JUAN del BICENTENARIO, SAN JUAN

A multi-purpose stadium opened on 16 March 2011.

22 ESTADIO BRIGADIER GENERAL E. LÓPEZ, SANTA FE

The ground was opened on 9 July 1946, as a football stadium, under its full name, 'Estadio Brigadier General Estanislao López'.

23 ESTADIO MONUMENTAL JOSÉ FIERRO, TUCUMÁN

This multi-purpose stadium, opened on 21 May 1922, is the home ground of the club Cancha (or Clube) del Atletico Tucumán.

MAJOR STADIUMS IN AUSTRALIA

1   BALLYMORE OVAL, BRISBANE

This mainly rugby stadium, opened in 1966, is owned by Queensland Rugby Union. The ground hosted five matches in Rugby World Cup 1987.

2   EXHIBITION GROUND, BRISBANE

The ground, formerly known as 'RNA Showgrounds', was opened in 1886 and was used for Internationals during the period 1899 to 1971.

3   LANG PARK, BRISBANE
renamed: SUNCORP STADIUM, BRISBANE

The stadium was opened in 1914 under the name 'John Brown Oval', before being re-named 'Lang Park' shortly afterwards.
In 1994, under sponsorship, it was renamed 'Suncorp Stadium' and was refurbished in 2003 in time to host nine matches in Rugby World Cup 2003.

4   BRUCE STADIUM / CANBERRA STADIUM

The stadium was opened in 1997 and named 'Bruce Stadium' until 2002 when it was renamed 'Canberra Stadium'.

5   THE GABBA CRICKET GROUND, BRISBANE

Brisbane Cricket Ground, known as 'The Gabba', was established in 1895, and was used for Internationals between 1907 and 2002.

6   COLONIAL STADIUM, MELBOURNE
renamed: TELSTRA DOME / ETIHAD STADIUM

The ground was opened on 9 March 2000 and named 'Colonial Stadium' before being renamed Telstra Dome on 1 October 2002. On 1 March 2009, with a new sponsor on board, it was renamed 'Etihad Stadium, Melbourne. It is also known as 'Docklands Stadium'.

7   OLYMPIC PARK STADIUM, MELBOURNE

This multi-purpose stadium, built in 1956, was used for rugby Internationals until 1994. It was demolished in 2011.

8   SUBIACO OVAL, PERTH
renamed: PATERSONS STADIUM, PERTH

The stadium, established on 9 May 1908, was redeveloped in 1995, 1997 and 1999 and hosted five matches in Rugby World Cup 2003. Since October 2010, under a naming rights contract, Subiaco Oval now is known as 'Patersons Stadium', Perth.

9   CONCORD OVAL, SYDNEY

The 'Oval', opened in 1985 was used for Internationals up to 1998 and also during the 1987 Rugby World Cup. It is often known as the Waratah Stadium.

MAJOR STADIUMS IN AUSTRALIA

10 SYDNEY CRICKET GROUND

Established as a sports ground in 1848, it was known as the SCG in 1894, and was used for rugby Internationals between 1899 and 1986.

11 SYDNEY FOOTBALL STADIUM
renamed: AUSSIE / ALLIANZ
STADIUM.

This football stadium was opened in 1988 and was renamed 'Aussie Stadium, Sydney' in early 2002. It then reverted to its original name on 7 July 2007. Currently however, it is known by its sponsorship name 'Allianz Stadium'.

12 ROYAL AGRICULTURAL
SHOWGROUND, SYDNEY

This ground, situated in Moore Park, was opened in 1882, and was used for rugby Internationals between 1921 and 1926.

13 SYDNEY SPORTS GROUND

The stadium opened in 1911 was used for rugby Internationals between 1914 and 1962. It was closed in 1986 and demolished in 1987.

14 STADIUM AUSTRALIA, SYDNEY
renamed: TELSTRA STADIUM,
SYDNEY
renamed: ANZ STADIUM, SYDNEY

The stadium built to host the Sydney 2000 Summer Olympic Games, was opened on 6 March 1999. It was renamed 'Telstra Stadium' in July 2002 when the telecommunications company acquired the naming rights. The stadium's name was changed again on 1 January 2008 to 'ANZ Stadium' in a seven-year sponsorship deal with the ANZ Bank.

15 YORK PARK LAUNCESTON,
TASMANIA

The sports ground was opened in 1921 and was renamed Aurora Stadium from 2004 to 2010 under a six-year naming agreement.

16 DAIRY FARMERS STADIUM,
TOWNSVILLE, QUEENSLAND

The ground opened in 1994, and was known as Stockland Stadium between 1995 and 1998 and Malanda Stadium during 1998.

17 WOLLONGONG SHOWGROUND,
NEW SOUTH WALES

The ground was opened in 1911 and took on the sponsored name of WIN Stadium Wollongong in 1997. It was upgraded in 2002.

MAJOR STADIUMS IN ENGLAND

1	VILLA PARK, BIRMINGHAM	The stadium, opened in 1897, is the home ground of Aston Villa Football Club. It will host two pool games in Rugby World Cup 2015.
2	RECTORY FIELD, BLACKHEATH	The multi-purposed ground, opened in 1873, was regularly used for rugby Internationals between 1884 and 1909.
3	BRIGHTON COMMUNITY STADIUM, BRIGHTON	Known under the sponsorship name of 'American Express Community Stadium', it will host two pool matches in Rugby World Cup 2015.
4	ASHTON GATE, BRISTOL	This football stadium, opened in 1904, staged its first rugby International in 1908, and was used in Rugby World Cup 1991 and in Rugby World Cup 1999.
5	SANDY PARK, EXETER	This rugby stadium opened on 1 September 2006 is the home ground of Exeter Chiefs' rugby club, and will host three pool games in RWC 2015.
6	KINGSHOLM, GLOUCESTER	The stadium, opened in 1891, staged its first rugby International in 1900. It was used in Rugby World Cup 1991, and will host four pool games in RWC 2015.
7	McALPINE STADIUM, HUDDERSFIELD	Opened in 1994, the stadium, renamed 'Galpharm Stadium' in 2005, is currently known as 'John Smith's Stadium' and was used in Rugby World Cup 1999.
8	ELLAND ROAD, LEEDS	The ground was opened in 1897 and has been the home of Leeds Football Club since 1919. The stadium will stage two pool games in Rugby World Cup 2015.
9	WELFORD ROAD, LEICESTER	Opened in 1892, as the home of Leicester Tigers, the ground staged its first rugby International match in 1902, and was used in Rugby World Cup 1991 and in Rugby World Cup 1999.
10	LEICESTER CITY STADIUM, LEICESTER	The stadium, built in 2002, and home of Leicester City Football Club, has since then staged seven rugby matches. The ground will host three pool games in Rugby World Cup 2015.
11	KENNINGTON OVAL, LONDON	This cricket ground, also known as 'The Oval', was established in 1845. It staged seven rugby Internationals between 1872 and 1879.

MAJOR STADIUMS IN ENGLAND

12 OLYMPIC STADIUM, LONDON — The stadium, built primarily to host the 2012 Olympic Games, was opened in 2011. It will stage four pool games and the bronze match in Rugby World Cup 2015.

13 TWICKENHAM, LONDON — The land was purchased in 1907, the rugby stadium was opened in 1909, and the first International was played on 15 January 1910. It underwent many redevelopments between 1927 and 1995, the most recent being in 2006. It was used in Rugby World Cups 1991 and 1999. The stadium will stage five pool games, two quarter-finals, both semi-finals and the final in Rugby World Cup 2015.

14 WEMBLEY STADIUM, LONDON — This football stadium was opened in 1923, renovated in 1963, and demolished in 2003. The new 'Wembley Stadium', opened on 9 March 2007, was chosen to host two matches in Rugby World Cup 2015.

15 STADIUM MK, MILTON KEYNES — This football ground, known locally as "Denbigh Stadium", was built in 2007. It will stage three pool games in Rugby World Cup 2015.

16 MANCHESTER CITY STADIUM, MANCHESTER — Known as the 'Etihad Stadium' for sponsorship reasons, it was opened as a football stadium in August 2003. It will host the England v Uruguay pool game in Rugby World Cup 2015.

17 OLD TRAFFORD, MANCHESTER — This football stadium was opened on 19 February 1910 and staged its first rugby International in 1997.

18 WHALLEY RANGE, MANCHESTER — This football stadium staged seven Home Nations rugby Internationals between 1880 and 1892.

19 ST JAMES' PARK, NEWCASTLE — The stadium has been the home of Newcastle United Football Club from the time it opened in 1892. It will host three pool matches in Rugby World Cup 2015.

20 CROSS GREEN, OTLEY — This multi-purpose stadium, home ground of Otley RFC, hosted the Pool A rugby International between Italy and the United States in Rugby World Cup 1991.

21 ATHLETIC GROUND, RICHMOND — The stadium was used for ten rugby Internationals between 1891 and 1909.

MAJOR STADIUMS IN FRANCE

1 STADE ARMANDIE, AGEN — The ground, opened on October 9, 1921, hosted one pool game in Rugby World Cup 1991. The stadium was then renovated between 2008 and 2010.

2 STADE JEAN DAUGER, BAYONNE — Opened in 1937, and renovated between 2006 and 2009, this multi-purpose stadium was used in a pool match in Rugby World Cup 1991.

3 STADE de la MÉDITERRANÉE, BÉZIERS — Opened in 1990, the stadium hosted a pool game in Rugby World Cup 1991, and two pool games in Rugby World Cup 1999. It was renovated between 2003 and 2007.

4 PARC des SPORTS AGUILÉRA, BIARRITZ — This multi-purpose ground was opened in 1906, expanded in 1962, and renovated during the period 2003 to 2006.

5 STADE MUNICIPAL du PARC LESCURE, BORDEAUX *renamed:* STADE CHABAN-DELMAS. BORDEAUX — This municipal sporting ground, opened on 12 June 1938, was renovated in 1935, 1987 and 1998. The stadium hosted two pool games in RWC 1999, was renamed 'Stade Chaban-Delmas' in 2001 and staged four pool games in RWC 2007.

6 STADE PARC MUNICIPAL des SPORTS, BRIVE . *renamed:* STADE AMÉDÉE-DOMENECH, BRIVE — Opened in 1921, and used for one pool game in RWC 1991, the stadium was renamed 'Stade Amédée-Domenech' in 2004, and expanded in 2011.

7 PARC des SPORTS MARCEL MICHELIN, CLERMONT-FERRAND — The stadium was opened in 1911, and renovated between 2006 and 2008. It was further renovated in 2010-11, and is the home of ASM Clermont Auvergne.

8 STADE LESDIGUIÈRES, GRENOBLE — The stadium was opened in 1968 and renovated in 1991. The ground hosted one pool match in Rugby World Cup 1991.

9 STADE FÉLIX BOLLAERT, LENS — Opened in 1933 and renovated in 2004, 'Stade Bollaert-Delelis' hosted a play-off game game in Rugby World Cup 1999 and three pool matches in Rugby World Cup 2007.

10
STADE NORD LILLE MÉTROPOLE — Built in 1976 and situated in Villeneuve-d'Ascq, the stadium staged a quarter-final match in Rugby World Cup 1991.

11
STADE de GERLAND, LYON — Opened in 1926 and renovated in 1960, 1980 and in 1998, this mainly football stadium hosted three pool matches in Rugby World Cup 2007.

MAJOR STADIUMS IN FRANCE

12 STADE VÉLODROME, MARSEILLE — Opened on 3 June 1937, and renovated in 1984 and 1998, the stadium staged four pool games and two quarter-final matches in Rugby World Cup 2007.

13 STADE de la MOSSON, MONTPELLIER — This mainly football stadium, opened in 1972 and renovated in 1997, hosted pool games in Rugby World Cup 2007.

14 STADE de la BEAUJOIRE, NANTES — The multi-purpose stadium, opened on 8 May 1984, staged three pool matches in Rugby World Cup 2007.

15 STADE COLOMBES, PARIS — Opened in 1907 as 'Stade du Matin', it was renamed Stade de Colombes' in 1920, and hosted the 1924 Olympics. In 1928 the stadium was renamed 'Stade Olympique Yves-du-Manoir' but it is still known as simply 'Stade Colombes'.

16 STADE DE FRANCE, PARIS — Opened on 28 January 1998 as the National Stadium of France, the ground is in the Saint Denis commune of Paris. It hosted a quarter-final match in Rugby World Cup 1999 and seven games, including both semi-finals and the final, in Rugby World Cup 2.

17 PARC DES PRINCES, PARIS — Opened as a multi-purpose stadium on 18 July 1897, and renovated in 1932, it became dedicated to football and rugby in 1967. Known as the National Stadium until 1998, the ground hosted a quarter-final in Rugby World Cup 1991 and five pool matches in Rugby World Cup 2007.

18 STADE GEOFFROY-GUICHARD, SAINT ÉTIENNE — This mainly football ground, opened on 13 September 1931 and renovated in 1984 and 1998, hosted three pool games in Rugby World Cup 2007.

19 STADE MAYOL, TOULON — This multi-purpose stadium, inaugurated on 28 March 1920 and renovated in 1947 and 1965, is the home ground of RC Toulonnais.

20 STADE ERNEST WALLON, TOULOUSE — The stadium also known as 'Stade des Sept Deniers' was opened in 1982, renovated in 2000, and used in a pool game in Rugby World Cup 1991.

21 STADE MUNICIPAL de TOULOUSE — This multi purpose stadium, opened in 1937 and renovated in 1998, hosted two pool games in Rugby World Cup 1999 and four pool games in Rugby World Cup 2007.

MAJOR STADIUMS IN IRELAND

1	BALLYNAFEIGH, BELFAST	The stadium was founded in 1877 and staged three rugby Internationals between 1891 and 1894.
2	BALMORAL SHOWGROUNDS, BELFAST	This venue was frequently used for rugby Internationals between 1898 and 1921. Eleven matches in all were played at the ground.
3	ORMEAU, BELFAST	The stadium staged seven rugby Internationals between 1877 and 1889, including the abandoned match against Scotland in 1885.
4	RAVENHILL, BELFAST *renamed:* KINGSPAN STADIUM, BELFAST	The stadium was opened in 1923 and was used continuously for rugby Internationals between 1924 and 1954. It was also used in both Rugby World Cup 1991 and Rugby World Cup 1999, and was renovated in 2009. It is now the home ground of Ulster Rugby. Ravenhill was upgraded during the period 2012 to 2014 and renamed in June 2014 as part of a ten year sponsorship deal with the Kingspan Group.
5	MARDYKE, CORK	The Cork County cricket ground, also used by University College Cork sports club, staged two rugby Internationals between 1911 and 1913.
6	MUSGRAVE PARK, CORK	The rugby stadium, opened in 1940, is one of two home grounds used by Munster Rugby, the other being in Limerick.
7	AVIVA STADIUM, DUBLIN	Mainly a rugby stadium, it was built on the site of 'Lansdowne Road' between 2007 and was opened on 14 May 2010.
8	CROKE PARK, DUBLIN	Headquarters of the Gaelic Athletic Association (GAA), the stadium was opened in 1913 and renovated in 2004. It was used for fourteen rugby Internationals between 2007 and 2010 during the Aviva Stadium construction project.
9	DONNYBROOK STADIUM, DUBLIN	The stadium was renovated in 2008, and became the home of Leinster Rugby until the club moved to the RDS Showgrounds.

MAJOR STADIUMS IN IRELAND

10 LANSDOWNE ROAD, DUBLIN

The rugby stadium was opened in 1872, but the first rugby International did not take place until 11 March 1878. The last International was played on 20 November 2006. The, then, oldest rugby International stadium in the world was finally demolished in 2007. It was used in Rugby World Cup 1991 and Rugby World Cup 1999.

11 LEINSTER CRICKET CLUB, RATHMINES, DUBLIN

The cricket club was founded in 1852 and the ground staged Ireland's first ever home rugby International on 13 December 1875.

12 RDS SHOWGROUNDS, DUBLIN

Opened in 1868 to host equestrian events, the arena, expanded in 2007 and 2008, is now the new home ground of Leinster Rugby.

13 UCD BOWL, DUBLIN

Part of the University College Dublin sports complex, the rugby ground section of the campus was renovated in 2007.

14 GALWAY SPORTSGROUND, GALWAY

This multi-purpose venue in the west of Ireland was opened in 1927, and is the home ground of Connacht Rugby.

15 THOMOND PARK, LIMERICK

The current stadium was opened in 1940, but the first rugby International was played on the old location on 19 March 1898. The stadium was used in Rugby World Cup 1999, and was modernised in 2008, to become the main home ground of Munster Rugby.

MAJOR STADIUMS IN ITALY

1   STADIO SANTA COLOMBA, BENEVENTO
renamed: STADIO CIRO VIGORITO

The ground was opened on 9 September 1979 as a football stadium, and it was renamed 'Stadio Ciro Vigorito' on 2 November 2010.

2   STADIO RENATO DALL'ARA, BOLOGNA

Opened in 1927 as a multi-purpose stadium, it is used by Bologna FC. In 1995 the ground hosted the Italy match against the All Blacks.

3   CENTRO SPORTIVO SAN MICHELE, CALVISANO
renamed: STADIO PERONI

Opened in 1972, the stadium is the home of Calvisano RFC, and was renamed 'Stadio Peroni' on 19 May 2012.

4   STADIO SANTA MARIA GORETTI, CATANIA

A multi-purpose stadium, home of Amatori Catania, it is used mostly for rugby and American football.

5   STADIO ARTEMIO FRANCHI, FLORENCE

Opened in 1931 as a football stadium and renovated in 1990, it was previously known as 'Stadio Comunale Artemio Franchi'.

6   STADIO COMUNALE LUIGI FERRARIS, GENOA

Opened on 22 January 1911, the stadium is also known as 'Stadio Luigi Ferraris' or just 'Marassi'. The ground was renovated in 1989.

7   STADIO TOMMASO FATTORI, L'AQUILA

This multi-purpose stadium opened in 1933, is the home ground of L'Aquila Calcio and L'Aquila Rugby.

8   ARENA CIVICA, MILAN
renamed: ARENA GIANNI BRERA

Opened on 18 August 1807, and renovated in 1945, this multi-purpose stadium was renamed 'Arena Gianni Brera' in 2003.

9   STADIO SAN SIRO, MILAN
renamed: STADIO GIUSEPPE MEAZZA

Opened on 19 September 1926, renovated in 1956 and 1989, the stadium was renamed 'Stadio Giuseppe Meazza' on 3 March 1980.

10   STADIO PLEBISCITO, PADOVA

The stadium, mainly used for rugby, is the home ground of Petrarca Padova rugby football club.

11   STADIO EUGANEO, PADOVA

Opened in 1994, this football stadium, home ground of Calcio Padova, replaced the historical 'Stadio Silvio Appiani'.

MAJOR STADIUMS IN ITALY

12 STADIO COMUNALE ENNIO TARDINI, PARMA

The football stadium opened on 16 September 1923. and renovated between 1990 and 1993, is the home of Parma FC.

13 STADIO XXV APRILE, PARMA

A dedicated rugby stadium opened in 2008, replaced 'Stadio Sergio Lanfranchi', and is the home ground of Zebre Rugby.

14 STADIO COMUNALE BELTRAMETTI, PIACENZA

Opened on 27 November 1966 as a rugby stadium, it is the home ground of Rugby Piacenza.

15 STADIO FLAMINIO, ROME

Opened in March 1959, the stadium was the venue for Italy's home games during the Six Nations competition between 2000 and 2011. The stadium was renovated in 2008, and was due expansion in 2012 which did not materialise.

16 STADIO OLIMPICO, ROME

Opened in 1937 as 'Stadio del Cipressi', the stadium was renovated and officially inaugurated on 17 May 1953, as 'Stadio dei Centomila'. In 1960, the stadium was given its current name when Italy staged the summer Olympics that year. It was further expanded in 1990.

17 STADIO COMUNALE MARIO BATTAGLINI, ROVIGO

Opened in 1970, as a multi-purpose facility, the stadium is the home ground of Rugby Rovigo.

18 STADIO COMUNALE DI MONIGO, TREVISO

Opened in 1973, mainly as a rugby stadium, it is the current home ground of Benetton Treviso rugby football club.

19 STADIO OLIMPICO di TORINO, TURIN

Opened on 14 May 1933, as 'Stadio Mussolini', and later as 'Stadio Comunale', it was renovated and reopened on 10 February 2006.

20 STADIO FRIULI, UDINE

This multi-purpose stadium was opened in 1976, replacing 'Stadio Moretti'. It was renovated in 1990, and also between 2012 and 2014.

21 STADIO LUIGI ZAFFANELLA, VIADANA

Opened in 1972, mainly as a rugby stadium, and owned by Rugby Viadana, it was the home ground of the now defunct Aironi rugby club.

MAJOR STADIUMS IN NEW ZEALAND

1 NORTH HARBOUR STADIUM, ALBANY

The stadium, opened on 8 March 1997, and situated in North Shore City near Auckland, hosted four pool games in Rugby World Cup 2011.

2 EDEN PARK, AUCKLAND

The ground was opened in 1900, and the first rugby International was played at that venue on August 27, 1921. The stadium staged many matches in RWC 1987 and in Rugby World Cup 2011, and is currently the only ground to have hosted two World Cup finals.

3 LANCASTER PARK OVAL, CHRISTCHURCH
renamed: JADE STADIUM, CHRISTCHURCH
renamed: A M I STADIUM, CHRISTCHURCH

The stadium was opened on 15 October 1881, and the first test at the venue took place on 29 September 1913. The ground was renovated many times between 1995 and 2009, and was renamed 'Jade Stadium' by its sponsor in 1998. It was renamed 'A M I Stadium' by another sponsor in 2007, but had to close in February 2011 because of an earthquake.

4 CARISBROOK, DUNEDIN

The ground, opened in 1883, staged three pool games in Rugby World Cup 1987, and closed in 2011. It was replaced by 'Forsyth Barr Stadium'.

5 FORSYTH BARR STADIUM, DUNEDIN

The stadium, opened on 5 August 2011, used the temporary non-commercial name 'Otago Stadium' during Rugby World Cup 2011.

6 RUGBY PARK, HAMILTON

Opened in 1925, the stadium hosted one pool game in Rugby World Cup 1987 and was replaced by 'Waikato Stadium' in 1999.

7 WAIKATO STADIUM, HAMILTON

Opened in 2002, to replace 'Rugby Park', the ground hosted three pool games in Rugby World Cup 2011.

8 RUGBY PARK STADIUM, INVERCARGILL

This rugby venue, which started as a cricket pitch in 1886, hosted one pool game in Rugby World Cup 1987 and three pool games in Rugby World Cup 2011.

9 McLEAN PARK, NAPIER

The ground, established in 1911 mainly as a cricket venue, hosted one pool game in Rugby World Cup 1987, and two pool games in Rugby World Cup 2011.

MAJOR STADIUMS IN NEW ZEALAND

10 TRAFALGAR PARK, NELSON

The ground was opened on 21 April 1888, renovated in 2008, and then upgraded in 2011 to host three pool games during Rugby World Cup 2011.

11 YARROW STADIUM, NEW PLYMOUTH

The stadium, opened in September 2002, used the non-commercial name of 'Stadium Taranaki' whilst hosting three pool games in Rugby World Cup 2011.

12 SHOWGROUNDS OVAL, PALMERSTON NORTH
remamed: ARENA 1, PALMERSTON NORTH
renamed: FMG STADIUM, PALMERSTON NORTH
renamed: ARENA MANAWATU PALMERSTON NORTH

The original ground, named 'Showgrounds Oval, Palmerston North' hosted one pool match in Rugby World Cup 1987. The stadium redeveloped in March 2005, was earlier known as 'Arena 1' and later as 'FMG Stadium', but is currently known as 'Arena Manawatu'. Under this name, the venue staged two pool games in Rugby World Cup 2011.

13 ROTORUA INTERNATIONAL STADIUM, ROTORUA

Rotorua Stadium, built in 1911, hosted the third-place game in Rugby World Cup 1987 and three pool matches in Rugby World Cup 2011.

14 ATHLETIC PARK, WELLINGTON

The stadium was opened on 6 April 1896, and demolished on 10 October 1999. The ground hosted four pool matches in Rugby World Cup 1987.

15 WESTPAC STADIUM (TRUST), WELLINGTON
renamed: WESTPAC STADIUM, WELLINGTON

The stadium was opened on 3 January 2000, with the original name incorporating the word 'trust', which was dropped in 2004. The new name was changed to the non-commercial name 'Wellington Regional Stadium', during Rugby World Cup 2011.

16 OKARA PARK, WHANGAREI

The ground was opened in 1965, renovated in 2008, and hosted two pool games in Rugby World Cup 2011.

MAJOR STADIUMS IN SCOTLAND

1 PITTODRIE STADIUM, ABERDEEN

The football stadium was opened in 1899 and renovated in 1993. The ground has also been used for rugby Internationals since 2008.

2 INVERLEITH, EDINBURGH

The ground was opened in 1899 and was used continuously for rugby Internationals between 1899 and 1925.

3 MEADOWBANK STADIUM, EDINBURGH

This multi-purpose sporting facility was opened in 1970 and was renovated in 1994 and also in 1999.

4 MURRAYFIELD, EDINBURGH

The Stadium was opened in 1925, and the first rugby International was played there on 21 March 1925. It was used in Rugby World Cup 1991, and following renovation in 1995, it staged further matches in Rugby World Cup 1999 and Rugby World Cup 2007.

5 POWDERHALL, EDINBURGH

The stadium was built in the 1870s and staged two rugby Internationals during the 1897 and 1898 seasons.

6 RAEBURN PLACE, EDINBURGH

Staged the first rugby International between Scotland and England in 1871 and was used continuously for rugby Internationals until 1895.

7 NETHERDALE STADIUM, GALASHIELS

Home to Gala Rugby Club, in the Scottish borders, the stadium hosted one rugby International match, between Uruguay and Spain, during Rugby World Cup 1999.

8 FIRHILL STADIUM, GLASGOW

The stadium was opened in 1909 and was the home ground of Glasgow Warriors Rugby Club between 2007 and 2012.

9 HAMILTON CRESCENT, GLASGOW

Staged the first soccer match between Scotland and England in 1872, and was used for four rugby Internationals between 1873 and 1885.

10 HAMPDEN PARK, GLASGOW

This famous Scottish International football stadium was opened in 1903, renovated in 1999 and used during Rugby World Cup 1999.

11 HUGHENDEN STADIUM, GLASGOW

This rugby stadium was opened on 24 May 1924, and was the home ground of Glasgow Warriors RFC between 2005 and 2007.

MAJOR STADIUMS IN SCOTLAND

12 OLD HAMPDEN PARK, GLASGOW

This football stadium named Cathkin Park, when opened in 1884, staged just one rugby International on 14 March 1896. The ground was closed in 1967.

13 SCOTSTOUN STADIUM, GLASGOW

The stadium, an athletics and rugby venue, was opened in 1915, and is the current home ground of Glasgow Warriors Rugby Football Club.

14 RUGBY PARK, KILMARNOCK

This football stadium, opened on 1 August 1899, renovated between 1994 and 1995, staged Scotland's rugby International against Tonga on 22 November 2014.

15 McDIARMID PARK, PERTH

This football stadium, opened in 1989, staged its first rugby International match between Scotland and Japan on 13 November 2004.

MAJOR STADIUMS IN SOUTH AFRICA

1 FREE STATE STADIUM, BLOEMFONTEIN
renamed: VODACOM PARK STADIUM

The original stadium was built in 1954 and was replaced in 1995 by the new 'Free State Stadium' in time to host three games in Rugby World Cup 1995. Renamed 'Vodacom Park' in 2002, the ground was expanded in 2007 and renovated in 2008.

2 NEWLANDS STADIUM, CAPE TOWN
renamed: NORWICH PARK, NEWLANDS
renamed: FEDSURE PARK, NEWLANDS

The ground was opened on 31 May 1890, and was upgraded several times between 1990 and 1995 in preparation for Rugby World Cup 1995. In an agreement with sponsors, the stadium was renamed 'Norwich Park' in 1996, and again in 2000 to 'Fedsure Park'. Investec became the sponsor in 2002, followed by Vodacom in 2005. Both agreed to retain the original name 'Newlands Stadium'. The ground hosted four matches, including a quarter-final and a semi-final, in Rugby World Cup 1995.

3 KINGS PARK STADIUM, DURBAN
renamed: ABSA STADIUM, DURBAN
renamed: THE ABSA STADIUM, DURBAN

Built in 1891, the stadium was opened by rugby icon Dr Danie Craven in 1958 as 'Kings Park Rugby Ground'. It was renovated throughout the 1990s, and its capacity was increased in 1995. In 2000, in a sponsorship deal, the stadium was renamed 'ABSA Stadium'. Then in 2005 it was renamed again to 'The ABSA Stadium', but is currently known simply as 'Kings Park Stadium'. The ground staged five games, including a quarter-final and a semi-final, in Rugby World Cup 1995.

4 BASIL KENYON STADIUM, EAST LONDON
renamed: ABSA STADIUM, EAST LONDON
renamed: BUFFALO CITY STADIUM, EAST LONDON

The stadium, built in 1934, was originally named 'Border Rugby Union Ground' and later named 'Basil Kenyon Stadium'. It was then named 'ABSA Stadium, East London' until 13 October 2009, when it was renamed 'Buffalo City Stadium' or 'BCM Stadium, East London'. The ground hosted three pool matches in Rugby World Cup 1995.

5 ELLIS PARK, JOHANNESBURG

The ground, established on 10 October 1927, was opened in 1928, then demolished, and rebuilt exclusively for rugby in 1982. The modernised stadium hosted five games in Rugby World Cup 1995, including a quarter-final and the final when South Africa beat New Zealand by 15 points to 12. Ellis Park was then rebranded 'CocaCola Park' on 4 July 2008, but the ground then reverted to its original name in 2012.

MAJOR STADIUMS IN SOUTH AFRICA

6 BOET ERASMUS STADIUM, PORT ELIZABETH
renamed: TELKOM PARK STADIUM, PORT ELIZABETH
renamed: EPRFU STADIUM, PORT ELIZABETH

The stadium, opened on 30 April 1960, was named 'Boet Erasmus' until 1999 when it was renamed 'Telkom Park' in a naming rights deal. It was further renamed 'EPRFU Stadium' in 2003, until it was officially closed in July 2010, to be replaced by the 'Nelson Mandela Bay Stadium'.

7 NELSON MANDELA BAY STADIUM, PORT ELIZABETH

The stadium staged its first event on 6 June 2009, nearly nine months before its official opening on 28 February 2010.

8 LOFTUS VERSFELD, PRETORIA
renamed: MINOLTA LOFTUS STADIUM, PRETORIA
renamed: SECURICOR LOFTUS STADIUM, PRETORIA

The stadium was opened in 1923 and named in honour of Robert Owen Loftus Versfeld in 1932 until its name change on 10 June 1998. It was then renamed 'Minolta Loftus' between 11 June 1998, and 4 February 2003, in a sponsorship deal with the Minolta Company. In a new sponsorship arrangement it was then renamed 'Securicor Loftus' from 5 February 2003, until 1 September 2005. Vodacom then took over the sponsorship, and agreed to use the original name. The ground hosted three pool matches, a quarter-final and the third place game in Rugby World Cup 1995.

9 OLYMPIA PARK, RUSTENBURG

This multi-purpose stadium, opened in 1989 and used for both football and rugby, hosted three pool matches in Rugby World Cup 1995.

10 ROYAL BAFOKENG SPORTS PALACE, RUSTENBURG

The sports palace, opened in 1999, is mainly used for football matches. It was renovated and expanded in 2009.

11 P A M BRINK STADIUM, SPRINGS

The ground was inaugurated on 3 July 1949, and is used mostly for football matches. Two Internationals have been played at the stadium: in 1964 and 2002.

12 DANIE CRAVEN STADIUM, STELLENBOSCH

Named after the famous Springbok scrum-half, the stadium built in 1979, staged the pool match between Australia and Romania in Rugby World Cup 1995.

MAJOR STADIUMS IN WALES

1 TALBOT ATHLETIC GROUND, ABERAVON

A multi-purpose ground, known as 'The Central Athletic Ground' in the 1900s, has been the home of Aberavon rugby football club since 1913.

2 BREWERY FIELD, BRIDGEND

This sports stadium, opened in 1920, is the home ground of Bridgend Ravens rugby football club.

3 ARMS PARK, CARDIFF
renamed: NATIONAL STADIUM, CARDIFF

The ground was opened in 1881 and renovated in 1912, 1934 and in 1956. The first International was played there on 12 April 1884, and the last International match against France took place on 23 March 1968. The stadium was then renamed 'National Stadium, Cardiff' in 1969, with the first match played on 8 March 1969. Although often referred to as the Arms Park in 1969, renovations at the stadium continued in stages during 1970, 1977 and 1980, and on completion the ground was officially opened, as 'The National Stadium', on 7 April 1994. The last match at the venue took place on 15 March 1997, just before it was demolished. The stadium had hosted four games, which included the third place match, in Rugby World Cup 1991.

4 MILLENNIUM STADIUM, CARDIFF

The new stadium, rebuilt on the National Stadium site, was opened in June 1999 in preparation for the 1999 Rugby World Cup, hosted by Wales. The first International took place on 26 June 1999, and the stadium staged matches during Rugby World Cup 1999 and Rugby World Cup 2007.

5 CARDIFF CITY STADIUM, CARDIFF

This relatively new multi-purpose stadium was opened on 22 July 2009, and is the home stadium of Cardiff Blues rugby club.

6 PARC EIRIAS, COLWYN BAY

The leisure centre, also known as known as 'Eirias Park', staged six International matches involving Tier 2 and 3 teams during November in 2012, 2013 and 2014.

7 EUGENE CROSS PARK, EBBW VALE

This rugby and cricket stadium was opened in 1919 and is the home ground of Ebbw Vale rugby football club.

8 PARC Y SCARLETS, LLANELLI

This new ground, which replaced Stradey Park, was opened 15 November 2008, and is the current home stadium of Llanelli Scarlets rugby club.

MAJOR STADIUMS IN WALES

9   STRADEY PARK, LLANELLI

The stadium was opened in 1879, and the first rugby International was played on 8 January 1887. The ground, home of Llanelli rugby football club until it was closed on 15 November 2008, was finally demolished in 2010. The stadium staged one pool game in both Rugby World Cup 1991 and Rugby World Cup 1999.

10   THE GNOLL, NEATH

The cricket club was formed in 1848 and rugby was played from 1871. The current multi-purpose ground is the home of Neath Rugby Football Club.

11   RODNEY PARADE, NEWPORT

Opened in 1877, this is the home of Newport-Gwent Dragons rugby club. The first rugby International took place at the ground on 12 January 1884.

12   PONTYPOOL PARK, PONTYPOOL

First used for rugby in 1946, it is the home of Pontypool rugby club. The ground hosted the pool match between Australia and Western Samoa in Rugby World Cup 1991.

13   SARDIS ROAD, PONTYPRIDD

Opened in September 1974, it is the home of Pontypridd rugby club. The ground hosted the pool match between Argentina and Western Samoa in Rugby World Cup 1991.

14   LIBERTY STADIUM, SWANSEA

The multi-purpose stadium was opened on 10 July 2005, and is the home ground of the Ospreys rugby club.

15   ST HELEN'S, SWANSEA

This rugby and cricket stadium, opened in 1873, staged Wales' first ever home rugby International on 16 December 1882. The ground continued to stage International matches until 1952, after which Welsh home matches were transferred to Cardiff.

16   THE RACECOURSE, WREXHAM

Opened in 1864, this football stadium, known as 'The Racecourse Ground', hosted the pool match between Samoa and Japan in Rugby World Cup 1999. The ground also staged three Internationals between Wales and Romania between 1997 and 2003.

INTERNATIONAL VENUES: LIST OF STADIUMS **A TO C**

AAMI Park - Melbourne

ABSA Stadium - Durban

ABSA Stadium - East London

Adams Park - High Wycombe

Adelaide Oval - Adelaide

AMI Stadium - Addington

AMI Stadium - Christchurch

ANZ Stadium - Sydney

Apia Park - Apia

Aranduroga Rugby Club - Corrientes

Arena Civica - Milan

Arena Giann Brera - Milan

Arena Manawatu - Palmerston North

Arms Park - Cardiff

Ashton Gate - Bristol

Athletic Club - San Pablo

Athletic Ground - Richmond

Athletic Park - Wellington

Aurora Stadium - Launceston

Ausgrid Stadium - Newcastle, NSW

Aussie Stadium - Sydney

Aviva Stadium - Dublin

Ballymore Oval - Brisbane

Ballynafeigh - Belfast

Balmoral Showgrounds - Belfast

Basil Kenyon Stadium - East London

BBVA Compass Stadium - Houston

Belgrano Stadium - Buenos Aires

BMO Stadium - Toronto

Boet Erasmus Stadium - Port Elizabeth

Boxer Stadium - San Francisco

Brewery Field - Bridgend

Brighton Community Stadium - Brighton

Brook's Field, Wilmington - North Carolina

Bruce Stadium - Canberra

Buck Shaw Stadium - Santa Clara, California

Buckhurst Park - Suva, Fiji

Buffalo City Stadium - East London

Camino Carrasco, Polo Club - Montevideo

Campo Ciudad Universitaria - Madrid

Campo de Pepe Rojo - Valladolid

Canberra Stadium - Canberra

Cardiff City Stadium - Cardiff

Cardigan Fields - Leeds

Carisbrook - Dunedin

Cataratas Rugby Club - Puerto Iguazu, Misiones

Central Coast Stadium - Gosford, NSW

Central Stadium - Krasnoyarsk

Centro Sportivo San Michele - Calvisano

Chalon-sur-Saone - Perpignan

Chanel College, Moamoa - Apia

Churchill Park - Lautoka, Fiji

Club Atlético Atlanta - Buenos Aires

Club Atlético San Isidro - Buenos Aires

Clube Atlético Ground - Sao Paulo

COC Stadium - Casablanca

CocaCola Park - Johannesburg

Colonial Stadium - Melbourne

Colorado Springs

Concord Oval - Sydney

County Ground - Gosforth

Cradock RC, Cradock - Eastern Cape

Cricket and Rugby Club - Buenos Aires

Cricket Ground - Melbourne

Cricket Ground - Sydney

Croke Park - Dublin

INTERNATIONAL VENUES: LIST OF STADIUMS C TO F

Cross Green - Otley, Yorkshire

Crown Flatt - Dewsbury

Crusaders Ground - Port Elizabeth

Crystal Palace - London

Dairy Farmers Stadium - Townsville

Danie Craven Stadium - Stellenbosch

Donnybrook Stadium - Dublin

Eclectic Cricket Ground - Kimberley

Eden Park - Auckland

Edgeley Park - Stockport

Elland Road - Leeds

Ellis Park - Johannesburg

EPRFU Stadium - Port Elizabeth

Epsom Showgrounds - Auckland

Estad. Mundialista J M Minella - Mar del Plata

Estadi Olímpic de Montjuïc - Barcelona

Estadi Olímpic Lluís Companys - Barcelona

Estadio Bautista Gargantini - Mendoza

Estadio Brig General E. López - Santa Fe

Estadio Centenario - Resistencia

Estadio Charrúa - Montevideo

Estadio Ciudad de la Plata - La Plata

Estadio de Las Fuerzas - Asunción

Estadio de Vallehermoso - Madrid

Estadio del Colegio San José - Asunción

Estadio Don Leon Kolbovski - Buenos Aires

Estadio Gabino Sosa - Rosario

Estadio G.E.B.A - Buenos Aires

Estadio General Pablo Rojas - Ascunción

Estadio Gigante de Arroyito - Rosario

Estadio Gran Parque Central - Montevideo

Estadio José Maria Minella - Mar del Plata

Estadio La Carrodilla - Mendoza

Estadio Luis Franzini - Montevideo

Estadio Malvinas Argentinas - Mendoza

Estadio Moldanado - Buenos Aires

Estadio Monumental A V Liberti - Buenos Aires

Estadio Monumental José Fierro - Tucumán

Estadio Monumental - River Plate, Buenos Aires

Estadio Mundialista JM Minella - Mar del Plata

Estadio Olimpico Château Carreras - Córdoba

Estadio Padre Ernesto Martearena - Salta

Estadio Parque Artigas - Paysandú

Estadio Playa Ancha - Valparaiso

Estadio Raúl Conti - Puerto Madryn

Estadio San Carlos de Apoquindo - Santiago

Estadio S. Juan del Bicentenario - San Juan

Estadio San Martin de San Juan - San Juan

Estadio Sausalito - Viña del Mar

Estádio Sérgio Conceição - Coimbra

Estádio Universitário de Coimbra - Coimbra

Estádio Universitário de Lisboa - Lisbon

Etihad Stadium, Docklands - Melbourne

Eugene Cross Park - Ebbw Vale

Exhibition Ground - Brisbane

Express Advocate Stadium - Gosford, NSW

Fallowfield - Manchester

Fedsure Park, Newlands - Cape Town

Ferro Carril Oeste Stadium - Buenos Aires

Fili Stadion - Moscow

Firhill Stadium - Glasgow

Fletcher's Field, Markham - Toronto

FMG Stadium - Palmerston North

FNB Stadium, Soweto - Johannesburg

Football Stadium - Sydney

Forsyth Barr Stadium - Dunedin

Franklin Gardens - Northampton

Frascati Rugby Stadium - Rome

INTERNATIONAL VENUES: LIST OF STADIUMS **F TO O**

Free State Stadium - Bloemfontein

Fritz-Grunebaum-Sportpark - Heidelburg

Galway Sports Ground - Galway

George Allen Memorial Field - Long Beach

Glover Field Anaheim - Los Angeles

Grand Stade - Lille Métropole

Great Strahov Stadium - Prague

Growthpoint Kings Park - Durban

Hamilton Crescent - Glasgow

Hampden Park - Glasgow

Hanazono Stadium - Osaka

Harder Stadium - Santa Barbara, California

Hartsfield Rugby Ground - Bulawayo

Headingley Stadium - Leeds

Heywood Road - Sale

Hughenden Stadium - Glasgow

Iffley Road - Oxford

Inverleith - Edinburgh

Jade Stadium - Christchurch

Johann van Riebeeck Stadium - Witbank

Kennington Oval - London

Kings Park - Durban

Kingsholm - Gloucester

Kingsland Rugby Park - Calgary

Kingsmead Ground - Durban

Kingspan Stadium, Belfast

Lancaster Park Oval - Christchurch

Lang Park - Brisbane

Lansdowne Road - Dublin

Leicester City Stadium - Leicester

Leinster CC, Rathmines - Dublin

Lia Manoliu Stadium - Bucharest

Liberty Stadium - Swansea

Life College Stadium - Atlanta, Georgia

Loftus Versfeld Stadium - Pretoria

Madejski Stadium - Reading

Mahamasina Stadium - Antananarivo

Makarska Stadium - Makaraska, Yugoslavia

Maksimir Stadium - Zagreb

Manchester City Stadium - Manchester

Mansfield Park - Hawick, Scotland

Mardyke - Cork

Mbombela Stadium - Nelspruit

McAlpine Stadium - Huddersfield

McDiarmid Park - Perth

McLean Park - Napier

Meadowbank Stadium - Edinburgh

Meanwood Road - Leeds

Millennium Stadium - Cardiff

Minolta Loftus Stadium - Pretoria

Mohawk Sports Park - Hamilton, Ontario

Murrayfield - Edinburgh

Musgrave Park - Cork

Nagai Stadium - Osaka

National Olympic Stadium - Tokyo

National Sports Stadium - Harare

National Stadium - Avarua, Rarotonga

National Stadium - Cardiff

National Stadium - Suva, Fiji

Nauka Stadion - Moscow

Netherdale Stadium - Galashiels, Scotland

Nelson Mandela Bay Stadium - Port Elizabeth

Newlands Stadium - Cape Town

North Harbour Stadium - Albany

Northland Events Centre - Whangarei, New Zealand

North West Stadium - Welkom

INTERNATIONAL VENUES: LIST OF STADIUMS O TO S

Norwich Park, Newlands - Cape Town

Observatory Park - Denver, Colorado

Okara Park - Whangarei, New Zealand

Old Hampden Park - Glasgow

Old Trafford - Manchester

Olën Park - Potchefstroom, South Africa

Olympia Park - Rustenburg

Olympic Park Stadium - Melbourne

Olympic Stadium - London

Ormeau - Belfast

Otago Stadium - Dunedin

Owl Creek Polo Field, Glenville - New York

P A M Brink Stadium - Springs

Parc des Princess - Paris

Parc des Sports Aguiléra - Biarritz

Parc des Sports de Sauclières - Béziers

Parc des Sports et de L'Amitié - Narbonne

Parc des Sports Marcel Michelin - Clermont-Ferrand

Parc Eirias - Colwyn Bay

Parc Municipal des Sports - Bayonne

Parc y Scarlets - Llanelli

Parque Federico Omar Saroldi - Montevideo

Parque Mahuida CARR La Reina - Santiago

Parramatta Stadium - Sydney

Patersons Stadium - Perth

Pittodrie Stadium - Aberdeen

Police Ground - Harare

Police Ground - Salisbury

Polo Ground, Flores - Buenos Aires

Pontypool Park - Pontypool

Potter's Park - Auckland

Powderhall - Edinburgh

Prince Chichibu Memorial Ground - Tokyo

Prince of Wales Country Club - Santiago

R A S Ground - Sydney

Raeburn Place - Edinburgh

Ravenhill - Belfast

RDS Showgrounds - Dublin

Recreation Ground - Bath

Rectangular Stadium - Melbourne

Rectory Field - Blackheath

Rentschler Field - Hartford, Connecticut

Richardson Stadium - Kingston, Ontario

Richardson's Field - Blackheath

River Plate Stadium - Buenos Aires

Robertson Stadium - Houston

Rockne Stadium, Northfield - Chicago

Rodney Parade - Newport

Rotorua International Stadium - Rotorua

Route du Médoc, Le Bouscat - Bordeaux

Royal Agricultural Showground - Sydney

Royal Bafokeng Sports Palace - Rustenburg

Rugby League Park - Christchurch

Rugby Park Stadium - Invercargill

Rugby Park - Hamilton

Rugby Park - Kilmarnock

San Carlos de Apoquindo - Santiago

San Pablo Athletic Ground - São Paulo

Sandy Park - Exeter

Sardis Road - Pontypridd

Scotstoun Stadium - Glasgow

Securicor Loftus Stadium - Pretoria

Showgrounds Oval - Palmerston North

Singer Family Park - Manchester, New Hampshire

Sixways Stadium - Worcester

Skilled Park, Robina, Gold Coast - Queensland

INTERNATIONAL VENUES: LIST OF STADIUMS S

Skra Stadium - Warsaw

Slava Stadion - Moscow

So Kon Po Stadium - Hong Kong

Soldier Field - Chicago

South West Stadium - Windhoek

Sparta Stadium - Moscow

Spartak Stadium - Kiev

Spartak Stadium - Moscow

Sports Ground - Sydney

Sports Ground, Avarua - Rarotonga

Sports Park Berg and Bos - Apeldoorn

Springbok Park - Bloemfontein

St Helen's - Swansea

St Ignatius, California Field - Berkeley

St James' Park - Newcastle

Stade Africain de Menzel - Bourghiba

Stade Aimé Giral - Perpignan

Stade Albert Domec - Carcassonne

Stade Amédée-Domenech - Brive

Stade Antoine-Béguère - Lourdes

Stade Armandie - Agen

Stade Auguste Bonal - Montbéliard

Stade Bourillot - Dijon

Stade Chaban-Delmas - Bordeaux

Stade Colombes - Paris

Stade d'Albert Domec - Carcassonne

Stade de France - Paris

Stade de Gerland - Lyon

Stade de L'Egassiairal - Narbonne

Stade de la Beaujoire - Nantes

Stade de la Chambrèrie - Valence

Stade de la Croix du Prince - Pau

Stade de la Méditerranée - Béziers

Stade de la Meinau - Strasbourg

Stade de la Mosson - Montpellier

Stade de Sapiac - Montauban Stade des Ponts, Jumeaux - Toulouse

Stade des Sports Aguiléra - Biarritz

Stade du Hameau - Pau

Stade du Moulias - Auch

Stade du Parc Lescure - Bordeaux

Stade du Ray - Nice

Stade E. Jean Baylet - Valence d'Agen

Stade Ernest Wallon - Toulouse

Stade Félix Bollaert - Lens

Stade Félix Mayol - Toulon

Stade Français - Santiago

Stade Geoffroy-Guichard - Saint Étienne

Stade Jacques Fouroux - Auch

Stade Jean Alric - Aurillac

Stade Jean Dauger - Bayonne

Stade Jules Deschaseaux - Le Havre

Stade le Bouscat - Bordeaux

Stade Leo Lagrange - Besançon

Stade Lesdiguières - Grenoble

Stade Louis II - Monte Carlo

Stade Marcel Michelin - Clermont Ferrand

Stade Marcel Saupin - Nantes

Stade Maurice Trélut - Tarbes

Stade Mayol - Toulon

Stade Méditerranée - Béziers

Stade Michel Bendichou - Colomiers

Stade Municipal de Toulouse - Toulouse

Stade Municipal du Parc Lescure - Bordeaux

Stade Municipal - Albi

Stade Municipal - Chalon-sur-Saone

INTERNATIONAL VENUES: LIST OF STADIUMS S

Stade Municipal - Chambéry

Stade Mustapha Ben Jannet - Monastir

Stade Nord Lille Métropole - Villeneuve-d'Ascq

Stade Océane - Le Havre

Stade Parc Municipal des Sports - Brive

Stade Patrice Brocas, Moulias - Auch

Stade Pershing,Vincennes - Paris

Stade Pierre-Antoine - Castres

Stade Roi Baudouin - Brussels

Stade Sébastien, Charléty - Paris

Stade Vélodrome - Marseille

Stade Yves-du-Manoir - Montpellier

Stadio Alberto Braglia - Modena

Stadio Angelo Massimino - Catania

Stadio Artemio Franchi - Florence

Stadio Arturo Collana - Naples

Stadio Brianteo - Monza, Milan

Stadio Cino e Lillo del Duca - Ascoli Piceno

Stadio Ciro Vigorito - Benevento

Stadio Comprensoriale - Fontanafredda

Stadio Comunale Beltrametti - Piacenza

Stadio Comunale Carlo Montano - Livorno

Stadio Comunale Censin Bosia - Asti

Stadio Comunale di Monigo - Treviso

Stadio Comunale, Ennio Tardini - Parma

Stadio Comunale Luigi Ferraris - Genova

Stadio Comunale Mario Battaglini - Rovigo

Stadio Comunale Rho - Rho

Stadio Comunale Sergio Lanfrachi - Parma

Stadio Danilo Martelli - Mantova

Stadio Dino Manuzzi, Cesana - Trieste

Stadio Euganeo - Padova

Stadio Flaminio - Rome

Stadio Friuli - Udine

Stadio Gigante de Arroyito - Rosario

Stadio Giglio - Reggio Emilia

Stadio Gino Pistoni-Ivrea - Turin

Stadio Giovanni Zini - Cremona

Stadio Giuseppe Meazza - Milan

Stadio Jesi Arriva - Jesi

Stadio Lamarmora - Biella-in-Piedmont

Stadio Leonardo Garilli - Piacenza

Stadio Luigi Zaffanella - Viadana

Stadio Lungobisenzio - Prato

Stadio Marc'Antonio Bentegodi - Verona

Stadio Mario Rigamonti - Brescia

Stadio Mompiano - Brescia

Stadio Nazionale del Roma - Rome

Stadio Olimpico di Torino - Turin

Stadio Olimpico - Rome

Stadio Omobono Tenni - Treviso

Stadio Oreste Granillo - Reggio di Calabria

Stadio Peroni - Calvisano

Stadio P. Perucca, St Vincent - Aosta

Stadio Pierluigi Penzo - Venice

Stadio Plebiscito - Padova

Stadio Renato Dall'Ara - Bologna

Stadio Rho - Rho

Stadio San Dona di Piave - Venice

Stadio San Paolo - Naples

Stadio San Siro - Milan

Stadio Santa Colomba - Benevento

Stadio Santa Maria Goretti - Catania

Stadio Silvio Appiani - Padova

Stadio St Vincent Perruca - Aosta

Stadio Testaccio - Rome

Stadio Tommaso Fattori - L'Aquila

Stadio XXV Aprile - Parma

INTERNATIONAL VENUES: LIST OF STADIUMS **S TO Y**

Stadion Krč - Prague

Stadion Maksimir - Zagreb

Stadion Sparta, Krč - Prague

Stadionul 1 Mai - Constanta

Stadionul 23 August - Bucharest

Stadionul ANEF - Bucharest

Stadionul Cotroceni - Bucharest

Stadionul Dinamo - Bucharest

Stadionul Farul - Constanta

Stadionul Giuleşti-Valentin Stănescu - Bucharest

Stadionul Municipal Gloria - Buzău

Stadionul Municipal - Brăilla

Stadionul Municipal - Braşov

Stadion Parcul Copilului - Bucharest

Stadionul Republican Chişinău - Moldova

Stadionul Republicii - Bucharest

Stadium Australia - Sydney

Stadium MK - Milton Keynes

Stadium Taranaki - New Plymouth

Stoop Memorial Ground - London

Stradey Park - Llanelli

Subiaco Oval - Perth

Suncorp Stadium - Brisbane

Swanguard Stadium - Burnaby Lake, BC

Tacuru Social Club Posadas - Misiones

Tahuna Park - Dunedin

Talbot Athletic Ground - Aberavon

Telkom Park Stadium - Port Elizabeth

Telstra Dome - Melbourne

Telstra Stadium - Sydney

Teufaiva Sport Stadium - Nuku'alofa

The ABSA Stadium - Durban

The Gabba Cricket Ground - Brisbane

The Gnoll - Neath, Wales

The Greenyards - Melrose, Scotland

The Kimberley Athletics Club - Kimberley

The Racecourse - Wrexham

The Sportsground - Galway

The Wanderers Ground - Johannesburg

Thomond Park - Limerick

Thunderbird Stadium - Vancouver

Toyota Park Stadium - Chicago

Trafalgar Park - Nelson

Tupapa Rugby Field - Avarua

Twickenham - London

Twin Elms Rugby Park - Nepean, Ontario

UCD Bowl - Dublin

Union Sportif Annecy Rugby - Annecy

University Ground - Sydney

Upper Park - Birkenhead Park

Varsity Stadium, Stanley Park - Toronto

Vélez Sarsfield Stadium - Buenos Aires

Vicarage Road - Watford

Viking Park - Canberra

Villa Park - Birmingham

Vodacom Park Stadium - Bloemfontein

Waikato Stadium - Hamilton

Wanderers Club Ground - Montevideo

Waverley Park - East London

Welford Road - Leicester

Wellington Regional Stadium - Wellington

Wembley Stadium - London

Westpac Stadium - Wellington

Westpac Trust Stadium - Wellington

Whalley Range - Manchester

WIN Stadium - Wollongong

Withdean Stadium - Brighton

Yarrow Stadium - New Plymouth

York Park, Launceston - Tasmania

York Stadium - Toronto

BIBLIOGRAPHY

Barrett, R. (ed).,	*The Daily Telegraph Chronicle of Rugby*	(Guinness Publishing Ltd., 1996)
Bath, R. (ed).,	*The Ultimate Encyclopaedia of Rugby*	(Carlton Books Ltd., 1997)
Bath, R.,	*The Scotland Rugby Miscellany*	(Vision Sports Publishing, 2007)
Bath, R.,	*The British & Irish Lions Rugby Miscellany*	(Vision Sports Publishing, 2007)
Bath, R.,	*The Treasures of International Rugby Union*	(Carlton Books Ltd., 2011)
Billot, J.,	*History of Welsh International Rugby*	(Roman Way Books, 1970)
Billot, J.,	*All Blacks in Wales*	(Ron Jones Publications, 1972)
Billot, J.,	*Springboks in Wales*	(Ron Jones Publications, 1974)
Bond, K., A Morton and J. Griffiths (eds).,	*IRB World Rugby Yearbook 2013*	(Vision Sports Publishing, 2012)
Bond, K., J. Murray and J. Griffiths (eds).,	*IRB World Rugby Yearbook 2014*	(Vision Sports Publishing, 2013)
Bond, K., R. Clark and J. Griffiths (eds).,	*IRB World Rugby Yearbook 2015*	(Vision Sports Publishing, 2014)
Chester, R. H. and N. A. C. McMillan,	*Men in Black*	(Pelham Books, 1978)
Chester, R. H. and N. A. C. McMillan,	*Centenary: 100 Years of All Black Rugby*	(Blandford Press, 1984)
Cleary, M. and J. Griffiths (eds).,	*Rothman's Rugby Union Yearbook 1995-1996*	(Rothmans Publications, 1995)
Cleary, M. and J. Griffiths (eds).,	*Rothman's Rugby Union Yearbook 1996-1997*	(Rothmans Publications, 1996)
Cleary, M. and J. Griffiths (eds).,	*Rothman's Rugby Union Yearbook 1997-1998*	(Rothmans Publications, 1997)
Cleary, M. and J. Griffiths (eds).,	*Rothman's Rugby Union Yearbook 1998-1999*	(Rothmans Publications, 1998)
Cleary, M. and J. Griffiths (eds).,	*Rothman's Rugby Union Yearbook 1999-2000*	(Rothmans Publications, 1999)
Cleary, M. and J. Griffiths (eds).,	*International Rugby Yearbook 2001-2002*	(Collins Willow, 2001)
Cleary, M. and J. Griffiths (eds).,	*International Rugby Yearbook 2002-2003*	(Collins Willow, 2002)
Cleary, M. and J. Griffiths (eds).,	*International Rugby Yearbook 2003-2004*	(Collins Willow, 2003)
Cole, R. and S. Farmer,	*The Wales Rugby Miscellany*	(Vision Sports Publishing, 2007)
Connor, J. and M. Hannan,	*Once Were Lions*	(Harper Sport, 2009)
Cronin, C.,	*The Ireland Rugby Miscellany*	(Vision Sports Publishing, 2007)
Davidson, J. McI.,	*A Compendium of Scotland's Matches*	(Polygon, 1994)
Day, B. and B Gallagher,	*Playfair Rugby Union Annual 1996-1997*	(Headline Book Publishing, 1996)
Day, B. and B Gallagher,	*Playfair Rugby Union Annual 1997-1998*	(Headline Book Publishing, 1997)
de Klerk, A.,	*International Rugby Encyclopaedia*	(30 deg South Publishers Pty Ltd., 2009)
Diffley, S.,	*The Men in Green: The Story of Irish Rugby*	(Pelham Books, 1973)
Edwards, G. and D. Parry-Jones (eds),	*The Golden Years of Welsh Rugby*	(Harrap Ltd., Publishers, 1982)
Evans, A.,	*The Barbarians: The United Nations of Rugby*	(Mainstream Publishing, 2005)
Evans, H.,	*Welsh International Matches 1881-2011*	(Y Lolfa Cyf., 2011)
Farmer, S. and B. Gallagher,	*Playfair Rugby Union Annual 1998-1999*	(Headline Book Publishing, 1998)
Farmer, S. and B. Gallagher,	*Playfair Rugby Union Annual 1999-2000*	(Headline Book Publishing, 1999)
Farmer, S.,	*The Official England Rugby Miscellany*	(Vision Sports Publishing, 2011)
First Editions, (ed.),	*Playfair Rugby Union Annual 1984-1985*	(Queen Anne Press, 1984)
Ford, D. and A. Hathaway,	*A Fans' Guide to World Rugby*	(New Holland Publishers UK Ltd., 2011)
Fox, D., K. Bogle and M. Hoskins,	*A Century of the All Blacks in Britain & Ireland*	(Tempus Publishing, 2006)
Godwin, T.,	*The Guinness Book of Rugby Facts & Feats*	(Guinness Superlatives Ltd., 1983)
Godwin, T.,	*The International Rugby Championship 1883-1983*	(Collins Willow, 1984)
Griffiths, J.,	*The Book of English International Rugby 1871-1982*	(Collins Willow, 1982)
Griffiths, J.,	*The Phoenix Book of International Rugby Records*	(Phoenix House, 1987)
Griffiths, J.,	*British Lions*	(Crowood Press, 1990)
Griffiths, J.,	*Rugby's Strangest Matches*	(Robson Books, 2000)

Guiney, D.,	*Rugby World Cup '91*	(Sportsworld Publishers, 1991)
Harrison, M.,	*Grand Slam: The Story of the Five Nations Championship*	(Aurum Press, 1999)
Hawkes, C.,	*World Rugby Union Records*	(Carlton Books Ltd., 2012)
Hawkes, C.,	*World Rugby Union Records Third Edition*	(Carlton Books Ltd., 2014)
Hopkins, J.,	*Life with the Lions*	(Hutchinson Publishing Group, 1977)
Jenkins, V.,	*Lions Rampant: The 1955 Tour of South Africa*	(Cassell & Co. Ltd., 1956)
Jenkins, V.,	*Lions Down Under: Tour of Australia & New Zealand 1959*	(Cassell & Co. Ltd., 1960)
Jenkins, V. (ed.),	*Rothmans Rugby Yearbook 1972*	(Brickfield Publications Ltd., 1972)
Jenkins, V. (ed.),	*Rothmans Rugby Yearbook 1973-1974*	(Brickfield Publications Ltd., 1973)
Jenkins, V. (ed.),	*Rothmans Rugby Yearbook 1974-1975*	(Brickfield Publications Ltd., 1974)
Jenkins, V. (ed.),	*Rothmans Rugby Yearbook 1975-1976*	(Brickfield Publications Ltd., 1975)
Jenkins, V. (ed.),	*Rothmans Rugby Yearbook 1976-1977*	(Brickfield Publications Ltd., 1976)
Jenkins, V. (ed.),	*Rothmans Rugby Yearbook 1977-1978*	(Brickfield Publications Ltd., 1977)
Jenkins, V. (ed.),	*Rothmans Rugby Yearbook 1978-1979*	(Brickfield Publications Ltd., 1978)
Jenkins, V. (ed.),	*Rothmans Rugby Yearbook 1979-1980*	(Brickfield Publications Ltd., 1979)
Jenkins, V. (ed.),	*Rothmans Rugby Yearbook 1980-1981*	(Brickfield Publications Ltd., 1980)
Jenkins, V. (ed.),	*Rothmans Rugby Yearbook 1981-1982*	(Rothmans Publications Ltd., 1981)
Jenkins, V. (ed.),	*Rothmans Rugby Yearbook 1982-1983*	(Rothmans Publications Ltd., 1982)
John, B. and P. Abbandonato,	*Barry John the King*	(Mainstream Publishing, 2000)
Jones, S. (ed.),	*Rothmans Rugby Yearbook 1983-1984*	(Rothmans Publications Ltd., 1983)
Jones, S. (ed.),	*Rothmans Rugby Yearbook 1984-1985*	(Rothmans Publications Ltd., 1984)
Jones, S. (ed.),	*Rothmans Rugby Yearbook 1985-1986*	(Rothmans Publications Ltd., 1985)
Jones, S. (ed.),	*Rothmans Rugby Yearbook 1986-1987*	(Rothmans Publications Ltd., 1986)
Jones, S. (ed.),	*Rothmans Rugby Yearbook 1987-1988*	(Rothmans Publications Ltd., 1987)
Jones, S. (ed.),	*Rothmans Rugby Union Yearbook 1988-1989*	(Rothmans Publications Ltd., 1988)
Jones, S. (ed.),	*Rothmans Rugby Union Yearbook 1989-1990*	(Rothmans Publications Ltd., 1989)
Jones, S. (ed.),	*Rothmans Rugby Union Yearbook 1990-1991*	(Rothmans Publications Ltd., 1990)
Jones, S. (ed.),	*Rothmans Rugby Union Yearbook 1991-1992*	(Rothmans Publications Ltd., 1991)
Jones, S. (ed.),	*Rothmans Rugby Union Yearbook 1992-1993*	(Rothmans Publications Ltd., 1992)
Jones, S. (ed.),	*Rothmans Rugby Union Yearbook 1993-1994*	(Rothmans Publications Ltd., 1993)
Jones, S. (ed.),Jones, S. (ed.),	*Rothmans Rugby Union Yearbook 1994-1995*	(Rothmans Publications Ltd., 1994)
Jones, S., T. English, N. Cain and D. Barnes,	*Behind the Lions*	(Arena Sport & Polaris Publishing Ltd., 201.)
Marks and Spencer,	*An A-Z of Rugby Rugby's Great Heroes and Entertainers*	(Marks & Spencer plc Publishing, 2008)
McLaren, B.,		(Hodder & Stoughton, 2003)
McLean, T. P.,	*The All Blacks*	(Sidgwick & Jackson, 1991)
Morgan, P. and J. Griffiths (eds),	*IRB World Rugby Yearbook 2007*	(Vision Sports Publishing, 2006)
Morgan, P. and J. Griffiths (eds),	*IRB World Rugby Yearbook 2008*	(Vision Sports Publishing, 2007)
Morgan, P. and J. Griffiths (eds),	*IRB World Rugby Yearbook 2009*	(Vision Sports Publishing, 2008)
Morgan, P. and J. Griffiths (eds),	*IRB World Rugby Yearbook 2010*	(Vision Sports Publishing, 2009)
Morgan, P. and J. Griffiths (eds),	*IRB World Rugby Yearbook 2011*	(Vision Sports Publishing, 2010)
Morgan, P. and J. Griffiths (eds),	*IRB World Rugby Yearbook 2012*	(Vision Sports Publishing, 2011)
Morgan, P. and A. Hathaway,	*The Rugby Companion*	(Igloo Books Ltd., 2004)
Oswald, N. and J. Griffiths (eds),	*The Essential History of Rugby Union: Scotland*	(Headline Book Publishing, 2003)
Owen, A. (ed.),	*Rugby Annual for Wales 1969-1970*	(Welsh Brewers Ltd. Publishing, 1969)
Owen, A. (ed.),	*Rugby Annual for Wales 1970-1971*	(Welsh Brewers Ltd. Publishing, 1970)
Owen, A. (ed.),	*Rugby Annual for Wales 1971-1972*	(Welsh Brewers Ltd. Publishing, 1971)

Owen, A. (ed.),	*Rugby Annual for Wales 1972-1973*	(Welsh Brewers Ltd. Publishing, 1972)
Owen, A. (ed.),	*Rugby Annual for Wales 1973-1974*	(Welsh Brewers Ltd. Publishing, 1973)
Owen, A. (ed.),	*Rugby Annual for Wales 1974-1975*	(Welsh Brewers Ltd. Publishing, 1974)
Owen, A. (ed.),	*Rugby Annual for Wales 1975-1976*	(Welsh Brewers Ltd. Publishing, 1975)
Owen, A. (ed.),	*Rugby Annual for Wales 1976-1977*	(Welsh Brewers Ltd. Publishing, 1976)
Owen, A. (ed.),	*Rugby Annual for Wales 1977-1978*	(Welsh Brewers Ltd. Publishing, 1977)
Owen, A. (ed.),	*Rugby Annual for Wales 1978-1979*	(Welsh Brewers Ltd. Publishing, 1978)
Owen, A. (ed.),	*Rugby Annual for Wales 1979-1980*	(Welsh Brewers Ltd. Publishing, 1979)
Owen, A. (ed.),	*Rugby Annual for Wales 1980-1981*	(Welsh Brewers Ltd. Publishing, 1980)
Owen, A. (ed.),	*Rugby Annual for Wales 1981-1982*	(Welsh Brewers Ltd. Publishing, 1981)
Owen, A. (ed.),	*Rugby Annual for Wales 1982-1983*	(Welsh Brewers Ltd. Publishing, 1982)
Owen, A. (ed.),	*Rugby Annual for Wales 1983-1984*	(Welsh Brewers Ltd. Publishing, 1983)
Owen, A. (ed.),	*Rugby Annual for Wales 1984-1985*	(Welsh Brewers Ltd. Publishing, 1984)
Owen, A. (ed.),	*Rugby Annual for Wales 1985-1986*	(Welsh Brewers Ltd. Publishing, 1985)
Owen, A. (ed.),	*Rugby Annual for Wales 1986-1987*	(Welsh Brewers Ltd. Publishing, 1986)
Owen, A. (ed.),	*Rugby Annual for Wales 1987-1988*	(Welsh Brewers Ltd. Publishing, 1987)
Owen, A. (ed.),	*Rugby Annual for Wales 1988-1989*	(Welsh Brewers Ltd. Publishing, 1988)
Owen, A. (ed.),	*Rugby Annual for Wales 1989-1990*	(Welsh Brewers Ltd. Publishing, 1989)
Owen, A. (ed.),	*Rugby Annual for Wales 1990-1991*	(Welsh Brewers Ltd. Publishing, 1990)
Owen, A. (ed.),	*Rugby Annual for Wales 1991-1992*	(Welsh Brewers Ltd. Publishing, 1991)
Owen, A. (ed.),	*Rugby Annual for Wales 1992-1993*	(Welsh Brewers Ltd. Publishing, 1992)
Owen, A. (ed.),	*Rugby Annual for Wales 1993-1994*	(Welsh Brewers Ltd. Publishing, 1993)
Owen, A. (ed.),	*Rugby Annual for Wales 1994-1995*	(Welsh Brewers Ltd. Publishing, 1994)
Owen, A. (ed.),	*Rugby Annual for Wales 1995-1996*	(Welsh Brewers Ltd. Publishing, 1995)
Owen, A. (ed.),	*Rugby Annual for Wales 1996-1997*	(Welsh Brewers Ltd. Publishing, 1996)
Owen, A. (ed.),	*Rugby Annual for Wales 1997-1998*	(Welsh Brewers Ltd. Publishing, 1997)
Owen, A. (ed.),	*Rugby Annual for Wales 1998-1999*	(Welsh Brewers Ltd. Publishing, 1998)
Owen, A. (ed.),	*Rugby Annual for Wales 1999-2000*	(Buy as you View Publishing, 1999)
Owen, A. (ed.),	*Rugby Annual for Wales 2000-2001*	(Buy as you View Publishing, 2000)
Owen, A. (ed.),	*Rugby Annual for Wales 2001-2002*	(Buy as you View Publishing, 2001)
Owen, A. (ed.),	*Rugby Annual for Wales 2002-2003*	(Buy as you View Publishing, 2002)
Owen, A. (ed.),	*Rugby Annual for Wales 2004-2005*	(Buy as you View Publishing, 2004)
Owen, A. (ed.),	*Rugby Annual for Wales 2005-2006*	(Newo Wales Books, 2005)
Owen, O. L. (ed.),	*Playfair Rugby Football Annual 1948-1949*	(Playfair Books Ltd. Publishing, 1948)
Owen, O. L. (ed.),	*Playfair Rugby Football Annual 1949-1950*	(Playfair Books Ltd. Publishing, 1949)
Owen, O. L. (ed.),	*Playfair Rugby Football Annual 1952-1953*	(Playfair Books Ltd. Publishing, 1952)
Owen, O. L. (ed.),	*Playfair Rugby Football Annual 1953-1954*	(Playfair Books Ltd. Publishing, 1953)
Owen, O. L. (ed.),	*Playfair Rugby Football Annual 1955-1956*	(Playfair Books Ltd. Publishing, 1955)
Owen, O. L. (ed.),	*Playfair Rugby Football Annual 1956-1957*	(Playfair Books Ltd. Publishing, 1956)
Owen, O. L. (ed.),	*Playfair Rugby Football Annual 1957-1958*	(Playfair Books Ltd. Publishing, 1957)
Owen, O. L. (ed.),	*Playfair Rugby Football Annual 1958-1959*	(Playfair Books Ltd. Publishing, 1958)
Owen, O. L. (ed.),	*Playfair Rugby Football Annual 1959-1960*	(Playfair Books Ltd. Publishing, 1959)
Owen, O. L. (ed.),	*Playfair Rugby Football Annual 1960-1961*	(Playfair Books Ltd. Publishing, 1960)
Owens, N. (ed.),	*Nigel Owens The Autobiography: Half Time*	(Y Lolfa Cyf, 2013)
Parker, A.C.,	*The Springboks 1891-1970*	(Cassell & Co. Ltd. Publishing, 1970)
Past Times,	*The Trivial History of Rugby*	(Past Times Publishing, 2002)

Past Times,	*Rugby Eccentrics*	(Past Times Publishing, 2002)
Paul, G,.	*Top 10 of everything Rugby*	(Exisle Publishing Ltd., 2012)
Reason, J.,	*The 1968 Lions: Tour of South Africa 1968*	(Eyre & Spottiswoode Publishers Ltd., 1968)
Reason, J.,	*The Victorious Lions: Tour of Australia & N Zealand 1971*	(Rugby Books, London Publishers, 1971)
Reason, J.,	*Backs to the Wall: Tour of South Africa 1980*	(Rugby Football Books Ltd., London, 1980)
Reason, J. and C. James,	*The World of Rugby*	(BBC Publications, 1979)
Rhys, C.,	*The Guinness Rugby Union Fact Book*	(Guinness Publishing Ltd., 1992)
Richards, H,	*A Game for Hooligans: The History of Rugby Union*	(Mainstream Publishing Company, 2007)
Ross, G. (ed.),	*Playfair Rugby Football Annual 1964-1965*	(Dickens Press Ltd., Publishing, 1964)
Ross, G. (ed.),	*Playfair Rugby Football Annual 1965-1966*	(Dickens Press Ltd., Publishing, 1965)
Ross, G. (ed.),	*Playfair Rugby Football Annual 1966-1967*	(Dickens Press Ltd., Publishing, 1966)
Ross, G. (ed.),	*Playfair Rugby Football Annual 1967-1968*	(Dickens Press Ltd., Publishing, 1967)
Ross, G. (ed.),	*Playfair Rugby Football Annual 1968-1969*	(Dickens Press Ltd., Publishing, 1968)
Ross, G. (ed.),	*Playfair Rugby Football Annual 1969-1970*	(Dickens Press Ltd., Publishing, 1969)
Ross, G. (ed.),	*Playfair Rugby Football Annual 1970-1971*	(Dickens Press Ltd., Publishing, 1970)
Ross, G. (ed.),	*Playfair Rugby Football Annual 1971-1972*	(Dickens Press Ltd., Publishing, 1971)
Ross, G. (ed.),	*Playfair Rugby Football Annual 1972-1973*	(Dickens Press Ltd., Publishing, 1972)
Ryan, M.,	*World Rugby*	(Flame Tree Publishing, 2007)
Smith, B.,	*World Cup 1998 Pocket Annual*	(Virgin Publishing, 1998)
Smith, B.,	*Rugby Union 1998-1999 Pocket Annual*	(Virgin Publishing, 1998)
Smith, B.,	*Rugby World Cup 1999 Pocket Guide*	(Virgin Publishing, 1999)
Spragg, I.,	*The Reduced History of Rugby*	(André Deutsch Ltd., 2005)
Starmer-Smith, N. and I. Robertson,	*The Whitbread Rugby World '89*	(Lennard Publishing, 1988)
Starmer-Smith, N. and I. Robertson,	*The Whitbread Rugby World '93*	(Queen Anne Press, 1992)
Starmer-Smith, N. and I. Robertson,	*The Whitbread Rugby World '94*	(Queen Anne Press, 1993)
Starmer-Smith, N. and I. Robertson,	*The Flowers Whitbread Rugby World '95*	(Queen Anne Press, 1994)
Thomas, A.,	*A Guide to the Rugby Union World Cup 1987*	(Christopher Davies Publishers Ltd., 1987)
Thomas, C.,	*The History of the British Lions*	(Mainstream Publishing Company, 1996)
Thomas, J. B. G.,	*Lions Courageous: Tour of Australia & N Zealand 1959*	(Stanley Paul & Co. Ltd., 1960)
Thomas, J. B. G.,	*Lions at Bay: Tour of Australia & N Zealand 1966*	(Pelham Books Ltd., 1966)
Thomas, J. B. G.,	*The Roaring Lions: Tour of Australia & N Zealand 1971*	(Pelham Books Ltd., 1971)
Thomas, J. B. G.,	*The Men in Scarlet: The Story of Welsh Rugby Football*	(Pelham Books Ltd., 1972)
Thomas, J. B. G.,	*The Greatest Lions: Tour of South Africa 1974*	(Pelham Books Ltd., 1974)
Van Esbeck, E.,	*Irish Rugby 1874-1999: A History*	(Gill & Macmillan, 1999)
Ward, T. with J. Scally,	*Life at Number 10*	(Blackwater Press, 2006)
Welch, I.,	*Great Moments of Rugby*	(G2 Entertainment Ltd., 2014)
Wemyss, A. (ed.),	*Barbarian Football Club: History & Records 1890-1955*	(Playfair Books Ltd. Publishing, 1955)
White, J.,	*The Six Nations Rugby Miscellany*	(Carlton Books Ltd., 1997)
Woolgar, J.,	*England: The Official R F U History*	(Virgin Books, 1999)
Wooller, W. (ed.),	*50 Years of the All Blacks*	(Phoenix House, 1954)
Wyatt, D. (ed.),	*The International Rugby Almanack 1994*	(Blandford Press, 1994)
Wyatt, D. and N. Keith (eds),	*The International Rugby Almanack 1995*	(Blandford Press, 1995)

BIBLIOGRAPHY

INTERNET RUGBY WEBSITES

www.worldrugby.org
http://rugbydata.com
www.espnscrum.com
www.supersport.com
www.opensideflanker.com
www.rugby365.com
www.rugbyinternational.net
www.lassen.co.nz
www.planetrugby.com

ARGENTINA	www.uar.com.ar
AUSTRALIA	www.rugby.com.au
ENGLAND	www.rfu.com
FRANCE	www.ffr.fr
IRELAND	www.irishrugby.ie
ITALY	www.federugby.it
NEW ZEALAND	www.nzru.co.nz
SCOTLAND	www.scottishrugby.org
SOUTH AFRICA	www.sarugby.co.za
WALES	www.wru.co.uk
CANADA	www.rugbycanada.ca
FIJI	www.fijirugby.com
GEORGIA	www.rugby.ge
JAPAN	www.jrfu.org
NAMIBIA	www.namibianrugby.com
ROMANIA	www.frr.ro
RUSSIA	www.rugby.ru
SAMOA	www.samoarugbyunion.ws
TONGA	www.tongarugbyunion.net
U S A	www.usarugby.org
URUGUAY	www.uru.org.uy

ALSO AVAILABLE FROM

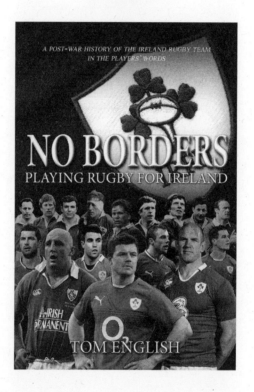

PUBLISHED BY ARENA SPORT

SEPTEMBER 2015

ALSO AVAILABLE FROM

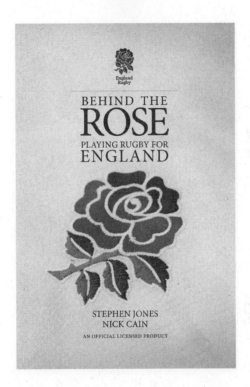

SHORTLISTED FOR 2015 RUGBY BOOK OF THE YEAR

'A handsome new book... a historical treasure trove' – *The Guardian*

'a superb book' – *ESPN Scrum*

'delves to the very heart of what it means to play for England ... a must-have' – *Planet Rugby*

'a riot of anecdote, inside track and genuine insights' – *The Rugby Paper*

ALSO AVAILABLE FROM

ARENA SPORT

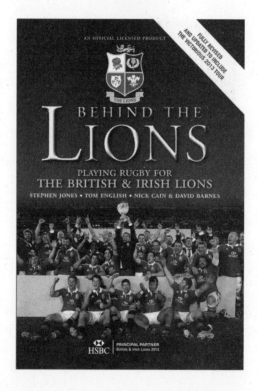

SHORTLISTED FOR 2013 RUGBY BOOK OF THE YEAR

'A fascinating collection of insights' – *The Sunday Times*

★★★★★ – *Rugby World*

'Utterly compelling' – *Planet Rugby*

'comfortably the most interesting and entertaining history of the Lions'
– *Irish Times*

ALSO AVAILABLE FROM

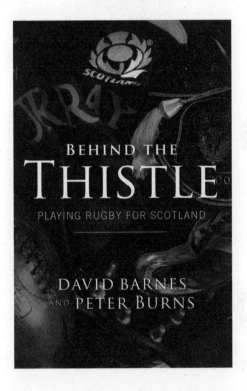

SHORTLISTED FOR 2011 RUGBY BOOK OF THE YEAR

'Takes the reader as close to the action as it is possible to get, short of invading the pitch' – *The Scotsman*

'A gem of a book' – *Sunday Herald*

'remarkable … an unmissable tome' – *Evening News*

ALSO AVAILABLE FROM

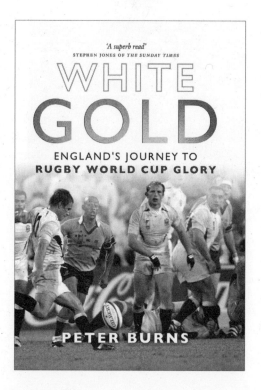

SHORTLISTED FOR 2014 RUGBY BOOK OF THE YEAR

'Marvellous ... you won't find a better read on the inner workings of Sir Clive Woodward's 2003 World Cup winning side ... Peter Burns has an astonishing eye for detail' – *Daily Mail*

'fascinating' – *Rugby World*

'A superb read' – Stephen Jones, *The Sunday Times*

'A fascinating analysis of one of British sport's greatest triumphs' – Tom English, *BBC Sport*